9th Workshop on Argument Mining (ArgMining 2022)

Gyeongju, South Korea and Online
17 October 2022

ISBN: 978-1-7138-9103-1

Printed from e-media with permission by:

Curran Associates, Inc.
57 Morehouse Lane
Red Hook, NY 12571

Some format issues inherent in the e-media version may also appear in this print version.

Printed with permission by Curran Associates, Inc. (2024)

For permission requests, please contact the Association for Computational Linguistics at the address below.

Association for Computational Linguistics
209 N. Eighth Street
Stroudsburg, Pennsylvania 18360

Phone: 1-570-476-8006
Fax: 1-570-476-0860

acl@aclweb.org

Additional copies of this publication are available from:

Curran Associates, Inc.
57 Morehouse Lane
Red Hook, NY 12571 USA
Phone: 845-758-0400
Fax: 845-758-2633
Email: curran@proceedings.com
Web: www.proceedings.com

COLING

International Conference on Computational Linguistics

Proceedings of the Conference and Workshops

COLING

Volume 29 (2022), No. 14

Proceedings of 9th Workshop on Argument Mining

The 29th International Conference on Computational Linguistics

October 17, 2022
Online and in Gyeongju, Republic of Korea

ISSN 2951-2093

Introduction

Argument mining (also known as "argumentation mining") is a growing research area within computational linguistics. At its heart, argument mining involves the automatic identification of argumentative structures in free text, such as the conclusions, premises, and inference schemes of arguments, as well as their pro- and con-relations. To date, researchers have investigated argument mining in many genres, such as legal documents, product reviews, news articles, online debates, Wikipedia articles, essays, academic literature, tweets, and dialogues. In addition, argument quality assessment and generation are also important problems. Argument mining gives rise to various practical applications of great importance. In particular, it provides methods that can find and visualize the main pro and con arguments in written text and dialogue and that enable argument search on the web for a topic of interest. In educational contexts, argument mining can be applied to written and diagrammed arguments for instructing and assessing students' critical thinking. In information retrieval, argument mining is expected to play a salient role in the emerging field of conversational search. Real-world applications include argument analysis in education, finance, law, public policy, and other social sciences, argument web search, opinion analysis in customer reviews, argument analysis in meetings, and scientific writing.

The community around ArgMining is constantly growing. This year's edition of the workshop had 37 valid submissions (27 in 2017, 32 in 2018, 41 in 2019, 30 in 2020, and 39 in 2021). Out of the 37 submissions, 12 full papers, 3 short papers, and 3 shared task papers were accepted, resulting in an overall acceptance rate of 49%. All accepted papers are included in the proceedings at hand.

Given the duration of the workshop (1 day) and its format (hybrid), we decided to give all the authors the opportunity to present their work orally. Long papers had 15 min for the talk and Q&A and short papers had 12 min for the talk and Q&A. We were delighted to have Prof. Dr. Hans Hoeken from the Department of Languages, Literature, and Communication, Utrecht University as the keynote speaker, on Mining for Persuasive Ingredients: What's the Right Mix.

The ArgMining 2022 workshop program also included a shared task on Predicting the Validity and Novelty of Arguments, chaired by Philipp Heinisch (University of Bielefeld), Philipp Cimiano (University of Bielefeld), Anette Frank (University of Heidelberg), and Juri Opitz (University of Heidelberg). A panel featured five domain experts from different domains: Laura Alonso Alemany (Universidad Nacional de Córdoba), Chung-Chi Chen (National Institute of Advanced Industrial Science and Technology), Beata Beigman Klebanov (Educational Testing Service), Joonsuk Park (University of Richmond), and Michael Yeomans (Imperial College London). A best paper award and scholarships were sponsored with thanks to NAVER and IBM. Awards are announced on the official workshop webpage: https://argmining-org.github.io/2022/index.html.

Gabriella Lapesa, Jodi Schneider, Yohan Jo, Sougata Saha
(ArgMining 2022 co-chairs)

Organizing Committee

Gabriella Lapesa, Universität Stuttgart
Jodi Schneider, University of Illinois Urbana-Champaign
Yohan Jo, Amazon
Sougata Saha, University at Buffalo

Program Committee

Rodrigo Agerri, University of the Basque Country
Khalid Al Khatib, University of Groningen
Roy Bar-Haim, IBM Research AI
Chris Biemann, University of Hamburg
Miriam Butt, University of Konstanz
Elena Cabrio, CNRS, Inria, I3S
Jonathan Clayton, University of Sheffield
Johannes Daxenberger, Technische Universität Darmstadt
Lorik Dumani, Trier University
Stephanie Evert, FAU Erlangen-Nürnberg
Neele Falk, University of Stuttgart
Andrea Galassi, University of Bologna
Michael Granitzer, University of Passau
Ivan Habernal, Technische Universität Darmstadt
Gerhard Heyer, University of Leipzig
Christopher Hidey, Columbia University
Lea Kawaletz, HHU Düsseldorf
Birgitta König-Ries, University of Jena
Manika Lamba, University of Delhi
Anne Lauscher, Bocconi University
John Lawrence, University of Dundee
Davide Liga, University of Bologna
Marie-Francine Moens, KU Leuven
Joonsuk Park, University of Richmond
Georgios Petasis, NCSR Demokritos, Athens
Olesya Razuvayevskaya, University of Cambridge
Chris Reed, University of Dundee
Julia Romberg, HHU Düsseldorf
Manfred Stede, University of Potsdam
Benno Stein, Bauhaus-Universität Weimar
Mohammed Taiye, Linnaeus University
Simone Teufel, University of Cambridge
Matthias Thimm, Fernuni Hagen
Dietrich Trautmann, University of Munich
Francielle Vargas, University of Sao Paulo
Eva Maria Vecchi, University of Stuttgart
Serena Villata, Université de Nice
Henning Wachsmuth, University of Paderborn
Gregor Wiedemann, Leibniz-Institut für Medienforschung
Hiroaki Yamada, Tokyo Institute of Technology

Shared Task Organizers

Philipp Heinisch, University of Bielefeld
Philipp Cimiano, University of Bielefeld
Anette Frank, University of Heidelberg
Juri Opitz, University of Heidelberg

Best Paper Committee

Ivan Habernal, Technische Universität Darmstadt
Naoya Inoue, JAIST
Evgeny Kotelnikov, Vyatka State University
Adam Wyner, Swansea University

Local Chair

JinYeong Bak, Sungkyunkwan University

Table of Contents

Conference Program

October 17, 2022

8:50–9:00 ***Opening Remarks***

9:00–10:20 ***Panel - Laura Alonso Alemany, Chung-Chi Chen, Beata Beigman Klebanov, Joonsuk Park, Michael Yeomans***

10:30–12:00 **Paper Session I**

ImageArg: A Multi-modal Tweet Dataset for Image Persuasiveness Mining
Zhexiong Liu, Meiqi Guo, Yue Dai and Diane Litman

Data Augmentation for Improving the Prediction of Validity and Novelty of Argumentative Conclusions
Philipp Heinisch, Moritz Plenz, Juri Opitz, Anette Frank and Philipp Cimiano

Do Discourse Indicators Reflect the Main Arguments in Scientific Papers?
Yingqiang Gao, Nianlong Gu, Jessica Lam and Richard H.R. Hahnloser

Analyzing Culture-Specific Argument Structures in Learner Essays
Wei-Fan Chen, Mei-Hua Chen, Garima Mudgal and Henning Wachsmuth

Perturbations and Subpopulations for Testing Robustness in Token-Based Argument Unit Recognition
Jonathan Kamp, Lisa Beinborn and Antske Fokkens

A Unified Representation and a Decoupled Deep Learning Architecture for Argumentation Mining of Students' Persuasive Essays
Muhammad Tawsif Sazid and Robert E. Mercer

12:00–13:00 ***Catered Lunch***

October 17, 2022 (continued)

13:00–14:00 Shared Task Papers

14:10–14:50 Paper Session II

October 17, 2022 (continued)

15:00–16:00 **Keynote: Mining for Persuasive Ingredients: What's the Right Mix? - Hans Hoeken**

16:15–17:45 **Paper Session III**

Detecting Arguments in CJEU Decisions on Fiscal State Aid
Giulia Grundler, Piera Santin, Andrea Galassi, Federico Galli, Francesco Godano, Francesca Lagioia, Elena Palmieri, Federico Ruggeri, Giovanni Sartor and Paolo Torroni

Multimodal Argument Mining: A Case Study in Political Debates
Eleonora Mancini, Federico Ruggeri, Andrea Galassi and Paolo Torroni

A Robustness Evaluation Framework for Argument Mining
Mehmet Sofi, Matteo Fortier and Oana Cocarascu

On Selecting Training Corpora for Cross-Domain Claim Detection
Robin Schaefer, René Knaebel and Manfred Stede

Entity-based Claim Representation Improves Fact-Checking of Medical Content in Tweets
Amelie Wührl and Roman Klinger

QualiAssistant: Extracting Qualia Structures from Texts
Manuel Biertz, Lorik Dumani, Markus Nilles, Björn Metzler and Ralf Schenkel

17:45–18:00 ***Closing Remarks + Best Paper Award***

18:00–20:00 ***Social @Whasoo Brewery***

ImageArg: A Multi-modal Tweet Dataset for Image Persuasiveness Mining

Zhexiong Liu*, Meiqi Guo*, Yue Dai*, Diane Litman
Department of Computer Science
University of Pittsburgh, Pittsburgh, Pennsylvania, 15260
{zhexiong.liu,meiqi.guo,yud42,dlitman}@pitt.edu

Abstract

The growing interest in developing corpora of persuasive texts has promoted applications in automated systems, e.g., debating and essay scoring systems; however, there is little prior work mining image persuasiveness from an argumentative perspective. To expand persuasiveness mining into a multi-modal realm, we present a multi-modal dataset, *ImageArg*, consisting of annotations of image persuasiveness in tweets. The annotations are based on a persuasion taxonomy we developed to explore image functionalities and the means of persuasion. We benchmark image persuasiveness tasks on *ImageArg* using widely-used multi-modal learning methods. The experimental results show that our dataset offers a useful resource for this rich and challenging topic, and there is ample room for modeling improvement.

#Gunviolence has serious and lasting social and emotional impacts on those who directly and indirectly experience it, a new study by UCD Firearm Violence Research Center @UCDavisHealth and @UCDavisEM found health.ucdavis.edu/vprp/UCFC/Fact

(a) A posted tweet text

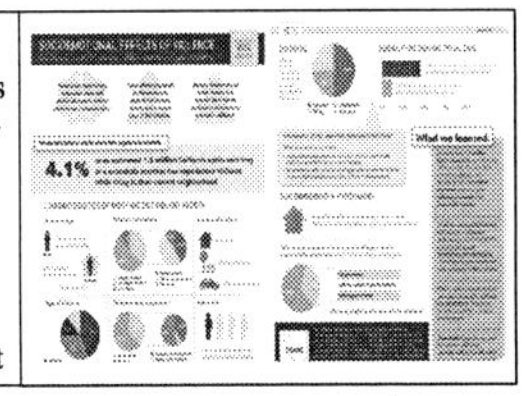

(b) An associated posted tweet image

Figure 1: (a) The tweet text uses gun violence to argue for *gun control*. (b) The image makes the argument more persuasive by providing supplementary statistics relating violence to gun ownership in California.

1 Introduction

Argumentation mining (AM) aims to analyze authors' argumentative stance by automatically identifying argumentative structures and their relationships (Green et al., 2014). As a fundamental component in AM, computational persuasiveness analysis has gained considerable momentum due to growing resources and downstream applications (Chatterjee and Agrawal, 2006; Park et al., 2014; Wei et al., 2016; Lukin et al., 2017; Chakrabarty et al., 2017; Lytos et al., 2019). Aiming at automatically evaluating how well one party can change another party's opinions or behaviors, computational persuasiveness tasks are critical yet challenging.

Recent work in AM has brought attention to mining persuasiveness in essays. Stab and Gurevych (2014) and Habernal and Gurevych (2017) developed the Argument Annotated Essays Corpus (AAEC) where stance, argument components, and argumentative relations were annotated. Carlile et al. (2018) extended AAEC annotations with persuasiveness scores, as well as with argumentative attributes that potentially impact persuasiveness (Eloquence, Specificity, Relevance, and Evidence) and the means of persuasion (Ethos, Pathos, or Logos). These are all text-based annotations, however, missing the opportunity to leverage other modalities (e.g., images) that potentially enhance the persuasiveness of the argument. For example, the image showing statistic charts in Fig. 1 makes the tweet text more convincing. To address the gap that image persuasivness has rarely been explored in the AM community, we create a new multi-modal dataset, *ImageArg*, that annotates image persuasiveness in tweets and extends persuasiveness mining to a multi-modal realm.

Regarding *ImageArg* construction, we first extend annotation schemes that are previously developed to capture the persuasive strength of text arguments in AAEC (Duthie et al., 2016; Wachsmuth et al., 2018; Carlile et al., 2018) to a new modality of image. Specifically, we develop a novel strategy (Sec. 3.2) to annotate multi-modal persuasiveness gains that measure if the persuasivness of a tweet's text increases after adding a visual image. Second, we devise a taxonomy to annotate image content (Sec. 3.3) that explicitly identifies image functionalities from a persuasive perspective. Furthermore,

*These authors contributed equally to this work.

Proceedings of the 9th Workshop on Argument Mining, co-located with the 29th International Conference on Computational Linguistics, pages 1–18
October 17, 2022.

we adapt existing text attributes used in Carlile et al. (2018) to annotate image persuasion modes (Sec. 3.4) by exploring different annotation strategies (Sec. 4.2). We evaluate the inter-rater agreement on our proposed annotation schemes as well as the quality of the annotated samples.

With *ImageArg*, we first report the basic statistics of the dataset and conduct a thorough analysis between different annotation dimensions (Sec. 4.3). We observe a strong correlation between human political ideology (i.e. stance towards a social topic) and the argumentative features in their posted tweets, as well as mutual influences between image content and persuasion mode. In addition, we benchmark model performance on multiple argumentative classification tasks annotated in *ImageArg* (Sec. 5.2). Specifically, we employ multi-modal learning methods to classify stance, image persuasiveness, image content, and image persuasion mode. Our benchmark results highlight the challenge of these tasks and indicate there is ample room for model improvement. We demonstrate the limitation of these general multi-modal methods and discuss possible future work. We further conduct a qualitative study on a real-world application, retrieving the most persuasive images given a tweet text, by using our trained classifiers (Sec. 5.3), which offers a starting point for developing an intelligent tool that recommends persuasive images to users based on their textual inputs. Our code and data is publicly available at: `https://github.com/MeiqiGuo/ArgMining2022-ImageArg`.

2 Related Work

Computational Persuasiveness While classical AM focuses on identifying argumentative components and their relations (Stab et al., 2014, 2018; Lawrence and Reed, 2020), recent work has developed interest in persuasiveness related tasks (Chatterjee et al., 2014; Park et al., 2014; Lukin et al., 2017; Carlile et al., 2018; Chakrabarty et al., 2019). In addition, Riley (1954), O'keefe (2015), and Wei et al. (2016) investigate ranking debate arguments on the same topic based on their persuasiveness, but they failed to investigate the factors that make arguments persuasive. Lukin et al. (2017) and Persing and Ng (2017) examine how audience variables (e.g., personality) influence persuasiveness through different argument styles (e.g., factual vs. emotional arguments), but only focus on the text modality. Higgins and Walker (2012) and Carlile et al. (2018) study the persuasion strategies, i.e., Ethos (credibility), Logos (reason), and Pathos (emotion), in the scope of reports or student essays. We follow their work developed for text corpora and extend the annotation schemes to the image modality. Although Park et al. (2014), Joo et al. (2014), and Huang and Kovashka (2016) utilize facial expressions and bodily gestures to analyze persuasiveness in social multimedia, their work is limited to the human portrait and fails to generalize to diverse image domains. Some prior work study persuasive advertisements in a multi-modal way (Hussain et al., 2017; Guo et al., 2021). Different from our argumentative mining goal, they focus on the sentiment, intent reasoning and persuasive strategies that are narrowly designed for ads. Thus, annotating a multi-modal tweet dataset focusing on image persuasiveness is under-explored in existing work, and has ample value for social science.

Multi-modal Learning The ability to process and understand multi-modal input for AI models has recently received much attention since the multi-modal signals are generally complementary for real-world applications (Aytar et al., 2016; Zhang et al., 2018; Alwassel et al., 2020). In the area of vision-language, tasks are mainly designed for evaluating models' ability to understand visual information as well as expressing the reasoning in language (Antol et al., 2015; Goyal et al., 2017; Hudson and Manning, 2019). In addition to the main stream, a few works study the relationship between image and text: Alikhani et al. (2019) annotates the discourse relations between text and accompanying imagery in recipe instructions; and Kruk et al. (2019) investigates the multi-modal document intent in instagram posts. However, multi-modal learning for AM has been under-explored due to a lack of multi-modal corpora. This drives us to build *ImageArg* and to analyze the effectiveness of multi-modal learning on AM tasks. With respect to modeling, researchers focus on learning good representation of each modality and developing effective fusion methods (Tsai et al., 2018; Hu et al., 2019; Tan and Bansal, 2019; Lu et al., 2020). In this work, we establish a benchmark performance for *ImageArg* by using fundamental and common encoders and fusion methods.

3 Annotation Scheme

We propose an annotation scheme to capture an image's impact on the persuasiveness of multi-modal

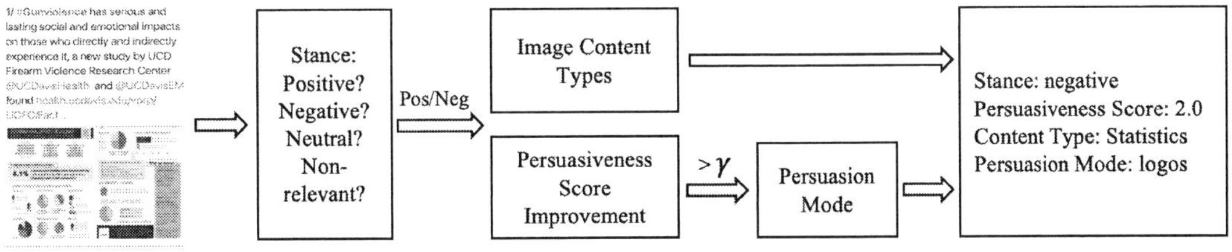

Figure 2: The overview of our annotation pipeline. Annotators start by annotating the argumentative stance of input tweets. Afterwards, tweets with either positive or negative stances are annotated for image content types and persuasiveness score improvement. The persuasion mode is further annotated if persuasiveness score improvement exceeds a given threshold γ. We use $\gamma = 0.5$ when we annotate data and test with different γ values for persuasiveness classification task (Table 6).

Support: ANOTHER BIG WIN FOR GUN SAFETY! Just after passing a bill to require background checks on all gun sales #HR8 the U.S House just passed #HR1446, a bill that would address the deadly Charleston loophole. This bill now heads to the Senate.

Oppose: #GunControl The THEORY that becoming a VICTIM is somehow morally superior to DEFENDING yourself or family! We support #SelfDefence #Legalgunownership #SafeCitizen

Figure 3: Examples of positive (support) and negative (oppose) tweets.

tweets. We build a corpus of Twitter posts on a social topic (e.g., *gun control*), then annotate the image within each post along four dimensions. The annotation pipeline is shown in Fig. 2. First, we determine **(1)** the **stance** of the entire tweet (Sec. 3.1). Specifically, we assume one tweet holds a consistent stance in its text and image since the author would intend to deliver a consistent argument. For those tweets annotated with a positive or negative stance, we also annotate **(2)** the **persuasiveness scores** of the tweet image (Sec. 3.2) and **(3)** the image **content type**. The content types identify image roles from an argumentative perspective (Sec. 3.3). Finally, we **(4)** identify the **persuasion mode** of an image that is annotated as persuasive. The persuasion mode indicates how the images persuade audiences (Sec. 3.4). Note that with this annotation pipeline, all tweets will first be annotated for stance. Then, only tweets with a clear stance will be annotated for content type and persuasiveness scores. Finally, only tweets where the images are persuasive will be annotated for persuasion mode.

3.1 Stance

We use existing methods (Mohammad et al., 2017) to verify if the image holds a clear stance on a given topic. Specifically, given a tweet (including text and images), we ask annotators to select among four stances that are extended from Mohammad et al. (2017): positive (i.e., support), negative (i.e., oppose), neutral, or irrelevant to the topic. We continue with the next annotation steps only if a tweet holds a positive or negative stance. Otherwise, it is discarded for our persuasion study. We show examples in Fig. 3.

3.2 Image Persuasiveness Scores

For a tweet that holds a positive or negative stance, we study the impact of its image by computing an image persuasiveness score improvment. We adopt five levels of text persuasiveness scores proposed in Carlile et al. (2018) in the annotation process: (L0) no persuasiveness (score = 0): the annotated target fails to convince the audience at all. (L1) medium persuasiveness (score = 1): the annotated target partially convinces the audience. (L2) persuasive (score = 2): the annotated target is convincing to the audience. (L3) high persuasiveness (score = 3): the annotated target is very convincing to the audience. (L4) extreme persuasiveness (score = 4): the annotated target is compelling to the audience.

Different from Carlile et al. (2018) that annotates the persuasiveness score directly, we propose a novel method to compute the image persuasiveness score. In particular, we calculate the differences with/without images to quantify image persuasiveness scores. We first ask annotators to choose one of 5 persuasiveness levels based on pure text from the tweet. Next, we ask annotators to give a second choice based on both text and image from the tweet. Suppose each sample has three annotations and each annotation has two persuasiveness scores: one for the text-only (s_t), the other for the image-text (s_{it}). We compute persuasiveness score differ-

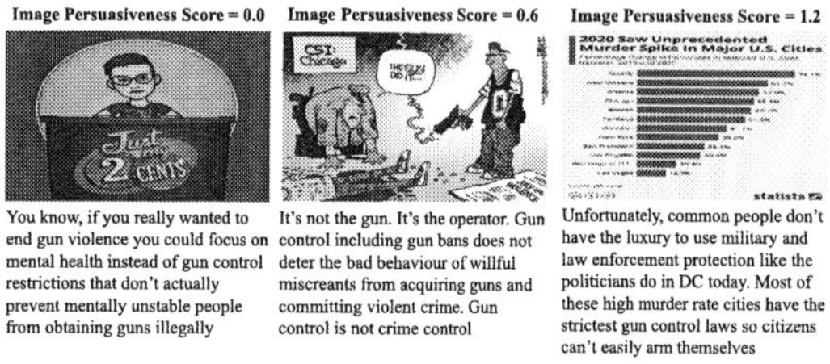

Figure 4: Examples of tweets with 0, 0.6, and 1.2 image persuasiveness scores.

ence $\Delta s_i = max(s_{it} - s_t, 0)$ for each annotation, as the persuasiveness gain from the image. Then, we compute the average of the three annotations (Δs_i) as the final image persuasiveness score. To interpret image persuasiveness, we use a threshold (γ) that encodes the score into a binary label (i.e., persuasiveness or not). If Δs_i is higher than the threshold (γ), it indicates that adding an image improves tweet persuasiveness, thus the image is considered as persuasive. We show examples with different image persuasiveness scores in Fig. 4.

3.3 Image Content Types

For persuasive samples, we investigate their image argumentative roles. In particular, we annotate the image content types from an argumentative perspective to describe what kind of evidence images provide to improve tweet persuasiveness (e.g., supportive data, authorized photos, etc.). We leverage Al Khatib et al. (2016)'s definition of argumentative roles of evidence to categorize image content: Statistics, Testimony, and Anecdote. However, we notice that the categories fail to capture all the image contents that frequently appear in tweet posts, for example, photographs. To this end, we propose a Slogan category highlighting text in images, and also propose Scene photo and Symbolic photo categories regarding image content in the visual modality. More details are specified as follows:

- **Statistics**: Images provide evidence by stating or quoting quantitative information, such as a chart or diagram showing data, that is related to the tweet text. In Fig. 5, the image provides quantitative statistics on gun fatalities.
- **Testimony**: Images quote statements or conclusions from an authority, such as a piece of articles or claims from an official document, that is related to the tweet text. For example, in Fig. 5, the testimony image cites a statement given by the transportation secretary.

Figure 5: Examples of image content types in tweets: statistics, testimony, anecdote, slogan, scene photo, and symbolic.

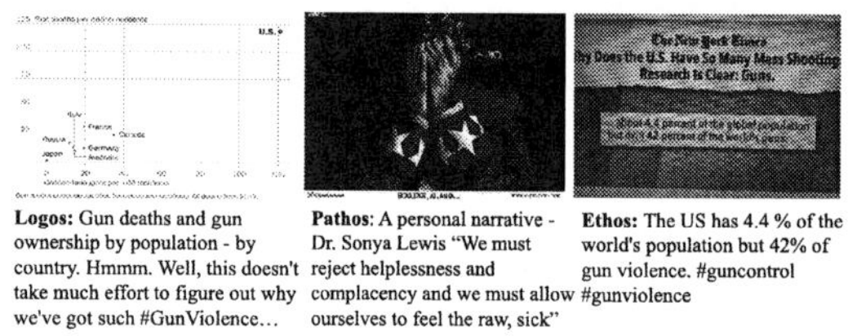

Figure 6: Examples of persuasion mode in tweet: logos, pathos, and ethos.

- **Anecdote**: Images provide information based on the author's personal experience, such as facts/personal stories, that are related to the tweet text. In Fig. 5, the anecdote image shows the fact that guns are developed since the period of the 2nd amendment, and therefore the laws for guns should be developed as well.
- **Slogan**: Images embed pieces of advertising/slogan text. In Fig. 5, the slogan image presents a phrase "Actually guns do kill people. Gun Reform Now".
- **Scene photo**: Images show a real scene or photograph that is related to the tweet text. In Fig. 5, the image shows a photo of a gun violence scene reported by CNN news.
- **Symbolic photo**: Images show a symbol/art that expresses the author's viewpoints in a non-literal way. In Fig. 5, the symbolic photo shows a pair of artificial bloodied hands holding bullets and a cross which symbolically reveals the brutality of gun violence.

3.4 Image Persuasion Modes

To investigate how images convince an audience (e.g., by providing strong logic, touching audiences emotionally, etc.), we annotate the persuasion modes of images by leveraging the definitions in Braet (1992) for Logos, Pathos, and Ethos. The modes form the rhetorical triangle, and both the textual and visual modalities follow these dimensions in the persuasiveness perspective. Fig. 6 shows examples, details are specified below:

- **Logos**: The image appeals to logic and reasoning, which persuades audiences with reasoning from a fact/statistics/study case/scientific evidence. In Fig. 6, the Logos image provides a chart that shows the high gun deaths and the high gun ownership by the population of the US, which implies a logical relationship between gun death and gun ownership.
- **Pathos**: The image appeals to emotion, i.e., evokes emotional impact that leads to higher persuasiveness. In Fig. 6, the Pathos image provides art that shows the grieved "Uncle Sam" saying "no" with helplessness, which evokes the desire to *gun control*.
- **Ethos**: The image appeals to ethics, which enhances credibility and trustworthiness. In Fig. 6, the Ethos image takes a screenshot of the source of a report from New York Times, which increases credibility.

4 Corpus Creation

4.1 Data Collection

We collect raw tweets containing both image and text across 3 topics (*gun control, immigration* and *abortion*) used in Mochales and Moens (2011) and Stab et al. (2018). Specifically, we retrieve tweets with images that contain pre-defined keywords[1] through TwitterAPI[2]. The raw data (286k tweets) are collected in a two-year window from 3/29/2019 to 3/29/2021. We retain tweets whose texts tend to be argumentative, with an argument confidence score larger than 0.9 by using ArgumentText Classify API[3]. 99.48% of tweets are discarded for having an argument confidence score below 0.9. These filtering processes ensure our annotation data has high argumentation-confidence and topic-relevance.

4.2 Annotation Strategies

We develop annotation strategies based on several rounds of pilot annotations. To ensure the annotation quality, we provide coding manual and examples for annotators (see the Appendix A for details). We employ qualified workers who passed a qualitative test that evaluates the workers' understanding on our annotation manual.

Task	Alpha	Count
Stance	64.5	87
Content type	71.1	38
Persuasion mode	19.9	38

Table 1: First pilot annotation inter-agreement on *gun control* topic. Persuasion modes are annotated as single choices from logos, pathos, and ethos.

Task	Alpha	Count
Stance	76.1	1003
Persuasiveness*	/	1003
Content type	64.6	1003
Logos	55.3	259
Pathos	51.0	259
Ethos	57.8	259

Table 2: Inter-agreement rate of each annotation task in our final corpus on *gun control* topic, and the number of samples with the corresponding annotation. (*) We only show numbers of persuasiveness since they are annotated with average persuasiveness scores from annotators rather than labels.

We start with the topic of *gun control*. In the first-round, we distribute 87 samples to two random annotators on MTurk. Table 1 shows Krippendorff's alpha (Krippendorff, 2011) score for inter-rater agreement[4]. Based on the interpretation of alpha scores in Landis and Koch (1977); Hartling et al. (2012), we conclude that stance and content type have a substantial inter-agreement but persuasion mode inter-agreement is slight. To investigate this issue, we modify our annotation guideline for persuasion mode. Instead of using three-class annotation (i.e., choosing one persuasion mode from 3 options), we move to three-label annotation that asks a binary question for each mode for each sample (i.e., annotating yes/no for each persuasion mode, individually). Moreover, the annotators are required to justify their choices by giving short comments. The improved results (on the final corpus from Sec. 4.3) are shown in Table 2, although the persuasion mode agreement (i.e., Logos, Pathos, and Ethos) is still lower than stance and content type. This is likely because annotators have different emotional reasoning (i.e., some annotators are easily evoked by images while others are not).

[1]We use keywords provided in Guo et al. (2020)'s work.
[2]https://developer.twitter.com/en/docs/twitter-api
[3]https://api.argumentsearch.com

[4]Note that the availability of annotation questions is based on the answer to the prior questions (Fig. 2) therefore each task has different sample numbers.

A: Togetherness; B: No A: Sadness; B: No A: Sadness & Anxiety; B: No

Figure 7: Annotator A annotates the above images as Pathos because these examples express emotions, while annotator B disagrees and marks as not Pathos.

For example, one annotator recognized strong emotional impact (e.g., togetherness, sadness, anxiety, etc.), while the other not as shown in Fig. 7.

We further perform pilot annotations for the topics of *immigration* and *abortion*, with the best annotation strategies that we developed for annotating *gun control*. We randomly choose 100 or 200 tweets respectively on *immigration* or *abortion* for the pilot study, and make a topic-specific instruction for the stance annotation that provides some topic-specific examples. The Inter-rater Agreement for both topics is shown in Table 3. We observe high Inter-rater Agreements on the stance annotation, which demonstrates the utility of our topic-specific instructions. The agreement on the content type is generally good, however, *abortion* has relatively lower agreement than the other two topics. One main reason is that authors prefer using photos to support their arguments. Such photos lead to ambiguity between scene photos and symbolic photos, as examples shown in Fig. 8. Moreover, we notice that the agreements on the persuasion modes are not satisfying. For *immigration*, Ethos has the lowest agreement, and one explanation is that there are few authentic resources that provide credible and trustworthy arguments on this topic; for *abortion*, the agreement on all three persuasion modes are relatively low, in particular, Logos surprisingly gets the lowest agreement.

These studies indicate that the inter-rater agreement on annotating persuasion mode is topic-dependent, and the relationship between topics and persuasion modes needs further investigation. We thus create the first version of *ImageArg* data using only the *gun control* topic, and leave the other two topics for future work.

4.3 Corpus Statistics and Analysis

We annotate 1003 samples that hold a support or oppose stance on *gun control* topic. 36% of data is discarded for not having an agreed support/oppose stance. We report the distribution of each annotation scheme in Fig. 9, and the inter-rater agreement

Task	Immigration		Abortion	
	Alpha	Count	Alpha	Count
Stance	61.5	100	68.7	200
Content type	65.8	53	56.6	76
Logos	56.7	23	25.0	48
Pathos	46.0	23	37.5	48
Ethos	30.8	23	28.2	48

Table 3: Inter-agreement rate of each annotation task on the topic *immigration* and *abortion*. The count represents the number of samples after filtering from previous questions.

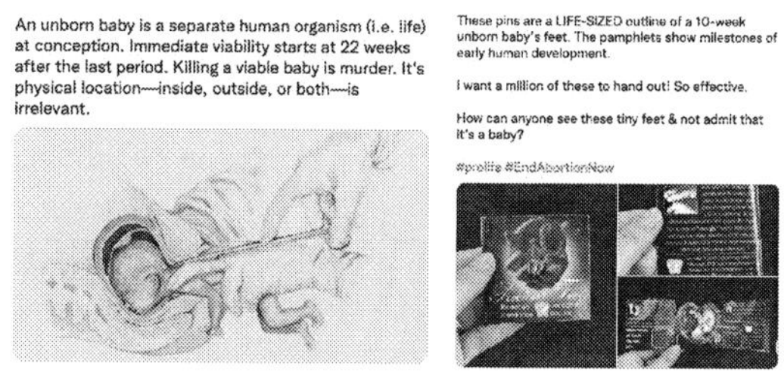

A: Scene Photo
B: Symbolic Photo

A: Scene Photo
B: Symbolic Photo

Figure 8: Samples of disagreed on the content type in the topic *abortion*.

evaluation in Table 2. The results reveal that the annotators have substantial agreement on the stance and content types, and moderate agreement on the image persuasion mode. Specifically, the stance annotations are balanced distributed as shown in Fig. 9 (a): 46.3% support and 54.7% oppose. As for image persuasiveness annotations, Table 4 shows sample distributions in different persuasiveness score intervals. We use a threshold γ to discretize numerical persuasiveness scores to binary labels (i.e., persuasiveness or not). The γ is set to 0.5 in our annotations since the persuasiveness score is an average of three annotators, thus γ greater than 0.5 suggests that there is at least two annotators annotating images persuasiveness with L1 or higher ($\geq$ 1) scores (as defined in Sec. 3.2) or at least one annotator annotating L2 or higher scores ($\geq$ 2). In terms of image content types, its distribution is shown in Fig. 9 (b): Symbolic photo (23.43%), Scene photo (21.93%), Anecdote (19.84%), Slogan (14.76%), Testimony (10.87%), Statistics (7.28%), Other (1.89%). We observe that images (i.e., symbolic photo/scene photo) occupy a high proportion of the samples, in contrast, data evidence (i.e., statistics) takes the relatively low ratio. One potential reason is that social media contents like tweets are generally short and informal, which prefers relatively simple evidence. Note that there are 19

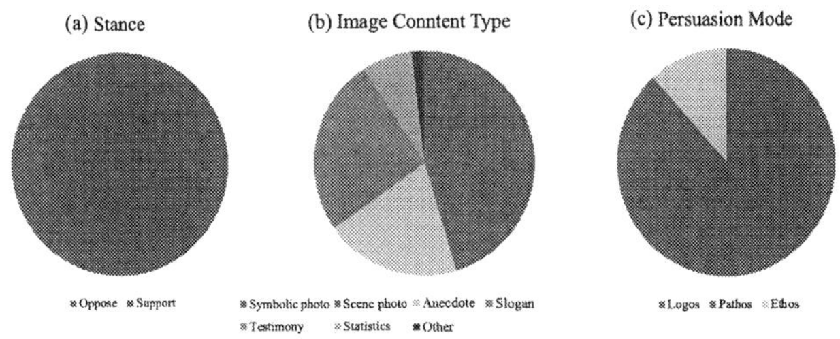

Figure 9: Distributions of (a) stance, (b) image content type, and (c) persuasion mode in our corpus on *gun control* topic.

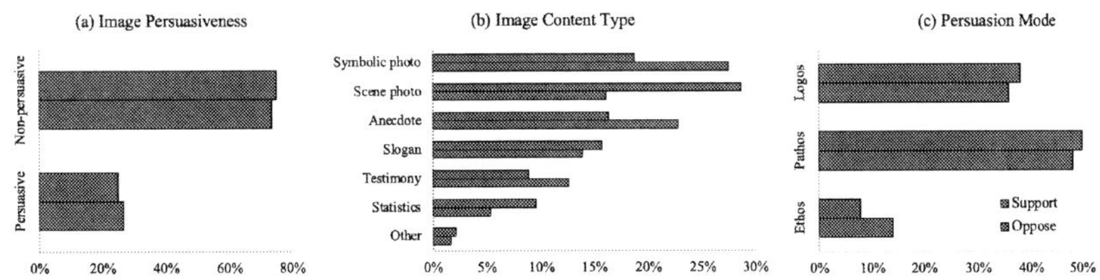

Figure 10: Distributions of (a) image persuasiveness, (b) content type and (c) persuasion mode regarding stances (support in blue and oppose in red) in our corpus on *gun control* topic.

Persuasiveness Score	Count	Percentage
0.0 - 0.1	336	33.50%
0.1 - 0.3	232	23.13%
0.3 - 0.5	176	17.55%
0.5 - 0.7	118	11.76%
0.7 - 0.9	66	6.58%
≥ 0.9	75	7.48%

Table 4: The annotated image persuasiveness score distribution on *gun control* topic in *ImageArg*.

"other" out of 1003 annotations that annotators were confused about; however, it does suggest that our image content type scheme works very well as only 1.89% are out of our defined labels. In terms of image persuasion mode, we only annotate images with persuasiveness score γ greater than 0.5, which produces 259 samples. As shown in Fig. 9 (c), we have 37.85% Logos, 50.60% Pathos, and 11.55% Ethos.

Additionally, we show how the stance impacts image persuasiveness, content type, and persuasion mode. In Fig. 10 (a), supporting and opposing *gun control* stance are almost evenly distributed with respect to persuasiveness and non-persuasiveness, which suggests that images generally support both positive and negative arguments. For the image content type in Fig. 10 (b), opposing *gun control* stance uses significantly more images with respect to Symbolic photos, Anecdote, and Testimony; however, supporting stance prefers images in the content of Scene photos and Statistics. Regarding persuasion mode in Fig. 10 (c), images in supporting *gun control* stance uses more Logos and Pathos but less Ethos than those in the opposing stance.

To further study the relevance between image content type and persuasion mode, we report their correlated distributions in charts. Fig. 11 (a) shows that most Logos samples use Statistics and Anecdote evidence. It meets the intuition that the logical reasoning can usually be clarified by introducing anecdotes and justified by providing supportive statistics. In terms of Pathos in Fig. 11 (b), the majority of samples utilize Scene and Symbolic photos. This is also reasonable since images generally promote emotional impression by presenting visual information. Regarding Ethos, Fig. 11 (c) shows Testimony takes the most ratio because statements from authorities can enhance trustworthiness. These correlations imply mutual influences between different annotation dimensions and raise demands for further study.

5 Experiments

5.1 Models and Tasks

We evaluate our corpus on *gun control* topic with binary classification tasks for Stance, Persuasiveness, Logos, Pathos, and Ethos and multi-class classification task for Image Content. Since data size is relatively small, we use pretrained image encoder ResNet50 (He et al., 2016) and text encoder BERT (Devlin et al., 2019) to fine-tune linear classifiers.

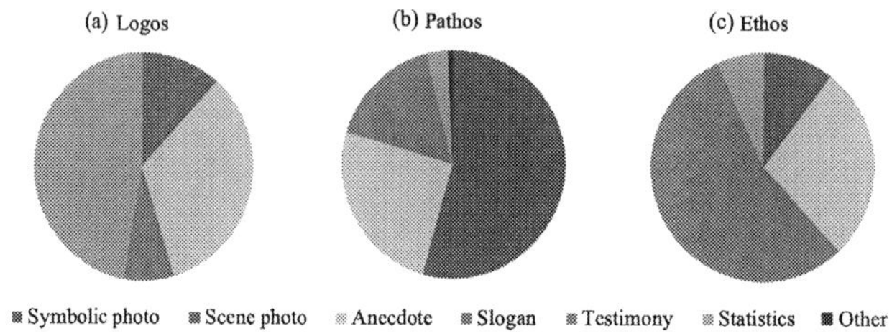

Figure 11: Distributions of image content type in different persuasion mode (a) Logos, (b) Pathos, and (c) Ethos in our corpus on *gun control* topic.

For fair comparison, we project both image and text embeddings into 1024 dimension before feeding into classification layers. We compare task performance on Text Modality (T-M), Image Modality (I-M), and Image-Text Multi-modality (M-M) that concatenates T-M and I-M. As for baseline (BASE), we report the performance when all samples are predicted as positive for binary classification, or predicted as the majority label for multi-class classification. We don't use the majority baseline for the binary classification task because the recall and F1 scores are always 0 if the majority label is negative, which is not interesting to compare with.

In the implementation, we follow the annotation strategy (Sec. 4.2) that uses threshold γ equal to 0.5 to encode persuasiveness scores into binaries. We remove Emoji, URLs, Mentions, and Hashtags in tweet texts, and discard 19 samples labeled with "Other" for the image content classification task. All images are resized to 224x224 dimension, and augmented (i.e., horizontal-flipped) only in training. Our models are implemented with Pytorch, and trained on a GeForce RTX 3080 GPU. We freeze BERT and ResNet50 encoders while training classifiers, and optimize the networks using Adam optimizer with $\beta_1 = 0.9, \beta_2 = 0.999, \epsilon = 10^{-8}$. The learning rate is 0.001 and the batch size is 16. We conduct 5-fold cross-validation (80% data in train; 20% data in test). We report 5-fold average Precision, Recall, F1, and AUC scores for binary classification and macro Precision, Recall, and F1 scores for multi-class classification on the test set.

5.2 Quantitative Results Analysis

Table 5 shows the classification benchmark results with standard deviation on *gun control* topic in *ImageArg* corpus.

Task-Stance Regarding stance, T-M has the highest performance in terms of AUC scores. It reveals that the image information is redundant to the text for identifying the stance; moreover, the image might introduce disturbing noise due to limited training samples.

Task	Model	Precision	Recall	F1	AUC
Stance (binary)	BASE	$0.470_{\pm 0.02}$	$\mathbf{1.000_{\pm 0.00}}$	$\mathbf{0.639_{\pm 0.02}}$	/
	T-M	$\mathbf{0.501_{\pm 0.05}}$	$0.740_{\pm 0.03}$	$0.596_{\pm 0.04}$	$\mathbf{0.527_{\pm 0.04}}$
	I-M	$0.443_{\pm 0.08}$	$0.147_{\pm 0.03}$	$0.218_{\pm 0.04}$	$0.472_{\pm 0.05}$
	M-M	$0.414_{\pm 0.04}$	$0.369_{\pm 0.06}$	$0.390_{\pm 0.05}$	$0.417_{\pm 0.03}$
Persua. (binary)	BASE	$0.257_{\pm 0.03}$	$\mathbf{1.000_{\pm 0.00}}$	$\mathbf{0.408_{\pm 0.04}}$	/
	T-M	$0.260_{\pm 0.01}$	$0.725_{\pm 0.11}$	$0.380_{\pm 0.01}$	$0.502_{\pm 0.03}$
	I-M	$\mathbf{0.313_{\pm 0.02}}$	$0.196_{\pm 0.05}$	$0.238_{\pm 0.05}$	$0.528_{\pm 0.03}$
	M-M	$0.296_{\pm 0.05}$	$0.486_{\pm 0.05}$	$0.364_{\pm 0.03}$	$\mathbf{0.534_{\pm 0.04}}$
Content (6-class)	BASE	$0.041_{\pm 0.00}$	$0.167_{\pm 0.00}$	$0.066_{\pm 0.00}$	/
	T-M	$0.198_{\pm 0.08}$	$0.201_{\pm 0.03}$	$\mathbf{0.165_{\pm 0.03}}$	/
	I-M	$\mathbf{0.235_{\pm 0.09}}$	$\mathbf{0.204_{\pm 0.02}}$	$0.151_{\pm 0.02}$	/
	M-M	$0.200_{\pm 0.02}$	$0.179_{\pm 0.01}$	$\mathbf{0.165_{\pm 0.01}}$	/
Logos (binary)	BASE	$\mathbf{0.405_{\pm 0.05}}$	$\mathbf{1.000_{\pm 0.00}}$	$\mathbf{0.575_{\pm 0.05}}$	/
	T-M	$0.364_{\pm 0.08}$	$0.613_{\pm 0.13}$	$0.456_{\pm 0.10}$	$0.439_{\pm 0.08}$
	I-M	$0.351_{\pm 0.22}$	$0.097_{\pm 0.07}$	$0.144_{\pm 0.10}$	$0.406_{\pm 0.08}$
	M-M	$0.262_{\pm 0.27}$	$0.047_{\pm 0.05}$	$0.077_{\pm 0.08}$	$\mathbf{0.508_{\pm 0.06}}$
Pathos (binary)	BASE	$0.554_{\pm 0.04}$	$\mathbf{1.000_{\pm 0.00}}$	$\mathbf{0.712_{\pm 0.04}}$	/
	T-M	$0.613_{\pm 0.11}$	$0.714_{\pm 0.08}$	$0.658_{\pm 0.09}$	$0.582_{\pm 0.10}$
	I-M	$\mathbf{0.666_{\pm 0.09}}$	$0.184_{\pm 0.07}$	$0.280_{\pm 0.07}$	$\mathbf{0.593_{\pm 0.09}}$
	M-M	$0.471_{\pm 0.42}$	$0.071_{\pm 0.10}$	$0.114_{\pm 0.15}$	$0.507_{\pm 0.12}$
Ethos (binary)	BASE	$0.128_{\pm 0.04}$	$\mathbf{1.000_{\pm 0.00}}$	$0.226_{\pm 0.06}$	/
	T-M	$0.168_{\pm 0.05}$	$0.817_{\pm 0.15}$	$\mathbf{0.272_{\pm 0.06}}$	$\mathbf{0.580_{\pm 0.09}}$
	I-M	$\mathbf{0.244_{\pm 0.16}}$	$0.233_{\pm 0.16}$	$0.221_{\pm 0.13}$	$0.459_{\pm 0.18}$
	M-M	$0.124_{\pm 0.15}$	$0.083_{\pm 0.11}$	$0.098_{\pm 0.12}$	$0.450_{\pm 0.09}$

Table 5: Classification benchmark results with standard deviation on *gun control* topic in *ImageArg* corpus. Note that the reported Persuasiveness results use threshold γ equal to 0.5. The Stance, Persuasiveness, and Image Content tasks use 1003 annotations; The Logos, Pathos, and Ethos use 259 annotations.

Task-Persuasiveness As for persuasiveness task, we observe that M-M performs slightly poorer than T-M regarding F1 score but relatively better in AUC score. This is because persuasiveness (positive/negative) labels are unbalanced if we use $\gamma = 0.5$ (as shown in Table 4). We show F1 scores drop with respect to threshold increases from 0.1 to 0.9 in Table 6.

Task-Content In terms of 6-class classification for image content, although all modalities outperform the baseline, the task is shown to be very challenging. It is surprising that the performance with I-M is lower than T-M. The reason might be that visual argumentative tasks demand more specific image encoders that learn sufficient knowledge on

Threshold (γ)	Pos. Ratio	F1 Score		
		T-M	I-M	M-M
0.1	66.50%	$\mathbf{0.681}_{\pm 0.02}$	$\mathbf{0.265}_{\pm 0.05}$	$\mathbf{0.536}_{\pm 0.03}$
0.3	43.37%	$0.538_{\pm 0.03}$	$0.251_{\pm 0.04}$	$0.459_{\pm 0.05}$
0.5	25.8%	$0.380_{\pm 0.01}$	$0.238_{\pm 0.05}$	$0.364_{\pm 0.03}$
0.7	14.1%	$0.246_{\pm 0.02}$	$0.168_{\pm 0.04}$	$0.233_{\pm 0.01}$
0.9	7.48%	$0.138_{\pm 0.03}$	$0.084_{\pm 0.03}$	$0.115_{\pm 0.01}$

Table 6: F1 scores with standard deviation and positive label ratio for Persuasiveness classification with respect to different threshold (γ).

persuasiveness and social science; however, the used image encoder is pretrained on a general object detection task on the ImageNet (Krizhevsky et al., 2012), thus our model is unable to learn well for this argumentative task with very limited training data.

Task-Logos Regarding logos, we observe that M-M gains the best AUC score but I-M has lower AUC than T-M. The reason might be that logos images usually contain statistic charts, as shown in Fig. 11 (a), that are relatively more difficult to encode than normal images (e.g., images with explicit objects), but multi-modal models might learn these patterns directly from textual inputs.

Task-Pathos As for pathos, I-M has the best performance in terms of AUC score, and T-M is quite close to I-M while M-M has the lowest. This suggests that the multi-modal representation fusion method we used might be too weak to conduct complex reasoning on the pathos task.

Task-Ethos The best performance in ethos is from T-M. It is intuitive because the image encoder pre-trained on object detection is unable to recognize the optical characters on the image, while this kind of images are common in ethos, e.g., testimony images in Fig. 11 (c).

5.3 Qualitative Results Analysis

We conduct qualitative analysis by retrieving the most persuasive images given a text. Specifically, we run the multi-modality (M-M) model, trained for the persuasiveness task, on the test set in each fold (out of 5 folds). The inputs are image-text pairs of which all candidate images are paired with the same text, and the outputs are image persuasiveness scores. Fig. 12 shows the actual, top, and bottom images with the highest and lowest persuasiveness scores, respectively. It is interesting to find that images with specific objects or scenes (image (b), and (c) in Fig. 12) boost the persuasiveness scores; however, images with slogans or symbolism have lower scores (image (d), and (e) in Fig.

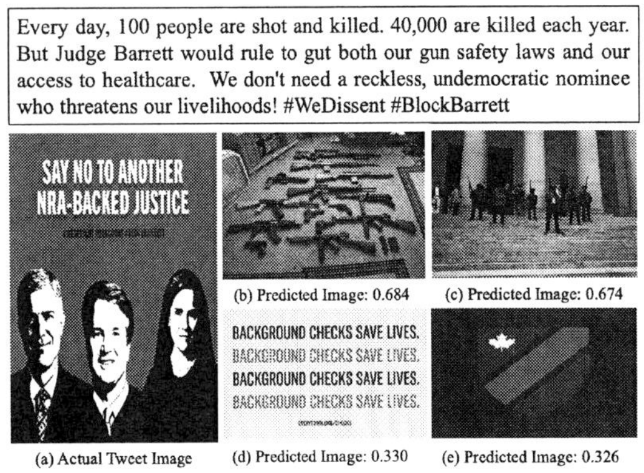

Figure 12: (a) the actual tweet image annotated with persuasiveness score 0 in *ImageArg*; (b) and (c) with top predicted persuasiveness scores; (d) and (e) with lowest predicted persuasiveness scores while retrieving images given the same tweet text.

12). This suggests that our image encoder is capable of capturing object information but not optical characters on images (e.g., slogans); therefore, our retrieved images with best persuasion scores are mostly related to gun-object images. Thus, learning an image encoder pre-trained on slogans and visual symbolism is a promising future direction to improve the performance. In the meanwhile, extracting text information from images by OCR tools and use it as an auxiliary modality may help models learn the context.

6 Conclusion and Future Work

We create a brand-new multi-modal persuasiveness dataset *ImageArg* that focuses on image functionality and persuasion mode for persuasive arguments. We extend the argumentative annotation scheme from text to vision, and demonstrate its feasibility. We then establish a benchmark on our defined tasks using computational models, with multiple input modalities. Our experimental results reveal that image persuasiveness mining is challenging and that there is ample room for model improvement. We identify the image encoder as a key modeling bottleneck through a series of qualitative and quantitative analysis, which offers a good starting point for further exploration on this rich and challenging topic. The first version of *ImageArg* has 1003 annotations on the *gun control* topic. In the future work, we will work on constructing datasets on the topics of *immigration* and *abortion*, and scaling up the annotations.

References

Khalid Al Khatib, Henning Wachsmuth, Johannes Kiesel, Matthias Hagen, and Benno Stein. 2016. A news editorial corpus for mining argumentation strategies. In *Proceedings of COLING 2016, the 26th International Conference on Computational Linguistics: Technical Papers*, pages 3433–3443.

Malihe Alikhani, Sreyasi Nag Chowdhury, Gerard de Melo, and Matthew Stone. 2019. Cite: A corpus of image-text discourse relations. In *Proceedings of the 2019 Conference of the North American Chapter of the Association for Computational Linguistics: Human Language Technologies, Volume 1 (Long and Short Papers)*, pages 570–575.

Humam Alwassel, Dhruv Mahajan, Bruno Korbar, Lorenzo Torresani, Bernard Ghanem, and Du Tran. 2020. Self-supervised learning by cross-modal audio-video clustering. *Advances in Neural Information Processing Systems*, 33:9758–9770.

Stanislaw Antol, Aishwarya Agrawal, Jiasen Lu, Margaret Mitchell, Dhruv Batra, C Lawrence Zitnick, and Devi Parikh. 2015. Vqa: Visual question answering. In *Proceedings of the IEEE international conference on computer vision*, pages 2425–2433.

Yusuf Aytar, Carl Vondrick, and Antonio Torralba. 2016. Soundnet: Learning sound representations from unlabeled video. *Advances in neural information processing systems*, 29.

Antoine C Braet. 1992. Ethos, pathos and logos in aristotle's rhetoric: A re-examination. *Argumentation*, 6(3):307–320.

Winston Carlile, Nishant Gurrapadi, Zixuan Ke, and Vincent Ng. 2018. Give me more feedback: Annotating argument persuasiveness and related attributes in student essays. In *Proceedings of the 56th Annual Meeting of the Association for Computational Linguistics (Volume 1: Long Papers)*, pages 621–631.

Abhisek Chakrabarty, Onkar Arun Pandit, and Utpal Garain. 2017. Context sensitive lemmatization using two successive bidirectional gated recurrent networks. In *Proceedings of the 55th Annual Meeting of the Association for Computational Linguistics (Volume 1: Long Papers)*, pages 1481–1491.

Tuhin Chakrabarty, Christopher Hidey, Smaranda Muresan, Kathleen Mckeown, and Alyssa Hwang. 2019. Ampersand: Argument mining for persuasive online discussions. In *Proceedings of the 2019 Conference on Empirical Methods in Natural Language Processing and the 9th International Joint Conference on Natural Language Processing (EMNLP-IJCNLP)*, pages 2933–2943.

Moitreya Chatterjee, Sunghyun Park, Han Suk Shim, Kenji Sagae, and Louis-Philippe Morency. 2014. Verbal behaviors and persuasiveness in online multimedia content. In *Proceedings of the Second Workshop on Natural Language Processing for Social Media (SocialNLP)*, pages 50–58.

Niladri Chatterjee and Saumya Agrawal. 2006. Word alignment in english-hindi parallel corpus using recency-vector approach: some studies. In *Proceedings of the 21st International Conference on Computational Linguistics and 44th Annual Meeting of the Association for Computational Linguistics*, pages 649–656.

Jacob Devlin, Ming-Wei Chang, Kenton Lee, and Kristina Toutanova. 2019. Bert: Pre-training of deep bidirectional transformers for language understanding. In *Proceedings of the 2019 Conference of the North American Chapter of the Association for Computational Linguistics: Human Language Technologies, Volume 1 (Long and Short Papers)*, pages 4171–4186.

Rory Duthie, Katarzyna Budzynska, and Chris Reed. 2016. Mining ethos in political debate. In *Computational Models of Argument: Proceedings from the Sixth International Conference on Computational Models of Argument (COMMA)*, pages 299–310. IOS Press.

Yash Goyal, Tejas Khot, Douglas Summers-Stay, Dhruv Batra, and Devi Parikh. 2017. Making the v in vqa matter: Elevating the role of image understanding in visual question answering. In *Proceedings of the IEEE conference on computer vision and pattern recognition*, pages 6904–6913.

Nancy Green, Kevin D Ashley, Diane Litman, Chris Reed, and Vern Walker. 2014. Proceedings of the first workshop on argumentation mining. In *Proceedings of the First Workshop on Argumentation Mining*.

Meiqi Guo, Rebecca Hwa, and Adriana Kovashka. 2021. Detecting persuasive atypicality by modeling contextual compatibility. In *Proceedings of the IEEE/CVF International Conference on Computer Vision*, pages 972–982.

Meiqi Guo, Rebecca Hwa, Yu-Ru Lin, and Wen-Ting Chung. 2020. Inflating topic relevance with ideology: A case study of political ideology bias in social topic detection models. In *Proceedings of the 28th International Conference on Computational Linguistics*, pages 4873–4885.

Ivan Habernal and Iryna Gurevych. 2017. Argumentation mining in user-generated web discourse. *Computational Linguistics*, 43(1):125–179.

Lisa Hartling, Michele Hamm, Andrea Milne, Ben Vandermeer, P Lina Santaguida, Mohammed Ansari, Alexander Tsertsvadze, Susanne Hempel, Paul Shekelle, and Donna M Dryden. 2012. Validity and inter-rater reliability testing of quality assessment instruments.

Kaiming He, Xiangyu Zhang, Shaoqing Ren, and Jian Sun. 2016. Deep residual learning for image recognition. In *Proceedings of the IEEE conference on computer vision and pattern recognition*, pages 770–778.

Colin Higgins and Robyn Walker. 2012. Ethos, logos, pathos: Strategies of persuasion in social/environmental reports. In *Accounting forum*, volume 36, pages 194–208. Elsevier.

Di Hu, Chengze Wang, Feiping Nie, and Xuelong Li. 2019. Dense multimodal fusion for hierarchically joint representation. In *ICASSP 2019-2019 IEEE International Conference on Acoustics, Speech and Signal Processing (ICASSP)*, pages 3941–3945. IEEE.

Xinyue Huang and Adriana Kovashka. 2016. Inferring visual persuasion via body language, setting, and deep features. *2016 IEEE Conference on Computer Vision and Pattern Recognition Workshops (CVPRW)*, pages 778–784.

Drew A Hudson and Christopher D Manning. 2019. Gqa: A new dataset for real-world visual reasoning and compositional question answering. In *Proceedings of the IEEE/CVF conference on computer vision and pattern recognition*, pages 6700–6709.

Zaeem Hussain, Mingda Zhang, Xiaozhong Zhang, Keren Ye, Christopher Thomas, Zuha Agha, Nathan Ong, and Adriana Kovashka. 2017. Automatic understanding of image and video advertisements. In *Proceedings of the IEEE Conference on Computer Vision and Pattern Recognition (CVPR)*.

Jungseock Joo, Weixin Li, Francis F Steen, and Song-Chun Zhu. 2014. Visual persuasion: Inferring communicative intents of images. In *Proceedings of the IEEE conference on computer vision and pattern recognition*, pages 216–223.

Klaus Krippendorff. 2011. Computing krippendorff's alpha-reliability.

Alex Krizhevsky, Ilya Sutskever, and Geoffrey E Hinton. 2012. Imagenet classification with deep convolutional neural networks. *Advances in neural information processing systems*, 25.

Julia Kruk, Jonah Lubin, Karan Sikka, Xiao Lin, Dan Jurafsky, and Ajay Divakaran. 2019. Integrating text and image: Determining multimodal document intent in instagram posts. In *Proceedings of the 2019 Conference on Empirical Methods in Natural Language Processing and the 9th International Joint Conference on Natural Language Processing (EMNLP-IJCNLP)*, pages 4622–4632.

J Richard Landis and Gary G Koch. 1977. The measurement of observer agreement for categorical data. *biometrics*, pages 159–174.

John Lawrence and Chris Reed. 2020. Argument mining: A survey. *Computational Linguistics*, 45(4):765–818.

Jiasen Lu, Vedanuj Goswami, Marcus Rohrbach, Devi Parikh, and Stefan Lee. 2020. 12-in-1: Multi-task vision and language representation learning. In *Proceedings of the IEEE/CVF Conference on Computer Vision and Pattern Recognition*, pages 10437–10446.

Stephanie Lukin, Pranav Anand, Marilyn Walker, and Steve Whittaker. 2017. Argument strength is in the eye of the beholder: Audience effects in persuasion. In *Proceedings of the 15th Conference of the European Chapter of the Association for Computational Linguistics: Volume 1, Long Papers*, pages 742–753.

Anastasios Lytos, Thomas Lagkas, Panagiotis Sarigiannidis, and Kalina Bontcheva. 2019. The evolution of argumentation mining: From models to social media and emerging tools. *Information Processing & Management*, 56(6):102055.

Raquel Mochales and Marie-Francine Moens. 2011. Argumentation mining. *Artificial Intelligence and Law*, 19(1):1–22.

Saif M Mohammad, Parinaz Sobhani, and Svetlana Kiritchenko. 2017. Stance and sentiment in tweets. *ACM Transactions on Internet Technology (TOIT)*, 17(3):1–23.

Daniel J O'keefe. 2015. *Persuasion: Theory and research*. Sage Publications.

Sunghyun Park, Han Suk Shim, Moitreya Chatterjee, Kenji Sagae, and Louis-Philippe Morency. 2014. Computational analysis of persuasiveness in social multimedia: A novel dataset and multimodal prediction approach. In *Proceedings of the 16th International Conference on Multimodal Interaction*, pages 50–57.

Isaac Persing and Vincent Ng. 2017. Why can't you convince me? modeling weaknesses in unpersuasive arguments. In *Proceedings of the 26th International Joint Conference on Artificial Intelligence*, pages 4082–4088.

Matilda White Riley. 1954. Communication and persuasion: psychological studies of opinion change.

Christian Stab and Iryna Gurevych. 2014. Annotating argument components and relations in persuasive essays. In *Proceedings of COLING 2014, the 25th international conference on computational linguistics: Technical papers*, pages 1501–1510.

Christian Stab, Christian Kirschner, Judith Eckle-Kohler, and Iryna Gurevych. 2014. Argumentation mining in persuasive essays and scientific articles from the discourse structure perspective. In *ArgNLP*, pages 21–25.

Christian Stab, Tristan Miller, Benjamin Schiller, Pranav Rai, and Iryna Gurevych. 2018. Cross-topic argument mining from heterogeneous sources. In *Proceedings of the 2018 Conference on Empirical Methods in Natural Language Processing*, pages 3664–3674.

Hao Tan and Mohit Bansal. 2019. Lxmert: Learning cross-modality encoder representations from transformers. In *Proceedings of the 2019 Conference on Empirical Methods in Natural Language Processing and the 9th International Joint Conference on Natural Language Processing (EMNLP-IJCNLP)*, pages 5103–5114.

Yao-Hung Hubert Tsai, Paul Pu Liang, Amir Zadeh, Louis-Philippe Morency, and Ruslan Salakhutdinov. 2018. Learning factorized multimodal representations. In *International Conference on Learning Representations*.

Henning Wachsmuth, Manfred Stede, Roxanne El Baff, Khalid Al Khatib, Maria Skeppstedt, and Benno Stein. 2018. Argumentation synthesis following rhetorical strategies. In *Proceedings of the 27th International Conference on Computational Linguistics*, pages 3753–3765.

Zhongyu Wei, Yang Liu, and Yi Li. 2016. Is this post persuasive? ranking argumentative comments in online forum. In *Proceedings of the 54th Annual Meeting of the Association for Computational Linguistics (Volume 2: Short Papers)*, pages 195–200.

Mingda Zhang, Rebecca Hwa, and Adriana Kovashka. 2018. Equal but not the same: Understanding the implicit relationship between persuasive images and text. In *Proceedings of the British Machine Vision Conference (BMVC)*.

A Coding Manual

A.1 Stance

We setup different instructions for stance annotations on different topics since we would like to provide detailed instructions and examples for different topics separately.

A.1.1 Stance: Gun Control

We aim to study the topic and the stance of tweets. Given a tweet accompanying with an image, you need to answer the stance of the tweet towards a given topic, as depicted in Figure 13. Please make sure that you have the basic knowledge about that social topic and you understand the key message that the tweet (i.e. both the text and the image) sends. Just skip the HIT if you are not sure.

Figure 13: Example of stance annotation on gun control

The question is about the stance. You need to decide whether the tweet is relevant or not to the social topic gun control. If it is relevant, then you need to annotate the stance: supports/opposes to/doesn't hold any stance.

A tweet is considered as relevant if it talks about anything that has to do with, but not limited to, the following issue categories: the Second Amendment, Gun control laws, etc. Tweets which contain the following hashtags are probably relevant to gun control: #NoBillNoBreak, #WearOrange, #EndGunViolence, #DisarmHate, #molonlabe, etc.

A tweet should be considered as irrelevant if it mentions a gun death event or a gun violence news, but the context is not necessarily about gun control.

Some examples for relevant tweets and their stance (we only show the text here, but you need to answer this question from both the text and image):

- *"Standing up for the second amendment and carrying a firearm for self defense."* This tweet asks the audience to stand up for the 2nd amendment, which opposes to gun control;
- *"I don't understand why we can't ban assault weapons. We all know they are only used for hunting people. #PrayForOrlando #guncontrolplease."* This tweet talks about banning weapons and contains the hashtag "#guncontrolplease", which supports gun control;
- *A common way to reduce violence in schools is to implement stronger security measures, such as surveillance cameras, security systems, campus guards and metal detectors. #violence #domesticviolence #gun #gunviolence #abuse #people #world #person #workplace."* This tweet is relevant to the topic, but we are not sure about its stance.

Some examples for non-relevant tweets (we only show the text here, but you need to answer this question from both the text and image):

- *"Love will always conquer hate. #PrayForOrlando #OrlandoShooting."* This tweet talks about gun violence but not about gun control;
- *"#Gunviolence has serious and lasting social and emotional impacts on those who directly and indirectly experience it."* This tweet points out the impact of gun violence but not about gun control.

A.1.2 Stance: Immigration

We aim to study the topic and the stance of tweets. Given a tweet accompanying with an image, you need to answer the stance of the tweet towards a given topic, as depicted in Figure 14. Please make sure that you have the basic knowledge about that social topic and you understand the key message that the tweet (i.e. both the text and the image) sends. Just skip the HIT if you are not sure.

The question is about the stance. You need to decide whether the tweet is relevant or not to the social topic immigration. If it is relevant, then you need to annotate the stance: supports/opposes to/doesn't hold any stance.

A tweet is considered as relevant if it talks about anything that has to do with, but not limited to, the following issue categories: Borders,

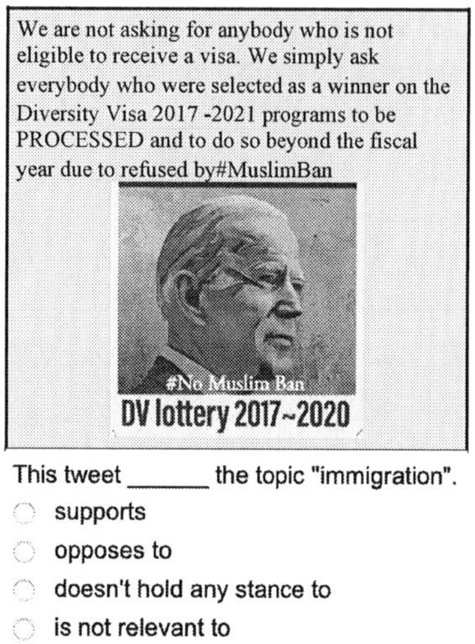

Figure 14: Example of stance annotation on immigration

Birthright citizenship, Immigrant Crime, DACA and the DREAM Act, Deportation debate, Economic impact, Immigration quotas, Immigrants' rights and access to services, Labor Market - American workers and employers, Law enforcement, Refugees, etc.

A tweet should be considered as irrelevant if it mentions a group of immigrant people such as Muslim, Syrian refugees but doesn't explicitly talk about immigration issues.

Some examples for relevant tweets and their stance (we only show the text here, but you need to answer this question from both the text and image):

- *"Man feels bad for new immigrant driver in Brampton that crashed into his truck, causing $6K worth of damages - he had no licence or insurance"*. This tweet is related to the topic of immigration under the category of Immigrant Crime, and it opposes to immigration.
- *"House Bill 3438 will finally give our immigrant students some desperately needed resources! Thank you State Representative Maura Hirschauer for introducing this bill! Now, let's make sure this bill becomes law!"* This tweet is related to the topic of immigration under the category of DREAM Act, and it supports immigration.
- *"I'm a woman that supports Trump to fix economy, immigration, school, military more. #MAGA3X"* We consider a tweet as relevant even if it mentions several topics in addition to immigration, and it opposes to immigration.

Some examples for non-relevant tweets (we only show the text here, but you need to answer this question from both the text and image):

- *"'Will I die, miss?' Terrified Syrian boy suffers suspected gas attack."* This tweet talks about a Syrian boy suffering a gas attack, which may be pointing to a war or terrorist event in Syria, not necessarily directly about an immigration issue.
- *"Virtual tour of Steinbach, in partnership with MANSO, Welcome Place, Eastman Immigrant Services and the Steinbach LIP, coming up March 9th, 2021. It's free so don't miss out!"* This tweet mentions Immigrant Services, but does not talk about any immigration issue.
- *"I called on [USERNAME] for increased vaccine access for South Philadelphia seniors and for members of our immigrant communities. We can't let physical distance and language barriers keep people from this lifesaving vaccine."* This tweet talks about vaccine access for the immigrant community but it doesn't hold any stance towards any immigration policy.

A.1.3 Stance: Abortion

We aim to study the topic and the stance of tweets. Given a tweet accompanying with an image, you need to answer the stance of the tweet towards a given topic, as depicted in Figure 15. Please make sure that you have the basic knowledge about that social topic and you understand the key message that the tweet (i.e. both the text and the image) sends. Just skip the HIT if you are not sure.

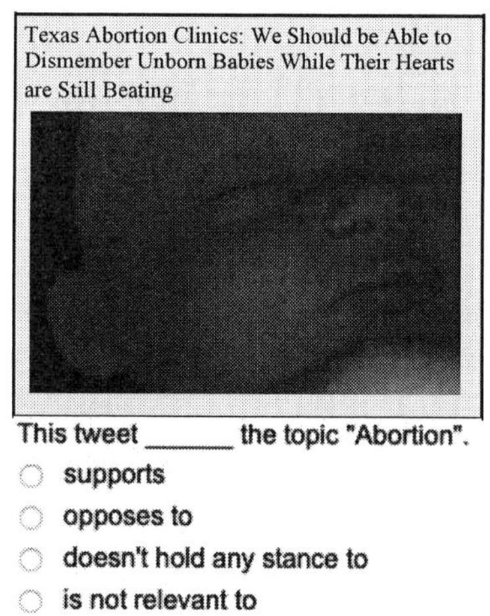

Figure 15: Example of stance annotation on abortion

The question is about the stance. You need to decide whether the tweet is relevant or not to the social topic abortion. If it is relevant, then you need to annotate the stance: supports/opposes to/doesn't hold any stance.

A tweet is considered as relevant if it talks about anything that discusses whether the abortion should be a legal option. If the arguments in the tweet text and image support that the abortion should be a legal option, then please choose "supports"; if arguments oppose to legal abortion, then choose "opposes to"; if arguments doesn't hold any stance for the topic then choose "doesn't hold any stance". Notice that a tweet is considered as irrelevant if it doesn't directly discuss whether the abortion should be a legal option or not, even though it may talk about related topics such as babies born alive after an abortion, birth control, etc.

A.2 Persuasiveness level and image content

We aim to study the persuasiveness level of images in tweets as well as their content. Given a tweet text shown as Figure 16, you need to give a persuasiveness score of it.

Nobody NEEDS to own an assault rifle.
#BanAssaultWeapons #GunViolence
#GunReformNow #BoulderMassacre

Figure 16: Example of a text only tweet

Then given a tweet accompanying an image shown as Figure 17, you need to give a persuasiveness score again.

Nobody NEEDS to own an assault rifle.
#BanAssaultWeapons #GunViolence
#GunReformNow #BoulderMassacre

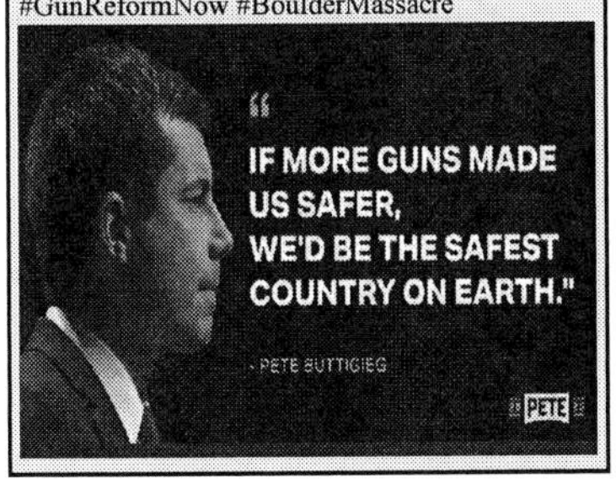

Figure 17: Example of a tweet accompanying an image

Finally, you need to select the content type of the image. The content type of an image represents what type of the information the image mainly carries. Specifically, you need to pick one out of six types below for each image.

Statistics: the image provides evidence by **stating or quoting quantitative information**, such as a chart/data analysis, that is related to the tweet text.

An image could be considered statistics if: 1) It carries quantitative information (number/statistics/etc). 2) The key purpose of the image is to deliver this quantitative information, in the case there are multiple content types involved.

For the examples shown in Figure 18, in the statistics example, the image mainly shows a chart and delivers quantitative information (homicides by firearm per 1 million people). In contrast, in the NOT statistics example, though there are numbers in the image, the main information is a news title and the shooting scene, but not these numbers.

Figure 18: Example of tweets with statistics image and a non-statistics image.

Testimony: the image **quotes statements or conclusions from an authority**, such as a piece of an article/claim from an official document, that is related to the tweet text.

The image can be considered as testimony if: 1) The content contains texts such as statements/conclusions/pieces of article. 2) These texts are original from other resources such as news/celebrities/official documents/etc. 3) The key purpose of the image is to quote the authorized statement, in the case there are multiple content types involved.

For the examples shown in Figure 19, in the Testimony tweet example, the image mainly cites a statement given by the transportation secretary. However, in the NOT Testimony tweet example, though it contains a piece of texts, these texts are not cited from an authority, therefore, it is not testimony.

Anecdote: the image provides information based on the **author's personal experience**, such as facts/personal stories, that are related to the tweet text.

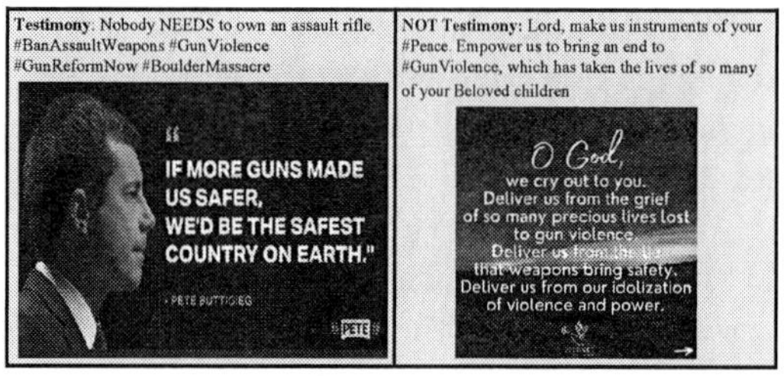

Figure 19: Example of tweets with testimony image and a non-testimony image.

An image can be considered as an anecdote if: 1) It delivers a personal experience, Or 2) it shows a fact/experience that comes from personal view/known by the author. 3) The key purpose of the image is to deliver personal experience, in the case there are multiple content types involved.

For the examples shown in Figure 20, the anecdote image shows the personal view on the fact that guns have been developed since the period of the 2nd amendment, and therefore the laws for guns should be developed as well. However, in the NOT anecdote example, though it comes from a personal statement, it does not describe any fact/experience/stories.

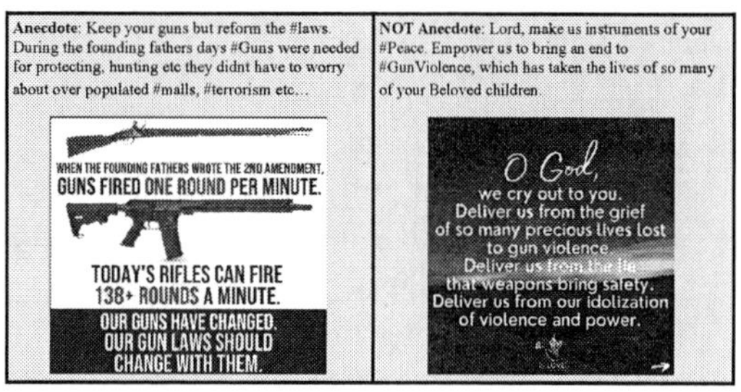

Figure 20: Example of tweets with anecdote image and a non-anecdote image.

Slogan: the image expresses a piece of **advertising phrase**.

An image can be considered as a slogan if: 1) It mainly delivers a piece of text as slogan; 2) The text is for advertising purposes as an advertising phrase/claim/statement. 3) The key purpose of the image is to deliver the piece of text, in the case there are multiple content types involved.

For the examples shown in Figure 21, the slogan image presents a phrase "Actually guns do kill people. Gun Reform Now", therefore it is a slogan. However, For the example of NOT Slogan, though the image is for advertising, it does not contain a phrase for that, therefore it is not a slogan.

Figure 21: Example of tweets with slogan image and a non-slogan image.

Scene photo: the image shows a **literal scene/photograph** that is related to the tweet text.

An image can be considered as a scene photo if: 1) It shows a literal photograph/scene. 2) The image is directly related to the text. 3) The key purpose of the image is to deliver the image content but not the text within, in the case there are multiple content types involved.

Symbolic photo: the image shows a **symbol/art** that expresses the author's viewpoints in a **non-literal** way.

An image can be considered as a symbolic photo if: 1) It shows a symbol/art. 2) It expresses the viewpoint from the author in an implicit way. 3) The key purpose of the image is to deliver the image content but not the text within, in the case there are multiple content types involved.

For example, in Figure 22, the scene photo image shows a real photograph of a gun violence scene reported by CNN news. In the Symbolic photo, though relevant to the text, it shows a photo/image that is related to the text in a non-literal way (blood signifies gun-killing and the hand posture signifies praying), therefore it is not a scene photo but a symbolic photo.

Figure 22: Example of tweets with scene photo image and a symbolic photo image.

The key difference between the Scene photo and Symbolic photo is **whether the photograph**

sends a message literally or symbolically. For a scene photo, the image directly expresses/supports the author's view without any rhetoric; for a symbolic photo, the image may have several possible interpretations and the audience can understand its symbolic meaning after considering the tweet text. Consider the example shown in Figure 23: for the scene photo, it directly shows a protest scene and the author opposes to the abortion by considering it as a lie. In the symbolic photo, the author shows a photo of Notre Dame as a symbol of anti-abortion. The photo is not directly related to abortion, but audience can understand its symbolic meaning after reading the text.

Figure 23: Another example of tweets with scene photo image and a symbolic photo image.

In the case there are multiple content types involved: You need to first identify the key purpose of the image (i.e. what is the most important information in the image). Then please select the content type of the key purpose. Table 7 shows the summary of content types for each key purpose.

Table 7: Summary of content types for each key purpose

Key Purpose		Content Type
Quantitative information in the image		Statistics
Textual information in the image	Statements or conclusions from an authority	Testimony
	Personal experiences/views	Anecdote
	Advertising phrases	Slogan
Graphical information in the image	Literal photograph	Scene Photo
	Non-literal/rhetorical photograph	Symbolic Photo

A.3 Persuasion Mode

We aim to study the **argumentative roles of images** in tweets. Given a tweet accompanying an image, we would ask you to choose the persuasion mode of the image. The persuasion mode of an image represents how the image convinces the audience. Specifically, we will ask you whether the image appeals to logic/emotion/credibility. Additionally, we will ask you why you make the choices.

Q1: Does the image make the tweet more persuasive by appealing to **logic and reasoning**?

The image appeals to logic and reasoning if it persuades audiences with reasoning from a fact/statistics/study case/scientific evidence. Specifically, if: 1) the image **contains information for logic and reasoning**; 2) the image **presents logic and reasoning**.

Also, we will ask you why you made the choice. i.e. Describing the logic/reasoning brought by the image. Such as following, by filling the blank in the textbox:

The logic/reasoning of the image is [the correlation between gun deaths and gun ownership by population].

For example shown in Figure 24, the left image provides a chart that shows the high gun deaths and the high gun ownership by the population of the US, which implies [a correlation between gun death and gun ownership which demonstrates that there will be less gun deaths with gun control.]. On the contrary, the right image shows the scene of the shooting but does not provide any reasoning or logic.

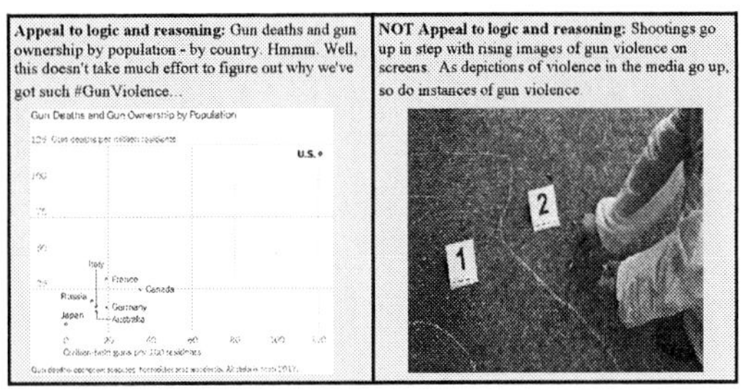

Figure 24: Example of tweets with logos image and non-logos image.

Q2: Does image make the tweet more persuasive by appealing to **emotion**?

The image appeals to **emotion**, if it puts audiences in a certain frame of mind by stimulating them to identify/empathize/sympathize with the arguments.

Specifically, if : 1) the image **invokes the audience with strong emotion**, such as sadness, happiness, compassion, worriness; 2) the image **makes the audience identify/empathize/sympathize** with the author/arguments.

Also, we will ask you why you made the choice. i.e. Describing the emotion(such as anger/amusement/sad/etc.) or impulsion(desire to do something) brought by the image. Such as following, by filling the blank within the [bracket]:

The image evokes my emotion/impulse of

[anger].

For example shown in Figure 25, the left image shows the grieved "Uncle Sam" saying "no" with helplessness, which evokes the [desire for gun control]. The right image provides an item that can revoke [compassion and forgiveness].

Figure 25: Example of tweets with pathos images.

Q3: Does image make the tweet more persuasive by **enhancing credibility and trustworthiness**?

The image **enhances credibility and trustworthiness**, if it makes people trust something more via authorized/trusted expertise/title/reputation.

Specifically, if 1) The image **cites reliable sources** of the event/story/opinion/stance, that can make the contents trustworthy. Reliable sources include news, research reports, celebrated dictum, etc. Sources which are not proved/well-known by the audience (.e.g. an organization logo) are not considered as reliable. 2) the image **shows authorities** that can convince the audience to believe the arguments.

Also, we will ask you why you made the choice. i.e. Describing the resources of the citation that enhances the credibility. Such as following, by filling the blank within the [bracket]:

The credibility is enhanced by [a citation to political report]

For example shown in Figure 26, the left image takes a screenshot of the source of a report from [New York Times], which increases credibility. The NOT Ethos right image shows the views but are not quoted sentences that do not provide the credibility to enhance the argument.

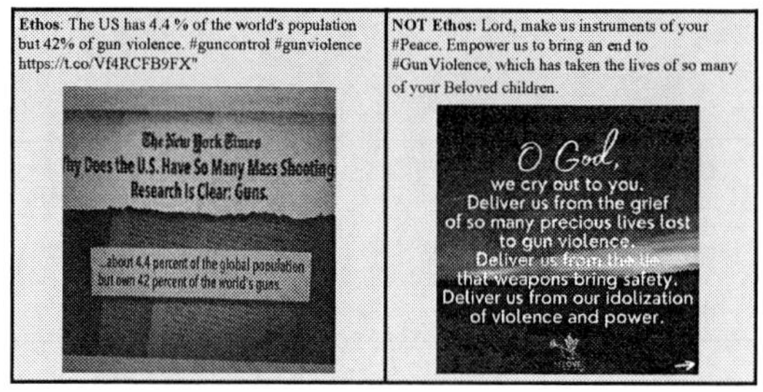

Figure 26: Example of tweets with ethos image and non-ethos image.

Data Augmentation for Improving the Prediction of Validity and Novelty of Argumentative Conclusions

Philipp Heinisch
Bielefeld University
pheinisch@techfak.uni-bielefeld.de

Moritz Plenz
Heidelberg University
plenz@cl.uni-heidelberg.de

Juri Opitz
Heidelberg University
opitz@cl.uni-heidelberg.de

Anette Frank
Heidelberg University
frank@cl.uni-heidelberg.de

Philipp Cimiano
Bielefeld University
cimiano@techfak.uni-bielefeld.de

Abstract

We address the problem of automatically predicting the quality of a conclusion given a set of (textual) premises of an argument, focusing in particular on the task of predicting the validity and novelty of the argumentative conclusion. We propose a multi-task approach that jointly predicts the validity and novelty of the textual conclusion, relying on pre-trained language models fine-tuned on the task. As training data for this task is scarce and costly to obtain, we experimentally investigate the impact of data augmentation approaches for improving the accuracy of prediction compared to a baseline that relies on task-specific data only. We consider the generation of synthetic data as well as the integration of datasets from related argument tasks. We show that especially our synthetic data, combined with class-balancing and instance-specific learning rates, substantially improves classification results (+15.1 points in F_1-score). Using only training data retrieved from related datasets by automatically labeling them for validity and novelty, combined with synthetic data, outperforms the baseline by 11.5 points in F_1-score.

1 Introduction

Recently, there has been interest in developing approaches that can automatically generate conclusions from textual premises (Syed et al., 2021; Heinisch et al., 2022a). Many of these systems rely on language models that are fine-tuned to the task of generating argument conclusions. As the space of possible conclusions that can be generated from a textual premise is a priori not constrained, it is key for a system to understand whether a conclusion candidate is adequate. In particular, models that can predict the quality of conclusions are needed to guide a generation system towards generating suitable argumentation conclusions.

While there has been work on identifying dimensions that characterize argument quality (Wachsmuth et al., 2017b), there are very few models that actually operationalize the (automatic) scoring of the quality of a conclusion. Gurcke et al. (2021) have analyzed whether the notion of "sufficiency" of an argument can be predicted, reaching an accuracy of 90% with transformer-based language models. Heinisch et al. (2022a) have relied on the notions of "validity" and "novelty" in their manual evaluation of conclusion quality – "validity" meaning that the conclusion is justified based on its premise and "novelty" that the conclusion contains novel content which is related to the premise. They have shown that there is a weak correlation between the automatically computed similarity between generated conclusion and reference conclusion, as measured by the BERTscore, on the one hand, and the criteria of manually rated validity and novelty on the other hand. One key problem is that it is difficult to obtain sufficient training data for such tasks, which is a necessary basis for training reliable models for these tasks.

In this paper, we focus on predicting the validity and novelty of argument conclusions. We propose a multi-task classification approach that jointly predicts validity and novelty in a single model that exploits synergies between both tasks.

Our main goal is to explore to what extent data augmentation can contribute to overcome the scarcity of manually labeled argument quality data. We propose and experimentally investigate two types of approaches. On the one hand, we investigate the impact of a synthetic data generation approach that modifies existing training data by generating 'altered copies' of its instances, e.g., by shifting or extending content between premise and conclusion in view of novelty, or by paraphrasing or negating parts of the argument in view of validity. Further, we augment the data labeled for novelty and validity by considering datasets from related argument mining tasks. In particu-

Proceedings of the 9th Workshop on Argument Mining, co-located with the 29th International Conference on Computational Linguistics, pages 19–33
October 17, 2022.

lar, we consider data from the ExplaGraph-dataset by Saha et al. (2021), the IBM-ArgumentQuality-dataset by Gretz et al. (2020b) and the Student-Essays-dataset, annotated for sufficiency of the conclusion by Stab and Gurevych (2017b). We describe how training data from these related tasks is mapped into a form that can be used to enhance the performance of our classifier for validity and novelty prediction. We experimentally evaluate the impact of both data augmentation strategies, showing that the generation of synthetic data outperforms a baseline system trained with only task-specific data by 15.1 points in F_1-score (38.3 vs. 23.2). Even when only using datasets from related tasks as training data, we improve results over the baseline by 11.5 points.

Our main contributions are:

- We present an approach for augmenting training data for validity and novelty, by creating synthetically generated instances. We do this by applying systematic transformations to the original, task-specific training data.
- We also explore various datasets in the field of argument mining, and show how to adapt them automatically to the task of validity and novelty prediction – in combination with specific training techniques, such as instance-adaptive learning rates.
- We perform an extensive automatic evaluation study of various combinations of datasets and training dataset sizes in combination with varying ratios of synthetic vs. non-synthetic instances. We obtain comparable classifier performances without even using the explicitly annotated validity-novelty-training split.
- To give further insight into our results, we present a case study that helps to better understand the effects of interleaving datasets, and of our adaptive training process.

2 Related Work

The task of automatic generation of arguments has received increasing attention in the last years (Gretz et al., 2020a; Schiller et al., 2021). In particular, research has considered the generation of a conclusion given a (textual) premise (Syed et al., 2021; Opitz et al., 2021; Heinisch et al., 2022a). These approaches rely on language models that are fine-tuned to the task of conclusion generation. The generation of conclusions can be seen as a search in the output space of a language model conditioned on the textual premise.

In the manual evaluation of approaches generating conclusions, Opitz et al. (2021) and Heinisch et al. (2022a) found that (generated) conclusions are often either not justified given their premise, or are often just a plain copy or paraphrase of the premise, hence lacking novelty. They conclude that validity and novelty are two main properties a conclusion should fulfill and that stand in a trade-off relation to each other.

A key question is thus how to guide the search or generation process towards i) conclusions that represent a legitimate inference from the premises, meaning that the conclusions are *valid*, and ii) conclusions that are not simple paraphrases of the premises, i.e., they are *novel* or *informative*. Having operationalized and thus automatically computable quality dimensions is key to generating high-quality conclusions.

While there is previous work that identifies quality criteria for arguments (Wachsmuth et al., 2017b; Gretz et al., 2020b), it has been shown that the annotation of such quality criteria is highly subjective (Wachsmuth et al., 2017a; Wachsmuth and Werner, 2020). Also, little work has been done on automatically rating the quality criteria for arguments. An exception is work by Gurcke et al. (2021) who – following Stab and Gurevych (2017b) – studied the operationalization of the criterion of sufficiency. Sufficiency measures whether the premises provide enough evidence for accepting or rejecting the conclusion, and is hence a criterion closely related to our notion of *validity*.

In this paper, we are concerned with developing a computational model that can jointly predict the validity and novelty of conclusions. Given that manually annotated data is scarce, relying on the manual studies by Heinisch et al. (2022a), we consider how task-specific datasets can be augmented with synthetic data and how to repurpose data from related argument mining tasks. Our work is thus related to and encouraged by data augmentation approaches in general. One example is the field of code-mixed languages, which often lacks available annotated training data. Here, Pratapa et al. (2018) showed how to create synthetic instances of code-mixing language by merging sentences from different languages with the help of syntactic parse trees. Another task that has been

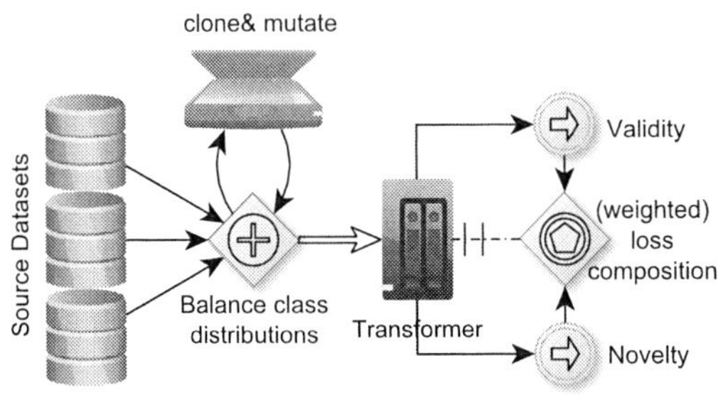

Figure 1: Architecture for validity-novelty multi-task-classification with modulated data augmentation.

shown to profit from automatically generated synthetic training data is grammatical error correction. Here, it has been shown that creating additional training data by corrupting error-free sentences leads to performance gains (Grundkiewicz et al., 2019; Stahlberg and Kumar, 2021). Finally, it has been shown that, by generating synthetic negative instances, one can bootstrap classifiers, e.g., to rate the output of a language model converting knowledge graph triples into natural language (Harkous et al., 2020). Building on prior evidence that generation of synthetic data can improve classifier performance, we investigate a clone&mutate technique that can artificially create new training instances of every class.

3 Methods

In this section, we present our methods for tackling the task of predicting validity and novelty as a classification task. We describe the learning objective and how we generate and modulate additional training data using data augmentation techniques. Figure 1 shows our proposed architecture.

3.1 Learning Objective

We adopt a multi-task classification setting to jointly predict validity and novelty. Inspired by Jin et al. (2020), our loss function includes a combined loss that controls the interaction of the separate individual task losses for novelty and validity, $L_{t_{val}}$ and $L_{t_{nov}}$, which we define by mean squared error. The interaction of the different losses is defined as follows:

$$\mathcal{L} = \alpha \mathcal{L}_{t_{val}} \mathcal{L}_{t_{nov}} + \beta \mathcal{L}_{t_{val}} + \gamma \mathcal{L}_{t_{nov}} \quad (1)$$

where α, β, γ are scalars > 0.

If the target validity or novelty is unknown for a training instance, the related loss $\mathcal{L}_{t_{val}}$ or $\mathcal{L}_{t_{nov}}$ in Equation 1 is set to 0 to avoid random model weight adjustments.

Extending the loss function - introducing dataset- and instance-specific weights We hypothesize that not all instances have the same relevance for the task at hand, so that the impact of each training instance should not be uniform. Therefore, we introduce a fixed weight w_i for each training instance i that is multiplied with the loss computed for the specific training sample i as follows:

$$\mathcal{L}_i = w_i \left(\alpha \mathcal{L}_{t_{val}} \mathcal{L}_{t_{nov}} + \beta \mathcal{L}_{t_{val}} + \gamma \mathcal{L}_{t_{nov}}\right) \quad (2)$$

We investigate three approaches for setting the instance weights. First, as a baseline, in the *uniform weighting* setting, we set the weight w_i uniformly to 1 for every instance. For *dataset-specific weighting* we set w_i to a value that is specific for each dataset and apply it to all instances contained therein. Finally, in the *individual weighting* setting, the weight is set individually for each sample.

3.2 Training Data

We explore the impact of using different source datasets as training data in which we represent each instance as a pair of a textual premise p and conclusion c. We test combinations of data having explicit values for validity and novelty, as well as data without such explicit values. We describe the used datasets including the procedures for setting the values for validity v, novelty n and the weights w in Section 4. To resolve the issue of class-imbalance when merging uneven source datasets, we rely on synthetic data generation as described below, to ensure a larger training dataset while maintaining class balance.

Synthetic generation of data: clone&mutate For augmenting the training data, we propose a procedure that selects training instances randomly and applies a clone&mutate operation to create new instances artificially.

The mutate-operations we apply are as follows:

- *Paraphrase* ($\tilde{\bullet}$)/ *Summarization* ($\ddot{\bullet}$): We apply a language model to change the wording in the premise and/or conclusion. We use the state-of-the-art model Pegasus (Zhang et al., 2020) fine-tuned on paraphrasing or summarization.

from↓ to→	v/n	v/¬n	¬v/n	¬v/¬n
v/n	$p := \tilde{p}$ ...	$c := \ddot{p}$	$c := \neg c$	$p := p + \neg c$
v/¬n		$c := \tilde{c}$ ...		$c := \neg c$
¬v/n		$c := \ddot{p}$ $p := p + \tilde{c}$	... $p := \acute{p}$	$p := p + \neg c$
¬v/¬n		$c := \ddot{p}$ $p := p + \tilde{c}$	$p \mapsto c$	... $c := \acute{c}$

Table 1: Operations for synthetic data generation. Given an instance with a known label **v**alidity and **n**ovelty (rows) and a target **v**alidity/ **n**ovelty-label (columns), each cell lists the set of available operations (Section 3.2) to perform the desired mutation. The union of the operations in the cells in the diagonal apply to any single cell along the diagonal.

- *Substitution ($\acute{\bullet}$):* We introduce synonyms and hypernyms of words in the premise or conclusion using WordNet[1] (Fellbaum, 1998). We also add non-content phrases such as *Hence* and remove punctuation cues with a certain probability. The degree to which words are substituted is determined by random choice.
- *Negation ($\neg\bullet$):* We negate the conclusion or premise by adding/ removing the word "not" while preserving grammaticality.
- *Copy-Conclusion ($+$):* We append the (paraphrased) conclusion to the premise.
- *Move-Premise ($\mapsto$):* We move the last sentence of the premise into the conclusion.

In Table 1 we explain which of the above operations we apply, depending on the intended change of validity and novelty. In case more than one operation is applicable, we randomly select one operation. For example, if we synthesize a new instance with an unchanged label for validity and novelty, we randomly either paraphrase or substitute the premise or the conclusion.

Some cells are empty in Table 1, indicating a lack of mutation operations to accomplish the intended change in validity and novelty. In such cases we sample a new instance for augmentation. Potentially, all these mutations introduce noise to a different extent, e.g. paraphrases not being close to the source text, or substituted hypernyms affecting the validity of the argument, etc. As a kind of confidence measure, we individually scale the weight of the synthetic instances both in the dataset-specific weight mode and in the instance-individual weight mode.

4 Datasets

This section presents the four datasets we use in our work. As a baseline, we rely on the relatively small dataset provided by Heinisch et al. (2022b), in which conclusions were explicitly annotated for validity and novelty (henceforth task-internal data). We further rely on task-external data: the ExplaGraphs dataset by Saha et al. (2021), the IBM Debater datasets by Gretz et al. (2020b) and the annotated essays dataset by Stab and Gurevych (2017a) (sorted by their relatedness to the validity-novelty-classification task in descending order). Appendix A shows examples from each dataset.

4.1 Task-internal Data

We use the dataset of the shared task on predicting validity and novelty provided by Heinisch et al. (2022b) as task-internal data. This dataset is an extension of the dataset provided by Heinisch et al. (2022a) in the context of a conclusion generation approach. They used a fine-tuned language model to generate conclusions that follow a particular frame, conditioned on premises as input. The quality of the generated conclusions was rated regarding their validity and novelty by three annotators. The dataset is rather small in size, consisting of 750 manually annotated instances in the training split. The label distribution is quite imbalanced, with 55% of conclusions being valid, 16% being novel, and only 2% of conclusions being both novel and valid. Some instances (6%) have a tie in the aggregated annotations because one or all annotators indicated *"don't know"* for the aspect in question. We treat a tie in validity as a unknown label and a tie in novelty as $\frac{1}{2}$ since the conclusion seems to contain degrees of novelty[2]. By treating such potentially novel instances as being novel for our statistics in Table 2, we can double the proportion of non-valid & novel instances to 4%.

Since this dataset was manually labeled for the task of validity- and novelty-prediction, we give each instance the highest weight of $w_i = 3$ in the dataset-specific weight configuration. In the

[1]For efficiency reasons, we do not apply word sense disambiguation while selecting the synset in WordNet but give preference to the most probable first synset and prioritize replacing words having few synsets.

[2]Normally, our target values for validity and novelty are either unknown, 0, or 1, with an exception in this dataset for the novelty to model the special case of a tie.

Dataset	#	v/n	v/¬n	¬v/n	¬v/¬n
		task-internal			
train	750	15%	38%	4%	39%
dev	198	19%	44%	22%	15%
test	520	25%	35%	18%	21%
		task-external			
Expla	2.8k	55%	0%	45%	0%
IBM	30k	50%		50%	
Essays	749	66%		34%	

Table 2: Statistics of the processed source datasets, showing the total number (#) of retrieved instances and instance distributions for **v**alidity and **n**ovelty.

individual weighting setting for this dataset, the weight of each instance is scaled proportionally to the instance annotator agreements from $w_i = 1$ (no agreement at all) up to $w_i = 5$ (full agreement for validity and novelty).

Our development split and test split originate from the same data source as the task-internal training split annotated with validity and novelty, but cover different debate topics. For development and test data, we only consider instances that at a minimum achieved votes with majority agreement for both validity and novelty. More details on the dataset are given in Table 2.

4.2 Task-external Data

For our task-external dataset, we combine instances from the following three datasets.

ExplaGraphs by Saha et al. (2021) is a dataset for stance prediction. Given a textual belief and argument, the task is to classify the relationship between these short texts into support and attack. A belief in their setup can be seen as a conclusion, the argument as a premise. To make the link between belief and argument explicit, the authors perform a manual annotation that provides, for each sample, a conceptual explanation graph linking premise and conclusion. When reusing their data, we consider pairs linked by a support relation to have a valid conclusion and those related by an attack relation to have a non-valid conclusion. We consider all instances as novel, since the authors claim high novelty of the conclusions, which is supported by the inserted explanation graphs. Because of the high data quality due to the manual creation process we decide to double-weight each instance with $w_i = 2$ in the dataset-specific weighting. For individual weighting, we also consider the given explanation graph: if the graph is separable into non-contiguous subgraphs by deleting a single commonsense-concept node, indicating an inference which could be easy to undermine and is therefore not so representative, we subtract 0.8 from the dataset-specific weight. In case the resulting graph is linear, hinting a trivial straight-lined inference without combining different concepts or aspects, we further subtract 0.2 from the weight.

IBM Debater - IBM-ArgQ-Rank-30kArgs by Gretz et al. (2020b) (IBM) This dataset is used for determining the quality of arguments from 471 topics. Each argument consists of a topic and a premise pro or con the topic in question. For our purposes, the topic can be regarded as the conclusion. In their dataset, the support or attack of the premise towards its conclusion is manually labeled. We consider conclusions in support vs. attack as valid and invalid, respectively. Since the dataset does not contain any indicators for novelty, we set novelty to *'unknown'*. Since this dataset does not relate to the task of novelty prediction and only indirectly to validity prediction, we do not give a weight preference for instances from this dataset ($w_i = 1$), except in the individual weighting case where we allowed to consider the instance-individual annotated argument quality. We set the weight of low-quality-arguments (which are often defeasible) to $w_i = \frac{1}{2}$, and increase the weight with increasing quality up to $w_i = \frac{3}{2}$. After a manual inspection, we found support instances to be more reliable in general, such that we further add $\frac{1}{3}$ to the weight in these cases. Using the same weighting scheme, we further extend the dataset with 150 instances from arguments from non-American cultures provided by Kiesel et al. (2022) to increase the cultural diversity in this quality dataset.

Essays dataset by Stab and Gurevych (2017a,b) This dataset is based on student essays in which annotators marked spans of premises, claims, and major claims, as well as the argumentative relation between the different spans. Hence, the data is often used for argument unit recognition and classification. In further work by Stab and Gurevych (2017b), the arguments were annotated in terms of sufficiency, to indicate whether the premises provide enough evidence for accepting/rejecting the claim. For our purposes, we consider the binary sufficiency criterion as validity, while setting novelty to *'unknown'*. Again, this dataset does not relate to the task of novelty prediction and covers only one partial aspect of validity in one specific text genre (cropped text parts from student essays). To avoid models tailoring too much on this data, we lower the weight for each instance to $w_i = \frac{3}{4}$ in the dataset-specific setting. As for individual weighting, we set the weight to $\frac{1}{2}$ in case no annotator agreement information was given for an instance and to $\frac{5}{6}$ and 1, corresponding to a majority-agreement and full-agreement, respectively.

5 Experiments and Evaluation

In this section, we present our experimental results with the goal of testing the following hypotheses:

- The available task-internal training data is not sufficient to solve the task of predicting validity and novelty in a supervised manner (without additional external knowledge).
- Augmenting the data with task-external and synthetic data improves the quality of the predictions.
- Different amounts of (synthetic) data influence the performance. We expect that an optimal mixing proportion yields high F_1-scores, even without task-internal training data.

5.1 Experimental Setup

For our experiments we use the pretrained language model `roberta-large` (Zhuang et al., 2021) as available in the transformers library (Wolf et al., 2020), predicting both validity and novelty by having two feed-forwarded classification heads post-processed by the Sigmoid-function to map the prediction into the interval of $[0, 1]$ for validity and novelty, respectively.

Evaluation metric For evaluation, we rely on the ValNov-score which is the macro F_1-score over the F_1-scores for each class as shown in Equation 3.

$$
\begin{aligned}
ValNov = (&F_1(\text{valid\&novel})+\\
&F_1(\text{valid\&not-novel})+\\
&F_1(\text{not-valid\&novel})+\\
&F_1(\text{not-valid\&not-novel}))/4
\end{aligned} \tag{3}
$$

We also measure the macro F_1-score for Validity (Val) and Novelty (Nov) separately.

Training We use the Adam optimizer with a maximum learning rate of 3e-5, a model weight decay of 3e-7, a batch size of 8 and early-stopping, checking the model performance on the development split each quarter of an epoch with patience of 4. We balance the source dataset and class distribution, allowing up to 20% instances having unknown validity or unknown novelty. We do not clone&mutate instances with unknown validity or novelty. Regarding the loss function in Equation 2, we set $\alpha = \beta = \gamma = 0.5$. We use binary target values $\{0, 1\}$ for validity and novelty.

Model selection The performance of our models varies substantially between runs due to randomized initialization. Some runs produce models that end up predicting only one class. To circumvent this problem, we run the training with different initialization for 12 runs, selecting the model with the best performance on the development set. More details can be found in the Appendix B.1.

5.2 Results and Evaluation

We run several experiments to evaluate our three hypotheses. First, we use only task-internal training data, then consider the integration of task-external and synthetic data, and finally, we vary training set sizes and data type proportions.

Baseline results (using only task-internal data) In this setting, our training set consists of 750 instances. This size is small compared to custom training sets for fine-tuning language models. Moreover, the number of instances per class is not balanced (Table 2). Hence, the results for the fine-tuned model are slightly worse compared to a random baseline of 24.5 ValNov-score. The best-performing model on the development split yields a ValNov-score of 23.2. Despite this low score, the F_1-score for classifying valid conclusions (61.5) outperforms the random baseline (49.5) and many other experimental settings. In contrast, the model completely fails to discriminate novelty: No novel instance was correctly predicted as novel. Introducing a class balance in the training data by undersampling removes this bias, and increases the F_1-score in novelty from 36.1 to 41.5 points which is still below the random baseline (49.8). The class-balanced training set contains only 137 instances, which results in a worse overall model performance of 21.4 ValNov-score. This first set of experiments highlights the need for techniques to overcome the problem of scarce labeled data and especially for solving the task of novelty prediction. We therefore aim to address the problem through augmentation of training data.

Augmenting training data with task-external and synthetic data Table 3 shows the results with different training set mixtures and instance weighting configurations, including the discussed baseline as reference.

Task-internal + synthetic training data: Augmenting task-internal data with synthetic instances by generating instances for underrepresented classes outperforms random guessing and our baseline model. We result in overall ValNov-scores of 33.3 / 38.1 / 38.3 without weight adjustments / weight adjustments only for synthetic instances / individual weight adjustments, respectively, outperforming the baseline by between 10.1 and 15.1 points. While there is a minor decrease on the prediction of validity, the prediction of novelty nearly doubles its F_1-score, yielding scores of up to 66.2 due to the additional novel instances in the synthetic data.

Task-external training data: Using task-external training data only without any task-internal data yields low ValNov-scores between 10 and 20.7, yielding worse results than the random baseline. This seems plausible as more than 93% of the datapoints lack a novelty label, with ExplaGraph being the only dataset including novelty information by exclusively presenting novel instances. It is only through the inclusion of synthetic data that we can increase performance to a ValNov-score of 22.6.

Task-internal + task-external training data: When combining task-internal and task-external training data, we generally observe minor improvements in the ValNov-score, having ValNov-scores of up to 25.1, which outperforms random guessing and our model baseline using internal training data only. One exception is the case of dataset-specific instance weighting, in which we regress to a model classifying all instances as valid and novel due to the (weighted) overpresence of valid and novel training instances. The settings in which synthetic training data is added worsen the ValNov-scores compared to the version of the system using internal and synthetic data only.

Effect of weighting Examining the impact of our weighting mechanisms, we see that the *dataset-specific weighting scheme* often worsens the results. For the task-internal condition in Table 3, we see no impact at all on ValNov-score. Considering the condition using internal and synthetic data, we do see an impact of dataset-specific weighting by +4.8 points in the ValNov-score by distinguishing between original and synthetic data in the impact of the learning rate. For the other conditions (external + synthetic data, internal + external + synthetic data) we see a detrimental impact of dataset-specific weighting. The *individual weighting scheme* has very mixed results in general. The internal+synthetic condition benefits from the individual weighting mechanisms as the ValNov-score increases by 0.2 points (from 38.1 to 38.3) and significantly increases the novelty score by 6.6 points (from 59.4 to 66.2), yielding the overall best result. For the other settings, the impact of individual weighting is very mixed, leading to similarly worse results compared to the dataset-specific weighting in the case of external data and internal+external+synthetic data. In the case of using external+synthetic data and internal+external data, however, individual weighting leads to higher ValNov-scores (+1.8 and +1.2 compared to disabled weight adjustments).

Effect of training data sizes for synthetic data Since our synthetic data generation method can generate an arbitrary number of instances, we explore the impact of different training data sizes on model performance. As sample sizes we consider a range from 100 instances to 100k instances (see Table 4). For all configurations, we see a clear increase in ValNov-score when moving from 100 to 1k training instances. We see improvements of between 4.1 points (internal+external data, individual weighting) to 19 points (internal data, individual weighting). Moving from 1k to 10k instances has a mixed impact. For some settings based on a large merged dataset of non-synthetic instances or individual weighting we see a further improvement (+1.6 for internal data with individual weighting, and +14.3 for in-&external with dataset-fixed weights). For other conditions we see a worsening of results moving from 1k to 10k instances. Interestingly, when moving from 10k to 100k instances, we see a worsening for nearly all conditions compared to the best results at 1k or 10k. Overall, the sweet-spot thus lies around 1k to 10k instances.

Data components	w/o weight ValNov	Val	Nov	dataset-specific weight ValNov	Val	Nov	individual weight ValNov	Val	Nov
internal	23.2	**61.5**	36.1	23.2	**61.5**	36.1	22.7	57.7	36.1
+ synthetic	33.3	57.4	59.0	38.1	60.2	59.4	**38.3**	57.2	**66.2**
external	20.7	58.5	36.4	10.0	37.7	30.3	10.0	37.7	30.3
+ synthetic	21.8	50.5	42.6	15.8	41.8	36.0	22.6	41.9	57.1
internal+external	23.9	53.8	41.5	10.0	37.7	30.3	25.1	59.3	43.2
+ synthetic	32.7	57.9	51.0	13.1	37.7	36.1	13.1	37.7	36.1

Table 3: F_1-score-results for augmenting the training data with task-external and synthetic data. Synthetic data (based on the given data components) includes the class-balance, providing data for underrepresented classes. Using synthetic data does not change the number of training instances here, only the instance class distribution.

Config	100	1k	10k	100k
internal (ind. w.)	17.4	36.4	38.0	29.4
external (set w.)	18.9	34.7	32.9	23.9
external (ind. w.)	19.7	33.8	30.3	25.4
int-+external (w/o w.)	18.8	23.0	17.9	34.4
int-+external (set w.)	19.2	23.8	38.0	33.8
int-+external (ind. w.)	21.7	25.8	25.6	26.9

Table 4: ValNov-scores for training sizes (+synthetic data) without instance weighting (w/o w.), w/ dataset-specific (set w.) and w/ individual weighting (ind. w.)

Summary of results Using the task-internal data without augmenting it with synthetic or external data is insufficient to solve the validity-novelty-prediction task (ValNov-score of 23.2). Augmenting the task-internal data with synthetic data, including the class-balancing effect, improves the prediction performance. In fact, our best configuration is the one using the task-internal data class-balanced by the synthetic data, reaching the overall best ValNov-score of 38.3 and a high novelty F_1-score of 66.2, in addition to a above-average validity prediction score of 57.2 that is only seven points away from the overall maximum (64.5 with 10,000 dataset-specific weighted internal-external-synthetic instances).

Adding additional external or more synthetic data does not improve performance in general. In fact, we see the different data proportions heavily influence the performance, especially the right amount of synthetic data seems to be crucial. While we see some improvements in having 1k and 10k instances, the performance is often negatively affected when adding further synthetic training data instances.

A quite remarkable result, however, is that in spite of not seeing improvements in the ValNov-score when using external data *in addition* to task-internal data, we observe that by using task-external data *instead of* task-internal data, we can get comparable results to training with task-internal data. Using 1,000 task-external and synthetic instances with dataset-specific weighting, we obtain a model with only 3.6 points less in the ValNov-score and an F_1-score of 65.2 in the novelty aspect, which is only 2.4 points below the overall maximum (10,000 individual weighted internal-synthetic instances).

5.3 Case Study

In a case study, we compare the predictions made by the *task-internal model* (trained with task-internal training data without any changes), the *task-internal-synthetic model* (750 individual-weighted task-internal instances class-balanced with synthetic instances), the *task-internal-external-synthetic model* (10,000 dataset-specific weighted task-internal and task-external instances class-balanced with synthetic instances) and *task-external-synthetic model* (1,000 dataset-specific weighted task-external instances class-weighted with synthetic instances). We consider different conclusion candidates for the premise:

> *"**Year-round school**: Many districts are finding that year-round schools are not cost-effective to operate unless the student population substantially exceeds traditional school capacity".*

The conclusion *"Many districts find year-round schools are not cost-effective"* is a valid but not novel summary of the premise – which is easy to detect by paraphrase-recognition capabilities. All our four models succeed in predicting the validity and lack of novelty of this conclusion.

In order to further understand the behavior of our models, we consider a conclusion that incorporates an inconsistency with respect to the above premise. However, the inconsistency is subtle and not trivial to detect. Consider the conclusion: *"Year-round schools are ineffective when student populations exceed capacity"* which contradicts the statement that "year-round schools would be cost-effective if student population would exceed capacity", which follows from the above premise. The conclusion thus represents a non-valid-non-novel example. All models with the exception of the task-internal-external-synthetic model fail to recognize the contradiction and classify the example as valid. We hypothesize that the task-internal-external-synthetic model captures this example because it has been largely trained with antonym-substitution (cost-effective vs. ineffective in the above example). However, the model slightly misclassifies the novelty with a probability of 56% being novel due to a tendency to classify non-valid instances as novel. We consider a more obviously inconsistent conclusion with an explicit negation: *"Year-round schools are not cost-effective for large schools"*. All models misclassify this example as valid, showing a general lack of logical reasoning capabilities. In particular, there is an obvious element of commonsense-knowledge (large school = school with high student capacity) that the models are lacking.

Finally, we consider a clearly off-topic conclusion: *"Offshore drilling is very valuable to the US economy"*, which is neither valid nor novel. All models successfully predict the non-validity of the conclusion, including the task-internal model that otherwise consistently votes for validity in our case study. Regarding the novelty aspect, only the task-external-synthetic model misclassified the example as novel because it never saw such completely unrelated conclusions in its training data.

We further analyze the models in Appendix B.3.

6 Conclusion

Predicting the validity and novelty of a given conclusion based on its premise is a challenging task. Using 750 class-unbalanced training instances annotated with validity and novelty does not provide enough evidence for tuning a large language model. Augmenting the task-internal training data to 10,000 instances using task-external and synthetic data increases the ValNov-score up to 38.0. Using task-internal and synthetic data to balance the training data increases this score to 38.3. However, the results achieved by data augmentation techniques are still very modest, showing that massive training data and modern language models alone are not sufficient for solving the task. While valid but non-novel instances can, to a large part, be detected using paraphrase recognition tests, many instances require logical inference and commonsense knowledge to properly classify validity and novelty. None of these capabilities are supported in the subsymbolic approach we chose in this work. In future work, we aim to investigate the impact of incorporating commonsense knowledge and deeper logical reasoning into the task of validity and novelty prediction.

References

Christiane Fellbaum, editor. 1998. *WordNet: An Electronic Lexical Database*. Language, Speech, and Communication. MIT Press, Cambridge, MA.

Shai Gretz, Yonatan Bilu, Edo Cohen-Karlik, and Noam Slonim. 2020a. The workweek is the best time to start a family – a study of GPT-2 based claim generation. In *Findings of the Association for Computational Linguistics: EMNLP 2020*, pages 528–544, Online. Association for Computational Linguistics.

Shai Gretz, Roni Friedman, Edo Cohen-Karlik, Assaf Toledo, Dan Lahav, Ranit Aharonov, and Noam Slonim. 2020b. A large-scale dataset for argument quality ranking: Construction and analysis. *Proceedings of the AAAI Conference on Artificial Intelligence*, 34(05):7805–7813.

Roman Grundkiewicz, Marcin Junczys-Dowmunt, and Kenneth Heafield. 2019. Neural grammatical error correction systems with unsupervised pre-training on synthetic data. In *Proceedings of the Fourteenth Workshop on Innovative Use of NLP for Building Educational Applications*, pages 252–263, Florence, Italy. Association for Computational Linguistics.

Timon Gurcke, Milad Alshomary, and Henning Wachsmuth. 2021. Assessing the sufficiency of arguments through conclusion generation. In *Proceedings of the 8th Workshop on Argument Mining*, pages 67–77, Punta Cana, Dominican Republic. Association for Computational Linguistics.

Hamza Harkous, Isabel Groves, and Amir Saffari. 2020. Have your text and use it too! end-to-end neural data-to-text generation with semantic fidelity. In *Proceedings of the 28th International Conference on Computational Linguistics*, pages 2410–2424, Barcelona, Spain (Online). International Committee on Computational Linguistics.

Philipp Heinisch, Anette Frank, Juri Opitz, and Philipp Cimiano. 2022a. Strategies for framing argumentative conclusion generation. In *Findings of the Association for Computational Linguistics: ACL-INLG 2022*. Association for Computational Linguistics.

Philipp Heinisch, Anette Frank, Juri Opitz, Moritz Plenz, and Philipp Cimiano. 2022b. Overview of the validity and novelty prediction shared task. In *Proceedings of the 9th*

Workshop on Argument Mining, Gyeongju, Republic of Korea. Association for Computational Linguistics.

Ning Jin, Jiaxian Wu, Xiang Ma, Ke Yan, and Yuchang Mo. 2020. Multi-task learning model based on multi-scale cnn and lstm for sentiment classification. *IEEE Access*, 8:77060–77072.

Johannes Kiesel, Milad Alshomary, Nicolas Handke, Xiaoni Cai, Henning Wachsmuth, and Benno Stein. 2022. Identifying the Human Values behind Arguments. In *60th Annual Meeting of the Association for Computational Linguistics (ACL 2022)*. Association for Computational Linguistics.

Juri Opitz, Philipp Heinisch, Philipp Wiesenbach, Philipp Cimiano, and Anette Frank. 2021. Explainable unsupervised argument similarity rating with Abstract Meaning Representation and conclusion generation. In *Proceedings of the 8th Workshop on Argument Mining*, pages 24–35, Punta Cana, Dominican Republic. Association for Computational Linguistics.

Adithya Pratapa, Gayatri Bhat, Monojit Choudhury, Sunayana Sitaram, Sandipan Dandapat, and Kalika Bali. 2018. Language modeling for code-mixing: The role of linguistic theory based synthetic data. In *Proceedings of the 56th Annual Meeting of the Association for Computational Linguistics (Volume 1: Long Papers)*, pages 1543–1553, Melbourne, Australia. Association for Computational Linguistics.

Swarnadeep Saha, Prateek Yadav, Lisa Bauer, and Mohit Bansal. 2021. ExplaGraphs: An explanation graph generation task for structured commonsense reasoning. In *EMNLP*.

Benjamin Schiller, Johannes Daxenberger, and Iryna Gurevych. 2021. Aspect-controlled neural argument generation. In *Proceedings of the 2021 Conference of the North American Chapter of the Association for Computational Linguistics: Human Language Technologies*, pages 380–396, Online. Association for Computational Linguistics.

Christian Stab and Iryna Gurevych. 2017a. Parsing Argumentation Structures in Persuasive Essays. *Computational Linguistics*, 43(3):619–659.

Christian Stab and Iryna Gurevych. 2017b. Recognizing insufficiently supported arguments in argumentative essays. In *Proceedings of the 15th Conference of the European Chapter of the Association for Computational Linguistics: Volume 1, Long Papers*, pages 980–990, Valencia, Spain. Association for Computational Linguistics.

Felix Stahlberg and Shankar Kumar. 2021. Synthetic data generation for grammatical error correction with tagged corruption models. In *Proceedings of the 16th Workshop on Innovative Use of NLP for Building Educational Applications*, pages 37–47, Online. Association for Computational Linguistics.

Shahbaz Syed, Khalid Al Khatib, Milad Alshomary, Henning Wachsmuth, and Martin Potthast. 2021. Generating informative conclusions for argumentative texts. In *Findings of the Association for Computational Linguistics: ACL-IJCNLP 2021*, pages 3482–3493, Online. Association for Computational Linguistics.

Henning Wachsmuth, Nona Naderi, Ivan Habernal, Yufang Hou, Graeme Hirst, Iryna Gurevych, and Benno Stein. 2017a. Argumentation quality assessment: Theory vs. practice. In *Proceedings of the 55th Annual Meeting of the Association for Computational Linguistics (Volume 2: Short Papers)*, pages 250–255, Vancouver, Canada. Association for Computational Linguistics.

Henning Wachsmuth, Nona Naderi, Yufang Hou, Yonatan Bilu, Vinodkumar Prabhakaran, Tim Alberdingk Thijm, Graeme Hirst, and Benno Stein. 2017b. Computational argumentation quality assessment in natural language. In *Proceedings of the 15th Conference of the European Chapter of the Association for Computational Linguistics: Volume 1, Long Papers*, pages 176–187, Valencia, Spain. Association for Computational Linguistics.

Henning Wachsmuth and Till Werner. 2020. Intrinsic quality assessment of arguments. In *Proceedings of the 28th International Conference on Computational Linguistics*, pages 6739–6745, Barcelona, Spain (Online). International Committee on Computational Linguistics.

Thomas Wolf, Lysandre Debut, Victor Sanh, Julien Chaumond, Clement Delangue, Anthony Moi, Pierric Cistac, Tim Rault, Rémi Louf, Morgan Funtowicz, Joe Davison, Sam Shleifer, Patrick von Platen, Clara Ma, Yacine Jernite, Julien Plu, Canwen Xu, Teven Le Scao, Sylvain Gugger, Mariama Drame, Quentin Lhoest, and Alexander M. Rush. 2020. Transformers: State-of-the-art natural language processing. In *Proceedings of the 2020 Conference on Empirical Methods in Natural Language Processing: System Demonstrations*, pages 38–45, Online. Association for Computational Linguistics.

Jingqing Zhang, Yao Zhao, Mohammad Saleh, and Peter Liu. 2020. Pegasus: Pre-training with extracted gap-sentences for abstractive summarization. In *Proceedings of the 2020 Thirty-seventh International Conference on Machine Learning*, pages 1–55, Vienna, Austria,. ICML.

Liu Zhuang, Lin Wayne, Shi Ya, and Zhao Jun. 2021. A robustly optimized BERT pre-training approach with post-training. In *Proceedings of the 20th Chinese National Conference on Computational Linguistics*, pages 1218–1227, Huhhot, China. Chinese Information Processing Society of China.

A Examples from the Task-internal and Task-external Datasets

In this section we give examples for each dataset presented in Section 4, showing how the examples have been mapped to our premise-conclusion schema with novelty and validity indicators.

A.1 Task-internal Dataset

Example 1:

(1) Premise: *Twin Towers reconstruction: Pentagon, hardly a symbol of peace, has been rebuilt. Twin towers weren't. The message that this sends to the public is hardly positive.*
Conclusion: *Pentagon rebuild sends wrong message of peace*

Validity: yes / Novelty: yes
Weight: dataset-specific: 3 / individual-weighted: 1.5

Example 2:

(2) Premise: *Twin Towers reconstruction: Pentagon, hardly a symbol of peace, has been rebuilt. Twin towers weren't. The message that this sends to the public is hardly positive.*
Conclusion: *Twin towers are hardly a symbol of peace*
Validity: no / Novelty: no
Weight: dataset-specific: 3 / individual-weighted: 3.25

A.2 Task-external Datasets

A.2.1 ExplaGraphs

Example 1:

(3) Premise: *It is not realistic to abandon television, as many people still get current new information from it.*
Conclusion: *Television viewing should be moderated, not banned.*
Validity: yes / Novelty: yes
Weight: dataset-specific: 2 / individual-weighted: 2

Example 2:

(4) Premise: *Intelligence tests lower self esteem.*
Conclusion: *Intelligence tests are harmless.*
Validity: no / Novelty: yes
Weight: dataset-specific: 2 / individual-weighted: 1.8

A.2.2 IBM-ArgQ_Rank-30kArguments

(5) Premise: *A country with a diverse population is better represented by a multi-party system.*
Conclusion: *We should adopt a multi-party system*
Validity: yes / Novelty: unknown
Weight: dataset-specific: 1 / individual-weighted: 1.27

Example 2:

(6) Premise: *telemarketers have to earn a living wage somehow. it is better than government assistance*
Conclusion: *We should ban telemarketing*
Validity: no / Novelty: unknown
Weight: dataset-specific: 1 / individual-weighted: 0.53

A.2.3 Essay dataset

(7) Premise: *All the living creatures live together on our mother Earth and she is the only one.*
Conclusion: *First , environmental protection is far more urgent than economic developments.*
Validity: yes / Novelty: unknown
Weight: dataset-specific: 0.75 / individual-weighted: 0.5

Example 2:

(8) Premise: *Arts include many forms and music as well as cinema are the most typical . These two art forms not only provide the public with entertainment but also contribute significantly to the economy .*
Conclusion: *But our standard of living also depend on another factor - spiritual life which is related closely with arts .*
Validity: no / Novelty: unknown
Weight: dataset-specific: 0.75 / individual-weighted: 0.5

B Further Details of the Experimental Setup and Results

We give further details about the model selection process for each experiment (B.1) and give further insights into the model performance (B.2) and test prediction (B.3). For additional information about the implementation consult our code located at `https://github.com/phhei/ValidityNoveltyRegressor`.

B.1 Model Selection

In our experiments, we observed a high variance of results across runs. The deviations are mainly caused by the random factors introduced in the synthetic data generation and partially caused by the random initialization of weights for the classification heads. We observed in particular that often fine-tuned models get stuck in local optima in some runs, often over-focusing on one specific class (e.g., valid&not-novel) and failing completely in all other three classes. We thus ran each configuration 12 times per default, reducing the number of runs further for increasing training data sizes, that is, six runs for 10,000 - 50,000 instances, and three runs in the case of 100,000 instances. We select the model achieving the highest ValNov-score on the development split among all runs.

Config	100 Val	100 Nov	1k Val	1k Nov	10k Val	10k Nov	100k Val	100k Nov
internal (ind. w.)	45.3	38.5	61.4	59.6	54.7	67.6	58.0	57.9
external (set w.)	47.6	40.8	57.0	65.2	57.3	53.9	44.8	51.6
external (ind. w.)	43.4	47.7	58.0	63.4	49.3	58.1	51.2	49.0
int-+external (w/o w.)	50.0	39.3	49.0	46.2	48.5	40.3	53.0	60.0
int-+external (set w.)	46.2	49.5	40.4	39.6	64.5	57.2	57.7	55.0
int-+external (ind. w.)	54.2	40.0	60.8	39.1	43.0	61.8	52.8	49.5

Table 5: F_1-scores for **val**idity and **nov**elty for different training sizes (+synthetic data) without instance weighting (w/o w.), w/ dataset-specific (set w.) and w/ individual weighting (ind. w.). For the ValNov-scores see Table 4.

We observed that selecting the final model based on the performance on the development split is a good indicator, especially for models trained on large training sets. In 58% of all cases, the best performing model on the development split was also the best performing model on the test split. In all other cases, the selected model achieves ∅88.8% of the ValNov-score that would have been achieved based on model selection on test data.

B.2 Further Details regarding Effect of Training Data Sizes for Synthetic Data

Table 5 shows the F_1-scores in addition to the ValNov-scores given in Table 4. Table 4 and 5 omit some source-data-weight-combinations, e.g. task-internal data in combination with the uniform weighting setting. We omit these combinations because they do not outperform the other weight settings given the same training data in any data set size. Table 3 hints at this trend already, with instance-individual weighting as the outperforming weighting setting when using only task-internal data in combination with synthetic data.

B.3 Further Analyses of the Test-predictions

We carried out a further analysis of the predictions on the task-internal test set of the baseline model (Section 5.2), the *task-internal model* (trained with the task-internal training data without any changes), the *task-internal-synthetic model* (750 individual-weighted task-internal instances class-balanced with synthetic instances), the *task-internal-external-synthetic model* (10,000 dataset-specific weighted task-internal and task-external instances class-balanced with synthetic instances), and *task-external-synthetic model* (1,000 dataset-specific weighted task-external instances class-weighted with synthetic instances). Figures 2-5 show the heatmaps and histograms for validity and novelty of the predictions and prediction errors of these four models.

The baseline model (Figure 2) succeeds in distinguishing between valid and non-valid conclusions in some cases. However, it fails completely in the case of novelty, as every instance is classified as non-novel (the predicted probability of a conclusion being novel is between 1% and 5%). This leads to very low scores regarding novelty prediction, yielding an F_1-score of 36.1. The baseline model is thus biased to detect valid but non-novel conclusions, for example repetitions of the premise.

The model trained on data augmented with synthetic instances (Figure 3) is more diverse in its predictions, mostly predicting examples as being valid, both novel and not novel. The model learns successfully to discriminate between novel and non-novel conclusions with an an F_1-score of 66.2, thus being a good summarization detector. However, the model avoids to classify a conclusion as not valid but novel, with an F_1-score of only 15.1 in this case. By avoiding such difficult cases, the model correctly predicts at least one of the two quality dimensions (novelty, validity) in many cases.

The task-internal-external-synthetic model (Figure 4) succeeds very well in recognizing conclusions that are valid but not novel (66.2 F_1-score). The corresponding training data includes a high number of examples which vary in terms of their validity label. The performance of the model on novelty prediction, however, remains weak.

When discarding the task-internal data and thus applying a model trained on task-external data to task-internal test data (Figure 5), this leads to high diversity and thus uncertainty in the predicted labels. In spite of this, it is quite remarkable that the model predicts at least one of the two quality dimensions correctly in many cases. However, the model has lower F_1-scores in recognizing valid-non-novel conclusions (59.9) and especially non-valid-non-novel conclusions (11.0). We hypothesize that this is due to the fact that the model has only seen synthetic instances in the latter class. Hence, the model rarely saw random off-topic conclusions which are not valid and not novel and part of the task-internal test data. The performance of the model on recognizing non-valid and novel conclusions (28.7 F_1-score) is however above the baseline. This is likely due to the many non-valid but novel instances in the ExplaGraphs dataset.

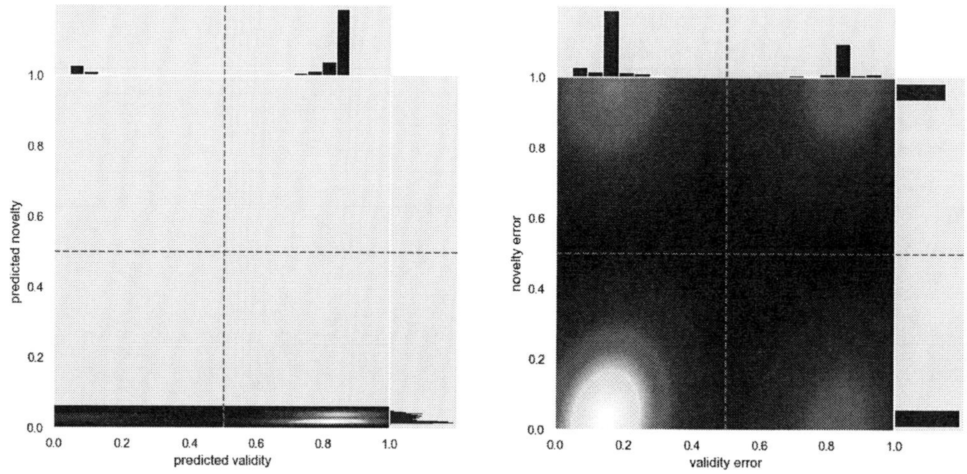

Figure 2: Heatmaps for the baseline-model *(task-internal model)*. The highest predicted value for novelty is 0.05. Therefore, the plots contain gray areas.

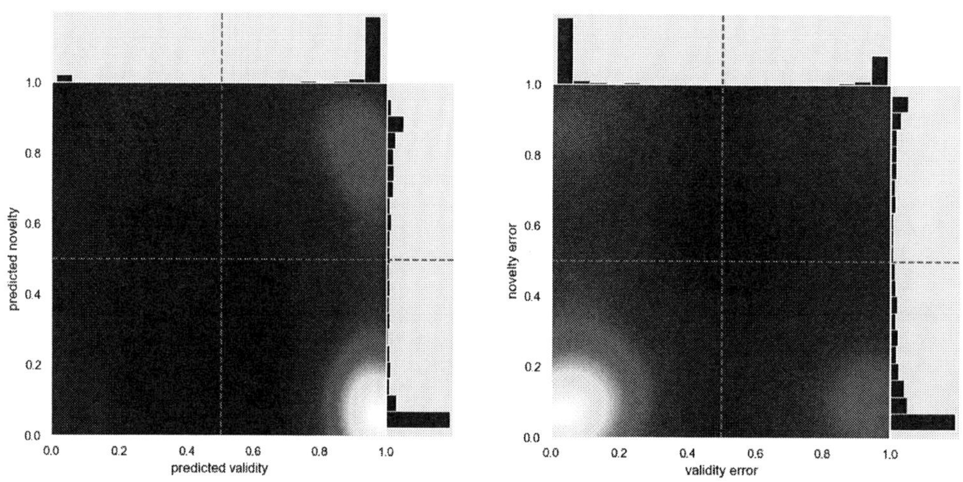

Figure 3: Heatmaps for the *task-internal-synthetic model.*

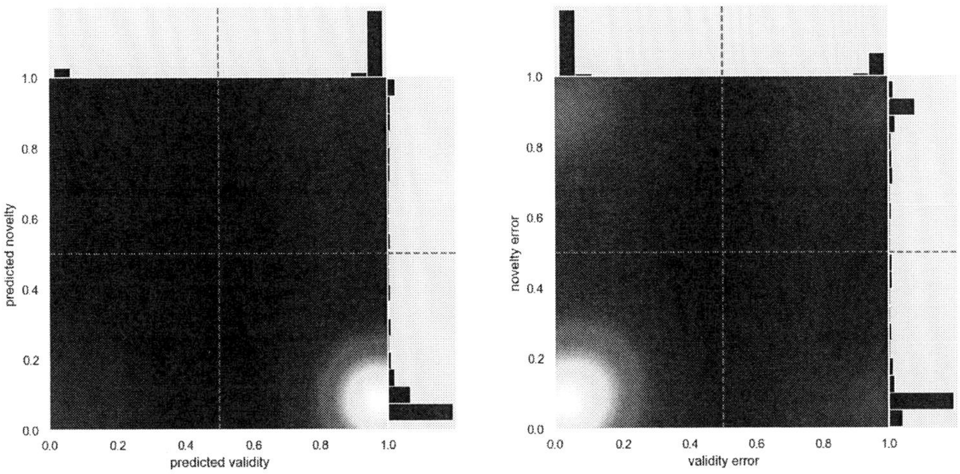

Figure 4: Heatmaps for the *task-internal-external-synthetic model.*

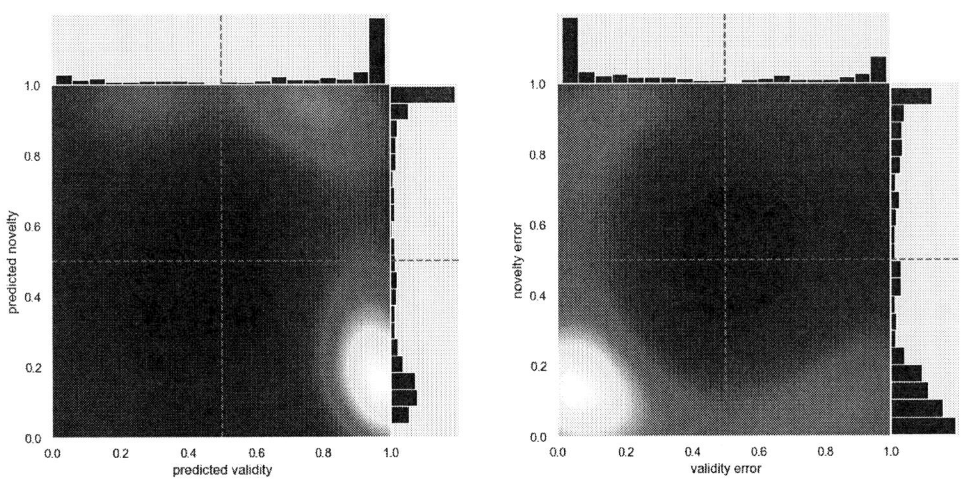

Figure 5: Heatmaps for the *task-external-synthetic model.*

Do Discourse Indicators Reflect the Main Arguments in Scientific Papers?

Yingqiang Gao[†], **Nianlong Gu**[†], **Jessica Lam**[†]
Richard H.R. Hahnloser[†]

[†]Institute of Neuroinformatics, University of Zurich and ETH Zurich, Switzerland
{ yingqiang.gao, nianlong, lamjessica, rich }@ini.ethz.ch

Abstract

In scientific papers, arguments are essential for explaining authors' findings. As substrates of the reasoning process, arguments are often decorated with discourse indicators such as "which shows that" or "suggesting that". However, it remains understudied whether discourse indicators by themselves can be used as effective markers of the local argument components (LACs) in the body text that support the main claim in the abstract, i.e., the global argument. In this work, we investigate whether discourse indicators reflect the global premise and conclusion. We construct a set of regular expressions for over 100 word- and phrase-level discourse indicators and measure the alignment of LACs extracted by discourse indicators with the global arguments. We find a positive correlation between the alignment of local premises and local conclusions. However, compared to a simple textual intersection baseline, discourse indicators achieve lower ROUGE scores and have limited capability of extracting LACs relevant to the global argument; thus their role in scientific reasoning is less salient as expected.[1]

1 Introduction

Arguments are made by presenting cascades of argument components (ACs) called *premises* and *conclusions*, where the premises are intentional justifications that lend credibility to the conclusions (Wyatt, 2001; Stede and Schneider, 2018). In scientific papers, arguments aim to make claims supported by evidences taken from experiments, observations, and references (Al Khatib et al., 2021), and are usually presented as premise-conclusion pairs that are linked via an argumentative relation (Prasad et al., 2008; Lee et al., 2016). In scientific papers, the main claim or *global argument* of a paper is drawn in the abstract and several *local argument components* (LACs) are formulated throughout the entire body text. However, extracting LACs that support the global argument is hard because of the difficulties in finding premise-conclusion pairs.

Example LAC in our dataset
Assuming that [gene duplications primarily evolve under purifying selection]premise, [the observed acceleration of evolution may be explained by epistatic interaction between gene copies]conclusion.
regex rule: *Assuming that* P, C

Table 1: An example of discoure indicator *Assuming that* which links the premise and conclusion together. P represents the premise and C the conclusion. Best viewed under color printing.

It has been claimed that discourse indicators can be used to extract ACs in unstructured text, such as news articles (Sardianos et al., 2015) and student essays (Stab and Gurevych, 2014; Persing and Ng, 2016). However, the alignment between premises and conclusions in scientific papers is often implicit, especially when several premises correspond to one particular conclusion. Moreover, the extraction rules for ACs strongly depend on the pre-defined argumentation scheme and often do not generalize well (Walton et al., 2008; Prakken, 2010). Kirschner et al. (2015) have annotated a small corpus of 24 scientific papers, but the argumentative relation scheme is only binary (attack or support) and thus cannot represent more complex argumentative relations. Finally, the relation between arguments in the abstract and the body text remains understudied. Therefore, although a lot of progress in mining arguments from unstructured texts (Reed and Rowe, 2004; Van Gelder, 2007; Bex et al., 2014; Ong et al., 2014; Persing and Ng, 2015) has been made, it remains unclear whether discourse indicators can extract LACs that support the global argument in structured texts such as sci-

[1]Data and code are available at https://github.com/CharizardAcademy/discourse-indicator

Proceedings of the 9th Workshop on Argument Mining, co-located with the 29th International Conference on Computational Linguistics, pages 34–50
October 17, 2022.

entific papers.

In this work, we create a sizeable scientific paper dataset consisting of biomedical papers with well-structured abstracts, which enables us to easily extract the global argument of papers. On this dataset, we propose an efficient discourse indicator-based LAC extraction pipeline. We first construct a set of regular expressions of argument-associated discourse indicators; then, for each regular expression, we define how the local premise and the local conclusion are organized either in the sentence or in two consecutive sentences that are linked by this discourse indicator. With this pre-defined set of rules, we extract and disentangle the local premise from the local conclusion, which serve as LACs (see Table 1). To evaluate the effectiveness of our discourse indicator-based LAC extraction pipeline for scientific papers in terms of reflecting the global argument, we first compute the ROUGE-N scores of the union of all LACs extracted by our pipeline with respect to the global argument, and further qualitatively evaluate the extracted LACs and compare with the baselines via human evaluation.

Our main **contributions** are: 1) We propose a set of regular expressions for over 100 word- and phrase-level discourse indicators for extracting LACs from the body text of scientific papers; 2) We show that counter-intuitively, LACs extracted by discourse indicators only poorly reflect the global argument, by the fact that LACs extracted with discourse indicators achieved lower ROUGE-N scores than a simple baseline approach; 3) Human evaluation results suggest that LACs extracted by discourse indicators are precise in the exact wordings, but do not have a high information coverage of the global argument.

2 Related Works

The task of extracting LACs is most similar to argument mining (Lawrence and Reed, 2015, 2017, 2020), which typically classifies sentences into argumentative and non-argumentative text according to their rhetorical and syntactic role. Argument mining usually depends on a carefully designed argumentation scheme, which is, in general, a pre-defined type of connection between premise and conclusion. Teufel et al. (1999) proposed the first argumentative scheme which was later expanded to 14 categories of ACs (e.g. AIM, SUPPORT, USE, etc.) in scientific texts (Teufel et al., 2009). In our work, we consolidate the argumentation scheme simply as premise-conclusion pairs.

Discourse indicators have been used as rhetorical features to determine the credibility of claimed premises in support of a conclusion (Freeman, 2000). As a milestone, Wyner et al. (2012) showed that premise-conclusion pairs could be located by discourse indicators. Eckle-Kohler et al. (2015) annotated a corpus including 88 German language documents of premise-conclusion pairs and found that particular discourse indicators are more closely linked to either premises or conclusions. Lawrence and Reed (2015) used a small set of discourse indicators to extract premise-conclusion pairs and achieved high precision in recognizing the connections between propositional segments. In their later work (Lawrence and Reed, 2017), they further leveraged contextual knowledge such as topic information by constructing an inferential matrix that indicated the propositional relations, including premise-conclusion pairs. Argument mining has also been studied in series of works of Moens et al. (Moens et al., 2007; Palau and Moens, 2009; Mochales and Moens, 2011), where sentences are classified into *Arguments* and *Non-arguments* in an unsupervised manner using syntactic and semantic features. In these studies, the extraction of ACs is mainly done on the sentence level.

Nevertheless, in these works discussed above, the contribution of discourse indicators alone is not clear, and often the power of discourse indicators are only partially studied for news articles (e.g. Eckle-Kohler et al. (2015)). Unlike news articles, which are often written in plain language and are easy to understand, the readability of scientific papers decreases over time (Plavén-Sigray et al., 2017). In this work, we focus on understanding the role of discourse indicators in scientific papers particularly, mainly on how they contribute to extracting LACs in the body text supporting the global argument in the abstract.

3 Methodology

This section outlines our approaches to extracting global arguments and LACs from scientific papers (see Figure 1 for the proposed pipelines). In this work, we use the term *global* and *local* to refer to argument components located in the abstract and the body text of a paper separately.

We make the following assumptions: 1) Every scientific paper has one global argument and several paired LACs. The global argument expresses

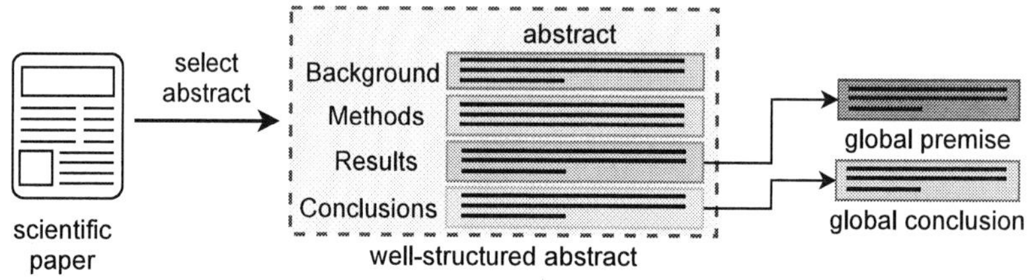

(a) Global argument extraction using well-structured abstracts.

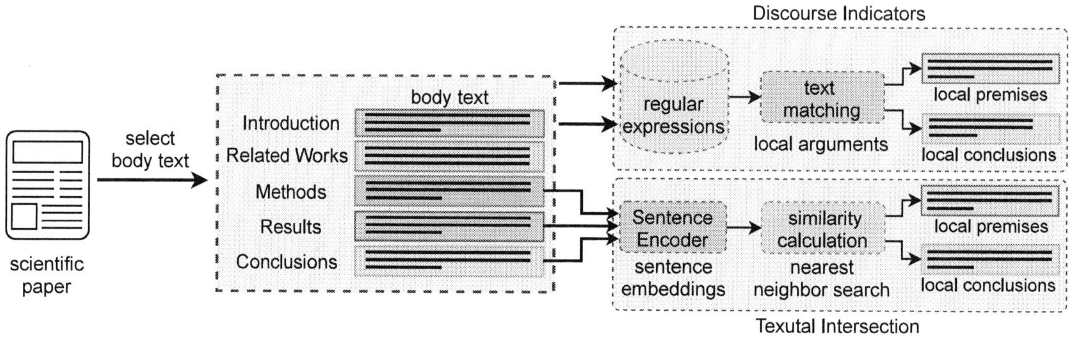

(b) LAC extraction using discourse indicators and textual intersection.

Figure 1: Our argument mining pipelines for biomedical papers: (a) global arguments are extracted from the well-structured abstracts with headers; (b) LACs are extracted from the body text. The textual intersection approach only makes use of *method*, *result* and *conclusion* sections, while the discourse indicator approach leverages the whole body text. We use well-structured abstracts to get the best human labeled global arguments we can find.

the paper's central claim, whereas LACs are individual statements that support the global argument from diverse perspectives; 2) The global argument locates in the paper's abstract, whereas LACs are distributed across the entire body text of the paper.

3.1 Mining Global Argument Components

In order to measure how well extracted LACs reflect the global argument, we first need to extract the global arguments from the abstracts because raw abstracts might also contain non-argumentative text. To ensure we have pure argumentative text extracted as the global argument, we use well-structured abstracts that contain both *result* and *conclusion* headers.

Since the naming convention of headers across different papers can vary greatly, we categorize headers such as "result" and "outcome" as *result* headers and headers such as "conclusion" or "concluding" as *conclusion* headers. A complete list of critical strings for *result/conclusion* headers is provided in appendix B. The text after the recognized headers are identified as the global argument: the text after the "result" header was extracted as the global premise and the text after the "conclusion" header as the global conclusion.

3.2 Mining Local Argument Components

Inspired by the work of Lawrence and Reed (2015, 2017), we use a broad set of over 100 discourse indicators both on the word level (e.g. *because*) and the phrase level (e.g. *assuming that*). Each discourse indicator extracts one local premise p_i^{local} and one local conclusion c_i^{local} on either the sub-sentence or the sentence level (see appendix C). The assessments were defined based on the mutual agreement of five experienced experts.

We concatenate the extracted local premises p_i^{local} $(i = 1, ..., .n)$ of all n matched discourse indicators to form the set of local premises P_{local}; similarly, we form the set of local conclusions C_{local} by concatenating all extracted local conclusions $c_i^{local}(i = 1, \ldots, n)$.

Textual Intersection Baseline As a baseline for LAC extraction, we propose an embedding-based approach to extract LACs solely from the *result* and *conclusion* sections. The idea is that sentences in the *result* section that are similar to sentences in the *method* section serve as local premises P_{local}.

The baseline extraction of LACs works as follows:

1. Similar to our definition of global argument, we used the same set of critical strings to parse the section names in the body text of scientific papers and recognize the *method*, *result*, and *conclusion* sections.

2. We remove stopwords, special symbols as well as extra blanks from the section paragraphs, then we tokenize the paragraphs into sentences using the NLTK[2] package (version 3.6.2).

3. For the i_{th} sentence s_m^i in the *method* section S_m and the j_{th} sentence s_r^j in the *result* section S_r, we compute 600-dimensional sentence embeddings e_m^i and e_r^j using a pre-trained universal text encoder, Sent2vec[3] (Pagliardini et al., 2018).

$$e_m^i = \text{Sent2vec}(s_m^i)$$
$$e_r^j = \text{Sent2vec}(s_r^j).$$

   We form the set of local premises P_{local} as a collection of *result* sentences that have similarity higher than a threshold value θ against any *method* sentence. Here sentence similarity is measured with the cosine similarity between the sentence embeddings:

$$P_{local} = \left\{ s_r^j \in S_r : \max_{s_m^i \in S_m} \text{sim}(e_m^i, e_r^j) \geqslant \theta \right\}$$

$$\text{where} \quad \text{sim}(e_m^i, e_r^j) = \frac{e_m^i \cdot e_r^j}{||e_m^i|| \cdot ||e_r^j||}.$$

4. We perform the same textual intersection step using the *result* and *conclusion* sentences. The set of local conclusions C_{local} is therefore a collection of *conclusion* sentences whose maximum cosine similarity against *result* sentences is greater than the threshold ϵ:

$$C_{local} = \left\{ s_c^k \in S_c : \max_{s_r^j \in S_r} \text{sim}(e_r^j, e_c^k) \geqslant \epsilon \right\}$$

$$\text{where} \quad \text{sim}(e_r^j, e_c^k) = \frac{e_r^j \cdot e_c^k}{||e_r^j|| \cdot ||e_c^k||}.$$

Both premise threshold θ and conclusion threshold ϵ were set to 0.1 to encourage extracting diverse LACs of rich semantics.

[2]Apache License 2.0, available at https://github.com/nltk/nltk

[3]BSD License, available at: https://github.com/epfml/sent2vec

4 Dataset

Our proposed argument mining pipelines are applied to the Semantic Scholar Open Research Corpus, i.e., S2ORC[4] (Lo et al., 2020), which is an extensive collection of 81.1M well-parsed peer-reviewed English papers, among which around 12.7M are complete with full text.

From the S2ORC corpus, we create a subset of nearly 28k papers in the biomedical domain with full text and structured abstracts available. We use papers with well-structured abstracts of biomedical papers to extract the global arguments due to the following reasons: 1) well-structured abstracts are the best massive human annotated source of global arguments we can get since these papers are peer-reviewed and usually multi-round editor-revised, therefore the quality of the argumentative text is ensured; 2) many journals specialized for biomedicine research naturally require the authors to construct the abstract in a structured manner, where the argumentative text is purposely decomposed into different units; 3) a previous study (Shieh et al., 2019) demonstrates the success of generating global conclusions from global premises using the well-structured abstracts of PubMed papers, thus enlightening the usefulness of well-structured abstracts for mining argument components.

For each paper in our dataset, we extract the LACs using both discourse indicators and textual intersection approaches. We also compute the upper bound of the ROUGE f-measure performance using the greedy strategy of Gu et al. (2022) that iteratively selects sentences to approximately maximize the sum of ROUGE-1 and ROUGE-2 f-measure scores. Table 2 shows the statistics of our proposed dataset *scinf-biomed*. Notice that for LACs extracted with discourse indicators, one local conclusion corresponds to one local premise due to our assessments of discourse indicators, whereas for the textual intersection approach, there is no one-to-one mapping between local conclusions and local premises. In Table 11 of appendix D we demonstrate the LACs extracted by the two proposed approaches.

5 Evaluation

To evaluate the performance of our proposed approaches, we perform the local-to-global comparison between the LACs and the global argument us-

[4]CC BY-NC 2.0 License, available at https://github.com/allenai/s2orc

Dataset	size	global args		local args (*d*)		local args (*t*)		local args (greedy)	
	#papers	#*con*	#*pre*	#*con*	#*pre*	#*con*	#*pre*	#*con*	#*pre*
scinf-biomed	27,924	61,809	133,480	71,245	75,379	179,654	319,272	63,245	136,282

Table 2: Statistics of the dataset of the extracted arguments. #papers represents the number of papers being selected, #*con* and #*pre* denote number of extracted local conclusions and local premises, *d* and *t* denote discourse indicators approach and textual intersection baseline. For LACs extracted using discourse indicators, #*con* and #*pre* are counted for non-empty local conclusions and local premises.

ing the summarization metric ROUGE scores as the automatic evaluation (Lin, 2004). Inspired by the pilot study on argument sufficiency of Gurcke et al. (2021), which showed that conclusion sentences generated from sufficient premises share more word-level commonalities, we choose ROUGE as the evaluation metric to measure the lexical relevance of the extracted LACs, based on the intuition that global arguments in the abstract can only be inferred from local arguments in the body text if they contain sufficient lexical information.

We first concatenate the LACs within their original order of occurrence in the body text, then we average the ROUGE-1, ROUGE-2, and ROUGE-Lsum scores[5] for precision, recall, and f-measure. All evaluations are performed separately for 1) the extracted local conclusions (against the global conclusions); 2) the extracted local premises (against global premises). Discourse indicators themselves are excluded from LACs while computing the ROUGE scores.

In addition, we are particularly interested in the n-gram precisions of the LACs compared to the global argument, since they provide information about whether n-grams in the global argument are favored in local conclusions or local premises. Therefore, we use the ROUGE-N precision as the metric to evaluate the lexical preferences of LACs.

6 Results and Discussion

6.1 Local-to-global comparison

In Table 3, we compare average ROUGE f-measures of the global argument against LACs (both local conclusions and local premises) extracted either with discourse indicators or with our baseline textual-intersection approach. The greedy oracle serves as the theoretical upper bound of the average ROUGE f-measures. In Table 4, we indicate how LACs extracted by the greedy oracle are distributed across sections.

approach	ROUGE-1	ROUGE-2	ROUGE-Lsum
greedy-*con*	62.10	43.75	56.93
indicator-*con*	23.76	5.88	21.72
intersection-*con*	**40.27**	**25.51**	**36.47**
greedy-*pre*	58.00	35.97	53.45
indicator-*pre*	23.76	4.85	20.92
intersection-*pre*	**38.09**	**20.08**	**33.81**

Table 3: Averaged ROUGE f-measures for local-to-global comparison of local conclusions (*con*) and local premises (*pre*) using discourse indicators and textual intersection with similarity thresholds $\theta = 0.1, \epsilon = 0.1$.

approach	sections	#sent	ratio
greedy-*con*	*conclusion*	33,036	52.2 %
	result	3,999	6.3 %
	method	2,247	3.6 %
greedy-*pre*	*result*	68,759	50.5 %
	method	11,163	8.2 %
	conclusion	6,332	4.7 %

Table 4: Statistics of the extracted LACs using the greedy approach. #sent means the number of sentences extracted from different sections, where ratio is the percentage to all greedily extracted LACs.

We found that local conclusions and local premises extracted with textual intersection achieve higher average ROUGE scores than those extracted by discourse indicators. This finding suggests that LACs retrieved with discourse indicators are not as well-aligned with the global argument as compared to LACs extracted by the textual intersection baseline. Thus, LACs linked by discourse indicators share less textual commonality with the global argument than those extracted by the textual intersection baseline.

LACs extracted by the two approaches tend to

[5]We use the python package rouge_score (version 0.0.4) to compute the ROUGE measures (Apache 2.0 License). https://pypi.org/project/rouge-score/

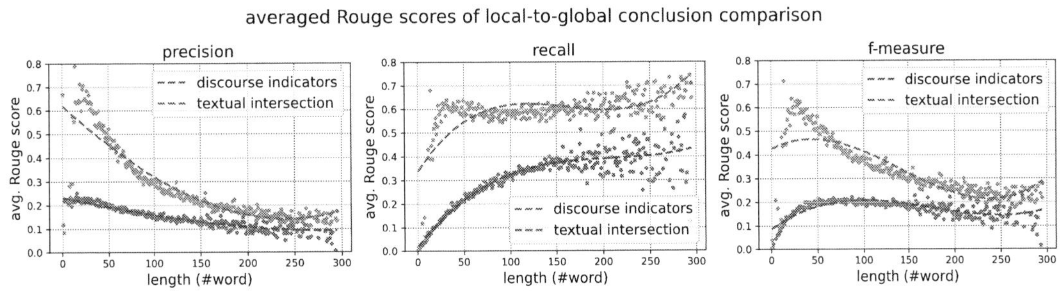

(a) Local conclusions compare against global conclusions.

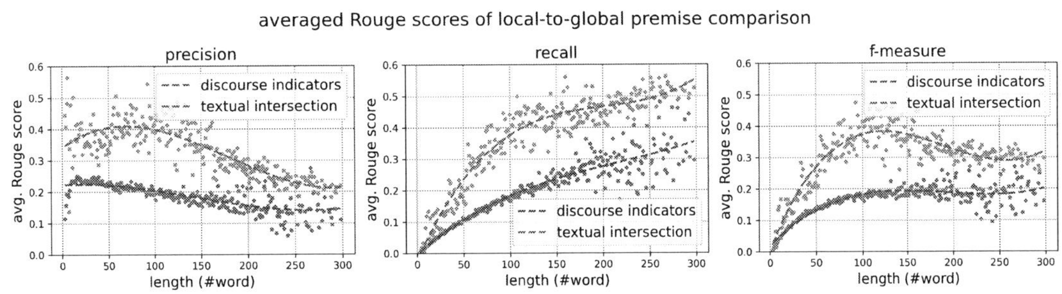

(b) Local premises compare against global premises.

Figure 2: Averaged Rouge scores for local-to-global comparison of premises and conclusions. We choose small similarity thresholds for the textual intersection ($\theta = 0.1$, $\epsilon = 0.1$) to encourage LACs of diverse semantics being extracted. The extracted local premises and local conclusions are limited to the first 300 words for a fair comparison. Best viewed under color printing.

have different lengths. To eliminate the influence of LAC length on ROUGE performance, we compared LACs extracted by the two approaches for a given length. Figure 2 illustrates the average ROUGE scores as a function of the length (number of unigrams) of concatenated LACs. To better visualize the overall trend, for each average ROUGE score, we fit the data with a third-order polynomial (dashed lines in Figure 2).

max. *pr*@10	ROUGE-1	ROUGE-2	ROUGE-Lsum
indicator-*con*	49.06	23.91	47.07
indicator-*pre*	37.02	9.34	35.15
max. *pr*@30	ROUGE-1	ROUGE-2	ROUGE-Lsum
indicator-*con*	34.86	9.60	33.46
indicator-*pre*	34.66	6.83	33.54
max. *pr*@60	ROUGE-1	ROUGE-2	ROUGE-Lsum
indicator-*con*	28.43	6.78	26.57
indicator-*pre*	31.52	5.61	29.97

Table 5: ROUGE-N precisions for local-to-global comparison of local conclusions (*con*) and local premises (*pre*) using top 10, 30, and 60 discourse indicators ranked by averaged ROUGE-N precisions.

We observed that regardless of LAC length, discourse indicators consistently achieved lower performance than the textual intersection baseline. This suggests that LACs linked by discourse indicators do not reflect the global argument well.

6.2 Analysis

We hypothesize that the inferior performance of discourse indicators can be attributed to two aspects: 1) not all discourse indicators are equally useful for the task; 2) discourse indicators are not exclusively used for constructing arguments.

To verify the first hypothesis, we first score each discourse indicator by the average ROUGE-N precision of LACs it extracts. Table 10 of appendix C shows that some discourse indicators like *wherefore* and *on this account* have high scores, whereas other discourse indicators such as *indicating that* and *this is shown by* have much lower scores. In Table 12 of appendix C, we provide an example of LACs extracted by these two discourse indicators.

We evaluated the LACs extracted by the top-k ($k = 10, 30, 60$) discourse indicators in terms of their average ROUGE-N precisions compared to

(a) Top 20 discourse indicators ranked by number of hits.

indicator	#hits	indicator	#hits	indicator	#hits	indicator	#hits
therefore	12,659	*results from*	3,567	*indeed*	2,120	*in conclusion*	1,612
thus	7,194	*resulting in*	3,005	*hence*	2,076	*indicating*	1,612
suggested that	5,324	*is based on*	2,736	*accordingly*	1,918	*demonstrates that*	1,223
because	4,730	*indicates that*	2,628	*in fact*	1,846	*can cause*	1,164
if	4,030	*since*	2,532	*due to*	1,821	*is supported by*	968

(b) Location of indicators (#hits) by sections.

sections	#hits total local conclusions	#hits total local premises	#hits/1k words local conclusions	#hits/1k words local premises
method	6,844	6,948	4.88	4.88
result	7,601	6,929	4.64	4.60
conclusion	5,860	4,434	5.94	5.43
other	50,940	57,068	4.14	4.10
$\sum$ sections	71,245	75,379	4.32	4.26

(c) Average n-gram precision per section.

section	avg. unigram precision		avg. bigram precision		avg. trigram precision	
	premise$_g$	conclusion$_g$	premise$_g$	conclusion$_g$	premise$_g$	conclusion$_g$
method	11.45±6.35	8.11±5.23	3.04±2.92	2.16±2.70	1.10±2.08	0.89±2.21
result	**12.83**±7.14	8.51±5.47	**3.59**±3.43	2.33±2.94	**1.39**±2.67	1.01±2.51
conclusion	12.22±6.91	**10.44**±6.67	3.32±3.61	**3.03**±3.06	1.35±2.92	**1.69**±3.35
other	11.57±6.19	8.62±5.15	2.96±2.80	2.20±2.53	1.05±2.00	0.93±2.10

Table 6: Precision of discourse indicators: (a) discourse indicators ranked by number of hits in the body text of papers; (b) number of discourse indicators in the sections, and the corresponding percentage indicator densities, for local conclusions and local premises within the same section; (c) average n-gram precision with standard deviation, reported for each section. Local premises in the *result* sections achieve higher precision than local premises in the *method* sections, ANOVA test for all n-grams are with $p < 0.01$. Local conclusions in the *conclusion* sections achieve higher precision than local conclusions in other sections. The subscript g denotes global argument.

the global argument. The more discourse indicators we include (the larger k), the lower the average ROUGE-N precision (see Table 5). We also see the average ROUGE-N scores of local conclusions decrease more than the scores of local premises. This suggests that the relevance of discourse indicators varies greatly, i.e., LACs linked by certain discourse indicators are much better aligned with the global argument than others.

To verify the second hypothesis, we compute the overall number of appearances of discourse indicators and the hit rate per 1000 words for different types of sections (see Table 6). We found that regardless of the section type, the hit rate is around 4 to 5, which reveals no distinct section preference of discourse indicators. This may be because scientific papers can contain arguments all through the body text, or because discourse indicators may be overused in non-argumentative occasions for decorative purposes where no scientific reasoning is needed.

As pointed out earlier, we are particularly interested in analyzing the n-gram precision of each LAC with the global argument, to detect re-uses of global-argument n-grams in the LACs.

In Table 6, we show the average n-gram precision in different sections. We see that unigram precision of both local premises and local conclusions are similarly distributed in *method* and *result* sections (see Figure 4 in appendix A), revealing no strong preference for either these section types. Nevertheless, the local premises extracted from the *result* sections achieve significantly higher precision with respect to the global premises than from the *method* and *conclusion* sections, revealing a preference for local premises to occur in the *result* sections. Similarly, the local conclusions extracted from the *conclusion* sections are better aligned with the global conclusions than the local conclusions from *method* and *result* sections, revealing a preference for local conclusions to be drawn in the *conclusion* section, as expected.

In addition, we studied correlations between the precisions of local premises and conclusions. We expected that when either the premise or conclusion of a local argument is well aligned with the global counterpart, then so will be the other component of the local argument. We therefore calculated the Pearson correlation coefficients between unigram precisions of local premises and of local conclusions in *method, result,* and *conclusion* sections. We find significant correlation coefficients in the range 0.3-0.4 (see Figure 4 in Appendix A), revealing a weak positive correlation between local premises and conclusions.

To depict the relation between local premises and local conclusions as a contour plot, we first meshed the unigram precisions in Figure 4 of appendix A into square cells of size 0.01x0.01. We then smoothed the unigram precisions using a 2D Gaussian kernel with $\sigma = 1$ and summed the values within each cell. Finally, we performed brute force computation to find the levels corresponding to the first one-third and the two-thirds of the summation of the mesh.

In Figure 3 we show the superimposed contours of the unigram precisions in *method, result,* and *conclusion* sections. We see that the 2/3 contour associated with *result* sections extends to larger premise precisions than the contours associated with other sections, in agreement with our finding that local premises located in *result* sections are best aligned with global premises.

7 Human Evaluation

Following the evaluation setups proposed by (Gu et al., 2022; Dong et al., 2018), we conducted a human evaluation on how well LACs extracted with the two proposed approaches reflect the global argument. The human evaluation is designed as a text comparison task where we asked the evaluators to choose between the LACs extracted by the two approaches in an interactive UI interface setting (see Figure 5 in appendix E), by carefully reading the text displayed on the interface.

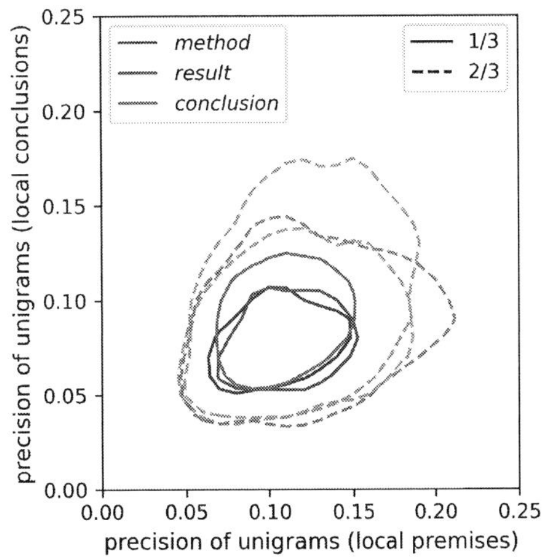

Figure 3: Superimposed contours of the unigram precisions of local premises and local conclusions in *method* (green), *result* (blue), and *conclusion* (red) sections. A solid contour delimits the first one-third of a given (summed) density and a dashed contour the first two-thirds. Best viewed under color printing.

We recruited 6 human evaluators with strong biology/neuroscience backgrounds. Each evaluator was asked to evaluate 25 randomly picked samples from our proposed scinf-biomed dataset. LACs extracted by discourse indicators and textual intersection were randomly displayed in separate text wrappers (Extractor A and Extractor B). In order to prevent the evaluators from inferring the LACs extraction method, we presented the LACs extracted with discourse indicators as complete sentences. To discount for LAC length (as in Figure 2), we truncated LACs to the first 100, 200, and 300 unigrams, respectively. The evaluators were asked to choose the better extractor (value of #1) for each of the following criteria:

- Coverage (Recall): how many different aspects/perspectives of the global argument are mentioned in the LACs;
- Non-redundancy (Precision): how precisely are those aspects/perspectives mentioned in the LACs;
- Overall: the better extractor based on subjective criteria including non-redundancy and coverage.

#unigram@100	Overall	Recall	Precision
indicator	**1.46**	1.54	**1.40**
intersection	1.54	**1.46**	1.60
#unigram@200	Overall	Recall	Precision
indicator	1.60	1.60	1.64
intersection	**1.40**	**1.40**	**1.36**⋆
#unigram@300	Overall	Recall	Precision
indicator	1.52	1.54	**1.42**
intersection	**1.48**	**1.46**	1.58

Table 7: Average rank of two approaches in human evaluation. Smaller rank corresponds to better performance. ⋆ indicates statistical significance ($p < 0.05$, Wilcoxon signed-rank test).

Table 7 shows the results of the human evaluation. On the overall score, textual intersection achieves better performance on longer LACs (up to 200 and 300 words), whereas the discourse indicator approach ranks higher on shorter LACs (up to 100 words). On coverage, textual intersection is also better, but on non-redundancy results are more mixed. Overall, we see that textual intersection has a slight advantage but that discourse indicators can be useful for retrieving shorter argument components.

8 Conclusion

In this work, we investigate the effectiveness of discourse indicators for retrieving LACs relevant to the global argument of scientific papers. We develop a set of regular expressions for over 100 word- and phrase-level discourse indicators and test the performance of extracting the LACs of scientific papers. Our preliminary results show that discourse indicators have a limited capability of capturing LACs that are well-aligned with the global argument and thus cannot be solely used to extract arguments from scientific papers.

In future works, we will explore the effectiveness of discourse indicators in different types of scientific paper, such as research article, case report, and technical notes, etc. At the moment a notable weakness of our work is the oversimplifying use of regular expressions to disentangle premises from conclusions, thus we believe that the extraction of LACs using discourse indicators may be improved using more sophisticated (hierarchical) parsing techniques. In addition, we will work on a gold standard dataset that consists human annotated premise-conclusion pairs for argument generation, at the same time investigate the power of other more advanced contextualized sentence encoders.

Acknowledgements

We acknowledge the support from Swiss National Science Foundation NCCR Evolving Language, Agreement No.51NF40_180888. We also thank the anonymous reviewers for their constructive comments and feedback.

References

Khalid Al Khatib, Tirthankar Ghosal, Yufang Hou, Anita de Waard, and Dayne Freitag. 2021. Argument mining for scholarly document processing: Taking stock and looking ahead. In *Proceedings of the Second Workshop on Scholarly Document Processing*, pages 56–65.

Floris Bex, John Lawrence, and Chris Reed. 2014. Generalising argument dialogue with the dialogue game execution platform. In *COMMA*, pages 141–152.

Yue Dong, Yikang Shen, Eric Crawford, Herke van Hoof, and Jackie Chi Kit Cheung. 2018. BanditSum: Extractive summarization as a contextual bandit. In *Proceedings of the 2018 Conference on Empirical Methods in Natural Language Processing*, pages 3739–3748, Brussels, Belgium. Association for Computational Linguistics.

Judith Eckle-Kohler, Roland Kluge, and Iryna Gurevych. 2015. On the role of discourse markers for discriminating claims and premises in argumentative discourse. In *Proceedings of the 2015 Conference on Empirical Methods in Natural Language Processing*, pages 2236–2242.

James B Freeman. 2000. What types of statements are there? *Argumentation*, 14(2):135–157.

Nianlong Gu, Elliott Ash, and Richard Hahnloser. 2022. MemSum: Extractive summarization of long documents using multi-step episodic Markov decision processes. In *Proceedings of the 60th Annual Meeting of the Association for Computational Linguistics (Volume 1: Long Papers)*, pages 6507–6522, Dublin, Ireland. Association for Computational Linguistics.

Timon Gurcke, Milad Alshomary, and Henning Wachsmuth. 2021. Assessing the sufficiency of arguments through conclusion generation. In *Proceedings of the 8th Workshop on Argument Mining*, pages 67–77.

Christian Kirschner, Judith Eckle-Kohler, and Iryna Gurevych. 2015. Linking the thoughts: Analysis of argumentation structures in scientific publications. In *Proceedings of the 2nd Workshop on Argumentation Mining*, pages 1–11.

John Lawrence and Chris Reed. 2015. Combining argument mining techniques. In *Proceedings of the 2nd Workshop on Argumentation Mining*, pages 127–136.

John Lawrence and Chris Reed. 2017. Mining argumentative structure from natural language text using automatically generated premise-conclusion topic models. In *EMNLP 2017: Conference on Empirical Methods in Natural Language Processing*, pages 39–48. Association for Computational Linguistics.

John Lawrence and Chris Reed. 2020. Argument mining: A survey. *Computational Linguistics*, 45(4):765–818.

Alan Lee, Rashmi Prasad, Bonnie Webber, and Aravind Joshi. 2016. Annotating discourse relations with the pdtb annotator. In *Proceedings of COLING 2016, the 26th International Conference on Computational Linguistics: System Demonstrations*, pages 121–125.

Chin-Yew Lin. 2004. Rouge: A package for automatic evaluation of summaries. In *Text summarization branches out*, pages 74–81.

Kyle Lo, Lucy Lu Wang, Mark Neumann, Rodney Kinney, and Daniel S Weld. 2020. S2orc: The semantic scholar open research corpus. In *Proceedings of the 58th Annual Meeting of the Association for Computational Linguistics*, pages 4969–4983.

Raquel Mochales and Marie-Francine Moens. 2011. Argumentation mining. *Artificial Intelligence and Law*, 19(1):1–22.

Marie-Francine Moens, Erik Boiy, Raquel Mochales Palau, and Chris Reed. 2007. Automatic detection of arguments in legal texts. In *Proceedings of the 11th international conference on Artificial intelligence and law*, pages 225–230.

Nathan Ong, Diane Litman, and Alexandra Brusilovsky. 2014. Ontology-based argument mining and automatic essay scoring. In *Proceedings of the First Workshop on Argumentation Mining*, pages 24–28.

Matteo Pagliardini, Prakhar Gupta, and Martin Jaggi. 2018. Unsupervised learning of sentence embeddings using compositional n-gram features. In *Proceedings of the 2018 Conference of the North American Chapter of the Association for Computational Linguistics: Human Language Technologies, Volume 1 (Long Papers)*, pages 528–540.

Raquel Mochales Palau and Marie-Francine Moens. 2009. Argumentation mining: the detection, classification and structure of arguments in text. In *Proceedings of the 12th international conference on artificial intelligence and law*, pages 98–107.

Isaac Persing and Vincent Ng. 2015. Modeling argument strength in student essays. In *Proceedings of the 53rd Annual Meeting of the Association for Computational Linguistics and the 7th International Joint Conference on Natural Language Processing (Volume 1: Long Papers)*, pages 543–552.

Isaac Persing and Vincent Ng. 2016. End-to-end argumentation mining in student essays. In *Proceedings of the 2016 Conference of the North American Chapter of the Association for Computational Linguistics: Human Language Technologies*, pages 1384–1394.

Pontus Plavén-Sigray, Granville James Matheson, Björn Christian Schiffler, and William Hedley Thompson. 2017. Research: The readability of scientific texts is decreasing over time. *eLife*, 6:e27725.

Henry Prakken. 2010. On the nature of argument schemes. *Dialectics, dialogue and argumentation. An examination of Douglas Walton's theories of reasoning and argument*, pages 167–185.

Rashmi Prasad, Nikhil Dinesh, Alan Lee, Eleni Miltsakaki, Livio Robaldo, Aravind K Joshi, and Bonnie L Webber. 2008. The penn discourse treebank 2.0. In *LREC*. Citeseer.

Chris Reed and Glenn Rowe. 2004. Araucaria: Software for argument analysis, diagramming and representation. *International Journal on Artificial Intelligence Tools*, 13(04):961–979.

Christos Sardianos, Ioannis Manousos Katakis, Georgios Petasis, and Vangelis Karkaletsis. 2015. Argument extraction from news. In *Proceedings of the 2nd Workshop on Argumentation Mining*, pages 56–66.

Alexander Te-Wei Shieh, Yung-Sung Chuang, Shang-Yu Su, and Yun-Nung Chen. 2019. Towards understanding of medical randomized controlled trials by conclusion generation. In *Proceedings of the Tenth International Workshop on Health Text Mining and Information Analysis (LOUHI 2019)*, pages 108–117.

Christian Stab and Iryna Gurevych. 2014. Identifying argumentative discourse structures in persuasive essays. In *Proceedings of the 2014 Conference on Empirical Methods in Natural Language Processing (EMNLP)*, pages 46–56.

Manfred Stede and Jodi Schneider. 2018. Argumentation mining. *Synthesis Lectures on Human Language Technologies*, 11(2):1–191.

Simone Teufel, Jean Carletta, and Marc Moens. 1999. An annotation scheme for discourse-level argumentation in research articles. In *Ninth Conference of the European Chapter of the Association for Computational Linguistics*, pages 110–117.

Simone Teufel, Advaith Siddharthan, and Colin Batchelor. 2009. Towards domain-independent argumentative zoning: Evidence from chemistry and computational linguistics. In *Proceedings of the 2009 conference on empirical methods in natural language processing*, pages 1493–1502.

Tim Van Gelder. 2007. The rationale for rationale™. *Law, probability and risk*, 6(1-4):23–42.

Douglas Walton, Christopher Reed, and Fabrizio Macagno. 2008. *Argumentation schemes*. Cambridge University Press.

Bonnie Webber, Rashmi Prasad, Alan Lee, and Aravind Joshi. 2019. The penn discourse treebank 3.0 annotation manual. *Philadelphia, University of Pennsylvania*.

Nicole Wyatt. 2001. Ralph h. johnson, manifest rationality: A pragmatic theory of argument. *Philosophy in Review*, 21(3).

Adam Wyner, Jodi Schneider, Katie Atkinson, and Trevor Bench-Capon. 2012. Semi-automated argumentative analysis of online product reviews. In *Computational Models of Argument*, pages 43–50. IOS Press.

A Distribution of Unigram Precisions

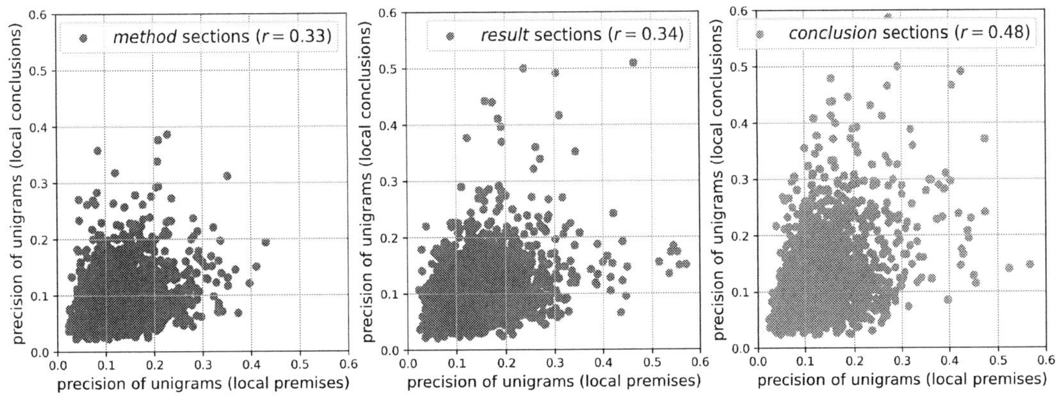

Figure 4: Distribution of unigram precisions of individual local conclusion and local premise occurring in the global conclusion and global premise. Each point in the figure represents a local premise (P) and a local conclusion (C) extracted by the same discourse indicator. r delimits the Pearson correlation coefficient of comparing unigram precisions for P to C. For all 3 type of sections, $p < 10^{-3}$ is observed.

B Sections

To detect *method, result,* and *conclusion* sections, we use the following anchors (critical strings for candidate section names) in Table 8. For instance, a section is considered to be a *method* section when its section name contains at least one of these section anchors.

Notice that to ensure no risk of having concluding text treated as local premises, all sections must be exclusive of the string *discussion.*

section	section anchors
method	method, procedure, data, theory, implementation
result	result, outcome, analysis, measure, evaluation
conclusion	conclusion, concluding, summary, remark, key point

Table 8: Critical strings for selecting related sections used in Table 6

C Discourse Indicators

(a) Discourse indicators part A

P. In view of that, C.	P. One can deduce that C.
P. One can infer that C.	P. One can conclude that C.
C. Its proof is that P.	P. As a result, C.
P, resulting in C.	P, in that case C.
C. This comes from P.	P. For this reason, C.
P. In consequence, C.	P. As conclusion, C.
P suggested that C.	P can cause C.

(b) Discourse indicators part B

C, since P.	Granted that P, C.
P, therefore C.	Supposing that P, C.
P. Therefore, C.	C, supposing that P.
P, wherefore C.	Assuming that P, C.
P, so that C.	C, assuming that P.
P, consequently C.	Because P, C.
P, entails that C.	C, because P.
As shown from P, C.	Here is why C: P.
C, if P.	P implies that C.
P, shows that C.	As indicated by P, C.
C, follows from P.	C, as indicated by P.
C, giving that P.	P, indicating that C.
Due to the reason that P, C.	On account of the reason that P, C.
C, due to the reason that P.	C, on account of the reason that P.
In view of the fact that P, C.	C may be deduced from P.
C, in view of the fact that P.	C may be inferred from P.
P, thereby showing that C.	C may be derived from P.
P, thus C.	C can be derived from P.
P establishes that C.	P proves that C.
P justifies that C.	C is supported by P.
In support of C, P.	P, which leads credence to C.
Inasmuch as P, C.	On the hypothesis that P, C.
P demonstrates that C.	C, on the hypothesis that P.
P indicates that C.	P signifies that C.
P, indicating that C.	P guarantees that C.
C is based on P.	On the basis of P, C.
In light of the fact that P, C.	C, on the basis of P.
P. In fact, C.	Convinced by the fact that P, C.
In fact that P, C.	Seeing that P, C.
C, for the reason that P.	C, seeing that P.
P, from which it follows C.	Owing to P, C.
Due to P, C.	C, owing to P.
C, due to P.	C, on the grounds that P.
C, considering P.	On the grounds that P, C.
P, which leads to C.	On account of the fact P, C.
P, which shows that C.	C, on account of the fact P.
P, which allows us to infer C.	P, means that C.
P, which implies C.	P, which points to C.
C. The reason is that P.	P. Accordingly, C.
P. From this we can deduce that C.	P. From this it follows that C.
P. This proves that C.	P. Hence, C.
P. Obviously, C.	P. Evidently, C.
P. In conclusion, C.	P. On this account, C.
C. This is shown by P.	P. This is being so C.
P. Indeed, C	*C, insofar as P.*
P. In short, C.	*P. In sum, C.*
P, in other words, C.	*Now that P, C.*

Table 9: Discourse indicators used in this work.

Table 9 lists all word- and phrase-level discourse indicators used in our work for LAC extraction. For each discourse indicator, $\mathbb{P}$ denotes the local premise and $\mathbb{C}$ the local conclusion. Based on linguistic facts and experience, the assessment was guided by five qualified scholars. Discourse indicators adapted exclusively from the Penn Discourse Treebank 3.0 (Webber et al., 2019) are marked in italic font.

Table 10 presents statistics of these discourse indicators ranked by: a) averaged length of extracted LACs; b) and c) average ROUGE-N scores. For local premises ($\mathbb{P}$) and local conclusions ($\mathbb{C}$) extracted by each discourse indicator, the averaged ROUGE-N scores are computed against the corresponding global premises and global conclusions, respectively.

(a) Top 5 discourse indicators that have at least 100 appearances (#hits), ranked by the average length of LACs (as number of words). $\mathbb{P}$ as local premises and $\mathbb{C}$ as local conclusions.

indicator	avg. length of $\mathbb{P}$	#hits total	indicator	avg. length of $\mathbb{C}$	#hits total
indicating that	29.30	741	in short	28.00	161
for these reasons	28.75	297	assuming that	27.63	105
so that	28.63	602	indeed	27.53	2,120
indeed	28.48	2,120	in conclusion	27.35	1,612
as a consequence	27.93	398	in fact	25.87	1,846

(b) Top 10 discourse indicators for $\mathbb{P}$ (local premises), ranked by the average Rouge-N score metrics.

indicator	pr	indicator	rc	indicator	fm
wherefore	39.86	which proves that	18.14	which proves that	19.91
in that case	35.30	which can be derived from	9.32	which can be derived from	12.81
one may infer that	34.81	means that	8.72	means that	12.38
in light of the fact that	31.56	in view of that	8.70	in that case	12.19
as indicated by*	29.91	which shows that	8.21	in view of that	11.91
indicating that*	29.75	indicating that*	8.12	indicating that*	11.20
this is shown by	28.20	in that case	7.37	this is shown by	10.45
may be inferred from	27.91	this is shown by	7.33	which proves that	10.19
which proves that	27.78	from this we can deduce that	7.16	wherefore	10.07
inasmuch as	27.76	consequently*	6.87	this proves that	10.06

(c) Top 10 discourse indicators for $\mathbb{C}$ (local conclusions), ranked by the average Rouge-N score metrics

indicator	pr	indicator	rc	indicator	fm
on this account	44.41	in conclusion*	26.35	in conclusion*	30.62
in view of that	43.57	one can conclude that	25.16	one can conclude that	28.78
in conclusion*	42.87	on this account	20.47	on this account	28.02
which proves that	36.31	in light of the fact that	18.79	in view of that	21.30
one can conclude that	33.62	demonstrates that*	15.97	demonstrates that*	19.95
demonstrates that*	33.02	in view of that	14.41	this is shown by	17.10
might be derived from	30.09	this is shown by	13.36	might be inferred from	15.84
wherefore	28.42	proves that	11.70	in sum	15.81
granted that	28.36	might be inferred from	10.97	wherefore	15.34
this is shown by	27.45	justifies that	10.73	which proves that	14.77

Table 10: Discourse indicators ranked by the Rouge-N scores: (a) top 5 discourse indicators that extract the longest LACs (length counted as the number of words) (b) top 10 discourse indicators in which local premises ($\mathbb{P}$) have the highest Rouge-N scores to the global premises (c) top 10 discourse indicators which local conclusions ($\mathbb{C}$) have the highest Rouge-N scores to the global conclusions. pr, rc, and fm stand for precision, recall, and f-measure, respectively. * in (b) and (c) denotes discourse indicators that have more than 100 appearances (# > 100).

D Dataset Example

LACs extracted using discourse indicators
The SRT estimated using the CPhT test was significantly higher (worse) for NAL-NL1 than for DSL [i/o] or DSL V, **indicating that** the NAL-NL1 prescription is less effective than the DSL prescriptions in making low level sounds intelligible.
High compression ratios, combined with high amounts of low-frequency gain, may also increase the audibility of background noise, and this may degrade speech understanding in noise via the upward spread of masking. ***Thus***, as compression ratios are increased, the potential benefits of increased audibility of speech may be offset by a variety of deleterious effects.
The lower gains **may help to** preserve the relative levels of the first and second formants, which may lead to improved vowel identification.
It is not feasible to restore the audibility of low-level sounds completely to normal for hearing-impaired children or adults, **due to** factors such as the internal noise of hearing aids (especially microphone noise), limitations in the gain that can be achieved without acoustic feedback, and the need to avoid excessive amounts of compression.
A problem with the use of questionnaires is that the outcomes may be influenced by the personality and attitude of the adult or child performing the evaluation. **Hence**, questionnaires may be useful for comparing results across groups, but are not so effective in evaluating the performance of individual children.
avg. ROUGE-N f-measures: 16.05 for local conclusions C, 26.89 for local premises P.
LACs extracted using textual intersection
A few children with moderate hearing loss scored close to ceiling for the-dB SPL stimuli. ANOVAs were conducted separately on the RAU-transformed scores for the presentation levels of and dBA with prescription as a within-subjects factor and severity of hearing loss as a between subjects factor. CAWL scores were derived from the number of phonemes correct for each of the target words. Figure shows the average levels in dBA required for correct identification of each of the Ling sounds, across all subjects, for each hearing aid prescription. For the level of dBA, there was no significant effect of prescription , but there was an effect of severity of hearing loss ...
The higher output levels prescribed by the DSL i/o and DSL V prescription methods relative to NAL-NL1 led to significantly better detection and discrimination of lowlevel sounds. Using age-appropriate closed-set and open-set speech tests, designed to avoid floor and ceiling effects, we found significant differences between scores for the different hearing aid prescription methods.
avg. ROUGE-N f-measures: 44.10 for local conclusions C, 31.90 for local premises P.
Global premises
Scores for the Consonant Confusion Test and CAPT consonant discrimination and consonant detection were lower for the NAL-NL1 prescription than for the DSL prescriptions. Scores for the CAPT vowel-in-noise discrimination test were higher for DSL V than for either of the other prescriptions. Scores for the Cambridge Auditory Word Lists did not differ across prescriptions for the level of 65 dBA, but were lower for the NAL-NL1 prescription than for either of the DSL prescriptions for the level of 50 dBA. The speech reception threshold measured using the Common Phrases Test and the levels required for identification of the Ling 5 sounds were higher (worse) for the NAL-NL1 prescription than for the DSL prescriptions.
Global conclusions
The higher gains prescribed by the DSL i/o and DSL V prescription methods relative to NAL-NL1 led to significantly better detection and discrimination of low-level speech sounds.

Table 11: An example biomedial paper in our proposed dataset *scinf-biomed*.

(a) Strong (*which proves that*) and weak (*indicating that*) discourse indicators for local-to-global premise comparison

Local Premise (P)	The circadian curves of cortisol secretion compared the day after the end of magnetotherapy and M3P3 magnetostimulation significantly differ from the M2P2 program -nearly by 100%, **which proves that** this type of magnetotherapy and magnetostimulation shows varied influence on cortisol secretion in men.
Global Premise	... Statistically significant difference was demonstrated in the participants after the application of magnetotherapy and magnetostimulation with M3P3 program compared to the men submitted to magnetostimulation, with M2P2 program, at 400 p.m. after 15 applications.
Local Premise (P)	Within the families of bipolar probands there is a higher than average rate of unipolar depressive disorders, **indicating that** bipolar susceptibility genes can be expressed in a broad spectrum of mood phenotypes.
Global Premise	... Systematic study of the coding and flanking intronic regions of 25 known genes within this latter region failed to identify any highly penetrant autosomal dominant disease-conferring mutations in these pedigrees.

(b) Strong (*one can conclude that*) and weak (*in sum*) discourse indicators for local-to-global conclusion comparison

Local Conclusion (C)	... **One can conclude that** RGCs express RS both developmentally and in the adult retina, indicating that local replenishment of RS protein evidently is desirable for maintaining retinal structure, even after retinal development is completed.
Global Conclusion	All major classes of adult retinal neurons ... strongly suggesting that retinoschisin in the inner retina is synthesized locally rather than being transported, as earlier proposed, from distal retinal photoreceptors ...
Local Conclusion (C)	Observations were repeated with the same biological replicate for each tissue. **In sum** this is a factorial arrangement of treatments (Diet by Genotype) laid out on a balanced Completely Randomized Design (CRD) with repeated measures on another treatment (Source of Tissue) amounting to a total of 2n = 40 observations.
Global Conclusion	These studies show that high-throughput metabolomics combined with appropriate statistical modeling and large scale functional approaches can be used to monitor and infer changes and interactions in the metabolome and genome of the host under controlled experimental conditions ... Based on our results, metabolic signatures and metabolic pathways of polyposis and intestinal carcinoma have been identified, which may serve as useful targets for the development of therapeutic interventions.

Table 12: Alignment of LACs extracted by strong and weak discourse indicators to the global argument.

E User Interface for Human Evaluation

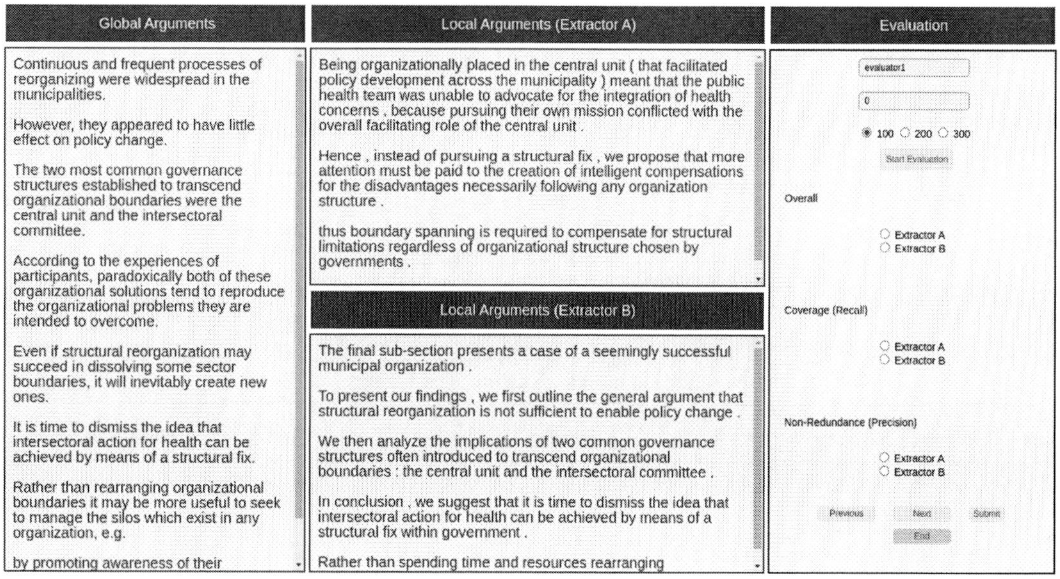

Figure 5: The user interface designed for the human evaluation. The annotators are asked to mark the anonymous extractor which they think is better in terms of overall quality, information coverage, and non-redundancy.

Analyzing Culture-Specific Argument Structures in Learner Essays

Wei-Fan Chen
Paderborn University
Department of Computer Science
cwf@mail.upb.de

Mei-Hua Chen
Tunghai University
Department of Foreign Languages and Literature
mhchen@thu.edu.tw

Garima Mudgal
Paderborn University
Department of Computer Science
garima@mail.upb.de

Henning Wachsmuth
Paderborn University
Department of Computer Science
henningw@upb.de

Abstract

Language education has been shown to benefit from computational argumentation, for example, from methods that assess quality dimensions of language learners' argumentative essays, such as their organization and argument strength. So far, however, little attention has been paid to cultural differences in learners' argument structures originating from different origins and language capabilities. This paper extends prior studies of learner argumentation by analyzing differences in the argument structure of essays from culturally diverse learners. Based on the ICLE corpus containing essays written by English learners of 16 different mother tongues, we train natural language processing models to mine argumentative discourse units (ADUs) as well as to assess the essays' quality in terms of organization and argument strength. The extracted ADUs and the predicted quality scores enable us to look into the similarities and differences of essay argumentation across different English learners. In particular, we analyze the ADUs from learners with different mother tongues, different levels of arguing proficiency, and different context cultures.

1 Introduction

Analyzing the argument structure of a text helps understand the individual points being made and the relationships between these points to identify the overall position that the writer supports (Lawrence and Reed, 2020). In practice, manual annotation of argument structure is a skilled work; the laborious and time-consuming process behind would make large-scale studies challenging. This is undoubtedly true for second-language writing research. Especially studies investigating language learners' use of arguments in the essays usually need to determine the occurrence of individual argument components, such as Paek and Kang (2017) and Liu and Wan (2020), see Section §2 for details.

Research on computational argumentation has drawn increased interest in recent years, with argumentative writing support being one of the main envisioned applications (Stab and Gurevych, 2017; Wambsganss and Niklaus, 2022). Computational methods to automatically mine argumentative discourse units (ADUs) and the relations between these units enable various applications in the context of language education (Wambsganss et al., 2021; Putra et al., 2021). Argument mining has been performed effectively on persuasive learner essays (Stab and Gurevych, 2014b), and argument quality assessment has been aided with claim generation (Gurcke et al., 2021). Given the close connection between argument structure and text quality (Putra et al., 2021), argumentative learner essays have also been studied in terms of quality dimensions such as organization (Persing et al., 2010) and argument strength (Persing and Ng, 2015).

So far, however, little attention has been paid to the cultural diversity of language learners with respect to the different argument structures they form. Cultural variation may originate from different geographical origins, mother tongues, societal systems, the ways people communicate in these systems, and many other aspects (Senthamarai and Chandran, 2015). Some of these aspects may be easy to access, others barely. Either way, culture is recognized known as a factor affecting the persuasiveness of arguments and the organization of ideas of language learners (Carlile et al., 2018; Putra et al., 2021). At the same time, the extent to which culture is reflected in a given text may depend on the learner's level of language proficiency. Bearing these points in mind, this paper goes beyond previous studies of learner argumentation, analyzing differences in the structure and quality of essay argumentation of culturally diverse learners.[1]

[1] Studying cultural differences in the context of text quality

Proceedings of the 9th Workshop on Argument Mining, co-located with the 29th International Conference on Computational Linguistics, pages 51–61
October 17, 2022.

To learn about cultural differences, we first build statistical and neural NLP models, following previous research, to classify ADUs in learner essays and to extract common structural argument patterns in terms of sequences of types of ADUs in a paragraph (hereafter, *ADU flows*). Moreover, in line with the a study of the impact of argument structure on text quality (Wachsmuth et al., 2016), we develop models to score the essays in terms of their organization and argument strength.

First, a state-of-the-art approach (Prakash and Madabushi, 2020) is adapted for mining ADUs from English texts, trained on the 402 persuasive student essays of Stab and Gurevych (2017) as well as on a corpus of Reddit ChangeMyView discussions (Hidey et al., 2017). Then, two scoring models are learned on 1000 essays from the ICLE corpus (Granger et al., 2009; Persing et al., 2010; Persing and Ng, 2015, Section §3). The trained models are compared with two strong baselines, including the current state of the art on the the respective tasks (Section §4), in order to get an idea of their reliability. The models then serve as the basis for the main analysis carried out in this paper.

In particular, applying the trained models to the entire ICLE corpus, we contrast the most frequent ADU flows that learners use depending on their cultural background, reflected in the author's first language, and in terms of whether that is a high or low-context language (Hall, 1976), as well as their proficiency levels, reflected in the scores of organization and argument strength (Section §5). In addition, we analyze the macro-structure of the essays to classify essays into climactic/anti-climactic (Suzuki, 2010) and horizontal/vertical (Suzuki, 2011). The results suggested that the most frequent ADU flows and their macro-structures correlate with the cultural background and language proficiency of learners, revealing various patterns. For example, speakers of European languages tend to use similar ADUs flows, and among them, speakers of Germanic language have even more similar ADUs flows.

Altogether, we make three contributions in this analysis-oriented paper:

1. We present computational methods that reliably mine ADUs from persuasive essays and that score the essays' quality.
2. We extend computational research on essay argumentation by the consideration of cultural differences between the essays' authors.
3. We provide meaningful insights into the similarities and differences of essay argumentation across different English learners.

The code of our experiments is available at: `https://github.com/webis-de/argmining22-culture-arg`.

2 Related Work

Most research on language learners' argumentation competence investigates essays of a small number of ESL learners in their own countries, such as Paek and Kang (2017) and Liu and Wan (2020). Paek and Kang (2017) study how Korean students use Toulmin elements in their English essays. The results show that Korean students relied heavily on claim and data due to the Korean culture-specific discourse. Liu et al. (2019) and Qin and Karabacak (2010) analyze Toulmin elements in Chinese students in their English argumentative writings. The researchers find that Chinese students mainly use data and subclaim but they barely use counterarguments and rebuttal to consider opposing views. In addition, influenced by Chinese culture, Taiwanese students prefer backing and modal besides data and claim (Cheng and Chen, 2009). The study of Abdollahzadeh et al. (2017) on Iranian graduate learners of English also shows that the students are prone to use data and claim the most.

On the other hand, numerous studies (Kim, 1997; Suzuki, 2010; Kim et al., 2011; Suzuki, 2011; Liu and Furneaux, 2014; Vajjala, 2018) have investigated the effects of culture on persuasive essays produced by native and non-native learners. For example, Kim (1997) studies the differences in Korean and American editorials while Suzuki (2010) conducts a similar study that compares the arguments written by Japanese and American. The results show that non-native students tend to transfer their first language rhetorical style into their English writing. Particularly, non-native speakers tend to use climactic and vertical macro-structures while English speakers tend to use anti-climactic and horizontal macro-structures. These terms are elaborated in Section §5.1.

The above mentioned studies suggest the learners' argument structures would differ depending on their mother tongue backgrounds. Language is the carrier of culture, and cultural features can be

is, by concept. an ethically sensitive endeavor. We point out already here that we do not assess whether people from some cultures argue "better" than others, but to learn about differences in arguing that may be important to provide adequate writing support (see Section §8 for details).

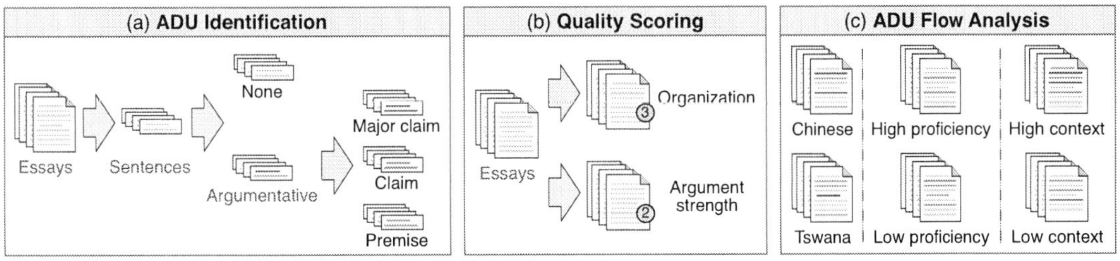

Figure 1: Overview of this paper: (a) We identify sentence-level argumentative discourse units (ADUs) in essays distinguishing four types: *none*, *major claim*, *claim*, and *premise* (Section §3.1). (b) We score the essays' quality in terms of *organization* and *argument strength* (Section §3.2). (c) We analyze ADU flows of cultural diverse learners in terms of first language (Section §5.1), arguing proficiency (Section §5.2) and language context (Section §5.3).

reflected in one's writing. Hall (1976) suggests the categorization of cultures into high context versus low context cultures[2] in order to understand their basic differences in communication style and cultural issues. In fact, the communication styles of people from different cultures range from explicit to ambiguous (Hall, 1976; Zou, 2019; Panina and Kroumova, 2015). That means one culture is more or less high-context (or low-context) than the other. Zou (2019) shows various cultures on a continuum, from where a tendency is observed that most Northern European countries are low-context whereas Asian countries are more high-context. Similarly, Senthamarai and Chandran (2015) classifies North America and much of Western Europe are low-context while Middle East, Asia, Africa, and South America are high-context. Given that the "thought patterns" (Kaplan, 1966) are expected as an integral part of their communication, the "cultural thought patterns" (Kaplan, 1966) may affect the persuasiveness of arguments and organization of ideas (Carlile et al., 2018; Putra et al., 2021).

With a better understanding of how learners from different cultural groups write arguments, language teachers could help learners enhance the quality of argumentative writing. Unfortunately, the impact of cultural differences on argument forms of learners from diverse mother tongue backgrounds is understudied. Typically, such studies rely heavily on manual annotation of argument structures. It is a skilled work. The laborious and time-consuming process would make large-scale studies challenging. Luckily this thorny issue could be addressed using argument mining technology. It has enabled a variety of applications (Wambsganss et al., 2021).

To achieve our goal, two main tasks are performed. Mining argumentative discourse units (ADUs) is the first task of most argumentation technologies. The argument annotated essays corpus (Stab and Gurevych, 2014a), has been widely used to find the boundaries of ADUs with sequential labeling (Stab and Gurevych, 2017; Ajjour et al., 2017), to identify the types of ADUs (Stab and Gurevych, 2014b), or recognize the relations between ADUs (Stab and Gurevych, 2014b). A subsequent computational argumentation task is to assess the essay quality. The International Corpus of Learner English (Granger et al., 2009) has been adopted to assess various quality dimensions of persuasive essays, such as organization (Persing et al., 2010), thesis clarity (Persing and Ng, 2013), prompt adherence (Persing and Ng, 2014) and argument strength (Persing and Ng, 2015). In this paper, we target the two fundamentally important dimensions: organization and argument strength.

We build on the setting of Wachsmuth et al. (2016), but analyze a large number of different learner populations. To the best of our knowledge, we are the very first paper aiming at providing an in-depth analysis of ADUs produced by learners from various cultures, and revealing the differences and similarities of argument structures among different learner populations and proficiency levels from the perspective of computational argumentation.

3 Method

This section presents the computational methods that we develop for identifying argumentative discourse units (ADUs) in student essays as well as for scoring quality dimensions of the essays. We discuss how the methods are trained and what features are used. Figure 1a and b illustrate their usage.

[2]High and low-context will be discussed in Section§ 5.3.

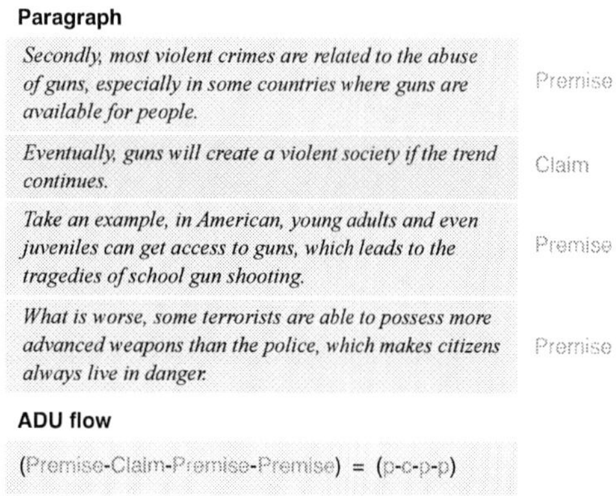

Figure 2: Argumentative discourse units (ADUs) and an ADU flow. The example is adapted from Wachsmuth et al. (2016). This paragraph contains three premises and one claim in the order of *premise-claim-premise-premise*.

3.1 ADU Identification

In this study, we see ADU identification as classifying each sentence of an essay into one of four types: *major claim*, *claim*, *premise*, and *none*. In line with Stab and Gurevych (2014b), we decompose the task into two stages, as in Figure 1a: the first separates all sentences into non-argumentative units (*none*) and argumentative units. In the second stage, another model classifies each argumentative unit into *major claim*, *claim*, and *premise*. Inspired by Prakash and Madabushi (2020), we use multi-layer perceptron (MLP) in both stages whose features are TF-IDF values of words and the sentence embedding vector encoded by RoBERTa (Liu et al., 2019).

After extracting the ADUs in an essay, we then identify the ADU flows as the ADU type sequence in a paragraph. As shown in Figure 2, given that there are ordered *premise, claim, premise, and premise* in the paragraph, the ADU flow here is *premise-claim-premise-premise*, or *p-c-p-p* for short.

3.2 Quality Scoring

As shown in Figure 1b, we use two scoring models to predict the quality of essays on a 4-point scale, in terms of their organization and argument strength, respectively. For scoring, we employ random forest regression (Breiman, 2001). The models' features combine distributed semantics with structure-oriented features handcrafted for the given task. In particular, for distributed semantics, we make use of the last hidden layer of BERT. Conceptually, this layer should encode the meaning of the input in the form of a vector. For the handcrafted features, we reimplement a set of features mostly proposed by Wachsmuth et al. (2016), namely:

- Frequencies of nouns, verbs, and adjectives in the essay
- ADU n-grams in the essay, with $n \in \{1, 2, 3\}$
- ADU compositions, i.e., frequencies of combinations of ADU types within paragraphs
- ADU flows, i.e., sequences of ADU types (or changes thereof) within paragraphs
- Paragraph flows, i.e., sequences of discourse functions: introduction, body, and conclusion (Persing et al., 2010)

ADU type	Training	Validation	Test	Total
Major Claim	520	93	80	693
Claim	1,698	306	190	2,194
- Claims (AAE)	1,016	183	190	1,389
- Claims (CMV)	682	123	0	805
Premise	2,515	441	450	3,406
None	997	172	168	1,337

Table 1: The number of ADU types in the training, validation, and test sets built from the employed corpora.

3.3 Data and Experiments

For ADU identification, we employ the Argument Annotated Essays (AAE) corpus of Stab and Gurevych (2017). As the number of claims is rather small in the corpus, we include claims from the ChangeMyView (CMV) corpus annotated by Hidey et al. (2017).[3] Following Wachsmuth et al. (2016), we treat ADU identification as a sentence-level classification task: A sentence is labeled with one of the classes if any part of the sentence is labeled with that class. After merging the two corpora, we randomly split them into training, validation, and test sets by a 70-15-15 split. The distribution of the ADU types in the datasets can be seen in Table 1.

As for the quality scoring task, we rely on the annotated subset of 1000 essays from the ICLE corpus (Persing et al., 2010; Persing and Ng, 2015). We use the same splitting and the 5-fold setting as Wachsmuth et al. (2016). The distribution of the scores can be seen in Table 2.

[3] We use the authors' updated corpus version: `https://github.com/chridey/change-my-view-modes`. Thus, the data distribution differs from Hidey et al. (2017).

Quality Dimension	1.0	1.5	2.0	2.5	3.0	3.5	4.0
Organization	24	14	35	146	416	289	79
Argument strength	2	21	116	342	372	132	15

Table 2: The number of essays of each score for argument strength and organization in the data employed from Persing et al. (2010) and Persing and Ng (2015).

ADU Identification	M.Cl.	Claim	Prem.	Macro
Baseline majority	0	0	67.3	22.4
Baseline SVM	54.6	23.5	70.4	49.5
Our method w/o CMV	77.6	57.5	83.9	73.0
Our method	85.0	67.8	88.5	80.4
Stab and Gurevych (2017)	89.1	68.2	90.3	82.6

Table 3: Effectiveness of two variations of our ADU identification method and the baselines. The columns show the F_1-score for major claims (M.Cl.), claims, premise (Prem.), and macro F_1-score.

4 Results

We seek to apply ADU identification and quality scoring in order to analyze the whole ICLE corpus with 6,085 essays in total. This section discusses the effectiveness of the trained models.

4.1 ADU Identification

We compare our method to two baselines, a majority baseline and an SVM based on word 1-, 2- and 3-grams, as well as to Stab and Gurevych (2017). As seen in Table 3, our approach outperforms both baselines with a large margin. It also shows that adding claims from CMV improves the performance in all regards. Compared to Stab and Gurevych (2017), our method does not perform better mainly because of the limited comparability. Our evaluation is performed at the sentence level whereas theirs is a token-based evaluation.

4.2 Quality Scoring

The effectiveness of our scoring models are compared to the results of Persing et al. (2010), Persing and Ng (2015), and Wachsmuth et al. (2016) in Table 4. With respect to argument strength and organization, our method performs better than Persing et al. (2010) and Persing and Ng (2015) but worse than Wachsmuth et al. (2016) in terms of MAE and MSE. Our organization scoring model is almost on par with the others. The difference could result from the features; we employ BERT encodings while Wachsmuth et al. (2016) fine-tuned handcrafted semantic features.

	Arg. Strength		Organization	
Approach	**MAE**	**MSE**	**MAE**	**MSE**
Persing et al. best	0.392	0.244	0.323	0.175
Wachsmuth et al. best	0.378	0.226	0.314	0.167
Our approach	0.385	0.229	0.346	0.193

Table 4: Effectiveness of our quality scoring methods compared to previous approaches in terms of mean absolute error (MAE) and mean squared error (MSE).

5 Analysis

The methods we developed and evaluated in the previous sections mainly serve as a means to carry out the analysis presented in this section. In particular, we applied the methods to all essays from the ICLE corpus (Granger et al., 2009). Based on their output, we analyze culture-specific argument structures in terms of what ADU flows learners use depending on three cultural aspects: the learners' *first language*, their *arguing proficiency*, and their *cultural context*. For each aspect, we also discuss the macro structures used in different cultures.

5.1 Differences across First Languages

One way to model culture is via the first language, that is, to assume all people with the same first language form one cultural group. While the ICLE corpus covers essays written by learners of 16 different first languages, we restrict our view to the five most representative ones: Chinese,[4] Tswana, Swedish, German and Italian.

ADU Flows Table 5 shows the five most frequent ADU flows in essays of learners of each considered first language. The essays from the European cultures (last three columns) comprise almost the exact same top ADU flows, with *premise (p)*, *claim (c)*, and *premise-premise (p-p)* as the top-3. In contrast, Chinese speakers largely start a paragraph with claims (*c*, *c-c*, and *c-p*), indicating a clear difference in argument structures compared European learners. Tswana speakers, finally, generally use more *premises* according to the output of our sentence-level ADU identifier.

Given that ADU flows are determined based on the ADUs within one paragraph each, the learners' paragraph splitting strategies may have affected the observed results. Table 6 shows statistics of paragraphs and their length across the cultures defined by the five languages. We see that the essays of all

[4]In this paper, we refer to both Chinese-Mandarin and Chinese-Cantonese as Chinese for simplicity.

Chinese		Tswana		Swedish		German		Italian	
c	4.2%	p-p	12.7%	p	3.8%	p	7.5%	p	11.3%
c-c	3.1%	p	11.5%	c	3.6%	c	7.1%	c	8.9%
c-p	2.5%	p-p-p	6.2%	p-p	3.3%	p-p	3.9%	p-p	4.3%
p	2.1%	c	4.2%	c-c	2.6%	n	2.9%	c-c	3.6%
n	2.0%	c-p	3.2%	p-p-p	2.3%	c-c	2.9%	n	3.5%

Table 5: First languages: The top-5 most frequent ADU flows and their occurrence in essays of learners from each of the five first languages. The letters *c*, *p*, and *n* stand for claim, premise, and none respectively.

	Chinese	Tswana	Swedish	German	Italian
# Essays	814	519	472	445	398
Paragraphs/essay	6.39	5.98	6.78	6.10	6.94
Sentences/parag.	4.46	3.25	4.52	4.39	3.33
Climactic	14%	7%	7%	6%	12%
Anti-Climactic	86%	93%	93%	94%	88%
Horizontal	58%	78%	68%	69%	71%
Vertical	42%	22%	32%	31%	29%

Table 6: First languages: The number of essays, average numbers of paragraphs per essay, and average number of sentences per paragraph in the essays of learners from the considered five languages. The lower part shows the proportion of essays that are climactic vs. anti-climactic as well as horizontal vs. vertical.

cultures have a similar number of paragraphs, likely due to the instructions on essay writing taught beforehand. Among the learners, Italians write the most with an average of 6.94 paragraphs, whereas Tswana speakers write the least: 5.98 paragraphs. Regarding the number of sentences in one paragraph, Italian and Tswana speakers write much fewer sentences compared to the other three languages in the table.

Macro Structures Additionally, we check for cultural differences in the macro-structure of the essays. On the hand, we counted how often they are *climactic* and how often *anti-climactic* (Suzuki, 2010). Climactic macro-structure refers to essays that have a writing style where the conclusion comes at the end (Suzuki, 2010). Statistically, English speakers generally tend to use an anti-climactic macro-structure where the conclusion appears at the beginning of articles. Computationally, we can see essays as climactic, if the extracted major claims are in the second half of the essay, and as anti-climactic otherwise.

On the other hand, we counted the numbers of *horizontal* and *vertical* essays (Suzuki, 2011). Horizontal macro-structure means the written arguments are not reason-based. In contrast, an essay is vertical, if the claims are supported by the premises (Suzuki, 2011). To distinguish the two cases, we assume that a claim is supported, if there is at least one premise appearing within the same paragraph. For example, the claim in Figure 2 is supported. With this in mind, we see an essay as having a horizontal macro-structure, if there are more claims being supported than the claims being unsupported.

Argument Strength				Organization			
Low		High		Low		High	
p	7.5%	c	5.6%	p	7.9%	p	7.3%
c	5.2%	p	5.4%	c	5.9%	c	6.6%
p-p	4.4%	p-p	3.5%	p-p	3.4%	p-p	5.9%
n	3.3%	c-c	2.6%	n	3.2%	c-c	3.8%
p-p-p	2.2%	c-p	2.2%	c-p	1.6%	c-p	3.4%

Table 7: Arguing proficiency: The top-5 most frequent ADU flows and their occurrence in essay of learners with low and high arguing proficiency, according to our argument strength and organization scoring methods.

With respect to the two kinds of macro-structures, Table 6 suggests that Tswana, Swedish, and German learners use fewer climactic essay constructions (6%–7%) than Chinese (14%) and Italian learners (12%). We also find that Tswana speakers use horizontal structures the most (78%), whereas Chinese speakers use them comparably little (58%).

Combining the results from Tables 5 and 6, we find a higher overall similarity between the argument structures of European cultures (Swedish, German, and Italian), matching intuition. Furthermore, among the three cultures, ADU flows and paragraph splitting strategies by Swedish and German speakers seem to be even closer. Our assumption is that the reason behind is these two languages belong to Germanic languages, whereas Italian has an entirely Roman origin.

5.2 Differences across Arguing Proficiencies

While we observed differences between learners of different first languages, they may partly also result from varying arguing proficiencies between the groups of learners. To further investigate this direction, we study ADU flows across proficiencies. In particular, we divided the essays based on their quality into two groups in two ways, once based on the argument strength scores and once based on the organization scores predicted by our methods. The

	Arg. Strength		Organization	
	Low	High	Low	High
# Essays	3 498	2 589	982	5 103
Paragraphs/essay	7.35	7.49	11.58	6.61
Sentences/paragraph	2.67	2.73	1.72	3.02
Climactic	10%	12%	11%	11%
Anti-Climactic	90%	88%	89%	89%
Horizontal	66%	57%	69%	61%
Vertical	34%	43%	31%	39%

Table 8: Arguing proficiency: The number of essays, average numbers of paragraphs per essay, and average number of sentences per paragraph in the essays of learners of different arguing proficiency. The lower part shows the proportion of essays that are climactic vs. anti-climactic as well as horizontal vs. vertical.

essays that scored above or equal to the average scores (2.71 and 2.98, respectively) were classified as more proficient, the others as less proficient.

ADU Flows Table 7 shows the top-5 ADU flows written by learners of different arguing proficiency. In terms of *organization*, both groups share very similar patterns except for the fourth most frequent ADU flows (*n* vs. *c-c*). The flow *n* indicates that less proficient learners seem more prone to use non-argumentative text units. The results based on the *argument strength* scores reveal that the less proficient learners state premises more often than the more proficient ones (7.5% vs. 5.4%). Also for this quality dimension, we observe that less proficient learners resort more often to non-argumentative text units.

Macro Structures Table 8 presents statistics of the essays written by the two groups of learners. We find that, in terms of *argument strength*, the average number of paragraphs in an essay (7.35 and 7.49) and the average number of sentences in a paragraph (2.67 and 2.73) are very similar between writers of different proficiencies. However, in terms of *organization*, more organized essays tend to have notably fewer paragraphs (6.61 as opposed to 11.58), but much more sentences in one paragraph (3.02 as opposed to 1.72). This suggests that a good paragraph splitting strategy is key to better organization, while there is no clear clue how it affects argument strength.

Analyzing macro-structures, we also see that the proportions of climactic and anti-climactic essays are very similar for different proficiencies, both for argument strength and for organization. In terms

Argument Strength				Organization			
Low		High		Low		High	
I-B4-C	13.6%	I-B3-C	16.3%	I	13.4%	I-B3-C	17.1%
I-B3-C	13.2%	I-B4-C	14.4%	I-C	10.7%	I-B4-C	16.5%
I-B5-C	9.6%	I-B5-C	9.9%	I-B10-C	4.8%	I-B5-C	11.5%
I-B2-C	8.7%	I-B2-C	7.9%	I-B-C	4.1%	I-B2-C	9.8%
I-B6-C	6.4%	I-B6-C	6.5%	I-B11-C	3.3%	I-B6-C	7.6%

Table 9: Arguing proficiency: The top-5 most frequent paragraph flows and their occurrence in essays of low and high proficiency learners, according to our argument strength and organization scoring methods. I, B, and C mean *Introduction*, *Body*, and *Conclusion*, respectively. The number after of B means the number of paragraphs having the body labels.

of horizontal or vertical structures, more proficient learners seem to use more vertical structures (43% and 39%, respectively) in these two argument quality dimensions than less proficient ones (34% and 31%, respectively).

In Table 9, finally, we investigate the top-5 most frequent *paragraph flows*. A paragraph flow is here defined as a sequence of paragraph labels identified by the method, which we used for the corresponding feature in Section §3.2. We observe that less proficient writers in organization tend to write either too many (like 10 or 11) or very few (1 or even 0) body paragraphs. This again suggests that less proficient writers miss proper paragraph-splitting skills. For the argument strength, we find that both high and low proficiency writers have similar patterns. Note that, given that the paragraph labeling method may label the paragraphs incorrectly, we cannot say whether both high and low-proficiency learners split their essays in the same way into paragraphs. However, the results tell us that paragraph labels are not a clear feature to distinguish between essays having weaker and stronger argument strength.

5.3 Differences across Cultural Contexts

Another way to model culture is to split learners by whether they come from a high- or low-context culture. According to Hall (1976), "high context transactions feature pre-programmed information that is in the receiver and in the setting, with only minimal information in the transmitted message. Low context transactions are the reverse". Zou (2019) sorts 15 languages from the lowest context culture to the highest. Since not all the languages in ICLE can be found in the sorted list, we select *Chinese* and *Japanese* to represent the high-context

High Context		Low Context	
claim	3.5%	premise	7.2%
claim-claim	2.6%	claim	6.7%
claim-premise	2.0%	premise-premise	4.0%
premise	2.0%	none	3.6%
none	1.9%	claim-claim	2.6%

Table 10: Cultural context: The top-5 most frequent ADU flows and their occurrence in essay of learners from high and low-context cultures.

Argument Strength				Organization			
High Context		Low Context		High Context		Low Context	
Low	High	Low	High	Low	High	Low	High
c	c	p	c	c	c	p	p
c-c	c-c	c	p	n	c-c	c	c
p	p-c	n	p-p	p	c-p	n	p-p
c-p	c-p	p-p	c-c	c-c	p	p-p	p-p-p
n	c-p-p	p-p-p	c-p	c-p	n	c-p	c-c

Table 11: Arguing proficiency and cultural context: The top-5 most frequent ADU flows in essays of learners from high- and low-context cultures, separately for essays of low and high proficiency, according to our argument strength and organization scoring methods.

cultures. For the low-context cultures, we select *German*, *Norwegian*, and *Czech*.

ADU Flows Table 10 shows the top-5 most frequent ADU flows in the high and low-context cultures. We find that learners from high-context cultures use more claims while low-context cultures use more premises in general. The reason behind this phenomenon may be that the pre-programmed information (premises in our case) is assumed to be known by the readers in the high-context culture. As a result, learners may, consciously or unconsciously, omit premises in their arguments.

Table 11 presents combined results for language proficiency and contextual cultures. In terms of the former, non-argumentative text units more frequently appear in the essays by less proficient learners from both cultural groups. The top ADU flow of high-context cultures is just a single claim (*c*), irrespective of the proficiency level. In contrast, both learners from low-context cultures tend to use more premises irrespective of proficiency.

Macro Structures Table 12 shows the macro-structure usage in the high and low-context cultures. We note that there is a tendency for high-context cultures to use more climactic (12% vs. 8%) and vertical (45% vs. 39%) structures in their writings. These findings fit the findings of Suzuki (2010)

	High Context	Low Context
# Essays	1 348	1 002
Paragraphs/essay	6.02	7.02
Sentences/paragraph	5.26	5.06
Climactic	12%	8%
Anti-Climactic	88%	92%
Horizontal	55%	61%
Vertical	45%	39%

Table 12: Cultural context: The number of essays, average numbers of paragraphs per essay, and average number of sentences per paragraph in the essays of learners from high and low-context cultures. The lower part shows the proportion of essays that are climactic vs. anti-climactic as well as horizontal vs. vertical.

	Argument Strength				Organization			
	High ctxt.		Low ctxt.		High ctxt.		Low ctxt.	
	Low	High	Low	High	Low	High	Low	High
Climactic	11%	16%	7%	9%	5%	13%	6%	8%
Anti-Clim.	89%	84%	93%	91%	95%	87%	94%	92%
Horizontal	56%	49%	66%	54%	44%	55%	54%	64%
Vertical	44%	51%	34%	46%	56%	45%	56%	36%

Table 13: Arguing proficiency and cultural context: The proportion of essays that are climactic vs. anti-climactic as well as horizontal vs. vertical from high- and low-context cultures, separately for essays of low and high proficiency, according to our argument strength and organization scoring methods.

and Suzuki (2011). However, we point out that the majority of the macro-structure in our dataset is still anti-climactic and horizontal. The difference between the high and low context does not change this majority.

Finally, Table 13 analyzes the macro-structures considering both the language proficiencies and contextual cultures. It can be seen that most essays use an anti-climactic structure. For high-context cultures, learners of high proficiency use notably more climactic structures than those of low proficiency, both for argument strength (16% vs. 11%) and for organization (13% vs. 5%). For low-context cultures, there is a similar tendency, but with smaller differences (9% vs. 7% and 8% vs. 6%, respectively).

In terms of horizontal and vertical structures, we observe fewer horizontal ones in essays with higher argument strength than in those with lower argument strength for both cultural groups. The low-proficiency learners in low-context cultures use the most horizontal structures (66%) within the argument strength table block. In contrast, we observe an opposite situation in organization: writers use more horizontal structures in higher organization essays than in lower ones for both cultural groups.

6 Conclusion

This study aims to advance the understanding of language learners' argumentation with respect to cultural differences. To investigate argument structures in learner essays, we have built models for ADU identification and quality scoring, aiming at analyzing all ICLE essays. The results reveal differences and similarities of argument structures across English learners from different cultural backgrounds and proficiency levels.

The empirical findings from this study make two significant contributions to educational applications. First, argumentation technology can be of effective assistance in reducing the manual annotation workload as well as in expanding the research scope. Second, the analysis helps gain a comprehensive understanding of the argument structures produced by learners from different language backgrounds. It appears that culture would have a substantial influence on learners' argumentation patterns in terms of argument strength and organization. Our preliminary findings could be a doorway to the intercultural understanding of language learners' argument structures. For example, future research could usefully explore appropriate instructional approaches to help learners from different cultural backgrounds.

7 Limitations

While we provide many interesting findings in this paper, we are aware that there are several limitations in our study.

First, our analysis is based on the results of our ADU identification and quality scoring methods. More advanced models would be able to extract possible underlying patterns. It is likely that the top-5 ADU flows of each culture could be different from those retrieved in the current study.

Moreover, we notice that other factors other than mother tongue languages could play a vital role in the analysis of learners' argumentation structures. For example, the *first foreign language* or the *second language used at home*, both available in the ICLE dataset, could also influence the cultural backgrounds of the learners. These language usages may let them argue differently. However, in this study we only limit our view to their native language. Future studies can utilize more meta information of learners in order to figure out more cultural differences from other perspectives.

Last but not least, we do not distinguish languages spoken by multiple countries, e.g., German spoken in Germany and Switzerland. There could be some subtle differences in their argumentation strategies as well. In this paper, we assume that the language used in different countries share similar patterns regardless of where they are from. In the future, researchers can do further analyses by zooming in on these differences.

8 Ethical Statement

Our study can raise a few potential ethical concerns, as discussed in the following.

First of all, we show statistics of argument micro-structures and macro-structures of different language groups. The results are not meant to be used to interpret that some cultural groups are better than others in any sense. Instead, the differences are a signal for understanding different cultural groups. While communicating with other people (e.g., in writing assistance), knowing the characteristics of their culture helps better understand them or what they may struggle with in expressing arguments. For example, knowing that low-context cultures expect many more premises in a statement, a speaker from a high-context culture can adjust the arguing strategies accordingly.

Secondly, our results should not be used to interpret that English learners from some cultural groups are good at arguing while some do not. We can conclude that some cultures use similar strategies to other cultures, and some cultures have their own strategies. While teaching languages, the results give hints for instructors on how to teach students accordingly. While designing argument mining models, the cultural group of the writers could be used as a feature in the models as well. Such applications of argument mining are expected to build on our findings.

Finally, we should be aware that the findings are based on whole cultural groups but not on individuals. We should not over-generalize or even stereotype people from different cultures in any situation. Still, people from a low-context culture may argue in the way that they are from a high-context culture. Any future research and application in this context should be aware of the individual differences.

Acknowledgments

This work was partially supported by the German Research Foundation (DFG) within the Collaborative Research Center "On-The-Fly Computing" (SFB 901/3) under the project number 160364472.

References

Esmaeel Abdollahzadeh, Mohammad Amini Farsani, and Maryam Beikmohammadi. 2017. Argumentative writing behavior of graduate efl learners. *Argumentation*, 31(4):641–661.

Yamen Ajjour, Wei-Fan Chen, Johannes Kiesel, Henning Wachsmuth, and Benno Stein. 2017. Unit segmentation of argumentative texts. In *Proceedings of the 4th Workshop on Argument Mining*, pages 118–128. Association for Computational Linguistics.

Leo Breiman. 2001. Random forests. *Machine learning*, 45(1):5–32.

Winston Carlile, Nishant Gurrapadi, Zixuan Ke, and Vincent Ng. 2018. Give me more feedback: Annotating argument persuasiveness and related attributes in student essays. In *Proceedings of the 56th Annual Meeting of the Association for Computational Linguistics*, pages 621–631, Melbourne, Australia. Association for Computational Linguistics.

Fei-Wen Cheng and Yueh-Miao Chen. 2009. Taiwanese argumentation skills: Contrastive rhetoric perspective. *Taiwan International ESP Journal*, 1(1):23–50.

Sylviane Granger, Estelle Dagneaux, Fanny Meunier, Magali Paquot, et al. 2009. *International corpus of learner English*, volume 2. Presses universitaires de Louvain Louvain-la-Neuve.

Timon Gurcke, Milad Alshomary, and Henning Wachsmuth. 2021. Assessing the sufficiency of arguments through conclusion generation. In *Proceedings of the 8th Workshop on Argument Mining*, pages 67–77, Punta Cana, Dominican Republic. Association for Computational Linguistics.

Edward T Hall. 1976. Beyond culture. garden city. *NY: Anchor.*

Christopher Hidey, Elena Musi, Alyssa Hwang, Smaranda Muresan, and Kathleen McKeown. 2017. Analyzing the semantic types of claims and premises in an online persuasive forum. In *Proceedings of the 4th Workshop on Argument Mining*, pages 11–21, Copenhagen, Denmark. Association for Computational Linguistics.

Robert B Kaplan. 1966. Cultural thought patterns in inter-cultural education. *Language learning*, 16(1-2):1–20.

Il-Hee Kim, Richard C Anderson, Brian Miller, Jongseong Jeong, and Terri Swim. 2011. Influence of cultural norms and collaborative discussions on children's reflective essays. *Discourse Processes*, 48(7):501–528.

Kyeongja Kim. 1997. A comparison of rhetorical styles in korean and american student writing. *Intercultural Communication Studies*, 6:115–150.

John Lawrence and Chris Reed. 2020. Argument mining: A survey. *Computational Linguistics*, 45(4):765–818.

Donghong Liu and Fang Wan. 2020. What makes proficient writers' essays more persuasive? A Toulmin perspective. *International Journal of TESOL Studies*, 2(1):1–13.

Xinghua Liu and Clare Furneaux. 2014. A multidimensional comparison of discourse organization in english and chinese university students' argumentative writing. *International Journal of Applied Linguistics*, 24(1):74–96.

Yinhan Liu, Myle Ott, Naman Goyal, Jingfei Du, Mandar Joshi, Danqi Chen, Omer Levy, Mike Lewis, Luke Zettlemoyer, and Veselin Stoyanov. 2019. Roberta: A robustly optimized bert pretraining approach. *arXiv preprint arXiv:1907.11692*.

Jin Kyung Paek and Yusun Kang. 2017. Investigation of content features that determine korean EFL learners' argumentative writing qualities. *English teaching*, 72(2):101–122.

Daria Panina and Maya Kroumova. 2015. Cross-cultural communication patterns in computer mediated communication. *Journal of International Education Research*, 11(1):1–6.

Isaac Persing, Alan Davis, and Vincent Ng. 2010. Modeling organization in student essays. In *Proceedings of the 2010 Conference on Empirical Methods in Natural Language Processing*, pages 229–239, Cambridge, MA. Association for Computational Linguistics.

Isaac Persing and Vincent Ng. 2013. Modeling thesis clarity in student essays. In *Proceedings of the 51st Annual Meeting of the Association for Computational Linguistics*, pages 260–269, Sofia, Bulgaria. Association for Computational Linguistics.

Isaac Persing and Vincent Ng. 2014. Modeling prompt adherence in student essays. In *Proceedings of the 52nd Annual Meeting of the Association for Computational Linguistics*, pages 1534–1543, Baltimore, Maryland. Association for Computational Linguistics.

Isaac Persing and Vincent Ng. 2015. Modeling argument strength in student essays. In *Proceedings of the 53rd Annual Meeting of the Association for Computational Linguistics and the 7th International Joint Conference on Natural Language Processing*, pages

543–552, Barcelona, Spain (Online). Association for Computational Linguistics.

Anushka Prakash and Harish Tayyar Madabushi. 2020. Incorporating count-based features into pre-trained models for improved stance detection. In *Proceedings of the 3rd NLP4IF Workshop on NLP for Internet Freedom: Censorship, Disinformation, and Propaganda*, pages 22–32, Barcelona, Spain (Online). International Committee on Computational Linguistics (ICCL).

Jan Wira Gotama Putra, Simone Teufel, and Takenobu Tokunaga. 2021. Annotating argumentative structure in English-as-a-foreign-language learner essays. *Natural Language Engineering*, pages 1–27.

Jingjing Qin and Erkan Karabacak. 2010. The analysis of toulmin elements in chinese efl university argumentative writing. *System*, 38(3):444–456.

T Senthamarai and MR Chandran. 2015. Context in communication: A linguistic study of the interaction between the chinese and the indians in chennai, india. *Journal of Research in Humanities and Social Science*, 3(12):32–35.

Christian Stab and Iryna Gurevych. 2014a. Annotating argument components and relations in persuasive essays. In *Proceedings of COLING 2014, the 25th international conference on computational linguistics*, pages 1501–1510, Dublin, Ireland. Dublin City University and Association for Computational Linguistics.

Christian Stab and Iryna Gurevych. 2014b. Identifying argumentative discourse structures in persuasive essays. In *Proceedings of the 2014 Conference on Empirical Methods in Natural Language Processing*, pages 46–56, Doha, Qatar. Association for Computational Linguistics.

Christian Stab and Iryna Gurevych. 2017. Parsing argumentation structures in persuasive essays. *Computational Linguistics*, 43(3):619–659.

Shinobu Suzuki. 2010. Forms of written arguments: A comparison between japan and the united states. *International Journal of Intercultural Relations*, 34(6):651–660.

Shinobu Suzuki. 2011. Trait and state approaches to explaining argument structures. *Communication Quarterly*, 59(1):123–143.

Sowmya Vajjala. 2018. Automated assessment of nonnative learner essays: Investigating the role of linguistic features. *International Journal of Artificial Intelligence in Education*, 28(1):79–105.

Henning Wachsmuth, Khalid Al Khatib, and Benno Stein. 2016. Using argument mining to assess the argumentation quality of essays. In *Proceedings of COLING 2016, the 26th International Conference on Computational Linguistics*, pages 1680–1691. The COLING 2016 Organizing Committee.

Thiemo Wambsganss and Christina Niklaus. 2022. Modeling persuasive discourse to adaptively support students' argumentative writing. In *Proceedings of the 60th Annual Meeting of the Association for Computational Linguistics (Volume 1: Long Papers)*, pages 8748–8760, Dublin, Ireland. Association for Computational Linguistics.

Thiemo Wambsganss, Christina Niklaus, Matthias Söllner, Siegfried Handschuh, and Jan Marco Leimeister. 2021. Supporting cognitive and emotional empathic writing of students. In *Proceedings of the 59th Annual Meeting of the Association for Computational Linguistics and the 11th International Joint Conference on Natural Language Processing*, pages 4063–4077, Online. Association for Computational Linguistics.

Yumei Zou. 2019. A study on english writing pattern under the impact of high-context and low-context cultures. In *5th International Conference on Arts, Design and Contemporary Education (ICADCE 2019)*, pages 758–762. Atlantis Press.

Perturbations and Subpopulations for Testing Robustness in Token-Based Argument Unit Recognition

Jonathan Kamp[1] **Lisa Beinborn**[1] **Antske Fokkens**[1,2]
[1]Computational Linguistics and Text Mining Lab, Vrije Universiteit Amsterdam
[2]Dept. of Mathematics and Computer Science, Eindhoven University of Technology
{j.b.kamp, l.beinborn, antske.fokkens}@vu.nl

Abstract

Argument Unit Recognition and Classification aims at identifying argument units from text and classifying them as *pro* or *against*. One of the design choices that need to be made when developing systems for this task is what the unit of classification should be: segments of tokens or full sentences. Previous research suggests that fine-tuning language models on the token-level yields more robust results for classifying sentences compared to training on sentences directly. We reproduce the study that originally made this claim and further investigate what exactly token-based systems learned better compared to sentence-based ones. We develop systematic tests for analysing the behavioural differences between the token-based and the sentence-based system. Our results show that token-based models are generally more robust than sentence-based models both on manually perturbed examples and on specific subpopulations of the data.

1 Introduction

Identifying argumentation units is difficult, both for humans and machines. The challenge starts with the question of what it means for a segment to be argumentative towards a given topic in the first place (Trautmann et al., 2020; Habernal et al., 2014, e.g.). Trautmann et al. (2020) propose a pragmatic approach for defining arguments and ask annotators to identify segments that can be placed in the <argument span> slot of the following template: *"<TOPIC> should be supported/opposed, because <argument span>"*. They compare models that are trained to label tokens as being part of argumentative segments to models that classify full sentences as containing argumentative segments (ARG) or not (non-ARG) (see Figure 1), ultimately arguing that token-based training is preferable. Their experiments suggest that a token-based approach is more robust when sentence boundaries are unknown or not precisely given.

Argumentative segments provide reasons for taking a positive (pro) or negative (against) stance on a topic. These arguments are highly topic-specific, but the decent accuracy of cross-topic models indicates that there are also topic-independent cues. Niven and Kao (2019) previously showed that transformer-based models learn to map specific cue words to a label and learn little about argumentation reasoning. It could be that this is the most we can expect in a cross-topic scenario. The question then remains where these cues are found: are they in the ARG segments themselves or are they also provided by the non-ARG context? When comparing token-based and sentence-based models, we expect token-based models to be better at picking up cues that are specific to ARG segments themselves, whereas sentence-based models may be more susceptible to cues from the non-ARG context, in particular, when these appear to announce an argumentation (e.g. *because I think that...*). Reliance on (non-ARG) cues is a particularly strong signal that general cues rather than reasoning are used.

In this paper, we dive further into this line of research. We rerun experiments with the best models of Trautmann et al. (2020) to ensure a fair basis of comparison, reproducing most of the original results and coming close for the rest. We then design multiple robustness tests comparing the behavior of token- and sentence-based models in mixed-segment sentences, i.e. sentences that contain at least one ARG segment and one non-ARG segment. We expect token-based models to be more robust because they are trained to distinguish between ARG and non-ARG segments within sentence boundaries and thus have access to more precise information as to what makes up an ARG segment during training. This hypothesis is confirmed by our perturbation tests, which also show different behavior on subpopulations of the data. We thus show that a relatively small, curated dataset of ad-

Proceedings of the 9th Workshop on Argument Mining, co-located with the 29th International Conference on Computational Linguistics, pages 62–73
October 17, 2022.

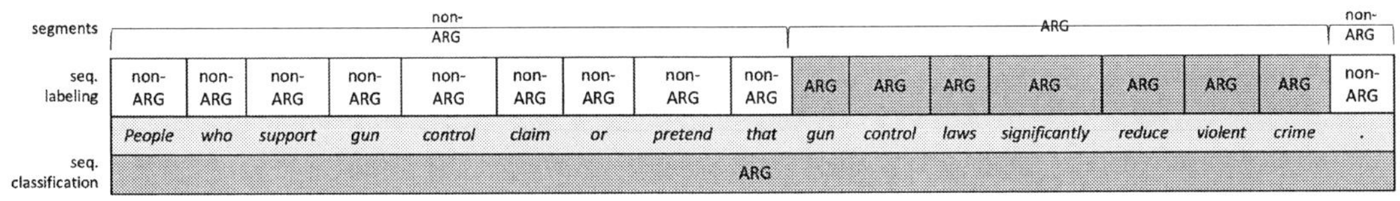

Figure 1: An example sentence from the AURC-8 (Trautmann et al., 2020) topic *gun control*. Each sentence in the dataset has one vector of token-wise gold labels (in- and output in a sequence *labeling* approach, i.e. **token-based**) as well as one sentence-wise gold label (in- and output in a sequence *classification* approach, i.e. **sentence-based**). ARG and non-ARG gold *segments* are sequences of tokens that carry the same label.

versarial examples can provide systematic insights into model behavior. Additional robustness tests with subpopulations of the data surprisingly do not yield clear differences between the two approaches.

2 Background and Related Work

In this section, we first present related work on argument unit recognition (§2.1) and then dive further into the concept of robustness tests (§2.2).

2.1 Argument Unit Recognition

Argumentation theory is about identifying how humans reach common ground and compromise, how societal information is exchanged, what the degree of subjectivity in viewpoints is and how polarised different stances can be. In the digital era, arguments from a wide range of sources are analysed. These sources range from debates on social media and (online) fora to technical documents used by professionals in the legal domain. Arguments roughly reflect the rationale behind a stance or decision, in relation to a certain topic or proposition. The field of computational argumentation attempts to model the argument patterns that are present in human language. Lauscher et al. (2021) distinguish between different tasks in argument modeling: ~mining, ~assessment, ~reasoning, and ~generation. Argument Unit Recognition and Classification is a task that can be positioned within argument *mining*, as argumentative from non-argumentative expressions are first distinguished, and a stance is then attributed to each of the identified arguments. Ajjour et al. (2017) show that the task of segmenting a text into argument units of different types remains particularly challenging in a cross-domain setting.

The first part of this research aims to reproduce the Argument Unit Recognition and Classification experiments by Trautmann et al. (2020), who train multiple transformer-based models on a novel argumentation dataset that is labeled at the token level: spans of tokens are then predicted as being pro, against or non-argumentative towards a given topic.

Argument mining has been thoroughly approached by (Bi-)LSTM modeling (Eger et al., 2017), SVMs and RNNs (Niculae et al., 2017). Apart from Trautmann et al. (2020), however, transformer-based architectures have been deployed more rarely. Poudyal et al. (2020) show how RoBERTa (Liu et al., 2019) can successfully be applied on the legal ECHR dataset on a claim-premise task. Ruiz-Dolz et al. (2021) test several flavors of BERT models (Devlin et al., 2019) on the same task, but on a less domain-specific debate corpus. Mayer et al. (2020a) compare different domain-generic and -specific transformer-based models in combination with CRF and GRU layers on medical texts. Similarly to Trautmann et al. (2020), they experiment with both sequence labeling and sequence classification, applying the former to a component detection task, and using the latter to classify relations between argument components.

The next subsection provides background and related work on the second contribution of our paper: testing robustness.

2.2 Robustness Testing

Goel et al. (2021) describe three ways of testing robustness: (1) testing on **subpopulations** of the test data the model is expected to perform poorly on; (2) **perturbing** the test data by creating adversarial examples (Zhang et al., 2020) that are expected to shed light on weaknesses of the model; (3) assessing model performance on pre-existing evaluation sets to establish **scalability** and **cross-domain** validity. We briefly discuss the role of each of these three in our work.

We design three **subpopulation** tests, two of which are based on similarity between training and test instances and one based on the ratio of argumentative tokens in a sentence. We also design three **perturbation** tests. The first design choice involves the level of granularity, which is usually on the word- or phrase-level. In our case, perturbation units are aligned with the granularity of the annotated spans, i.e. the ARG or non-ARG segments remain intact but are combined in different ways. A second point of attention in creating perturbations is the risk of altering the grammar or semantics in an unintended way. Automatic metrics have been utilised to determine whether linguistic aspects are preserved after perturbation, such as the Jaccard similarity coefficient, grammar and syntax related measurements and edit-based measurements (Zhang et al., 2020). These may be relatively fast to use, especially on a large scale, but might fall short in tasks where generating adversarial candidates goes beyond relatively simple, single word substitutions. We therefore opt for manual verification of our samples. Trautmann et al. (2020) include the third type of robustness test already in that they apply **cross-topic** evaluation. Since we are mostly interested in the models' generic ability in identifying argumentative segments, we apply our robustness tests in the cross-topic setting only.

A handful of studies have applied robustness tests to transformer-based models on an argument mining task. Schiller et al. (2021) apply paraphrases, spelling alterations and negation stress tests on a stance detection task. Niven and Kao (2019) apply a negation stress test on a Argument Reasoning Comprehension Task, where negating a warrant (i.e. a type of argument) should result in predicting the inverted label. Mayer et al. (2020b) protract robustness testing into adversarial training: by inserting or replacing simple linguistic elements in the original data, such as nouns, scalar adverbs and punctuation, they use the perturbed examples for retraining the model, achieving higher performance. Mayer et al. (2020b) show the effectiveness of single, token-level perturbations, while aiming to control for *same-meaning* preservation between the original and perturbed example pairs. Instead, we focus on the different argumentative load that different parts of a sentence carry to guide our perturbations, and ensure that the result of each perturbation is semantically sound (yet not unaltered). Finally, the in-domain versus cross-domain comparison is a more frequent type of testing, but it is often approached from a generalisability perspective (*how well does the model perform on cross-domain data?*), which has a slightly different connotation from a robustness perspective (*how well does the model defend itself from specific adversaries in cross-domain data?*). Our work can be seen as an extension to Trautmann et al. (2020), who find that token-based models are more robust against sentence segmentation errors than sentence-based models. Our robustness tests go beyond their work in that they show that token-based models are also more robust compared to sentence-based models in well-formed sentences with manipulated combinations of ARG and non-ARG segments. Furthermore, the phenomena that we are testing robustness on are more likely to occur than scenarios in which sentence boundaries are not given.

3 Reproduction Experiments

This section describes our reproduction study, including the dataset used (§3.1), the experimental setup (§3.2), the model evaluation metrics (§3.3), and the requirements for a successful reproduction together with our results (§3.4).

3.1 Dataset Description

The AURC-8 dataset developed by Trautmann et al. (2020) is divided over eight topics: *1. abortion 2. cloning 3. marijuana legalization 4. minimum wage 5. nuclear energy 6. death penalty 7. gun control 8. school uniforms.* In their manual labeling process, annotators were presented with candidate sentences in which arguments related to one given topic were possibly present. Argument spans were annotated according to the slot-filling template *"<TOPIC> should be supported/opposed, because <argument span>"*. This results in spans annotated as PRO (a supporting argument) or CON (an opposing argument). Spans that remain unlabeled are assigned NON (a non-argumentative segment). As an example, both underlined spans in the following sentence about *death penalty* are labeled as CON segments: '*It does not deter crime and it is extremely expensive to administer .*' Instead, the first underlined span in the following sentence about *gun control* is labeled as a CON segment whereas the second span is labeled as PRO: '*Yes , guns can be used for protection but laws are meant to protect us , too .*' In both example sentences, the spans of adjacent non-underlined tokens form the NON segments. The dataset consists of 1,000 example sentences per topic. Of the 8,000 total sentences, 3,500 (43.75%) are annotated as ARG and 4,500 (56.25%) as non-ARG. The portion of ARG sentences is divided over 658 examples (14.62%) containing exclusively PRO segments, 621 examples (13.80%) containing exclusively CON segments and 3,221 (71.58%) containing any combination of PRO, CON and NON segments.[1]

The models are run on two different splits of the data: in-domain and cross-domain. In the in-domain setup, the first 70% of the examples from each of the Topics 1-6 is assigned to training, the next 10% to the development set, and the last 20% to the test set. The cross-domain setup assigns all sentences from Topics 1-5 to training, Topic 6 to development, whereas Topic 7 and 8 form the test set.[2]

3.2 Experimental Setup

We use two training approaches: token-based and sentence-based.

Token-based Models are trained on the sequence of token-wise gold labels, in a sequence-labeling fashion. The input to the model are tokenised sentences.

Sentence-based Models are trained on a sentence-level gold label, in a sequence-classification fashion. The sentence-level gold label is a modification of the token-level gold labels. Let t_L be the set of labels assigned to individual tokens in a sentence, and f_{PRO} and f_{CON} the number of tokens in the sentence that are labeled as PRO and CON, respectively. Then, the sentence label s_L is obtained as follows:

$$
\begin{array}{ll}
t_L = \{NON\}, & s_L := NON \\
t_L = \{NON, PRO\}, & s_L := PRO \\
t_L = \{NON, CON\}, & s_L := CON \\
t_L \supseteq \{PRO, CON\}: & \\
\quad \text{if } f_{PRO} > f_{CON}, & s_L := PRO \\
\quad \text{if } f_{CON} > f_{PRO}, & s_L := CON \\
\quad \text{if } f_{PRO} = f_{CON}, & s_L := random^3
\end{array}
$$

The input instance fed to the sentence-based model is the same tokenised sentence used as input in the token-based model. Instead of feeding along a sequence of token-wise labels, we feed its unique s_L. The output is a predicted s_L.

We re-train the models based on the architecture that performed best in the original paper: BERTLARGE (Devlin et al., 2019). We also train a token-based model with a CRF layer.[4] In the original results, the CRF layer improved segmentation. The model without CRF more often broke segments up into multiple single-word segments.

For each domain split, for each model setup we carry out series of 5 training runs with a different random seed for each run. We report mean F1-scores and standard deviation for each series of runs. Hyperparameter settings are reported in Appendix A.

3.3 Model Evaluation

The models are evaluated on two metrics: token-F1 and sentence-F1.[5] Token-F1 is calculated as the average over the per-class F1-scores for all tokens in the evaluation set. Sentence-F1 is the average over per-class F1-scores for all sentences in the evaluation set. Whereas token-F1 is straightforward for the token-based setup, and sentence-F1 is for the sentence-based setup, one extra step is needed to retrieve the sentence labels from the token-based predictions, and token labels from the sentence-based predictions. When using the token-based model, we obtain the sentence labels from the assigned tokens using the same approach as described in §3.2. After applying the sentence-based model, we obtain token labels by assigning the predicted sentence label to all tokens of the sentence.

3.4 Reproduction Results and Considerations

We consider the mean F1-scores over three runs from Trautmann et al. (2020) as the benchmark for the reproduction comparisons. We follow Moore and Rayson (2018) and provide F1-distributions reporting the mean and standard deviation from our experiments. It remains a methodological challenge to determine a threshold within which a score can be defined as successfully reproduced. We follow Reuver et al. (2021) and consider the reproduction successful if given a distribution of reproduced F1-scores D, the original mean F1-score falls within two standard deviations from the mean

[1] In this calculation, NON segments that are solely formed by punctuation marks are ignored.

[2] Visit Appendix A for additional details on dataset versioning and pre-processing of the data.

[3] A random choice from $\{PRO, CON\}$ is made.

[4] We were not able to re-implement the CRF layer for the sentence-based approach and could therefore not include this.

[5] Trautmann et al. (2020) also include a third metric: segment-F1. Given that the description of their implementation remains underspecified and since the metric is not strictly relevant to our work, we report the original segment-F1 results in Appendix A along with our own segment-F1 implementation.

setting		model	token-F1: token -based setup	token-F1: sentence -based setup	sentence-F1: token -based setup	sentence-F1: sentence -based setup
in-domain	orig	BERTLARGE	.683	.627	.709	.715
		BERTLARGE+CRF	.696	.622	.711	.725
	repr	BERTLARGE	.698 (.003)	**.614** (.008)	**.708** (.004)	**.713** (.012)
		BERTLARGE+CRF	**.696** (.003)	-	**.711** (.006)	-
cross-domain	orig	BERTLARGE	.596	.544	.598	.602
		BERTLARGE+CRF	.620	.519	.610	.573
	repr	BERTLARGE	**.587** (.008)	**.529** (.011)	**.604** (.009)	.566 (.017)
		BERTLARGE+CRF	.578 (.008)	-	**.609** (.007)	-

Table 1: Original results (white background) compared to reproduction results (non-white background) on the test set. Models are divided over an in- and cross-domain setting. Reproduction results show the mean scores from 5 runs, along with the standard deviation (within parentheses). The reproduction scores where the original score falls within two standard deviations from the mean are given in bold.

of D. We provide all individual decisions on the test set for a more accurate comparison, since F1-scores can still stem from different behavior on sub-populations of the data.

At a first glance, the differences between the original and replicated results are relatively small for both token-based and sentence-based models. One pattern from the original paper is not reproduced, namely, the positive effect on performance by the CRF layer on the token-based model. In the light of the threshold of two standard deviations, we observe in Table 1 that reproductions are partially successful. On the test set, 5 out of 6 F1-scores are reproduced in the in-domain setting, and 4 out of 6 in the cross-domain setting. Success rate of reproduction does not seem to depend on training setup either: 6 out of 8 for token-based versus 3 out of 4 for sentence-based. Scores that are not reproduced come close as they fall within half a decimal from the original.[6]

4 Robustness Testing

We test robustness in a cross-domain setting. By isolating this problem from topic-dependent content biases, the models are expected to focus more on indicators that are representative of a generic notion of argumentation. While a token-based model is explicitly instructed that there are fine-grained argumentative differences within a sentence, a sentence-based model is not. Therefore, we expect the sentence-based models to have more difficulty in predicting the cues that are argumentative on a micro-level (i.e. tokens, segments), which translates to difficulties at the macro-level (i.e. the sentence). Our robustness tests precisely operate at a micro-level: adding, replacing or removing segments should impact the sentence-based model more negatively than the token-based model.

We apply robustness tests to the two cross-domain token-based models (BERTLARGE, BERTLARGE+CRF) and the sentence-based model (BERTLARGE). We investigate robustness for the task as a binary prediction problem (Argument Unit Recognition) and remove the stance component: ARG entails both labels PRO and CON, and non-ARG corresponds to NON. As anticipated in §2.2, we categorise the robustness tests according to two classes: *perturbations* on the test set (§4.1) and *subpopulations* of the test set (§4.2).

4.1 Perturbations on the Test Set

We craft a $before$-dataset and $after$-dataset in the following way. First, artificial candidate test sets are generated through deletion, recombination or label-based pre-selection of segments. The segments are sampled from the original test set. Second, we manually label or complete the candidate examples. We create three types of tests **T1**, **T2** and **T3**. We report on the impact of the perturbation through Δacc, i.e. the difference between the accuracy *before* and the accuracy *after* the perturbation has been applied. Hence, each example in

[6] See Table 5 in Appendix A for a complete overview of the reproduction results. It can be observed that none of the segment-F1 metrics are reproduced, probably caused by a slightly different implementation of how these scores are calculated.

either the *before-* or *after*-dataset has one gold label (at the sentence-level) on which the models are evaluated.

T1 - Announcing Segments Observations in the original test set show that non-ARG segments can broadly be divided in segments that announce (ANN) an immediately subsequent ARG segment, and segments that do not (non-ANN). For instance, ANN segments are phrases the include literal argument indicators such as *evidence, claim, argument, reason* followed by a copula, and phrases that include reporting verbs. Examples:

> **ANN**
> *... a major argument against this topic is...*
> *... he thinks that...*
>
> **non-ANN**
> *... this document was written in 2022 and...*
> *... but...*

ANN segments are an example of information that is known to be non-ARG by the token-based model, but not by the sentence-based model where it falls under a coarse-grained, sentence-level ARG label. Since ANN segments mostly co-occur with ARG segments, the sentence-based model is likely to mix them up. The token-based model may also use an ANN segment as signal that an ARG is following, but has better chances of using information from the following segment itself to identify when this is not the case. We test this by creating counter-examples that concatenate ANN segments to a subsequent *non*-ARG segment. This results in non-ARG sentence-level labels, for instance, *'Pro-abortion politicians think that...'* + *'...the debate has become very delicate.'*. If our theory is correct, the token-based model would generally be able to classify the two segments separately as non-ARG, resulting in a non-ARG label for the sentence, whereas the sentence-model is more prone to label the sentence as ARG based on the ANN segment.

	concatenation	sentence gold
before	ANN non-ARG seg. + ARG seg.	ARG
after	ANN non-ARG seg. + non-ARG seg.	non-ARG

We first extracted candidate $< a, b >$ pairs, where a is an ARG segment, b is a non-ARG segment and a is immediately followed by b in the same sentence from the original AURC-8 dataset. Pairs that do not form a full sentence are manually discarded. Subsequently, we manually labeled the non-ARG segments as (non-)ANN, until reaching 100 ANN annotations for the *gun control* topic and 100 for *school uniforms*. Each ANN segment (e.g. *'Pro-abortion politicians think that...'*) is then manually completed with a novel non-ARG segment (e.g. *'...the debate has become very delicate.'*) to form a full non-ARG sentence and is added to the *after*-dataset. The respective $< a, b >$ pairs are added to the *before*-dataset.

T2 - Concatenate Non-Argumentative Sentence Here we test robustness by concatenating an ARG segment with a pure non-ARG sentence. In between the two segments, the connector *'and besides,'* is used to create a well-formed sentence. This results in constructions where the ARG segment ends up in a context of a relatively high number of non-ARG tokens. Such a concatenation would result in e.g.: *'Uniforms force conformity'*+ *'and besides,'* + *'it's a great service for parents as I was able to pick up lots of good stuff for little money.'* The token-based model is expected to classify the two segments as ARG and non-ARG respectively, resulting in a sentence-wise ARG label prediction. The sentence-based model might be more biased by the high ratio of non-ARG tokens that are present in the sentence, potentially resulting in a sentence-wise non-ARG prediction.

	concatenation	sentence gold
before	ARG seg.	ARG
after	ARG seg. + connector + non-ARG sent.	ARG

We populate a candidate dataset with concatenations of an ARG segment, the connector and a pure non-ARG sentence, in that order. The components in each concatenation (except for the connector, which is constant) are on the same topic and are sampled from the original test set. The ARG segment should be a full stand-alone sentence. From this candidate dataset, we then select 50 examples for *gun control* and 50 for *school uniforms* that are sound, stand-alone sentences to be added to the *after*-dataset. The *before*-dataset consists of the respective ARG segments.

T3 - Remove Non-Argumentative Segment In this test, we remove the non-ARG context around the remaining ARG segment creating uncontextualised argument units. We expect this perturbation to have less impact on the token-based model, as its decision is potentially less informed by the missing non-ARG segments.

	concatenation	sentence gold
before	ARG seg. + non-ARG seg. / non-ARG seg. + ARG seg.	ARG
after	ARG seg.	ARG

We extract pairs consisting of an ARG and a non-ARG segment from the original corpus. Both elements of each pair stem from the same source sentence and are originally adjacent. We manually check them to ensure that both the pair and the ARG segment alone form well-formed sentences. We select a total of 200 examples with an approximate 50%-50% split of examples where non-ARG precedes or follows the ARG segment, as well as an approximate 50%-50% split between the two topics. The pairs form the *before*-dataset whereas the ARG segments alone form the *after*-dataset.

4.2 Subpopulations of the Test Set

A subpopulation is a group of test instances that is selected based upon a criterion that is expected to influence the performance of the model. We take it a step further: we consider each instance in the test set a subpopulation on its own and assign it a value from a continuous variable in the data. In our case, the continuous variable is a semantic similarity score between train and test data, and the ratio of noisy (non-argumentative) tokens per sentence, two aspects that generally impact language classification tasks. The point-biserial correlation coefficient r_{pb} is then calculated between this continuous variable and the dichotomous prediction correctness. Thus, r_{pb} is expected to be lower for a model when the continuous variable forms less of a bias on its decisions compared to its effect on another model.

T4 - Similarity Train-Test Same Labels The outcome of this test provides an indication of the impact of semantic similarity between training and test data on the decision of the model. For each of the mixed-segment sentences in the test set, a pairwise semantic similarity coefficient is calculated in relation to each of the sentences in the training set. If the maximum semantic similarity coefficient for one test sentence corresponds to a training instance with the same label (ARG), the test sentence is stored in the *T4-set* along with its coefficient. The correlation between prediction correctness of mixed-segment sentences from the *T4-set* and their respective maximum similarity coefficients is then computed. We expect the sentence-based model to be more affected by it than the token-based model, given that semantic similarity at the macro-level of the sentence may be a more prominent indicator for the former model. A token-based setup, on the other hand, should be able to classify segments within the sentence as it can rely on explicit ARG vs non-ARG information. This translates to a correlation coefficient that is expected to be higher for the sentence-based model than for the token-based model.

The semantic vector representation of a sentence is given by its averaged token vectors.[7] Sentence similarity corresponds to the cosine similarity between the two semantic vector representations of a sentence pair.

T5 - Similarity Train-Test Opposite Labels For T5, the maximum similarity coefficient is calculated in relation to the instances in the training set that have an opposite label (non-ARG) to the mixed-segment sentences. Similarly to the *T4-set*, a *T5-set* is created accordingly. This aspect is expected to have more impact on the sentence-based model than the token-based model, hence yielding a weaker correlation for the latter.

T6 - Argumentative Token Ratio Through T6, prediction correctness is correlated with the argumentative token ratio in mixed-segment sentences from the test set. This ratio is calculated as the number of ARG tokens over the number of all tokens. In line with the expectations in T4 and T5,

[7] `spacy.io/models/en` → `en_core_web_lg` `v3.3.0`.

the token-based model should be less affected by this sentence-level aspect, resulting in a weaker correlation coefficient compared to the sentence-based model.

4.3 Results Robustness Tests

The perturbation results of T1, T2, T3 are collected in Table 2, where Δacc quantifies the impact of each perturbation. Specifically, Δacc represents the difference in accuracy by the models on sentences before and after the perturbation has been applied. It can be observed that an overall negative Δacc pattern is present across the grid, which is expected behavior. The maximum absolute negative impact is $\Delta acc = -.077$, achieved through T3 on the token-based model without CRF layer. From a relative point of view, the sentence-based model is impacted most with -11.7% on T3.

As an answer to our initial expectations, the token-based model with CRF layer is more robust to perturbations than the sentence-based model on two out of three tests: T1 (Announcing Segments) and T3 (Remove Non-Argumentative Segment). This is quantified in terms of both absolute Δacc (-.022 on T1, -.068 on T3) and relative Δacc (-2.5% on T1, -9.2% on T3). In comparison, the token-based model without CRF is impacted more heavily than the sentence-based model in absolute terms (-.043 versus -.027 on T1; -.077 versus -.076 on T3), but is more robust in relative terms on T3 (-10.1% versus -11.7%). Although the CRF layer has not proven to clearly increase the token-based model performance (not observable in Table 1, nor in Table 2), it appears to improve the robustness of the model.

Interestingly, the token-based model without CRF layer is the only one to considerably improve performance on the T2 *after*-dataset. This behavior is unexpected since all *after*-sets were meant to *trick* the models rather than to help them. A possible explanation might be that the connector '*and besides,*' is often included in the annotated ARG spans in AURC-8 training instances. This could represent a general downside of token-based models: picking up a small cue in the sentence as ARG, therefore predicting the sentence-wise label as ARG.

The results of subpopulation tests T4, T5 and T6 are given in Table 3. We hypothesised that continuous aspects in the data (such as semantic similarity between full sentences in training and test or the argument token ratio of a sentence) would correlate more strongly with predictions by the sentence-based model compared to the token-based model. This hypothesis could not be confirmed. Apart from being close to 0, which indicates no correlation, the *rpb* coefficients for the token-based model are also close to the coefficients for the sentence-based model on the same tests T4-6, which indicates no difference in bias between the models. The perturbation results (T1-3), however, provide an indication that there are differences between subpopulations. Specifically, both token-based models achieve a higher accuracy on each single *before*- and *after*-dataset, which are specific subpopulations of the data. This clear difference in performance can be explained by the fact that these tests do not cover pure, non-argumentative sentences on which the sentence-based model might be stronger (as can be inferred from the comparable sentence-F1 scores between the two types of models in Table 1). We therefore believe more research on subpopulations is needed. In particular, we may investigate alternative implementations of the continuous variables, such as using Sentence-bert (Reimers and Gurevych, 2019) for representing the semantics of individual instances or also looking at the number of semantically similar examples in the training data.

5 Conclusion

In this study, we partially reproduced the results of Trautmann et al. (2020) and introduced new robustness tests that showed how token-based models are generally more robust than models trained at a sentence level on an Argument Unit Recognition task. We applied two type of tests: perturbations and subpopulations. With regards to the perturbations, we found that 1) removing the non-ARG segment from a mixed-segment sentence, and 2) replacing the ARG segment with a non-ARG segment in *announcing* phrases such as '*Their main argument is <ARG>*' or '*Most politicians against gun legislation think that <ARG>*' negatively impact a sentence-based model more than a token-based model. We did not find a difference in bias among the two types of models with regards to semantic similarity between training and evaluation data, and high argumentative token ratios at the sentence level. Instead, we showed that the development of perturbation test sets itself can shed light on specific subpopulations of the data: our token-based

	T1			T2			T3		
model	*before*	*after*	Δacc	*before*	*after*	Δacc	*before*	*after*	Δacc
token-based BERTLARGE	.875 (.018)	.832 (.033)	**-.043** **-4.8%**	.760 (.035)	.830 (.037)	**+.070** **+9.2%**	.760 (.022)	.683 (.037)	**-.077** **-10.1%**
token-based BERTLARGE+CRF	.878 (.021)	.856 (.024)	**-.022** **-2.5%**	.790 (.015)	.760 (.028)	**-.030** **-3.8%**	.740 (.036)	.672 (.023)	**-.068** **-9.2%**
sentence-based BERTLARGE	.835 (.034)	.808 (.053)	**-.027** **-3.2%**	.638 (.059)	.640 (.064)	**+.002** **+0.3%**	.652 (.047)	.576 (.034)	**-.076** **-11.7%**

Table 2: Impact perturbations on cross-domain token-based and sentence-based models. Mean accuracy and standard deviation (within parentheses) over 5 runs is reported for each model. Accuracy is calculated on the test set before applying the perturbation (*before*) and after applying the perturbation (*after*). Δacc represents the absolute and relative (%) difference between *before* and *after*.

	T4	T5	T6
model	r_{pb}	r_{pb}	r_{pb}
token-based BERTLARGE	-.068 (.031)	.027 (.009)	.028 (.023)
token-based BERTLARGE+CRF	-.031 (.016)	.013 (.029)	.046 (.010)
sentence-based BERTLARGE	-.014 (.034)	-.037 (.044)	.042 (.037)

Table 3: Impact subpopulations on cross-domain token-based and sentence-based models. *rpb* indicates the point-biserial correlation coefficient between prediction correctness and a given aspect of the sentence. The range of *rpb* is $[-1, 1]$, where the two extremes indicate a perfect negative and positive correlation, respectively. The coefficients in the table are the means from 5 runs per model, along with the standard deviations (within parentheses).

models performed better on both mixed-segment sentences and single argumentative segments.

By approaching the task from a challenging, cross-domain perspective, we isolated the problem from model reliance on topic-dependent content. Our analyses reveal that it is difficult to define a common denominator for the notion of argumentativeness across topics. They highlighted the importance of the type of knowledge we expect to be learned by a computational model of argumentation. Structural choices in the annotation setup can lead to systematic gaps in the dataset that allow the model to take superficial shortcuts (Gardner et al., 2020). Robustness tests are a means to detect such gaps and, as a side effect, help in unraveling conceptual vagueness.

Acknowledgements

Jonathan Kamp's and Antske Fokkens' research was funded by the Dutch National Science Organisation (NWO) through the project InDeep: Interpreting Deep Learning Models for Text and Sound (NWA.1292.19.399). Lisa Beinborn's research was funded by NWO through the project CLARIAH-PLUS (CP-W6-19-005). We would like to thank Dietrich Trautmann and his co-authors for making their clear code and dataset publicly available, and for the email correspondence. We also thank the anonymous reviewers for their valuable contribution.

References

Yamen Ajjour, Wei-Fan Chen, Johannes Kiesel, Henning Wachsmuth, and Benno Stein. 2017. Unit segmentation of argumentative texts. In *Proceedings of the 4th Workshop on Argument Mining*, pages 118–128.

Jacob Devlin, Ming-Wei Chang, Kenton Lee, and Kristina Toutanova. 2019. BERT: Pre-training of deep bidirectional transformers for language understanding. In *Proceedings of the 2019 Conference of the North American Chapter of the Association for Computational Linguistics: Human Language Technologies, Volume 1 (Long and Short Papers)*, pages 4171–4186, Minneapolis, Minnesota. Association for Computational Linguistics.

Steffen Eger, Johannes Daxenberger, and Iryna Gurevych. 2017. Neural end-to-end learning for computational argumentation mining. In *Proceedings of the 55th Annual Meeting of the Association for Computational Linguistics (Volume 1: Long Papers)*, pages 11–22, Vancouver, Canada. Association for Computational Linguistics.

Matt Gardner, Yoav Artzi, Victoria Basmov, Jonathan Berant, Ben Bogin, Sihao Chen, Pradeep Dasigi, Dheeru Dua, Yanai Elazar, Ananth Gottumukkala, et al. 2020. Evaluating models' local decision boundaries via contrast sets. In *Findings of the Association for Computational Linguistics: EMNLP 2020*, pages 1307–1323.

Karan Goel, Nazneen Fatema Rajani, Jesse Vig, Zachary Taschdjian, Mohit Bansal, and Christopher Ré. 2021. Robustness gym: Unifying the NLP evaluation landscape. In *Proceedings of the 2021 Conference of the North American Chapter of the Association for Computational Linguistics: Human Language Technologies: Demonstrations*, pages 42–55, Online. Association for Computational Linguistics.

Ivan Habernal, Judith Eckle-Kohler, and Iryna Gurevych. 2014. Argumentation mining on the web from information seeking perspective. In *ArgNLP*.

Anne Lauscher, Henning Wachsmuth, Iryna Gurevych, and Goran Glavaš. 2021. Scientia potentia est–on the role of knowledge in computational argumentation. *arXiv preprint arXiv:2107.00281*.

Yinhan Liu, Myle Ott, Naman Goyal, Jingfei Du, Mandar Joshi, Danqi Chen, Omer Levy, Mike Lewis, Luke Zettlemoyer, and Veselin Stoyanov. 2019. Roberta: A robustly optimized bert pretraining approach. *arXiv e-prints*, pages arXiv–1907.

Tobias Mayer, Elena Cabrio, and Serena Villata. 2020a. Transformer-based argument mining for healthcare applications. In *ECAI 2020*, pages 2108–2115. IOS Press.

Tobias Mayer, Santiago Marro, Elena Cabrio, and Serena Villata. 2020b. Generating adversarial examples for topic-dependent argument classification 1. In *Computational Models of Argument*, pages 33–44. IOS Press.

Andrew Moore and Paul Rayson. 2018. Bringing replication and reproduction together with generalisability in NLP: Three reproduction studies for target dependent sentiment analysis. In *Proceedings of the 27th International Conference on Computational Linguistics*, pages 1132–1144, Santa Fe, New Mexico, USA. Association for Computational Linguistics.

Vlad Niculae, Joonsuk Park, and Claire Cardie. 2017. Argument mining with structured SVMs and RNNs. In *Proceedings of the 55th Annual Meeting of the Association for Computational Linguistics (Volume 1: Long Papers)*, pages 985–995, Vancouver, Canada. Association for Computational Linguistics.

Timothy Niven and Hung-Yu Kao. 2019. Probing neural network comprehension of natural language arguments. In *Proceedings of the 57th Annual Meeting of the Association for Computational Linguistics*, pages 4658–4664, Florence, Italy. Association for Computational Linguistics.

Prakash Poudyal, Jaromir Savelka, Aagje Ieven, Marie Francine Moens, Teresa Goncalves, and Paulo Quaresma. 2020. ECHR: Legal corpus for argument mining. In *Proceedings of the 7th Workshop on Argument Mining*, pages 67–75, Online. Association for Computational Linguistics.

Nils Reimers and Iryna Gurevych. 2019. Sentence-bert: Sentence embeddings using siamese bert-networks. In *Proceedings of the 2019 Conference on Empirical Methods in Natural Language Processing and the 9th International Joint Conference on Natural Language Processing (EMNLP-IJCNLP)*, pages 3982–3992.

Myrthe Reuver, Suzan Verberne, Roser Morante, and Antske Fokkens. 2021. Is stance detection topic-independent and cross-topic generalizable? - a reproduction study. In *Proceedings of the 8th Workshop on Argument Mining*, pages 46–56, Punta Cana, Dominican Republic. Association for Computational Linguistics.

Ramon Ruiz-Dolz, Jose Alemany, Stella M Heras Barberá, and Ana García-Fornes. 2021. Transformer-based models for automatic identification of argument relations: A cross-domain evaluation. *IEEE Intelligent Systems*, 36(6):62–70.

Benjamin Schiller, Johannes Daxenberger, and Iryna Gurevych. 2021. Stance detection benchmark: How robust is your stance detection? *KI-Künstliche Intelligenz*, 35(3):329–341.

Dietrich Trautmann, Johannes Daxenberger, Christian Stab, Hinrich Schütze, and Iryna Gurevych. 2020. Fine-grained argument unit recognition and classification. In *Proceedings of the AAAI Conference on Artificial Intelligence*, volume 34, pages 9048–9056.

Wei Emma Zhang, Quan Z Sheng, Ahoud Alhazmi, and Chenliang Li. 2020. Adversarial attacks on deep-learning models in natural language processing: A survey. *ACM Transactions on Intelligent Systems and Technology (TIST)*, 11(3):1–41.

A Appendix

Software and Hyperparameters Our code and data are available at `github.com/jbkamp/repo-Rob-Token-AUR`. The implementation for the token-based model was retrieved from `github.com/trtm/AURC`, and we adapted it to train a sentence-based model through the `transformers.BertForSequenceClassification` class, at `huggingface.co`. For both, we used the large cased pre-trained model with whole word masking at `huggingface.co`. We used the same settings across models: learning rate was kept at 1e-5, dropout rate at 0.1 and the maximum length of the tokenised BERT input was set at 64 tokens. Optimizer adopted: AdamW. The batch size was set at 32 and models were trained for a maximum of 100 epochs with early stopping if the performance did not improve significantly after the 10th epoch.

Dataset Versioning Trautmann et al. (2020) published their results based on the AURC-8 dataset, requested and obtained via e-mail correspondence. A second version at `github.com/trtm/AURC/tree/master/data` of the AURC-8 dataset was uploaded in a later moment with, *cleaner parsing and encoding* (`github.com/trtm/AURC#readme`, last consulted on June 16th 2022) but with the same number of labels and sentences. The two datasets differ to a low degree: 4.91% of the sentences are not equal ($n = 393$). Of this subset, all elements show a better cleaning of punctuation tokens compared to the original. To the best of our knowledge, this is the only difference between the original and the updated dataset. Therefore, we prefer using the updated, cleaner version of the dataset. We remove duplicate sentences within and across training set, development set and test set, per split (see resulting counts in Table 4).

Segment-F1 In order to compute the segment-F1 score, we average over all sentence-wise segment-F1 scores, for each sentence in the evaluation set. To obtain a sentence-wise segment-F1 score we consider all pairs $< y, \hat{y} >$, where y is the sequence of true labels for a segment and $\hat{y}$ is the sequence of predicted labels for that segment. Let r be the overlap ratio between y and $\hat{y}$:

$$r = \frac{|y \cap \hat{y}|}{|y|} \tag{1}$$

We only compute r for segments where the label of y is PRO or CON. If $r > .5$ and labels are the same, $\hat{y}$ is considered a true prediction; otherwise, a false prediction. The sentence-wise segment-F1 is the number of true predictions over all predictions for that sentence. If the sentence does not contain PRO nor CON segments, and no PRO nor CON is predicted, the segment-F1 score for the sentence is 1.0. See Table 5 for a full overview of the results, including token-F1, segment-F1 and sentence-F1.

		in-domain			cross-domain		
#	topic	train	dev	test	train	dev	test
1	abortion	700	99	200	800	0	0
2	cloning	696	100	200	800	0	0
3	marijuana legalization	699	100	200	800	0	0
4	minimum wage	699	100	200	800	0	0
5	nuclear energy	699	100	200	800	0	0
6	death penalty	700	100	200	0	800	0
7	gun control	0	0	0	0	0	1,000
8	school uniforms	0	0	0	0	0	1,000

Table 4: The eight topics from the AURC-8 dataset (Trautmann et al., 2020) along with the number of sentence instances per data split after duplicates removal.

	token-F1				**segment-F1**				**sentence-F1**			
	token -based setup		*sentence -based setup*		*token -based setup*		*sentence -based setup*		*token -based setup*		*sentence -based setup*	
model	**dev**	**test**	**dev**	**test**	**dev**	**test**	**dev**	**test**	**dev**	**test**	**dev**	**test**
in-domain BERTLARGE	.732	.683	.671	.627	.749	.709	.599	.567	.738	.709	.759	.715
in-domain BERTLARGE+CRF	.743	.696	.637	.622	.750	.724	.552	.547	.744	.711	.731	.725
in-domain BERTLARGE	.717 (.004)	.698 (.003)	.628 (.005)	**.614** (.008)	.776 (.011)	.749 (.005)	.514 (.009)	.500 (.004)	.715 (.008)	**.708** (.004)	.726 (.007)	**.713** (.012)
in-domain BERTLARGE+CRF	.716 (.003)	**.696** (.003)	-	-	.766 (.003)	.743 (.008)	-	-	.718 (.008)	**.711** (.006)	-	-
cross-domain BERTLARGE	.604	.596	.550	.544	.653	.626	.487	.473	.606	.598	.628	.602
cross-domain BERTLARGE+CRF	.615	.620	.505	.519	.681	.649	.456	.464	.627	.610	.569	.573
cross-domain BERTLARGE	.581 (.011)	**.587** (.008)	.515 (.012)	**.529** (.011)	.630 (.007)	.603 (.011)	.424 (.014)	.433 (.004)	**.591** (.016)	**.604** (.009)	.596 (.010)	.566 (.017)
cross-domain BERTLARGE+CRF	.584 (.009)	.578 (.008)	-	-	.627 (.012)	.593 (.004)	-	-	.601 (.011)	**.609** (.007)	-	-

Table 5: Full overview of the original results (white background) compared to reproduction results (non-white background). Models are divided over an in-domain setting and a cross-domain setting. Reproduction results show the mean scores from 5 runs, along with the standard deviation (within parentheses). The reproduction scores where the original score falls within two standard deviations from the mean are given in bold.

A Unified Representation and a Decoupled Deep Learning Architecture for Argumentation Mining of Students' Persuasive Essays

Muhammad Tawsif Sazid and **Robert E. Mercer**
Department of Computer Science
The University of Western Ontario
London, Ontario, Canada

Abstract

We develop a novel unified representation for the argumentation mining task facilitating the extracting from text and the labelling of the non-argumentative units and argumentation components—premises, claims, and major claims—and the argumentative relations—premise to claim or premise in a support or attack relation, and claim to major-claim in a for or against relation—in an end-to-end machine learning pipeline. This tightly integrated representation combines the component and relation identification sub-problems and enables a unitary solution for detecting argumentation structures. This new representation together with a new deep learning architecture composed of a mixed embedding method, a multi-head attention layer, two biLSTM layers, and a final linear layer obtain state-of-the-art accuracy on the Persuasive Essays dataset. Also, we have introduced a decoupled solution to identify the entities and relations first, and on top of that a second model is used to detect distance between the detected related components. An augmentation of the corpus (paragraph version) by including copies of major claims has further increased the performance.

1 Introduction

Arguments are composed of statements, called claims, that take a position on a controversial subject and other statements, referred to as premises, that support or rebut the claims. When arguments are presented in text form, these argument components are realized as contiguous text spans. The writing also contains non-argumentative text spans. The argument and non-argumentative text spans are collectively referred to as argumentative discourse units (ADUs). Argumentation mining is usually viewed as the identification of argumentative structures: separating the argumentative ADUs from the non-argumentative ADUs, classifying the argumentative ADUs as premises and claims, and finding the relationships among the argumentative ADUs. Since we are using the Persuasive Essay (PE) dataset (Stab and Gurevych, 2017) these subtasks can be made more precise: 1) segment the argument components from the non-argumentative text, 2) label each argument component as a Major-Claim, Claim, or Premise, 3) determine which premises are in a relationship with claims or premises using a text distance measure, and 4) classify the stance of the relations between argument components.

Since we are using the Persuasive Essay (PE) dataset (Stab and Gurevych, 2017) we will use the description of these tasks as given by Eger et al. (2017): 1) segmenting the ADUs: separate the argumentative text spans from the non-argumentative text, 2) labeling each argument component as a Major-Claim, Claim, or Premise, 3) determining which premises are in a relationship with claims or premises and representing this relation as the text distance (the number of sentences before or after) between a premise and its related argument component (in the PE corpus, which major-claim is related to a claim is not annotated using the text distance method), and 4) classifying the stance of the relations between argument components ('for' and 'against' for the relationship between claims and major-claims; 'support' and 'attack' between premises and claims or other premises).

Previous research has approached the development of a computational argumentation mining method from two distinct viewpoints. Input for the first approach is plain text and this approach solves all four of the subtasks mentioned above. Stab and Gurevych (2017) provide the PE dataset, which we use in the development of our method. Eger et al. (2017) produce the state-of-the-art method to which we compare our new method. Recently, Persing and Ng (2020), using the PE dataset, have developed an unsupervised machine learning method that provides all but the stance information for the

Proceedings of the 9th Workshop on Argument Mining, co-located with the 29th International Conference on Computational Linguistics, pages 74–83
October 17, 2022.

relations.

The second view of argumentation mining assumes the first subtask has been done (Peldszus, 2014; Peldszus and Stede, 2015; Stab and Gurevych, 2017; Niculae et al., 2017; Potash et al., 2017; Kuribayashi et al., 2019; Bao et al., 2021).

The method proposed here takes the first approach, solving all four subtasks. As there are subtasks, previous argumentation mining works have decoupled various subtasks, solved them separately, and then combined the solutions. The end-to-end learning method proposed here differentiates itself from these previous works by approaching the problem with a unified representation. Our research contributions are summarized as follows:

1. Each token in the natural language text is encoded as a binary vector that captures all aspects of the argumentation mining task: the ADU type, the position in the argument component text span, the stance of the argument component, and the distance to the related argument component. The deep learning model computes a vector for each token which, when properly interpreted, provides the information required to assemble the text spans and relations thereby identifying the argument structure for the argument mining task. By combining all aspects of the argumentation mining task in this representation, a model is learned that has improved performance.

2. By constructing a novel dense representation of the problem we are able to achieve a better than previous performance using a stacked embedding model comprising two biLSTM layers, a multi-head attention layer, 3 linear layers with ReLU activation and 1 final linear layer (Unified-AM)[1].

3. We introduce a joint model (Decoupled-AM) approach[2]. We train both Unified-AM and a second model composed of a normalization layer, two biLSTM layers, three linear layers with Dropout and ReLU activations, and one final linear layer. While Unified-AM is detecting components and relations, the second model detects distances between the related components using different layer outputs provided by Unified-AM. In this setting, we have trained both models together from scratch.

4. Our previous work (Sazid and Mercer, 2022) only worked with the paragraph version of the PE dataset. Here we also test our novel representation and model on the essay version.

5. We develop an augmentation technique (paragraph version) based on the n-gram tokens that indicate the starting of the major claim tokens[3]. This further improves the results.

With the new formulation of the problem, our original Unified-AM and the Decoupled-AM reach state-of-the-art argument mining performance on detecting and labelling argument components and relations for the PE corpus.

2 Related Work

Computational argumentation mining deals with finding argumentation structures in text. Palau and Moens (2009) established that argument mining would need to detect claims and premises and their relationships. Stab and Gurevych (2014, 2017) provided the PE dataset, a corpus annotated with a scheme that includes claims, premises, and also attack or support relations. Stab and Gurevych (2017) addressed the argumentation problem by training independent models for each of the subtasks and then combining them with an Integer Linear Programming Model for the end-to-end task. Eger et al. (2017) achieved state-of-the-art performance on the PE corpus by addressing the problem as a sequence tagging problem. They have the best accuracy of **61.67%** by using a modified version of the LSTM-ER model, introduced by Miwa and Bansal (2016), which uses a stacked architecture of Sequence and Tree LSTMs.

Persing and Ng (2016) presented the first findings on end-to-end argument mining in student essays using a pipeline approach by performing joint inference using an Integer Linear Programming (ILP) framework. Ferrara et al. (2017) introduced an unsupervised approach, topic modeling, to detect claims and premises. Persing and Ng (2020) have also developed an unsupervised machine learning method that provides all but the stance information for the relations.

[1]Unified-AM code is available at `https://github.com/tawsifsazid/Unified-Representation-for-Argumentation-Mining`.

[2]Decoupled-AM code is also available at `https://github.com/tawsifsazid/Unified-Representation-for-Argumentation-Mining`.

[3]The augmented dataset is available at `https://github.com/tawsifsazid/Unified-Representation-for-Argumentation-Mining`.

A number of works have investigated approaches for subtasks 2, 3, and 4. Early work is epitomized by Peldszus (2014) and Peldszus and Stede (2015) where they develop a novel methodology for predicting argument structure by dividing it into different sub-tasks (relation, central claim, role, and function classification). Potash et al. (2017) presented the first neural network-based approach to argumentation mining, focusing on extracting links between argument components and classifying types of argument components as a secondary goal. Niculae et al. (2017) jointly approach unit type detections and relation predictions on their new CDCP dataset and the PE dataset. Kuribayashi et al. (2019) focuses on Argumentation Structure Parsing (ASP). Their analysis of other works regarding the span representation led them to the development of a simple task-dependent addition for the ASP. Bao et al. (2021) avoid previous inefficient enumeration operations for detecting relational attributes. For that, they introduce a transition-based methodology that follows an incremental procedure for building graphs based on argumentation.

We note from Ahmed et al. (2018) how additional handcrafted features can boost the accuracy on certain sequence tagging tasks. Kuribayashi et al. (2019) and Persing and Ng (Persing and Ng, 2020) also noted the importance of discourse connectives in the argumentation mining task.

3 Research Methodology

Here we present the method that we have developed to generate the argumentation structure for the PE data set. First, the data set is described. Then, we introduce the multi-label representation that allows us to consider argumentation mining as a single unified problem. Lastly, instead of presenting the final model with an ablation study, we present our method in a bottom-up style, starting with a base architecture to which we add, providing in Table 2 the performance increase given by that addition since we want to discuss the motivation for these additions. We compare the final model's performance with that achieved by Eger et al. (2017).

3.1 Data Set Description

The PE dataset that we are using in this paper was created by Stab and Gurevych (2017) and was used in Eger et al. (2017). The essays are written on controversial topics so that the authors can make their opinions and take their stances. The corpus has been tagged with the BIO scheme, the type of components, stances, and distances from premise to claim or premise (Eger et al., 2017; Stab and Gurevych, 2017). There are essay and paragraph versions of the data set. We have worked with both versions of the corpus. The data set contains 1,587 paragraphs totaling 105,988 tokens in the train-set and 449 paragraphs, 29,537 tokens in the test-set[4]. The development set has 12,657 tokens available in 199 paragraphs. In the essay version of the corpus, there are 285 essays in the train-set. The development and the test set have 35 and 79 essays, respectively.

The argumentation structure can be viewed as a forest with each tree rooted by one of the author's major claims. The claims are connected to all of the major claims with either 'for' or 'against' relations. Premises are related to exactly one claim or premise. Premises either 'support' or 'attack' the claims or premises. One important piece of information is that the argumentation structure is completely contained in the paragraph except for some relations from claims to major claims which are not in the same paragraph. The corpus is imbalanced as Eger et al. (2017) have mentioned.

3.2 New Problem Formulation

To integrate all of the sub-problems (argumentative and non-argumentative unit classification; major-claim, claim, and premise component classification; relation identification, and distance between 2 entities) into a single problem, we construct a binary vector of size 33 for our target labels (first described in Sazid and Mercer (2022)). We are addressing the argumentation mining problem as a sequence tagging problem and classifying each word or token as beginning argumentative / continuation argumentative / non-argumentative, premise / claim / major-claim, support / attack, for / against, relative distance between the current component and the component it relates to. The maximum and minimum distances from premise to claim suggested in Eger et al. (2017) are +11 and -11, respectively. Thus, we have constructed a dense unified representation of the argumentation mining problem. Table 1 provides the novel representation.

By formulating the argumentation mining task as a multi-label problem, we have enabled the options to solve the argumentation problem in a unified or in a decoupled way. We have tried both strategies

[4]Differs slightly from that reported in Eger et al. (2017).

Token	O	B	I	MC	C	P	Sup	For	At	Ag	Distance Value -11	...	Distance Value 3	...	Distance Value +11
For	1	0	0	0	0	0	0	0	0	0	0	0	0	0	0
instance	1	0	0	0	0	0	0	0	0	0	0	0	0	0	0
,	1	0	0	0	0	0	0	0	0	0	0	0	0	0	0
children	0	1	0	0	0	1	1	0	0	0	0	0	1	0	0
immigrated	0	0	1	0	0	1	1	0	0	0	0	0	1	0	0
to	0	0	1	0	0	1	1	0	0	0	0	0	1	0	0
a	0	0	1	0	0	1	1	0	0	0	0	0	1	0	0
new	0	0	1	0	0	1	1	0	0	0	0	0	1	0	0
country	0	0	1	0	0	1	1	0	0	0	0	0	1	0	0

Table 1: Example of the Novel Compact Representation of the Argumentation Problem. O: Non-Argumentative Token, B: Beginning of Argument Component, I: Continuation of Argument Component, MC: Major Claim Component, Cl: Claim Component, P: Premise Component, Sup: Support Relation Identifier, For: For Relation Identifier, At: Attack Relation Identifier, Ag: Against Relation Identifier, Distance Values: -11 to +11. The sentence being encoded "For instance, children immigrated to a new country ..." has three introductory non-argumentative tokens, the premise starting with "children" supports an argument component three sentences later in the paragraph.

and compare our results related to the experiments.

3.3 Interpretation Function for the Multi-label Outputs of the Model

We have formulated the argumentation problem in a unified way. As a result, it has become a multi-class, multi-label problem. As it becomes a multi-label problem when we create a unified representation, we just want to choose the index for each of the categories that has the highest logit value in that specific category (components, stances, and distance). For this, we have created an interpretation function.

For each token, this function first decides whether the token is to be considered non-argumentative or part of an argument component. If it is to be considered argumentative, the beginning and continuation designations are determined. Then, depending on the argument component type, the stance is determined, and if it is a premise, the distance is as well.

3.4 Description of the Deep Learning Model and the Hyper-Parameters

Figure 1 represents our final argumentation model architecture (Unified-AM) which we have created for detecting argumentation structures and solve all the subtasks jointly.

We have also developed a decoupled model (Decoupled-AM) (research contribution 3) where we first predict the components and relations. Then we detect the distance between the predicted components based on it. For this methodology, we have used two models. The first model is identical to the Unified-AM and we introduce a second model which predicts the distances. In this particular experiment, we have trained both models from scratch. In this experiment, Unified-AM is used to predict the first 10 labels and the loss is calculated for those 10 labels only. The second model predicts the last 23 labels (distances) and the loss is calculated for only these last 23 labels. After that, the two loss values are summed and then this summed loss value is used to calculate the gradients to initialize the back propagation for both models simultaneously. The components and stances (first 10 labels) predicted by Unified-AM and the distances (last 23 labels) predicted by the second model are concatenated to finally produce the 33-labelled output.

Our deep learning model architecture includes: stacked embedding, axial positional embedding, a multi-head attention layer, a 2-layered biLSTM, 3 linear layers with dropouts and ReLU activations and the final linear layer. The output of the model is optimized with BCEWithLogitsLoss.

For its capability of retaining long-distance information from sequential texts, we use biLSTM for the paragraph level for the argumentation mining task. Before adding the axial positional embedding and the multi-head attention layer, our preliminary experimentation determined the number of biLSTM layers by using a trial and error methodology, i.e., we have tried two layers of biLSTM with one linear layer, one biLSTM layer with one linear layer, and so on. We have found two biLSTM

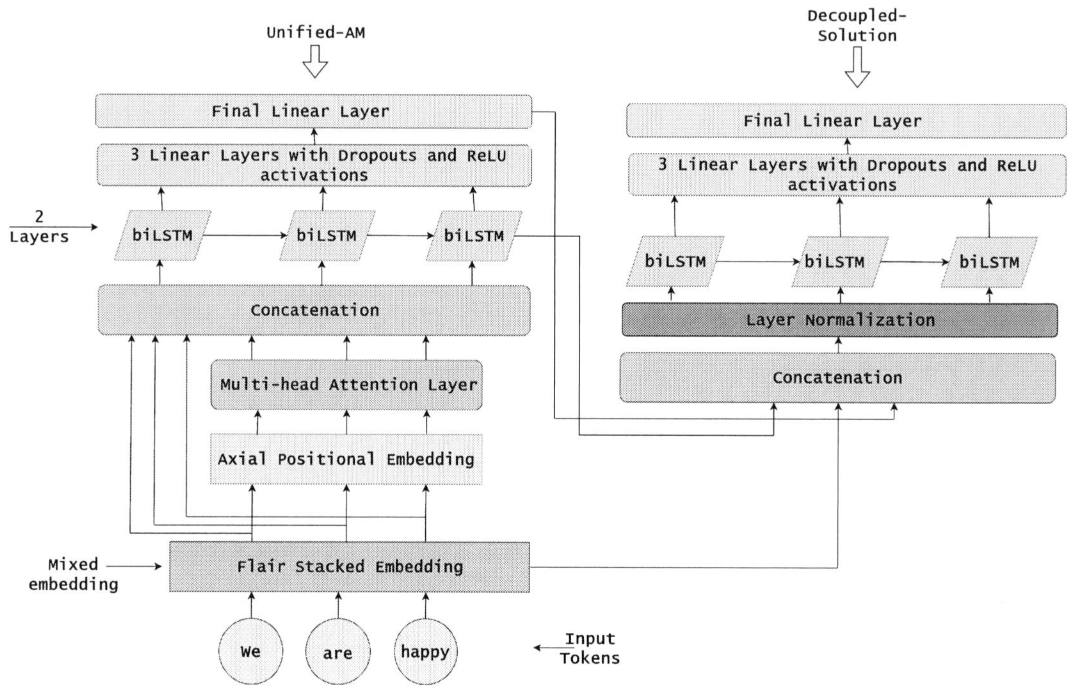

Figure 1: The Final Argumentation Mining Model Architecture with Decoupled Distance Prediction

layers, 3 linear layers with non-linear activation functions, and one final linear layer achieve the best accuracy.

Figure 1 includes a mixed embedding but in the model design we first experimented with a plain embedding layer instead. Lample et al. (2016), have shown that a combination of different embeddings may work better than using only one embedding class. For the pre-trained mixed embedding, we use the memory-efficient stacked embedding class that Akbik et al. (2019) introduced in their Flair framework for combining the FastText and Byte-pair embeddings. As our corpus contains unknown words in the test set and the whole corpus contains many suffix and prefix dependent words, we used these two types of embedding together.

The final design decision was to include the multi-head attention (Vaswani et al., 2017) and the axial positional embedding for the positional information (Ho et al., 2019; Kitaev et al., 2020). For our 400-dimension embedding class we use four heads for the multi-head attention layer for both of the experiments. This completes the description of the architecture.

To show the effects of each of these design decisions, we compare the number of wrong-predictions between our non-pre-trained embedding model, the pre-trained stacked embedding model, both without multi-head attention, and the final Unified-AM model. Table 2 shows the error analysis of these three stages of architecture design for the non-argumentative units, argumentative components, and relations. For each of the mentioned argumentative units we present the total number of errors (false negatives + false positives). For relations (support, attack, for, and against), we have combined the errors from each class and report this combined value. There are somewhat fewer wrong predictions when the stacked embedding is incorporated into the model. Without stacked embedding, the total number of wrong predictions for all of the classes on the paragraph level is **23,363**. With the addition of stacked embedding the total number of wrong predictions becomes **17,286**. After using this pre-trained embedding, the error rate is reduced by **26.01%**. The total number of errors for the Unified-AM model is **16,649**. This model further reduces the error rate by **3.69%**.

After trying several hyperparameter values for each of the different components we have chosen the final values. We use dropout values of 0.5 for the linear layers, and 0.65 for the biLSTM layer of our architecture. We use the default dropout value (0.0) for the multi-head attention layer. We use

Table 2: Error Analysis and Comparison of the Three Models (False Positives + False Negatives)

	Number of Wrong Predictions				
	Major Claim	**Claim**	**Premise**	**Relations**	**Non Argumentative**
Trained Embedding	1306	4011	4787	10004	3255
Stacked Embedding	1176	3215	3122	7653	2120
Unified-AM	1111	3082	2953	7301	2202

the ReLU activation function in-between the linear layers. A learning rate of 0.001 has been used in all of the experimental design stages. The Adam optimizer is used throughout. During training, we have used random shuffling for all of the final experiments. We have trained our model around 1000-1100 epochs for all of the experiments except the data augmentation experiment (see Tables 4, 6). For determining the default training epochs (1000-1100) we have closely observed the development set accuracy value after every 5 epochs. If after some epochs the development set accuracy stops increasing or starts fluctuating somewhat between a small range of accuracy values, we have stopped the training procedure. We also observe the training loss and find that when it reaches around 0.0005 loss value, the model has the highest development set accuracy. If we further train and decrease the loss value, it does not help to improve the accuracy value of the development set. As we have also increased the original PE corpus (paragraph version) by augmenting the data in our augmentation experiments (see Section 4.2), we also increase the training epochs to reach around the 0.0005 training loss which has given us improvements regarding the C-F1, R-F1 and F1 scores.

4 Experiments and Results

4.1 Experiments on the original version of the PE corpus

We have experimented with the new unified-representation of all of the sub-tasks of argumentation mining and trained our final model architectures. In one of our experiments, we have only trained the original Unified-AM (Sazid and Mercer, 2022) to jointly solve all of the sub-tasks (all 33 labels) of argumentation mining. In Table 3, we present individual precision, recall and F1 score for the four ADUs and the four relations that are available in the PE corpus (both paragraph and essay versions) for the original Unified-AM model. We observe low precision and recall scores for the claim tokens even though the class is not the least frequent one in the PE corpus. This is similar to the observed low agreement score among the human annotators for the claim tokens (Stab and Gurevych, 2017). Unified-AM also finds it difficult to predict the claim tokens in the corpus.

And in the other experimental setup, we have used a second model to detect the distance values (the last 23 labels) separately by using information about the components and relations (the first 10 labels) from the Unified-AM.

With the original Unified-AM, we achieve a token level accuracy of 66.79% in our argumentation mining task. On the other hand, the Decoupled-AM achieves the highest token level accuracy of **67.50%**. Also, we have improved C-F1, R-F1 scores regarding the task with Decoupled-AM.

Table 4 summarizes the result for these experiments, including the F1 measure for the component and relation tasks, and a global F1 score. The results from Eger et al. (2017) have been included for comparison. Now, compared to the Eger et al. (2017) decoupled method for computing the relation identification, this task in our original Unified-AM and Decoupled-AM is coupled with the component identification task due to the unified representation of the problem, which has led to the better performance. We have used the distance values from -11 to +11 that were observed by Eger et al. (2017) in the PE data set.

We have also experimented on the essay-level of the argumentation corpus and our original Unified-AM model has achieved the highest token level accuracy, C-F1, and R-F1 scores. The experiments on the essay version of the corpus show the robustness of the unified representation of all the subtasks with our model. When we experiment on the essay version of the corpus, our scores and results have not decreased like the LSTM-ER model and its decoupled solution. Our Decoupled-AM has not performed well on the essay version of the corpus compared to the original Unified-AM. Table 5 summarizes the results for the experiments related to the essay version of the argumentation corpus.

Table 3: Precision, Recall and F1-score for the Argumentation Mining Classes for Unified-AM

Class	Paragraph Level			Essay Level			Token Percentage
	Precision	Recall	F1 Score	Precision	Recall	F1 Score	
Non-Argumentative	88.38	88.27	88.33	89.26	91.27	90.25	32.20
Major-Claim	73.87	74.18	74.02	70.34	72.05	71.19	7.41
Claim	65.37	58.05	61.48	56.11	49.34	52.51	15.41
Premise	88.01	90.87	89.42	87.18	88.32	87.74	44.99
Support	86.79	89.69	88.22	85.09	88.35	86.69	42.61
For	60.96	57.05	58.94	56.41	50.76	53.43	12.77
Attack	32.52	26.77	29.37	27.08	7.10	11.25	2.38
Against	60.81	29.97	40.15	21.01	10.23	13.76	2.64

Table 4: Comparison of LSTM-ER (Eger et al., 2017), Unified-AM, and Decoupled-AM on the Paragraph Level

Model	Corpus	Token Accuracy	C-F1 (100%)	C-F1 (50%)	R-F1 (100%)	R-F1 (50%)	F1 (100%)	F1 (50%)
LSTM-ER	Original	61.67%	70.83	77.19	45.52	50.05	55.42	60.72
Unified-AM	Original	66.79%	68.88	78.22	51.14	56.41	60.00	67.32
Decoupled-AM	Original	**67.50%**	**71.24**	**79.98**	**52.71**	**57.92**	**61.97**	**68.95**
Unified-AM	Augmented	**68.03%**	**71.35**	**80.21**	**54.27**	**59.46**	**62.81**	**69.83**
Decoupled-AM	Augmented	65.53%	68.59	77.94	50.22	56.24	59.41	67.10

4.2 Data Augmentation Experiment on the Paragraph Version of the PE Corpus

We now turn to the final argumentation model performance improvement. Adding linguistic information to a model has been successful for low level NLP tasks (Ahmed et al., 2018). We have observed (as did Kuribayashi et al. (2019), and Persing and Ng (2020)) that many major claims are prefaced by a reasonably small set of n-grams. An n-gram is a continuous sequence of *n* words. Some examples of the n-grams that are found in the PE corpus are: 'I firmly believe that', 'In conclusion ,', 'Hence ,', and 'Firstly ,'. We consider augmenting the paragraph version of the corpus by using these n-grams to increase the frequency of the Major Claim component type which is the least frequent component available in the PE corpus.

In this experimental setup, we have augmented the paragraph level PE dataset. Below, we describe the augmentation technique that we have used to augment the PE corpus. We also compare the performance between Unified-AM, Decoupled-AM on both the augmented and original corpora.

We have augmented the paragraph-level corpus with new paragraphs. These new paragraphs are copies of those paragraphs that contain one of the 108 n-gram tokens that occur immediately before the major claim tokens but have had the n-gram randomly swapped with a same size n-gram token. This augmentation increases the number of major claim tokens in the whole corpus but with different introductory n-grams. We have hypothesized that if we increase the root element, i.e., the major claim components of the corpus, by swapping frequently occurring n-gram tokens that appear immediately before the component, it would help the model to accurately detect this type of component and differentiate between the three types of components that are available in the PE corpus. We have shown below an example of the original paragraph and the augmented paragraph after applying the described augmentation method:

Original Paragraph: "It is always said that competition can effectively promote the development of economy . In order to survive in the competition , companies continue to improve their products and service , and as a result , the whole society prospers . However , when we discuss the issue of competition or cooperation , what we are concerned about is not the whole society , but the development of an individual's whole life . *I **firmly** believe that* we should attach more importance to cooperation during primary education."

Augmented Paragraph: "It is always said that competition can effectively promote the development of economy . In order to survive in the compe-

Table 5: Comparison of LSTM-ER (Eger et al., 2017), Unified-AM, and Decoupled-AM on the Essay Level

Model	Corpus	Token Accuracy	C-F1 (100%)	C-F1 (50%)	R-F1 (100%)	R-F1 (50%)	F1 (100%)	F1 (50%)
LSTM-ER	Original	54.17%	66.21	73.02	29.56	32.72	40.87	45.19
Unified-AM	Original	**62.88%**	**67.78**	**76.20**	**48.24**	**52.49**	**58.01**	**64.35**
Decoupled-AM	Original	57.89%	64.67	75.51	40.01	46.10	52.34	60.75

Table 6: Token level Comparison between the Original and the Augmented Datasets

Model	**Corpus (Paragraph Version)**	**Correct Major-Claim Tokens**	**Correct Claim Tokens (with Stance)**	**Correct Premise Tokens (with Stance)**	**Correct Non-Argumentative Tokens**
Unified-AM	Original	1542	2057	7329	8217
Unified-AM	Augmented	1597	2344	**7956**	**8196**
Decoupled-AM	Original	**1595**	**2397**	**7720**	**8226**
Decoupled-AM	Augmented	1594	2355	7334	8074

tition , companies continue to improve their products and service , and as a result , the whole society prospers . However , when we discuss the issue of competition or cooperation , what we are concerned about is not the whole society , but the development of an individual's whole life . *I **truly** believe that* we should attach more importance to cooperation during primary education."

Description of the Augmentation Process: In this particular example we have substituted the 4-gram *"I firmly believe that"* with an equal size randomly chosen 4-gram *"I truly believe that"* from our collected n-gram list. The words following in that particular sentence are major claim tokens.

By using data augmentation, we have increased the number of Major Claim tokens by approximately 4000. Also, because claims, premises, and non-argumentative components occur in these paragraphs, the number of Claim, Premise, and Non-argumentative tokens have increased by around 2000, 1000, and 8000, respectively.

After creating the augmented corpus, we have trained our Unified-AM model first (see Figure 1) on the corpus. We have achieved the highest token level accuracy on the paragraph-level argumentation corpus. Previously, without augmentation, we have achieved 67.50% token level accuracy on the PE dataset (see Table 4) and after applying the augmentation methodology we have achieved the highest token level accuracy of **68.02%**. Also, all other performance measures have been improved. Table 4 shows the results related to the augmented datasets. Comparing Unified-AM's performance between the augmented corpus and the original corpus (see Table 4), the model has much higher token level accuracy, C-F1, R-F1, and F1 scores when we apply augmentation techniques on the training corpus. We have reached the highest component C-F1(100%) score of **71.35%** where Eger et al. (2017) has obtained 70.83%. After training Unified-AM, we move on to the next experimental setup and train our Decoupled-AM on the augmented corpus. Decoupled-AM has not performed well on the augmented corpus compared to Unified-AM. The reason is: Decoupled-AM needs more training time compared to the Unified-AM when we are experimenting for the augmented corpus. Training both the models together from scratch on a larger corpus needs sufficient amount of time and resources.

We present in Table 6, the token level improvements and compare them with the original PE corpus results. In the test set, we have 2,134 major claim tokens, 4,238 claim tokens, 13,728 premise tokens, and 9,437 non-argumentative tokens. Our goal is to increase the major claim tokens which can be considered as the root of the argumentation structure. The results provided in Table 6 show the overall token level improvements that we get compared to the original paragraph version of the PE corpus for both Unified-AM and Decoupled-AM.

5 Error Analysis

We have done some error analysis and comparison between various neural architectures to see how dif-

Table 7: F1 scores on the BIO labeling task

	STag_BLCC	LSTM-ER	ILP	HUB	Unified AM	Unified-AM Augmented Paragraph	Decoupled-AM	Decoupled-AM Augmented Paragraph
Essay	90.04	**90.57**	-	-	90.52	-	89.99	-
Paragraph	88.32	**90.84**	86.67	88.60	89.69	89.88	90.30	89.11

ferently all of the models perform on the argumentation task. Also, we have measured the distance prediction accuracy of the Unified-AM model and compare it with that of Eger et al. (2017).

We observe a higher accuracy of predicting longer distance in the paragraphs. One of the key strategies that we have followed for all of these experimental setups: We ensure the models share all of their learned parameters while solving any particular subtask (component detection and labelling, relation classification, or accurate distance prediction) of the main Argumentation Mining problem. This denser representation of the whole argumentation task enables our neural models to share all of the parameters while making predictions for each of the subtasks which has led to a high performance. Eger et al. (2017) showed that LSTM-ER model's probability of correctness given true distance is below 40% and it becomes below 20% when the distances are larger than 3. But in our case, our analysis shows above 50% accuracy for distances 1, 2, and 3 (for Unified-AM). Our final model (see Figure 1) has higher accuracy regarding smaller distances but its prediction accuracy declines as we observe larger distance values in the PE corpus.

For major-claim, premise, and claim, there are two different tags in the PE corpus, B: Beginning of a component and I: Continuation of a component. Non-Argumentative tokens are tagged as 'O' in the BIO scheme. We compare the component segmentation task (subtask 1) results with other works that have been mentioned in Eger et al. (2017). Table 7 shows the results for the models. We see that LSTM-ER has the highest macro-F1 score when we consider only the BIO labeling task.

6 Conclusions and Future Work

In this work, we show that rather than using a complex stacked architecture for a problem which has different subtasks (where all the subtasks are related to each other), we can have a compact and unified representation of all the sub-problems and can tackle it as a single problem with less complicated architectures. We obtain an improved performance over Eger et al. (2017) in recognizing the argument components and relations. We further improve this result by introducing the Flair stacked embedding (Akbik et al., 2019) to represent the text input. We introduce a multi-head attention layer to the neural architecture which leads us to the highest accuracy on the PE corpus. Observing that the imbalanced corpus may be creating problems for this model to learn certain underrepresented features of the corpus, we have used the standard technique of data augmentation to achieve further gains in performance. We have created one augmented version of the PE training corpus by using different combinations of the n-grams that occur immediately before approximately two-thirds of the major claim components (see Section 4.2) in the paragraph version of the corpus. By using the augmentation methodology, we further improve the Unified-AM model's performance on the test set. We have obtained the highest token level accuracy, C-F1, R-F1, and the global F1 score (which is the combination of both C-F1 and R-F1 scores) on the paragraph version of the PE corpus by applying the augmentation technique. We have obtained better results on the original essay version of the corpus. Shared parameter values across different subtasks enhanced the accuracy score and also the model's capability for accurate detection of components, relations and distance. Our work has shown a robust method which jointly solves the component and relation identification tasks on the essay and paragraph levels of the Persuasive Essays corpus.

Future work includes a modified, yet unified, representation for other corpora and using contextual embeddings to enhance the representations of the argumentative texts.

Acknowledgements

This research is partially funded by The Natural Sciences and Engineering Research Council of Canada (NSERC) through a Discovery Grant to Robert E. Mercer. We also acknowledge the helpful comments provided by the reviewers.

References

Mahtab Ahmed, Muhammad Rifayat Samee, and Robert E. Mercer. 2018. Improving neural sequence labelling using additional linguistic information. In *2018 17th IEEE Int. Conf. on Machine Learning and Applications*, pages 650–657.

Alan Akbik, Tanja Bergmann, Duncan Blythe, Kashif Rasul, Stefan Schweter, and Roland Vollgraf. 2019. Flair: An easy-to-use framework for state-of-the-art nlp. In *Proceedings of the 2019 Conference of the North American Chapter of the Association for Computational Linguistics (Demonstrations)*, pages 54–59.

Jianzhu Bao, Chuang Fan, Jipeng Wu, Yixue Dang, Jiachen Du, and Ruifeng Xu. 2021. A neural transition-based model for argumentation mining. In *Proc. of the 59th Annual Meeting of the Association for Computational Linguistics and the 11th International Joint Conf. on Natural Language Processing (Volume 1: Long Papers)*, pages 6354–6364.

Steffen Eger, Johannes Daxenberger, and Iryna Gurevych. 2017. Neural end-to-end learning for computational argumentation mining. In *Proc. of 55th Ann. Meet. of Assoc. for Comp. Ling. (Vol. 1: Long Papers)*, pages 11–22.

Alfio Ferrara, Stefano Montanelli, and Georgios Petasis. 2017. Unsupervised detection of argumentative units though topic modeling techniques. In *Proceedings of the 4th Workshop on Argument Mining*, pages 97–107.

Jonathan Ho, Nal Kalchbrenner, Dirk Weissenborn, and Tim Salimans. 2019. Axial attention in multidimensional transformers. *arXiv preprint arXiv:1912.12180*.

Nikita Kitaev, Lukasz Kaiser, and Anselm Levskaya. 2020. Reformer: The efficient transformer. In *International Conference on Learning Representations*, page 12pp.

Tatsuki Kuribayashi, Hiroki Ouchi, Naoya Inoue, Paul Reisert, Toshinori Miyoshi, Jun Suzuki, and Kentaro Inui. 2019. An empirical study of span representations in argumentation structure parsing. In *Proceedings of the 57th Annual Meeting of the Association for Computational Linguistics*, pages 4691–4698.

Guillaume Lample, Miguel Ballesteros, Sandeep Subramanian, Kazuya Kawakami, and Chris Dyer. 2016. Neural architectures for named entity recognition. In *Proceedings of the 2016 Conference of the North American Chapter of the Association for Computational Linguistics: Human Language Technologies*, pages 260–270.

Makoto Miwa and Mohit Bansal. 2016. End-to-end relation extraction using LSTMs on sequences and tree structures. In *Proc. of the 54th Ann. Meet. of the Assoc. for Comp. Ling. (Vol. 1: Long Papers)*, pages 1105–1116.

Vlad Niculae, Joonsuk Park, and Claire Cardie. 2017. Argument mining with structured SVMs and RNNs. In *Proc. of the 55th Annual Meeting of the Assoc. for Computational Linguistics (Volume 1: Long Papers)*, pages 985–995.

Raquel Mochales Palau and Marie-Francine Moens. 2009. Argumentation mining: the detection, classification and structure of arguments in text. In *Proc. of the 12th International Conference on Artificial Intelligence and Law*, pages 98–107.

Andreas Peldszus. 2014. Towards segment-based recognition of argumentation structure in short texts. In *Proceedings of the First Workshop on Argumentation Mining*, pages 88–97.

Andreas Peldszus and Manfred Stede. 2015. Joint prediction in MST-style discourse parsing for argumentation mining. In *Proc. of the 2015 Conference on Empirical Methods in Natural Language Processing*, pages 938–948.

Isaac Persing and Vincent Ng. 2016. End-to-end argumentation mining in student essays. In *Proc. of the 2016 Conf. of the N. American Chap. of the Assoc. for Comp. Ling. Human Language Technologies*, pages 1384–1394.

Isaac Persing and Vincent Ng. 2020. Unsupervised argumentation mining in student essays. In *Proceedings of the 12th Language Resources and Evaluation Conference*, pages 6795–6803.

Peter Potash, Alexey Romanov, and Anna Rumshisky. 2017. Here's my point: Joint pointer architecture for argument mining. In *Proc. of the 2017 Conf. on Empirical Methods in Natural Language Processing*, pages 1364–1373.

Muhammad Tawsif Sazid and Robert E. Mercer. 2022. A unified representation and deep learning architecture for argumentation mining of students' persuasive essays. In *to appear*, CEUR Workshop Proceedings.

Christian Stab and Iryna Gurevych. 2014. Annotating argument components and relations in persuasive essays. In *Proc. of the 25th International Conference on Computational Linguistics: Technical Papers*, pages 1501–1510.

Christian Stab and Iryna Gurevych. 2017. Parsing argumentation structures in persuasive essays. *Computational Linguistics*, 43(3):619–659.

Ashish Vaswani, Noam Shazeer, Niki Parmar, Jakob Uszkoreit, Llion Jones, Aidan N Gomez, Łukasz Kaiser, and Illia Polosukhin. 2017. Attention is all you need. In *Advances in neural information processing systems*, pages 5998–6008.

Overview of the 2022 Validity and Novelty Prediction Shared Task

Philipp Heinisch
Bielefeld University
pheinisch@techfak.uni-bielefeld.de

Anette Frank
Heidelberg University
frank@cl.uni-heidelberg.de

Juri Opitz
Heidelberg University
opitz@cl.uni-heidelberg.de

Moritz Plenz
Heidelberg University
plenz@cl.uni-heidelberg.de

Philipp Cimiano
Bielefeld University
cimiano@techfak.uni-bielefeld.de

Abstract

This paper provides an overview of the Argument Validity and Novelty Prediction Shared Task that was organized as part of the 9th Workshop on Argument Mining (ArgMining 2022). The task focused on the prediction of the validity and novelty of a conclusion given a textual premise. Validity is defined as the degree to which the conclusion is justified with respect to the given premise. Novelty defines the degree to which the conclusion contains content that is new in relation to the premise. Six groups participated in the task, submitting overall 13 system runs for the subtask of binary classification and 2 system runs for the subtask of relative classification. The results reveal that the task is challenging, with best results obtained for Validity prediction in the range of 75% F_1 score, for Novelty prediction of 70% F_1 score and for correctly predicting both Validity and Novelty of 45% F_1 score. In this paper we summarize the task definition and dataset. We give an overview of the results obtained by the participating systems, as well as insights to be gained from the diverse contributions[1].

1 Introduction

An important challenge within the field of argument mining is the assessment of the quality of an argument. In recent years, several systems have emerged that make mined arguments accessible to an end user, either via search engines (Wachsmuth et al., 2017b), debate summarization systems (Bar-Haim et al., 2020), dialogue systems (Rach et al., 2021), or by other means. In order to establish confidence and trust on the side of the user, the ability to distinguish high-quality arguments from low-quality ones is important.

Wachsmuth et al. (2017a) investigated the notion of quality for argumentation and proposed 3 dimensions along which the quality of arguments can be rated: cogency, reasonableness, and effectiveness, introducing corresponding subcategories for each dimension. However, there have not been many attempts to operationalize the notion of quality so far, e.g., by an exact definition of a metric that assesses the quality or by means of an automatic procedure to determine the quality. Exceptions are datasets manually labeled with coarse scores denoting overall quality, which have been used for supervised learning (Toledo et al., 2019; Gretz et al., 2020b) or attempts to determine single subdimensions, such as sufficiency (a subdimension of cogency) (Stab and Gurevych, 2017b; Gurcke et al., 2021).

Motivated by this gap, the authors of this paper decided to propose a new shared task and submitted it to the 9th Argmining Workshop. Instead of tackling the entire wide field of argument quality or isolating a single quality aspect, we focus on the conclusion in the context of its argument, and assess its quality in the Validity and Novelty Prediction Shared Task. This task consists of the prediction of these two important conclusion quality dimensions.

Following Opitz et al. (2021), we define Validity as the degree to which the conclusion is justified with respect to the given premise, and Novelty as the degree to which the conclusion contains premise-related content that is not explicitly stated in the premise.

The two notions stand in a trade-off to each other as it is straightforward to maximize one of them at the expense of the other. Copying or paraphrasing parts of the premise as a conclusion will yield high validity but no novelty. Expanding a concept of the premise with commonsense knowledge as a conclusion can potentially yield high novelty but may not satisfy validity. Previous research in Opitz et al. (2021) and Heinisch et al. (2022) has indeed shown that it is difficult to generate conclusions that satisfy both criteria, which require proper inference based on and expanding the premise.

[1]The shared task website including the data and result table is located at https://phhei.github.io/ArgsValidNovel/

Proceedings of the 9th Workshop on Argument Mining, co-located with the 29th International Conference on Computational Linguistics, pages 84–94
October 17, 2022.

We divide the task of predicting validity and novelty into two subtasks. The first subtask consists in the binary prediction of whether a conclusion is valid resp. novel or not. The second subtask is framed as a comparative task, tasking systems to predict which of two given conclusions is more valid resp. more novel compared to the other, or whether they form a tie. The best achieved F_1 score for binary prediction of both validity and novelty is 45.16, by van der Meer et al. (2022), and the best achieved F_1 score averaging the scores for relative validity and novelty is 41.5, by the team NLP@UIT[2] – while the best scores for predicting Validity and Novelty as single prediction targets yield substantially higher results, with up to 74.6 points F_1 score for Validity, and 70 points F_1 score for Novelty. This large contrast shows that the joint objective is challenging. Judging from the properties of the high-scoring systems for the individual quality aspects, we conclude that this challenging task requires strong text understanding capabilities, as well as (symbolic) background knowledge, which our received submissions are addressing, by taking a first step towards tackling this fundamental task for many downstream applications in Computational Argumentation.

In the following, we describe the task as organized in the context of the 9th Argument Mining Workshop. We describe the datasets used, as well as the different systems that have participated in the task. We provide an overview of the results the systems have obtained and make explicit the lessons we can learn from the shared task results, so that these observations can guide the community in their future choice of methods to address this and related tasks.

2 Related work

Argument quality Within the growing field of Computational Argumentation, an important concern is to assess the quality of arguments. In their seminal work, Wachsmuth et al. (2017a) established important dimensions for rating the quality of arguments. They proposed three quality dimensions: *cogency* (related to logics), *effectiveness* (relating to rhetoric) and *reasonableness* (relating to dialetics) – which they sub-divided into 11 fine-grained quality aspects. In a recent survey, Vecchi et al. (2021) extend the notion of argument quality to account for their function in deliberative processes, in the sense that good arguments should "ensure the discourse to unfold productively", e.g., by bringing *new aspects* into the discussion.

Several works have proposed computational models to rate the quality of arguments. While Toledo et al. (2019) and Gretz et al. (2020b) target rather coarse overall quality scores based on single quality labels, other systems were designed to assess specific quality aspects, such as *convincingness* (Habernal and Gurevych, 2016), *relevance* (Wachsmuth et al., 2017c) or *cogency*, the logical coherence of an argument (Lauscher et al., 2020).

While these works assess the quality of an argument as a whole, Stab and Gurevych (2017b) focused on the quality of the premises of an argument, in terms of their *sufficiency*, asking whether an argument's premises provide enough evidence for accepting or rejecting its claim or conclusion. They provide annotations of argument sufficiency on the argument essays (Stab and Gurevych, 2017a) and develop a classifier that achieves 84% accuracy for detecting (in)sufficiently supported arguments as a whole, including their (in)sufficient premises. Gurcke et al. (2021) revisited this quality criterion (sufficiency) in a new task formulation: *conclusion generation* from (in)sufficient premises, where the aim is to determine the sufficiency of a premise by examining the quality of the generated conclusion including the premise.

Argument conclusion generation Follow-up research investigated argument conclusion generation from different angles, focusing on the generation of **conclusions with specific properties**, such as *plausibility* (next to stance) (Gretz et al., 2020a), *informativeness* (beyond validity) (Syed et al., 2021), or realizing a specific *frame* (Heinisch et al., 2022).

Measuring *novelty and validity* of conclusions Opitz et al. (2021) found that assessing the novelty and validity of conclusions in the context of a premise poses a challenging problem for automatic metrics. Their work aimed at assessing the similarity of arguments by taking their conclusions into account – which they generated with a fine-tuned T5 pre-trained language model. However, while the automatically generated conclusions were able to increase the similarity rating performance, the gain was rather small. In a manual evaluation study they found a key problem in the *quality* of the generated conclusions: they were often either *novel*, or *valid*, but rarely both, thus either adding little in-

[2]No description paper was submitted for this system.

formation (no novelty), or introducing misleading information (no validity). The fact that novelty and validity are complementary, and, to some degree, dueling aspects is further corroborated by Heinisch et al. (2022) who show that it is challenging to automatically generate conclusions that are *both* valid and novel.

We therefore believe that the development of methods that can assess these key quality aspects of conclusions poses a challenging and interesting task for the community. In particular, the results of the task may not only provide strong baselines and future improvement perspectives of such metrics, but also provide useful guidance about the improvement of conclusion generation methods.

3 Task Details

3.1 Task Description

Given a textual premise and conclusion candidate, the VALNOV task consists in predicting two aspects of a conclusion: its *validity* and *novelty*.

Validity is defined as the degree to which the conclusion is *justified* with respect to the given premise. A conclusion is considered to be valid if it is supported by inferences that link the premise to the conclusion, based on logical principles or commonsense or world knowledge, which may be defeasible. A conclusion will be trivially considered valid if it repeats or summarizes the premise – in which case it can hardly be considered as *novel*.

Novelty defines the degree to which the conclusion contains content that is *new in relation to the premise*. As extreme cases, a conclusion candidate that repeats or summarizes the premise or is unrelated to the premise will not be considered novel.

We structured the shared task into two subtasks. **Subtask A** considers a *coarse-grained categorization* of validity and novelty by predicting binary labels denoting whether a conclusion candidate is *valid* or *not valid* and *novel* or *not novel*. In **Subtask B** we aim at a more fine-grained analysis without losing the advantages of using discrete labels for evaluation. Here, we give two conclusion candidates instead of one and task the systems to predict whether one, and if so, which conclusion is *more* valid and novel than the other, respectively, resulting in a ternary prediction task with categories: {*Conclusion 1 is better, Tie, Conclusion 2 is better*}, for each quality aspect.

Split	#	v/n	v/¬n	¬v/n	¬v/¬n
train	750	14%	39%	2%	39%
dev	202	19%	43%	22%	14%
test	520	25%	35%	18%	21%

Table 1: Data statistics for subtask A, considering **v**alidity and **n**ovelty.

		Validity		
		C1	**tie**	**C2**
Novelty	**C1**	8%	4%	6%
	tie	12%	32%	10%
	C2	9%	7%	12%

Table 2: Test data statistics for subtask B, considering validity and novelty.

3.2 Data

The data used in the Validity and Novelty shared task originates from a manual annotation study by Heinisch et al. (2022). They used as a basis the argumentative dataset of Ajjour et al. (2019), which had been collected from the high-quality, mostly political arguments from `debatepedia.org`. Heinisch et al. (2022) used the topic and premises from this data and generated automatic conclusions from them, which they then presented to human annotators to judge their validity and novelty, as well as the original conclusions, or conclusions randomly sampled from the remaining instances. The annotators had a higher education entrance qualification and some experience in the field of argument mining. Each data instance was labeled by three annotators for validity and novelty, where they could choose from the options {yes, I don't know, no} and {Conclusion 1 is better, tie, Conclusion 2 is better} for Subtask A and Subtask B, respectively. The annotators labeled validity and novelty separately and independently from each other. In order to reduce the annotation workload and to offer a more fine-grained analysis for validity and novelty prediction, we presented five to ten different conclusions (Subtask A) and conclusion combinations (Subtask B) for each premise, sometimes having only minor surface differences in the presented conclusions.

Since the annotation of validity and especially novelty introduces a degree of subjectiveness, as in many annotation tasks in the field of argument mining (Gurcke et al., 2021), we published the agreements for each instance. For Subtask A, we distinguish four classes of agreement: "defeasible" (there is no agreement due to one or three "I don't know"-labels), "majority" (two out of three annotators agree), "confident" (two out of three annotators agree and the third annotator labels "I don't know"), and "very confident" (full agreement). Defeasible instances are uncommon (1-4%) and were discarded for the test split. Two out of three samples have very confident validity labels, and every second sample yields a very confident novelty label. An exception is the test-split, with 41% very confident novelty labels and 58% majority novelty labels. We found similar agreements in Subtask B, except for a slightly increased chance (5%) to have one vote for Conclusion 1, one Vote for a Tie, and one vote for Conclusion 2 for validity and novelty, respectively. In such cases, we set the final label to "tie" in validity and novelty, respectively, instead of "unknown". For all other annotator decision distributions, we consider the label with the highest number of votes.

We split the data into train, development, and test data by avoiding a topic-overlap between train (22 overlapping topics for Subtasks A and B, respectively) and development (eight and seven overlapping topics for Subtasks A and B, respectively) data. For Subtask A and B, the development- and test data share eight topics, including the premises but different conclusions. In addition, the test split introduces seven novel topics. The train split and the test split have no topics in common. Overall, we have annotations for 750 train samples, 202 development samples, and 520 test samples for Subtask A and 600 train samples, 72 development samples, and 283 test samples for Subtask B. Further data statistics are in Table 1 and Table 2 for Subtask A and Subtask B, respectively.

We published the train- and development data split for developing the systems and released the test split without reference labels for the final prediction submissions. We revealed the test labels afterward.

3.3 Metrics

For evaluation, we consider standard metrics relying on the F_1 score measured on the predictions made on the predefined test split. For subtask A, our main metric for ranking the submissions is the macro F_1-score for predicting both validity and novelty, resulting in four different combinations (valid and novel, valid and not novel, not valid and novel, not valid and not novel). We also report the macro F_1 scores for validity and novelty separately. For subtask B, we respect the more fine-grained character and rely on the average of the separately calculated macro F_1 scores for validity and novelty.

4 Submissions and Results

In total, we received 13 submissions, from six participating teams[3] for Subtask A, and an additional submission each for Subtask B from two teams that participated in Subtask A. In addition we provide baselines for both subtasks, by fine-tuning the RoBERTa-base-language model (Zhuang et al., 2021) on the Shared Task training data, once to predict validity and and once novelty independently of each other (more details in Appendix A).

Note that some teams did not provide a system description paper. We nevertheless include their results and short descriptions based on the teams' submission information.

4.1 Subtask A

All the submitted systems rely on machine learning in some way.

Many of the submitted systems have built on large language models, mostly RoBERTa (Zhuang et al., 2021)), based on the transformer architecture. Some submitted systems fine-tuned large language models trained on the Natural Language Inference (NLI) and/or Argument Relation classification (ArgRel) task. In order to couple the predictions for both tasks (validity and novelty), it seems intuitive to propose a joint architecture based on Multi-Task-Learning which one of the submitted systems opts for. A further option is to rely on auto-regressive language model such as GPT-3, conditioning them on selected prompts to predict the quality labels as a generative task.

Beyond applying state-of-the-art machine learning architectures and models on the task, some participants have looked into the question how to incorporate background knowledge into the task. Two participating teams have looked in particular into how to extract paths from background knowledge resources such as ConceptNet (Speer et al., 2017) or WikiData (Vrandečić and Krötzsch, 2014) and incorporate these paths as features into a classifier.

We describe the participating systems in more detail in the following.

[3]We allowed each team to submit up to five different system runs.

Team submissions	Short Description	ValNov	Validity	Novelty
CLTeamL-3	GPT-3$_{\boldsymbol{Val\&Nov}}$+$_{NLI}$RoBERTa$_{\boldsymbol{Val\&Nov}}$	**45.16**	**74.64**	61.75
AXiS@EdUni-1	FFNN$_{Val\&Nov}$ w/ $_{NLI}$BART & WikiData	43.27	69.80	62.43
ACCEPT-1	SVM$_{Val\&Nov}$ w/ ConceptNet & SBERT	43.13	59.20	**70.00**
CLTeamL-5	GPT-3$_{\boldsymbol{Val\&Nov}}$+$_{ARC}$RoBERTa$_{\boldsymbol{Val\&Nov}}$	43.10	**74.64**	58.90
CSS*	$_{NLI}$RoBERTa$_{Val\&Nov}$	42.40	70.76	59.86
AXiS@EdUni-2	FFNN$_{Val\|Nov}$ w/ $_{NLI}$BART & WikiData	39.74	66.69	61.63
CLTeamL-2	$_{NLI}$RoBERTa$_{Val\&Nov}$	38.70	65.03	61.75
CLTeamL-1	GPT-3$_{Val\&Nov}$	35.32	**74.64**	46.07
CLTeamL-4	$_{ARC}$RoBERTa$_{Val\&Nov}$	33.11	56.74	58.95
ACCEPT-3	SVM$_{Val\&Nov}$ w/ ConceptNet	30.13	58.63	56.81
ACCEPT-2	SVM$_{Val\|Nov}$ w/ ConceptNet & SBERT	29.92	56.80	48.10
NLP@UIT	SBERT	25.89	61.72	43.36
Baseline	RoBERTa$_{Val\|Nov}$	23.90	59.96	36.12
Harshad	BERT$_{Val}$ + novelty := validity	17.35	56.31	39.00
-	overall system-average excluding the baseline	35.94	62.74	52.97

Table 3: Results (macro-F1-scores) for subtask A including short descriptions for each system. A "&"-sign indicates a jointly trained Validity-Novelty-Predictor, a "|"-sign validity and novelty predictions independent of each other.
*The CSS team revised their predictions after the submission deadline due to detecting a formatting failure of their previously submitted prediction file

Team CLTeamL described in van der Meer et al. (2022), submitted five system runs. They experimented with prompting GPT-3 in a few-shot scenario for both prediction targets (validity and novelty). They combine prompting with in-context learning, providing four samples from the training data that obtained majority annotator agreement, and a test sample to be classified. They also experimented with fine-tuning a multi-task RoBERTa-model on i) the NLI task, or ii) argument relation classification (ArgRel). The fine-tuned models are optionally further refined by contrastive learning.

Submission *CLTeamL-1* uses the validity and novelty predictions obtained from GPT-3 prompts. While GPT-3 performs well in predicting validity (F_1-score of 74.64), it fails in predicting novelty (F_1-score of 46.07) and, therefore, achieves a modest ValNov score of 35.32. Submission *CLTeamL-2* only uses the fine-tuned NLI RoBERTa model. This yields reverse results, with a lower score for validity (65.03) but a better score for novelty prediction (61.75). Submission *CLTeamL-3* combines GPT-3 prompting for validity and the NLI-based fine-tuned RoBERTa, further enhanced with contrastive learning for novelty. With this, the system achieves the *overall best shared task results* for ValNov (45.16), as well as the best results for validity (74.64) and the 3rd best score for novelty (61.75). Relying on a RoBERTa model fine-tuned on the ArgRel instead of the NLI task makes the overall results wose (submission *CLTeamL-4* without GPT-3, submission *CLTeamL-4* with GPT-3 for validity).

Team AXiS@EdUni-1 submitted two system runs (Saadat-Yazdi et al., 2022). The system combines diverse components in a joint prediction system: i) NLI knowledge via a fine-tuned BART NLI system, which computes NLI prediction scores in two directions from premise to conclusion and vice versa; ii) neural models predicting a) semantic distance of premise and conclusion via SBERT, and b) validity and novelty by fine-tuning BERT on the training set; finally iii) knowledge from the WikiData knowledge graph, by extracting knowledge paths between premise and conclusion concepts to determine a) the semantic distance of premise and conclusion (average path length), and b) an irrelevancy score from unconnected conclusion concepts.

The features obtained from each component are fed to a small FFNN to jointly predict validity and novelty (*AXiS-1*). Submission *AXiS-2* combines the predictions of two separately trained FFNNs for validity and novelty. *AXiS-1*, with an overall F_1-score of 43.27, clearly outperforms the *AXiS-2* system with separate validity and novelty predictions (39.47). With this, *AXiS-1* ranks 2nd in the overall task, 2nd for novelty and 3rd for validity. Notably, AXiS-1 obtains the first place when considering all systems that do not leverage GPT-3.

System ablations show that i) NLI from premise to conclusion has stronger impact on results, while the reversed direction also contributes. Semantic distance has a stronger impact on validity, while irrelevancy mostly contributes for the joint ValNov score. Comparing the impact of features from neural vs. knowledge graph resources indicates that neural features have stronger impact, while both feature types contribute to the overall system score.

Team ACCEPT submitted three system runs.[4] *ACCEPT-1* is based on a contextualized graph construction connecting the premise and the conclusion using commonsense knowledge from ConceptNet (Speer et al., 2017). The algorithm to construct the connecting commonsense graph extracts concepts from the premise and conclusion and searches ConceptNet for shortest paths between premise and conclusion concepts, using SBERT to ensure semantic relatedness of the extracted paths to the argument. 13 classic graph features extracted from the constructed knowledge graph, as well as the SBERT similarity between premise and conclusion form a feature vector. This feature vector is fed to a linear SVM classifier for joint ValNov prediction.

Submission *ACCEPT-1* yields the 3rd-best shared task results (43.1), with the overall best novelty score of 70, while validity ranks close to the baseline NLI RoBERTa model (59.2). Two additional runs ablate i) the SBERT component for graph construction (*ACCEPT-3*), which incurs a large drop for novelty and a slight reduction for validity, and ii) separate feature extraction and prediction of validity and novelty scores (*ACCEPT-2*), which decreases the overall ValNov-score by 13 points (from 43.1 to 30.1).

Team CSS submitted one approach (Alshomary and Stahl, 2022). The system relies on a large RoBERTa model fine-tuned for NLI. In a transfer learning setting, this model is further fine-tuned on the training data of the shared task. Two prediction heads, one for validity and one for novelty, are used. For each prediction head, the other metric is used as an auxiliary task. Each prediction head is trained with its own set of hyper-parameters, but the RoBERTa model is shared. *CSS* ranks fifth in Subtask A with a ValNov score of 42.4. The model achieves a strong Validity score of 70.8, and a Novelty score of 59.9.

[4]No description paper was submitted for these systems.

Submission	Val/Nov	Validity	Novelty
NLP@UIT	41.50	44.60	38.39
AXiS@EdUni	29.16	32.47	25.86
Baseline	21.46	19.82	23.09

Table 4: Results (avg/ macro-F1-scores) for subtask B.

Remaining submissions Team **NLP@UIT** and team **HARSHAD** submitted one submission each, using fine-tuned transformer models. Team **NLP@UIT** has minor success with training an SBERT (Reimers and Gurevych, 2019) system (25.9 ValNov-score), while team **HARSHAD** underperforms the baseline with a BERT model finetuned for validity (56.31), which they also use to rate the novelty aspect (39.00), a result that underpins the dueling nature of the two aspects.

Combining the best approaches for each aspect Copying the highest-ranked validity predictions from the third submission of Team **CLTeamL** (van der Meer et al., 2022) and the highest-ranked novelty predictions from the first approach of Team **ACCEPT**, we compute a ValNov-score by joining their respective independent predictions, which represents an increase of 8.1 macro-F_1 points in predicting both validity and novelty correctly (53.3). This combination of these two systems' outputs performs best for correctly identifying valid and non-novel samples, with an F_1 score of 66.2 for this class.

4.2 Subtask B

For subtask B (Table 4) we got only two submissions. Team **NLP@UIT** was successful by training SBERT (Reimers and Gurevych, 2019) with a triplet loss objective function. It obtains the highest F_1-scores for validity (44.6) and novelty (38.39). Team **AXiS@EdUni**, with the second best system in Subtask A, reuse their system to predict validity and novelty for both conclusions presented in a sample. Since the output of their system is continuous, mapped to one specific class for subtask A, they can compare the validity and novelty predictions for each conclusion, taking the conclusion with a higher predicted score as superior in validity and novelty, respectively. Hence, they never assign a sample as a tie for validity and novelty, respectively, which lowers their results to the second best ValNov-score (29.2) in this subtask.

5 Discussion

The results for the submitted systems suggest that the prediction of validity seems to be an easier task compared to the prediction of novelty, as many submitted system reach higher scores on validity than on novelty prediction for both subtasks (computed mean scores of 62.74 for validity vs. 52.97 points F_1-scores for novelty, across all system submissions in Subtask A). Most of the submitted systems (CLTeamL, AXiS@EdUni-1, CSS, HARSHAD) rely on large pre-trained languages models (e.g. GPT-3, RoBERTa, BART) that are i) fine-tuned on task-specific data, ii) pre-trained on related tasks (NLI, ArgRel), iii) or are used as generators conditioned on selected prompts, as well as combinations of these.

Systems relying on large language models achieve strong results in terms of validity prediction. The fact that the best results are achieved with the huge GPT-3 system, pretrained with a massive amount of textual data, and relying on prompts to condition the generation without being fine-tuned for the specific task is remarkable. Pre-training on the related task of NLI has been shown, in many submissions, to be beneficial for the task, whereas Argument Relation Classification was not found to be similarly effective (see results for CLTeamL). Further, Multi-Task-Learning, aimed towards exploiting interactions between both quality labels has been shown to improve performance, having a joint instead of separate prediction of the two target labels, which corroborates their complementary nature.

Analysis of validity prediction In general, the results demonstrate that systems relying on large language models can achieve reasonable results in terms of *validity* predictions, hinting at the fact that they are capable of recognizing some sort of inference. This is supported by the fact that such models are familiar with coherence due to their pretraining process and have been shown to yield good results on popular natural language inference tasks in general (Raffel et al., 2020). Nevertheless, recent work has shown that models tend to rely on statistical cues rather than actually learning valid and general rules of inference (Niven and Kao, 2019; Zhang et al., 2022).

Analysis of novelty prediction Regarding the prediction of *novelty*, the systems based on large language models show worse performance. The best result in terms of novelty is achieved by a system from Team ACCEPT that integrates symbolic knowledge from external commonsense knowledge sources, followed by Team AXiS@EdUni, which uses the WikiData knowledge graph. This suggests that the prediction of novelty requires deeper reasoning abilities in combination with background and common sense knowledge.

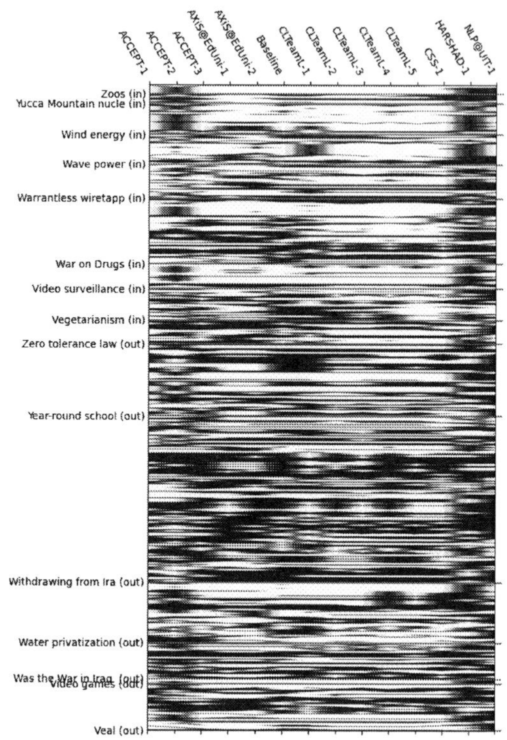

Figure 1: Error heatmap of each prediction and submitted system. The x-axis lists the submitted systems and the y-axis the instances grouped by topics. A topic marked with *out* does not occur in the other splits of the dataset, *in*-topics are also included in the validation-split. Red and dark areas represent misclassified instances.

Analysis of the difficulty of test topics and test instances for Subtask A We investigate the effect of individual instances and topics on the performance of the submitted systems with respect to the ValNov-score in Figure 1. In general, we observe that some instances seem more challenging than others. While 14% of all instances are correctly classified by at least 11 systems (out of 14), 23% of all instances are hard to classify (three or fewer systems correctly classifying them). 5% of all instances are never correctly classified. While detecting off-topic conclusions as neither valid nor novel is easy for all systems, detecting many non-valid but novel instances is challenging. Also, some non-novel-non-valid instances are always misclassified in case of topic-related conclusions. One of those challenging examples is "*Economically speaking, using unwanted calves for veal is more efficient and socially desirable result than simply wasting this good and valuable meat.*" with the conclusion "*Veal is more economical than wasting good meat*". On the surface level, the conclusion looks like a valid-non-novel summarization, but it does not make sense in this wording for us humans. This example highlights the risks of relying on statistical cues. We also observe that the prediction success also depends on the complexity of the premise, explaining the larger misclassified areas in Figure 1. However, besides a common ground of difficulty shared by all systems, 3% of all instances are mostly correctly classified by the systems integrating background knowledge (ACCEPT-1 to AXis@EdUni-2 in Figure 1) but consistently misclassified of those that focus on large language models (CLTeam-1 to CSS-1 in Figure 1) and 2% of all instances for the reverse case.

Looking at the topic level, we observe that some topics are more challenging than others. For example, the discussion about "Withdrawing from Iraq" requires lots of (expert) background knowledge about US foreign policy and is, in addition, not a current topic anymore.[5] Looking at this topic, only 4.6 out of 14 systems correctly classify an instance on average. On the other hand, "Wind energy" is a much more common and current topic, with 7.3 systems correctly predicting the instances in this topic on average. The fact that "Withdrawing from Iraq" is an important topic in the test split that does not occur in the other splits intensifies the effect the low performance of some systems on novel topics (5.3 systems on average classify examples in novel test topics correctly versus 7.2 systems in test topics shared with the development set), by also showing that systems have difficulties in generalizing to unseen topics. A large amount of topics shared between train and test would surely increase results on test data, but would provide a misleading picture regarding the ability of systems to generalize across topics.

[5]Outdated discussions or topics with fading relevance can harm the performance of modern language models due to the pressure of keeping them in sync with the real world (Lazaridou et al., 2021) and the phenomena of catastrophic forgetting.

6 Conclusion

In this paper we have described the shared task on validity and novelty prediction that has been carried out as part of the 9th Argument Mining Workshop. Six groups participated in the task, submitting 15 system runs overall, with a preference for the more course-grained first subtask with binary labels for validity and novelty. The results suggest that validity is easier to predict compared to novelty. Large language models which are few-shot prompted or fine-tuned on the provided task-specific data, especially by applying transfer-learning from natural inference tasks, perform reasonably well on the task of predicting validity. However, such systems have a notably worse performance on predicting novelty. Systems that complement large pre-trained language models with external commonsense or world knowledge, by contrast, perform much better for novelty. This suggests that the recognition of novel content is challenging, requiring deeper understanding and inference involving background, common sense or even domain-specific knowledge.

Acknowledgements

This work has been funded by DFG within the project ACCEPT, which is part of the priority program "Robust Argumentation Machines" (RATIO).

References

Yamen Ajjour, Milad Alshomary, Henning Wachsmuth, and Benno Stein. 2019. Modeling frames in argumentation. In *Proceedings of the 2019 Conference on Empirical Methods in Natural Language Processing and the 9th International Joint Conference on Natural Language Processing (EMNLP-IJCNLP)*, pages 2922–2932, Hong Kong, China. Association for Computational Linguistics.

Milad Alshomary and Maja Stahl. 2022. Argument novelty and validity assessment via multitask and transfer learning. In *Proceedings of the 9th Workshop on Argument Mining*, Gyeongju, Republic of Korea. Association for Computational Linguistics.

Roy Bar-Haim, Yoav Kantor, Lilach Eden, Roni Friedman, Dan Lahav, and Noam Slonim. 2020. Quantitative argument summarization and beyond: Cross-domain key point analysis. In *Proceedings of the 2020 Conference on Empirical Methods in Natural Language Processing (EMNLP)*, pages 39–49, Online. Association for Computational Linguistics.

Shai Gretz, Yonatan Bilu, Edo Cohen-Karlik, and Noam Slonim. 2020a. The workweek is the best time to start a family – a study of GPT-2 based claim generation. In *Findings of the Association for Computational Linguistics: EMNLP 2020*, pages 528–544, Online. Association for Computational Linguistics.

Shai Gretz, Roni Friedman, Edo Cohen-Karlik, Assaf Toledo, Dan Lahav, Ranit Aharonov, and Noam Slonim. 2020b. A large-scale dataset for argument quality ranking: Construction and analysis. *Proceedings of the AAAI Conference on Artificial Intelligence*, 34(05):7805–7813.

Timon Gurcke, Milad Alshomary, and Henning Wachsmuth. 2021. Assessing the sufficiency of arguments through conclusion generation. In *Proceedings of the 8th Workshop on Argument Mining*, pages 67–77, Punta Cana, Dominican Republic. Association for Computational Linguistics.

Ivan Habernal and Iryna Gurevych. 2016. Which argument is more convincing? analyzing and predicting convincingness of web arguments using bidirectional LSTM. In *Proceedings of the 54th Annual Meeting of the Association for Computational Linguistics (Volume 1: Long Papers)*, pages 1589–1599, Berlin, Germany. Association for Computational Linguistics.

Philipp Heinisch, Anette Frank, Juri Opitz, and Philipp Cimiano. 2022. Strategies for framing argumentative conclusion generation. In *Findings of the Association for Computational Linguistics: ACL-INLG 2022*. Association for Computational Linguistics.

Anne Lauscher, Lily Ng, Courtney Napoles, and Joel Tetreault. 2020. Rhetoric, logic, and dialectic: Advancing theory-based argument quality assessment in natural language processing. In *Proceedings of the 28th International Conference on Computational Linguistics*, pages 4563–4574, Barcelona, Spain (Online). International Committee on Computational Linguistics.

Angeliki Lazaridou, Adhiguna Kuncoro, Elena Gribovskaya, Devang Agrawal, Adam Liska, Tayfun Terzi, Mai Gimenez, Cyprien de Masson d'Autume, Tomás Kociský, Sebastian Ruder, Dani Yogatama, Kris Cao, Susannah Young, and Phil Blunsom. 2021. Mind the gap: Assessing temporal generalization in neural language models. In *Advances in Neural Information Processing Systems 34: Annual Conference on Neural Information Processing Systems 2021, NeurIPS 2021, December 6-14, 2021, virtual*, pages 29348–29363.

Timothy Niven and Hung-Yu Kao. 2019. Probing neural network comprehension of natural language arguments. In *Proceedings of the 57th Annual Meeting of the Association for Computational Linguistics*, pages 4658–4664, Florence, Italy. Association for Computational Linguistics.

Juri Opitz, Philipp Heinisch, Philipp Wiesenbach, Philipp Cimiano, and Anette Frank. 2021. Explainable unsupervised argument similarity rating with Abstract Meaning Representation and conclusion generation. In *Proceedings of the 8th Workshop on Argument Mining*, pages 24–35, Punta Cana, Dominican Republic. Association for Computational Linguistics.

Niklas Rach, Carolin Schindler, Isabel Feustel, Johannes Daxenberger, Wolfgang Minker, and Stefan Ultes. 2021. From argument search to argumentative dialogue: A topic-independent approach to argument acquisition for dialogue systems. In *Proceedings of the 22nd Annual Meeting of the Special Interest Group on Discourse and Dialogue, SIGdial 2021, Singapore and Online, July 29-31, 2021*, pages 368–379. Association for Computational Linguistics.

Colin Raffel, Noam Shazeer, Adam Roberts, Katherine Lee, Sharan Narang, Michael Matena, Yanqi Zhou, Wei Li, and Peter J. Liu. 2020. Exploring the limits of transfer learning with a unified text-to-text transformer. *Journal of Machine Learning Research*, 21(140):1–67.

Nils Reimers and Iryna Gurevych. 2019. Sentence-bert: Sentence embeddings using siamese bert-networks. In *Proceedings of the 2019 Conference on Empirical Methods in Natural Language Processing*. Association for Computational Linguistics.

Ameer Saadat-Yazdi, Xue Li, Sandrine Chausson, Vaishak Belle, Björn Ross, Jeff Z. Pan, and Nadin Kökciyan. 2022. Kevin: A knowledge enhanced validity and novelty classifier for arguments. In *Proceedings of the 9th Workshop on Argument Mining*, Gyeongju, Republic of Korea. Association for Computational Linguistics.

Robyn Speer, Joshua Chin, and Catherine Havasi. 2017. Conceptnet 5.5: An open multilingual graph of general knowledge. In *Proceedings of the Thirty-First AAAI Conference on Artificial Intelligence*, pages 4444–4451.

Christian Stab and Iryna Gurevych. 2017a. Parsing argumentation structures in persuasive essays. *Computational Linguistics*, 43(3):619–659.

Christian Stab and Iryna Gurevych. 2017b. Recognizing insufficiently supported arguments in argumentative essays. In *Proceedings of the 15th Conference of the European Chapter of the Association for Computational Linguistics: Volume 1, Long Papers*, pages 980–990, Valencia, Spain. Association for Computational Linguistics.

Shahbaz Syed, Khalid Al Khatib, Milad Alshomary, Henning Wachsmuth, and Martin Potthast. 2021. Generating informative conclusions for argumentative texts. In *Findings of the Association for Computational Linguistics: ACL-IJCNLP 2021*, pages 3482–3493, Online. Association for Computational Linguistics.

Assaf Toledo, Shai Gretz, Edo Cohen-Karlik, Roni Friedman, Elad Venezian, Dan Lahav, Michal Jacovi, Ranit Aharonov, and Noam Slonim. 2019. Automatic argument quality assessment - new datasets and methods. In *Proceedings of the 2019 Conference on Empirical Methods in Natural Language Processing and the 9th International Joint Conference on Natural Language Processing (EMNLP-IJCNLP)*, pages 5625–5635, Hong Kong, China. Association for Computational Linguistics.

Michael van der Meer, Myrthe Reuver, Urja Khurana, Lea Krause, and Selene Báez Santamaría. 2022. Will it blend? mixing training paradigms & prompting for argument quality prediction. In *Proceedings of the 9th Workshop on Argument Mining*, Gyeongju, Republic of Korea. Association for Computational Linguistics.

Eva Maria Vecchi, Neele Falk, Iman Jundi, and Gabriella Lapesa. 2021. Towards argument mining for social good: A survey. In *Proceedings of the 59th Annual Meeting of the Association for Computational Linguistics and the 11th International Joint Conference on Natural Language Processing (Volume 1: Long Papers)*, pages 1338–1352, Online. Association for Computational Linguistics.

Denny Vrandečić and Markus Krötzsch. 2014. Wikidata: A free collaborative knowledgebase. *Commun. ACM*, 57(10):78–85.

Henning Wachsmuth, Nona Naderi, Yufang Hou, Yonatan Bilu, Vinodkumar Prabhakaran, Tim Alberdingk Thijm, Graeme Hirst, and Benno Stein. 2017a. Computational argumentation quality assessment in natural language. In *Proceedings of the 15th Conference of the European Chapter of the Association for Computational Linguistics: Volume 1, Long Papers*, pages 176–187, Valencia, Spain. Association for Computational Linguistics.

Henning Wachsmuth, Martin Potthast, Khalid Al-Khatib, Yamen Ajjour, Jana Puschmann, Jiani Qu, Jonas Dorsch, Viorel Morari, Janek Bevendorff, and Benno Stein. 2017b. Building an argument search engine for the web. In *Proceedings of the 4th Workshop on Argument Mining*, pages 49–59, Copenhagen, Denmark. Association for Computational Linguistics.

Henning Wachsmuth, Benno Stein, and Yamen Ajjour. 2017c. "PageRank" for argument relevance. In *Proceedings of the 15th Conference of the European Chapter of the Association for Computational Linguistics: Volume 1, Long Papers*, pages 1117–1127, Valencia, Spain. Association for Computational Linguistics.

Honghua Zhang, Liunian Harold Li, Tao Meng, Kai-Wei Chang, and Guy Van den Broeck. 2022. On the paradox of learning to reason from data. ArXiv.

Liu Zhuang, Lin Wayne, Shi Ya, and Zhao Jun. 2021. A robustly optimized BERT pre-training approach with post-training. In *Proceedings of the 20th Chinese National Conference on Computational Linguistics*, pages 1218–1227, Huhhot, China. Chinese Information Processing Society of China.

A Details about the baseline model for both subtasks

We fine-tuned a RoBERTa-base-model (`https://huggingface.co/roberta-base`) once for validity prediction and once for novelty prediction by using the training data for Subtask A and Subtask B, respectively. In Subtask A, we ignored the training data with *"unknown"* labels. We tuned each RoBERTa model for three epochs and loaded the best performing model regrading the loss score on the development split at the end. The baseline can be reproduced by running the python script located at `https://github.com/phhei/ArgsValidNovel/blob/gh-pages/BaselinePrediction/main.py`.

B Further analysis of the test predictions for Subtask A

Besides Figure 1 presenting misclassfied areas with respect to the ValNov-score (a instance is misclassified if the prediction for validity or for novelty is incorrect), we show Figure 2 for classification errors in validity predictions and Figure 3 for classification errors in the novelty predictions.

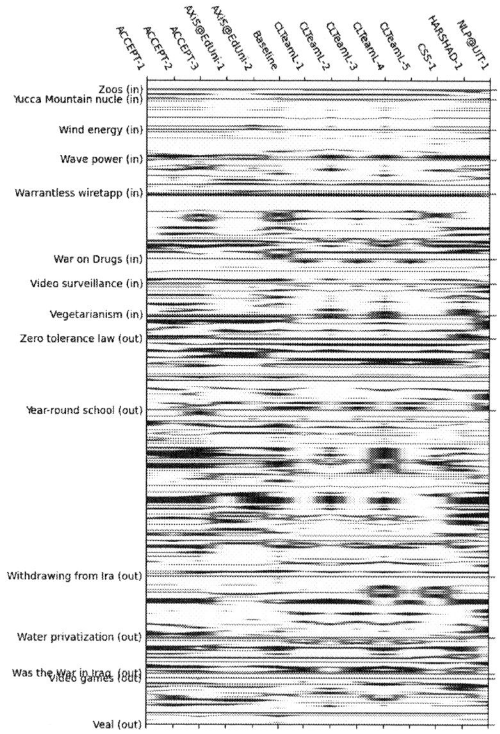

Figure 2: Error heatmap of each prediction and submitted system. The x-axis lists the submitted systems and the y-axis instances grouped by topic. A topic marked with *out* does not occur in the other splits of the dataset, *in*-topics are also included in the validation-split. Red and dark areas represent misclassified instances validity.

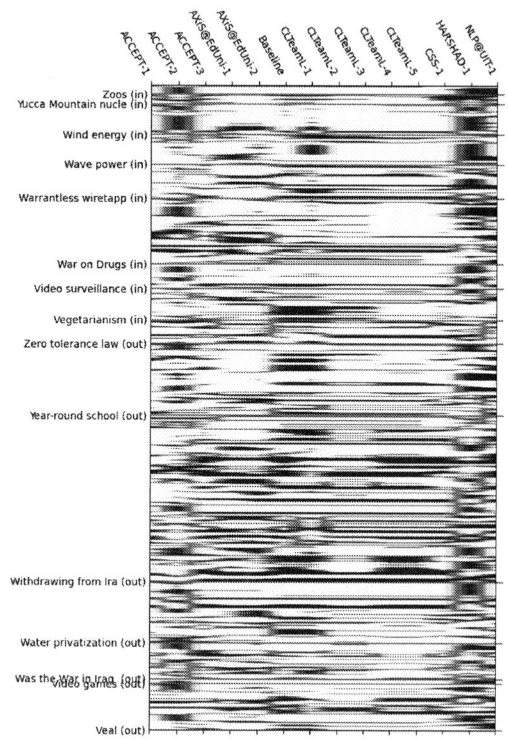

Figure 3: Error heatmap of each prediction and submitted system. The x-axis lists the submitted systems and the y-axis the instances group by topic. A topic marked with *out* does not occur in the other splits of the dataset, *in*-topics are also included in the validation-split. Red and dark areas represent misclassified instances novelty.

Will It Blend? Mixing Training Paradigms & Prompting for Argument Quality Prediction

Michiel van der Meer
Leiden University
m.t.van.der.meer@liacs.leidenuniv.nl

Myrthe Reuver
Vrije Universiteit Amsterdam
myrthe.reuver@vu.nl

Urja Khurana
Vrije Universiteit Amsterdam
u.khurana@vu.nl

Lea Krause
Vrije Universiteit Amsterdam
l.krause@vu.nl

Selene Báez Santamaría
Vrije Universiteit Amsterdam
s.baezsantamaria@vu.nl

Abstract

This paper describes our contributions to the Shared Task of the 9th Workshop on Argument Mining (2022). Our approach uses Large Language Models for the task of Argument Quality Prediction. We perform prompt engineering using GPT-3, and also investigate the training paradigms multi-task learning, contrastive learning, and intermediate-task training. We find that a mixed prediction setup outperforms single models. Prompting GPT-3 works best for predicting argument validity, and argument novelty is best estimated by a model trained using all three training paradigms.

1 Introduction

As debates are moving increasingly online, automatically processing and moderating arguments becomes essential to further fruitful discussions. The research field of automatic extraction, analysis, and relation detection of argument units is called Argument Mining (AM, Lawrence and Reed, 2020).

The shared task of the 9th Workshop on Argument Mining (2022) focuses on argument quality (Wachsmuth et al., 2017). Argument quality can be broken down into multiple dimensions, each with its own purpose, or be extended to *deliberative quality* (Vecchi et al., 2021). The shared task includes two aspects of the *logical* argument quality dimension: *validity* and *novelty*. Given a premise and a conclusion, a valid relationship indicates that sound logical inferences link the premise and conclusion. A novel relationship indicates that new information was introduced in the conclusion that was not present in the premise. Prediction of an argument's validity and novelty can be either through binary classification (Task A) or by explicit comparison between two arguments (Task B). We focus on Task A.

A system that is able to estimate validity and novelty could be a building block in AM for online deliberation. For instance, in assisting humans to detect arguments in online deliberative discussions (van der Meer et al., 2022; Falk et al., 2021) or presenting diverse viewpoints to users in a news recommendation system (Reuver et al., 2021a).

We address the task of validity and novelty prediction through a variety of approaches ranging from prompting, contrastive learning, intermediate task training, and multi-task learning. Our best-performing approach is a mix of a GPT-3 model (through prompting) and a contrastively trained multi-task model that uses NLI as an intermediate training task. This approach achieves a combined Validity and Novelty F1-score of 0.45.

2 Related Work: Paradigms & Prompting

Given the two related argumentation tasks (novelty and validity), a Multi-Task Learning (MTL) setup (Crawshaw, 2020) is a natural approach. Multi-task models use training signals across several tasks, and have been applied before in argument-related work with Large Language Models (LLMs) (Lauscher et al., 2020; Cheng et al., 2020; Tran and Litman, 2021). We use shared encoders followed by task-specific classification heads. The training of these encoders was influenced by the following two lines of work.

First, intermediate task training (Pruksachatkun et al., 2020; Weller et al., 2022) fine-tunes a pre-trained LLM on an auxiliary task before moving on to the final task. This can aid classification performance, also in AM (Shnarch et al., 2022).

Second, contrastive learning is shown to be

Proceedings of the 9th Workshop on Argument Mining, co-located with the 29th International Conference on Computational Linguistics, pages 95–103
October 17, 2022.

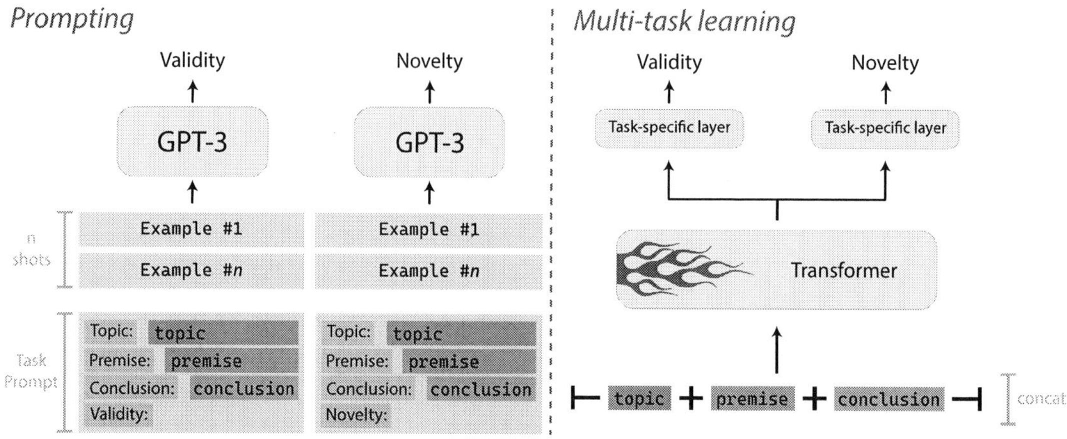

Figure 1: The two argument quality prediction setups used in our submissions. At inference time, predictions from different approaches may be mixed.

a promising approach (Alshomary et al., 2021; Phan et al., 2021) in a previous AM shared task (Friedman-Melamed et al., 2021). Contrastive learning is used to improve embeddings by forcing similar data points to be closer in space and dissimilar data points to be further away. Such an approach may cause the encoder to learn dataset-specific features that help in downstream task performance.

In addition to MTL, we look at prompt engineering for LLMs, which has shown remarkable progress in a large variety of tasks in combination with (Brown et al., 2020) or without few-shot learning (Sorensen et al., 2022). For this task we draw inspiration from ProP (Alivanistos et al., 2022), an approach that ranked first in the "Knowledge Base Construction from Pre-trained Language Models" challenge at ISWC 2022.[1] ProP reports the highest performance with (1) larger LLMs, (2) shorter prompts, (3) diverse and complete examples in the prompt, (4) task-specific prompts.

3 Data and Training Paradigms

3.1 Data

The task data is in American English and consists of Premise, Conclusion, Topic, and a Novel and Validity label. As highlighted in Table 1, arguments that are both non-valid and novel are underrepresented in the data. We use the original training and validation distribution as provided and do not use any over- or undersampling strategies. Instead, we opt to resolve the data imbalance by adopting different training paradigms (see Section 3.2).

[1]LM-KBC, `https://lm-kbc.github.io/`

Split	Size	Distribution	Topics	Topic Overlap w. train	Topic Overlap w. dev
train	750	331/18/296/105	22	–	0
dev	202	33/44/87/38	8	0	–
test	520	110/96/184/130	15	0	8

Table 1: Shared task data overview. **Distribution** indicates the class distribution of {non-valid, non-novel}/{non-valid, novel}/{valid, non-novel}/{valid,novel} counts. The red count indicates a severe data imbalance in the training set.

The content included in the dataset concerns common controversial issues popular on debate portals (Gretz et al., 2020), with topics varying from "TV Viewing is Harmful to Children" to "Turkey EU Membership".

The training data also contains classes labelled "defeasibly" valid and "somewhat" novel, which are not in the development or test set. We map these to negative labels (i.e. not novel or not valid) to refrain from discarding data. However, we do not measure the effect of this decision on performance.

3.2 Training Paradigms

In our submissions, we mix different training paradigms to obtain our final approach. A schematic overview is given in Figure 1. Below, we outline each of the paradigms individually.

Multi-task Learning Since both validity and novelty are related, a shared encoder is used to process the text input into an embedding, which is fed to task-specific layers. We do not use any parameter freezing, allowing gradients from either task to pass through the entire encoder. During training, a single task is sampled uniformly at random, and a batch is sampled containing instances for that task.

Intermediate task training In our case, we use two related tasks for intermediate task training: Natural Language Inference (NLI) and argument relation prediction. For NLI, we use a released RoBERTa model (Liu et al., 2019) trained on the MNLI corpus (Williams et al., 2018), predicting whether two sentences show logical entailment. This is related because making sound logical inferences plays a role in validity. The released argument relation RoBERTa model (Ruiz-Dolz et al., 2021) was trained on the relationship (inference, contradiction, or unrelated) between two sentences in a debate (Visser et al., 2020). This is related to novelty and validity. For instance, unrelated arguments may be novel but not valid, and vice versa.

Contrastive Learning We use SimCSE's (Gao et al., 2021) supervised setting to further fine-tune the previously mentioned RoBERTa MNLI model in a contrastive manner. To train the model we take triples of premises and conclusions in the form of premise, conclusion with a positive novelty rating, and conclusion with a negative novelty rating.

4 Approach

4.1 Submitted Approaches

Approach 1: GPT-3 Prompting In our prompt-engineering approach, we use OpenAI's GPT-3[2] (Brown et al., 2020) for few-shot classification of novelty and validity labels. We construct a prompt by concatenating the topic, premise, and conclusion in a structured format, and request either a validity or novelty label in separate prompts. In addition, we show four static examples before asking for a label from the model, selected from short, difficult examples (i.e. those with the lowest annotation agreement) in the training dataset.

Approach 2: NLI as Intermediate-task, Contrastive learning and Multi-Task Learning This model consists of a shared encoder with task-specific classification heads. We initialize the shared encoder using a pretrained RoBERTa model on the MNLI corpus. We then perform contrastive learning with a triplet loss. Afterward, the model is fine-tuned using MTL on the shared task training data. During training, we switch uniformly at random during training between the novelty and validity tasks.

Approach 3: Mixing Approach 1 (GPT-3) & Approach 2 (NLI+contrastive+MTL) Our Mixed Approach uses Approach 1 (prompt engineering) for validity labels, and Approach 2 (fine-tuned model) for novelty labels.

Approach 4: ArgRel as Intermediate-task and Multi-Task Learning This model uses intermediate-task training on the argument relation prediction task followed by Multi-Task Learning in the same set-up as in Approach 1, but without contrastive learning.

Approach 5: Mixing Approach 1 (GPT-3) & Approach 4 (ArgRel+MTL) This approach uses Approach 1 (prompt engineering) for validity and Approach 4 (ArgRel+MTL) for novelty labels.

4.2 Non-submitted Approaches

Baseline: SVM Support Vector Machines (SVMs) are strong baselines for argument mining tasks with relatively small multi-topic datasets (Reuver et al., 2021b). We train an SVM separately for validity and novelty as a competitive baseline.

4.3 Implementation details

We use Python3 and the HuggingFace `transformers` (Wolf et al., 2020) framework for training our models. The SVM baseline instead uses sklearn (Pedregosa et al., 2011). Our code is publicly available.[3] All models trained use RoBERTa (large) (Liu et al., 2019) as the base model, and the intermediate task trained models are obtained directly from the HuggingFace Hub.[4] We provide hyperparameters for fine-tuned trained models in Appendix A.

Model selection was done based on the combined (validity and novelty) F1 performance on the development set. All experiments were run for 10 epochs, after which the best-performing checkpoint was selected for use in creating predictions on the test set. The training was performed on machines including either two GTX2080 Ti GPUs, or four GTX3090 GPUs.

[2] `https://beta.openai.com/playground`

[3] `https://github.com/m0re4u/argmining2022`

[4] `https://huggingface.co/`

Model	F1		
	Validity	Novelty	Combined
SVM (TF-IDF + stemming)	0.60	0.08	0.21
GPT-3 (CLTeamL-1)	0.75	0.46	0.35
NLI+contrastive+MTL (CLTeamL-2)	0.65	0.62	0.39
GPT-3 & NLI+contrastive+MTL (CLTeamL-3)*	**0.75**	**0.62**	**0.45**
ArgRel+MTL (CLTeamL-4)	0.57	0.59	0.33
GPT-3 & ArgRel+MTL (CLTeamL-5)	0.75	0.59	0.43

Table 2: Test set performance. CLTeamL-*n* indicates an official submission with *n* corresponding to the Approach number also in Section 4.1. Bold scores indicate the best-performing approach in the shared task. "Combined" indicates the Shared Task organizer's scoring metric for both tasks.

5 Experiments and Results

We compare our approaches' performance on the test set with the shared task's metric (Combined F1 of Validity and Novelty). Additionally, we analyze our approaches' errors and their connection to labels, annotator confidence, and topic.

5.1 Test set performance

See Table 2 for performance on the test set. We also present a not-submitted SVM as a baseline.

5.2 Error Analysis

We perform additional error analysis on three approaches (Approach 1, 2, and 3). We analyze errors in terms of (1) label-specific performance, (2) annotator confidence, and (3) topics. Additional results are in Appendix B.

Per-label performance We observe complementary strengths for the GPT-3 model and our MTL approach in Tables 3. The MTL model is remarkably stronger than GPT-3 at identifying *novel* arguments, even when considering this is a low-frequency class. We see a similar trend in terms of misclassifications (Table 4), as the MTL model has a 40% lower error rate for the novelty label.

Model	F1 Validity		F1 Novelty	
	valid	non-valid	novel	non-novel
GPT-3	0.78	0.62	0.28	0.67
MTL	0.80	0.50	0.48	0.75

Table 3: Per-label performance on the test set.

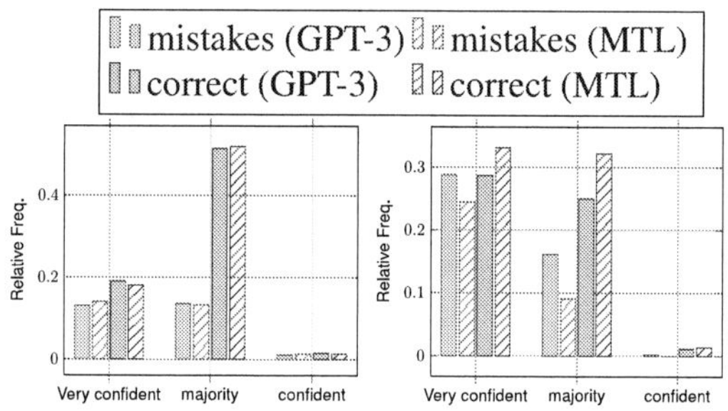

(a) Validity (b) Novelty

Figure 2: Relative accuracy rates divided over label confidence scores.

(a) GPT-3

		Predicted -	Predicted +
True	-	237	57
True	+	184	42

(b) MTL

		Predicted -	Predicted +
True	-	265	29
True	+	145	81

Table 4: Confusion matrices for the novelty labels.

Annotator confidence See Figure 2 for the relationship between annotator confidence and classification error. Surprisingly, examples labeled as very confident (easy for human annotators) are not consistently correctly classified by any approach. For novelty, GPT-3 gets about half of these examples wrong.

Topics The 3 topics with the highest error rates differ between approaches and tasks. For validity, GPT-3 struggles with "Was the Iraq War Worth it?" (44.8%), while MTL with "Vegetarianism" (40%). For novelty, GPT-3 also struggles with "Vegetarianism" (60%), and MTL with "Withdrawing from Iraq" (44.7%) and "Vegetarianism" (44%).

6 Conclusion

We highlight two main conclusions.

(1) **Different models have different strengths relating to the two tasks**. A prompting approach with a generative model worked best for validity, while contrastive supervised learning worked best for novelty. The two tasks are related enough to be able to effectively use one multi-task learning model, but merging predictions from multiple heterogeneous models leads to the best score.

(2) **Specific intermediate-tasks before fine-tuning work well for low-resource argument mining tasks**. NLI seems clearly related to validity prediction. For the novelty tasks, other tasks related to argument similarity (Reimers et al., 2019) might be equally informative.

7 Access and Responsible Research

A core consideration in NLP research when sharing results is the accessibility and reproducibility of the solution. While our code is openly available, the approaches including GPT-3 require access to commercially trained models. We used free trial OpenAI accounts (allowing $18 of free GPT-3 credit), but larger datasets and additional tasks can quickly make this approach infeasible. We also considered the freely accessible LLM BLOOM[5]. BLOOM does not require payment, but does require more GPU memory than what was available to us – making it inaccessible.

Ultimately, GPT-3 and related LLMs have several biases and risks of use, including the generation of false information (Tamkin et al., 2021) and the fact that their training on internet language leads to a very limited set of language, ideas, and perspectives represented (Bender et al., 2021), with even racist, sexist, and hateful views (Gehman et al., 2020). This is especially important to mention, as the task description mentions a future use case of generating new arguments.

[5]`https://huggingface.co/bigscience/bloom`

Acknowledgements

This research was funded by the Vrije Universiteit Amsterdam and the Netherlands Organisation for Scientific Research (NWO) through the *Hybrid Intelligence Centre* via the Zwaartekracht grant (024.004.022), the *Rethinking News Algorithms* project via the Open Competition Digitalization Humanities & Social Science grant (406.D1.19.073), and the *Spinoza* grant (SPI 63-260) awarded to Piek Vossen. We would also like to thank the reviewers for their excellent feedback that enhanced this paper. All remaining errors are our own.

References

Dimitrios Alivanistos, Selene Báez Santamaría, Michael Cochez, Jan-Christoph Kalo, Emile van Krieken, and Thiviyan Thanapalasingam. 2022. Prompting as probing: Using language models for knowledge base construction.

Milad Alshomary, Timon Gurcke, Shahbaz Syed, Philipp Heinisch, Maximilian Spliethöver, Philipp Cimiano, Martin Potthast, and Henning Wachsmuth. 2021. Key point analysis via contrastive learning and extractive argument summarization. In *Proceedings of the 8th Workshop on Argument Mining*, pages 184–189.

Emily M Bender, Timnit Gebru, Angelina McMillan-Major, and Shmargaret Shmitchell. 2021. On the dangers of stochastic parrots: Can language models be too big? In *Proceedings of the 2021 ACM Conference on Fairness, Accountability, and Transparency*, pages 610–623.

Tom Brown, Benjamin Mann, Nick Ryder, Melanie Subbiah, Jared D Kaplan, Prafulla Dhariwal, Arvind Neelakantan, Pranav Shyam, Girish Sastry, Amanda Askell, et al. 2020. Language models are few-shot learners. *Advances in neural information processing systems*, 33:1877–1901.

Liying Cheng, Lidong Bing, Qian Yu, Wei Lu, and Luo Si. 2020. Ape: argument pair extraction from peer review and rebuttal via multi-task learning. In *Proceedings of the 2020 Conference on Empirical Methods in Natural Language Processing (EMNLP)*, pages 7000–7011.

Michael Crawshaw. 2020. Multi-task learning with deep neural networks: A survey. *arXiv preprint arXiv:2009.09796*.

Neele Falk, Iman Jundi, Eva Maria Vecchi, and Gabriella Lapesa. 2021. Predicting moderation of deliberative arguments: Is argument quality the key? In *Proceedings of the 8th Workshop on Argument Mining*, pages 133–141.

Roni Friedman-Melamed, Lena Dankin, Yufang Hou, Ranit Aharonov, Yoav Katz, and Noam Slonim. 2021. Overview of the 2021 key point analysis shared task. In *Conference on Empirical Methods in Natural Language Processing*.

Tianyu Gao, Xingcheng Yao, and Danqi Chen. 2021. SimCSE: Simple contrastive learning of sentence embeddings. In *Empirical Methods in Natural Language Processing (EMNLP)*.

Samuel Gehman, Suchin Gururangan, Maarten Sap, Yejin Choi, and Noah A Smith. 2020. Realtoxicityprompts: Evaluating neural toxic degeneration in language models. In *Findings of the Association for Computational Linguistics: EMNLP 2020*, pages 3356–3369.

Shai Gretz, Roni Friedman, Edo Cohen-Karlik, Assaf Toledo, Dan Lahav, Ranit Aharonov, and Noam Slonim. 2020. A large-scale dataset for argument quality ranking: Construction and analysis. In *Proceedings of the AAAI Conference on Artificial Intelligence*, volume 34, pages 7805–7813.

Anne Lauscher, Lily Ng, Courtney Napoles, and Joel Tetreault. 2020. Rhetoric, logic, and dialectic: Advancing theory-based argument quality assessment in natural language processing. In *Proceedings of the 28th International Conference on Computational Linguistics*, pages 4563–4574, Barcelona, Spain (Online). International Committee on Computational Linguistics.

John Lawrence and Chris Reed. 2020. Argument mining: A survey. *Computational Linguistics*, 45(4):765–818.

Yinhan Liu, Myle Ott, Naman Goyal, Jingfei Du, Mandar Joshi, Danqi Chen, Omer Levy, Mike Lewis, Luke Zettlemoyer, and Veselin Stoyanov. 2019. Roberta: A robustly optimized bert pretraining approach. *arXiv preprint arXiv:1907.11692*.

Ilya Loshchilov and Frank Hutter. 2018. Decoupled weight decay regularization. In *International Conference on Learning Representations*.

F. Pedregosa, G. Varoquaux, A. Gramfort, V. Michel, B. Thirion, O. Grisel, M. Blondel, P. Prettenhofer, R. Weiss, V. Dubourg, J. Vanderplas, A. Passos, D. Cournapeau, M. Brucher, M. Perrot, and E. Duchesnay. 2011. Scikit-learn: Machine learning in Python. *Journal of Machine Learning Research*, 12:2825–2830.

Hoang Phan, Long Nguyen, and Khanh Doan. 2021. Matching the statements: A simple and accurate model for key point analysis. In *Proceedings of the 8th Workshop on Argument Mining*, pages 165–174.

Yada Pruksachatkun, Jason Phang, Haokun Liu, Phu Mon Htut, Xiaoyi Zhang, Richard Yuanzhe Pang, Clara Vania, Katharina Kann, and Samuel R. Bowman. 2020. Intermediate-task transfer learning with pretrained language models: When and why does it work? In *Proceedings of the 58th Annual Meeting of the Association for Computational Linguistics*, pages 5231–5247, Online. Association for Computational Linguistics.

Nils Reimers, Benjamin Schiller, Tilman Beck, Johannes Daxenberger, Christian Stab, and Iryna Gurevych. 2019. Classification and clustering of arguments with contextualized word embeddings. In *Proceedings of the 57th Annual Meeting of the Association for Computational Linguistics*, pages 567–578.

Myrthe Reuver, Nicolas Mattis, Marijn Sax, Suzan Verberne, Nava Tintarev, Natali Helberger, Judith Moeller, Sanne Vrijenhoek, Antske Fokkens, and Wouter van Atteveldt. 2021a. Are we human, or are we users? the role of natural language processing in human-centric news recommenders that nudge users to diverse content. In *Proceedings of the 1st Workshop on NLP for Positive Impact*, pages 47–59.

Myrthe Reuver, Suzan Verberne, Roser Morante, and Antske Fokkens. 2021b. Is stance detection topic-independent and cross-topic generalizable?-a reproduction study. In *Proceedings of the 8th Workshop on Argument Mining*, pages 46–56.

Ramon Ruiz-Dolz, Jose Alemany, Stella M Heras Barberá, and Ana García-Fornes. 2021. Transformer-based models for automatic identification of argument relations: A cross-domain evaluation. *IEEE Intelligent Systems*, 36(6):62–70.

Eyal Shnarch, Ariel Gera, Alon Halfon, Lena Dankin, Leshem Choshen, Ranit Aharonov, and Noam Slonim. 2022. Cluster & tune: Boost cold start performance in text classification. In *Proceedings of the 60th Annual Meeting of the Association for Computational Linguistics (Volume 1: Long Papers)*, pages 7639–7653.

Taylor Sorensen, Joshua Robinson, Christopher Michael Rytting, Alexander Glenn Shaw, Kyle Jeffrey Rogers, Alexia Pauline Delorey, Mahmoud Khalil, Nancy Fulda, and David Wingate. 2022. An information-theoretic approach to prompt engineering without ground truth labels.

Alex Tamkin, Miles Brundage, Jack Clark, and Deep Ganguli. 2021. Understanding the capabilities, limitations, and societal impact of large language models. *arXiv preprint arXiv:2102.02503*.

Nhat Tran and Diane Litman. 2021. Multi-task learning in argument mining for persuasive online discussions. In *Proceedings of the 8th Workshop on Argument Mining*, pages 148–153.

Michiel van der Meer, Enrico Liscio, Catholijn M. Jonker, Aske Plaat, Piek Vossen, and Pradeep K. Murukannaiah. 2022. Hyena: A hybrid method for extracting arguments from opinions. In *Proceedings of the first International Conference on Hybrid Human-Artificial Intelligence (HHAI 2022)*, pages 1–15, Amsterdam, the Netherlands. IOS Press.

Eva Maria Vecchi, Neele Falk, Iman Jundi, and Gabriella Lapesa. 2021. Towards argument mining for social good: A survey. In *Proceedings of the 59th Annual Meeting of the Association for Computational Linguistics and the 11th International Joint Conference on Natural Language Processing (Volume 1: Long Papers)*, pages 1338–1352.

Jacky Visser, Barbara Konat, Rory Duthie, Marcin Koszowy, Katarzyna Budzynska, and Chris Reed. 2020. Argumentation in the 2016 us presidential elections: annotated corpora of television debates and social media reaction. *Language Resources and Evaluation*, 54(1):123–154.

Henning Wachsmuth, Nona Naderi, Yufang Hou, Yonatan Bilu, Vinodkumar Prabhakaran, Tim Alberdingk Thijm, Graeme Hirst, and Benno Stein. 2017. Computational argumentation quality assessment in natural language. In *Proceedings of the 15th Conference of the European Chapter of the Association for Computational Linguistics: Volume 1, Long Papers*, pages 176–187, Valencia, Spain. Association for Computational Linguistics.

Orion Weller, Kevin Seppi, and Matt Gardner. 2022. When to use multi-task learning vs intermediate fine-tuning for pre-trained encoder transfer learning. In *Proceedings of the 60th Annual Meeting of the Association for Computational Linguistics (Volume 2: Short Papers)*, pages 272–282.

Adina Williams, Nikita Nangia, and Samuel Bowman. 2018. A broad-coverage challenge corpus for sentence understanding through inference. In *Proceedings of the 2018 Conference of the North American Chapter of the Association for Computational Linguistics: Human Language Technologies, Volume 1 (Long Papers)*, pages 1112–1122. Association for Computational Linguistics.

Thomas Wolf, Lysandre Debut, Victor Sanh, Julien Chaumond, Clement Delangue, Anthony Moi, Pierric Cistac, Tim Rault, Rémi Louf, Morgan Funtowicz, et al. 2020. Transformers: State-of-the-art natural language processing. In *Proceedings of the 2020 conference on empirical methods in natural language processing: system demonstrations*, pages 38–45.

A Hyperparameters

GPT-3 Prompt We used the model `text-davinci-002` with a temperature of 0 and no penalties on frequency and presence. We experimented with various prompt designs (e.g. dynamic or longer examples, more/fewer examples, joint prompting of novelty and validity) but manual inspection showed the best results for the present setup described in the paper (i.e. separate prompts, static prompt style).

Transformers We report the hyperparameters for each approach in Table 5 that differ from the default. In all Transformer models, we used the AdamW optimizer (Loshchilov and Hutter, 2018).

Model	LR	epochs	g.acc.
CLTeamL-2	1e-05	9	1
CLTeamL-3 (novelty)	1e-05	9	1
CLTeamL-4	5e-06	6	4
CLTeamL-5 (novelty)	5e-06	6	4

Table 5: Hyperparameters for our approaches that involve gradient-based learning.

SVM The best performing model on the validation set is one with a C parameter of 0.09 for validity and 4.7 for novelty. The text representation concatenates the two texts, in a TF-IDF and stemmed (with the SnowBall stemmer as implemented in NLTK) representation.

B Additional results

For every analysis, we show the results for approaches *CLTeamL-1* and *CLTeamL-2*, which can be combined into *CLTeamL-3* by merging their results (take validity and novelty, respectively for *1* and *2*).

B.1 Per-label Performance

See Tables 6 and 7.

B.2 Label confusion

See Tables 4 and 8.

B.3 Seed Variance

While the results for the task were obtained using a single model, we investigate training stability over multiple seeds. We show the results and variance from five different seeds for our best-performing MTL model. The results can be seen in Figure 3.

	Prec.	Rec.	F1	Support
non-valid	0.583	0.670	0.623	179
valid	0.812	0.748	0.779	341
non-novel	0.816	0.570	0.671	421
novel	0.199	0.455	0.277	99

Table 6: Performance statistics for approach *CLTeamL-1*.

	Prec.	Rec.	F1	Support
non-valid	0.364	0.806	0.502	93
valid	0.943	0.693	0.799	427
non-novel	0.901	0.646	0.753	410
novel	0.358	0.736	0.482	110

Table 7: Performance statistics for approach *CLTeamL-2*.

Training is relatively stable, but individual models may have small performance differences on the test set.

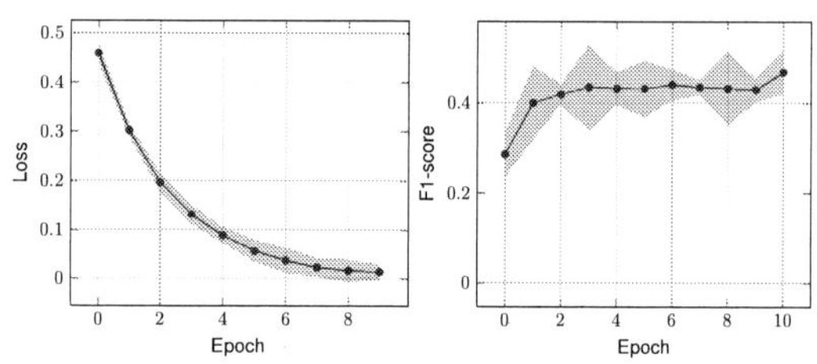

Figure 3: Training loss and combined F1 score for multiple training runs of *CLTeamL-2* with different seeds.

B.4 Topics

The three most error-prone topics were different for approaches. Notable is that "Vegetarianism" is an error-prone topic across tasks and approaches.

GPT-3 - Validity "Was the Iraq War Worth it?" (unseen) with 44.8% errors, "Year Round School" (unseen), 39.7% errors, and "Withdrawing from

(a) GPT-3

		Predicted -	Predicted +
True	-	120	86
True	+	59	255

(b) MTL

		Predicted -	Predicted +
True	-	75	131
True	+	18	296

Table 8: Confusion matrices for the validity labels.

Iraq" (unseen), 38.1% errors.

GPT-3 - Novelty "Yucca Mountain nuclear waste" (62.5% error rate), "Vegetarianism" (60% error rate), "Wiretapping in the U.S. (59.2% error rate).

MTL - Validity "Zero Tolerance Law" (42.1%), "Vegetarianism" (40% error rate) and "Yucca Mountain nuclear waste" (37.5% error rate).

MTL - Novelty "Withdrawing from Iraq" (44.7% error rate), "Vegetarianism" (44% error rate), "Wiretapping in the United States" (44% error rate)

Topics not in dev, only in test "Video games', "Zero tolerance law', "Was the War in Iraq worth it?', "Withdrawing from Iraq', "Year-round school', "Veal', "Water privatization'.

KEViN: A Knowledge Enhanced Validity and Novelty Classifier for Arguments

Ameer Saadat-Yazdi[1] and **Xue Li**[1] and **Sandrine Chausson**[1]
Vaishak Belle[1] and **Björn Ross**[1] and **Jeff Z. Pan**[1,2] and **Nadin Kökciyan**[1]
[1]School of Informatics, University of Edinburgh
[2] Huawei Edinburgh Centre, CSI, Huawei
(ameer.saadat, xue.shirley.li, sandrine.chausson,
vbelle, b.ross, j.z.pan, nadin.kokciyan)@ed.ac.uk

Abstract

The ArgMining 2022 Shared Task is concerned with predicting the validity and novelty of an inference for a given premise and conclusion pair. We propose two feed-forward network based models ($\mathcal{KEV}i\mathcal{N}_1$ and $\mathcal{KEV}i\mathcal{N}_2$), which combine features generated from several pre-trained transformers and the WikiData knowledge graph. The transformers are used to predict entailment and semantic similarity, while WikiData is used to provide a semantic measure between concepts in the premise-conclusion pair. Our proposed models show significant improvement over RoBERTa, with $\mathcal{KEV}i\mathcal{N}_1$ outperforming $\mathcal{KEV}i\mathcal{N}_2$ and obtaining second rank on both subtasks (A and B) of the ArgMining 2022 Shared Task.

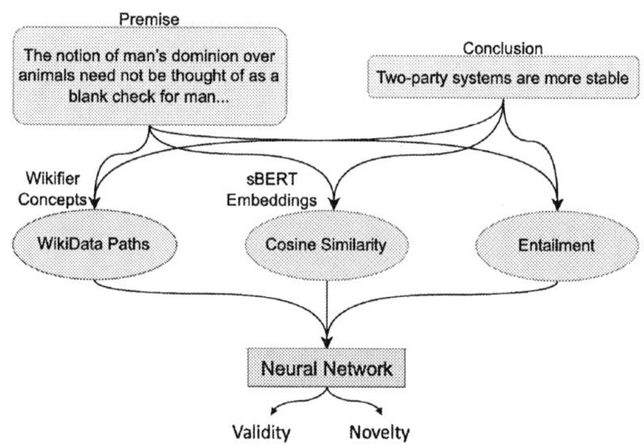

Figure 1: $\mathcal{KEV}i\mathcal{N}_1$ uses WikiData knowledge, and pre-trained transformers to predict similarity and entailment prior to feeding the data into the neural network.

1 Introduction

A number of frameworks have been proposed to evaluate the quality of natural language arguments. Many of these frameworks consider some notion of logical soundness (validity), (Wachsmuth et al., 2017). The ArgMining 2022 shared task also highlights the importance of novelty in measuring the usefulness of a conclusion in order to avoid redundant or non-informative conclusions. These metrics were more formally introduced in (Opitz et al., 2021) to assess the quality of arguments.

In our work, we combine the power of pre-trained language models with external knowledge sources to provide additional information for predictions (Wang et al., 2019; Pan et al., 2019). For this, we extract paths from WikiData (Vrandečić and Krötzsch, 2014) that link the premise to the conclusion, and generate numerical features from these paths.

Having generated several sets of features using WikiData and pre-trained models, we proceed to use these features as inputs to a small feed-forward network trained to predict validity and novelty. Our results show a significant improvement from simply fine-tuning a pre-trained model on the task, and we identify that textual entailment serves as a strong indicator of argument validity, while a combination of textual entailment and knowledge graph distance serves to improve the model's ability to detect novelty[1].

We trained and tested two versions of our model on Task A (binary classification). The first model, $\mathcal{KEV}i\mathcal{N}_1$, predicts both validity and novelty using the same network (Figure 1). The second model, $\mathcal{KEV}i\mathcal{N}_2$, uses two separate networks, which were trained separately for each label, and then combines their predictions. Both models show significant improvement over RoBERTa with $\mathcal{KEV}i\mathcal{N}_1$ significantly outperforming $\mathcal{KEV}i\mathcal{N}_2$. We additionally evaluated the $\mathcal{KEV}i\mathcal{N}_1$ model trained on Task A on the testing set of Task B, the corresponding details and results are given in the Appendix.

[1]Our code is available on GitLab: `https://git.ecdf.ed.ac.uk/xli3310/KEViN_2022`.

Proceedings of the 9th Workshop on Argument Mining, co-located with the 29th International Conference on Computational Linguistics, pages 104–110
October 17, 2022.

Split	Val	¬Val	Nov	¬Nov	Total
train	401	320	123	595	750
dev	125	74	82	118	202
test	314	206	226	294	520

Table 1: Data split from Task A. Note that the training and development sets also contain ambiguous examples that are neither valid/novel nor non-valid/-novel.

2 Task and Data Description

The ArgMining 2022 Shared Task consists of two subtasks: for a given textual premise, 1) classifying a conclusion as being valid/novel (Task A) and 2) comparing conclusions in terms of validity/novelty (Task B). For both tasks, the premise consists of multiple sentences while the conclusion is a single statement. *Validity* requires that there exists a sound logical inference linking the premise to the conclusion; *Novelty*, on the other hand, requires the conclusion to contain new information compared to the premise, and as such to be more than a simple paraphrase[2]. Table 1 provides the class counts per data split for Task A, while Table 2 provides examples of premise/conclusions pairs to illustrate the concepts of validity and novelty.

3 Feature Extraction

In this section, we explain the process for extracting the features that were used as input to our feed-forward network.

3.1 Neural Features

A subset of the features we used as input for our classifier were extracted using large pre-trained neural networks.

3.1.1 Textual Entailment

Given a text t and hypothesis h, the task of Recognising Textual Entailment (RTE), also called Natural Language Inference (NLI), consists of determining whether t entails h ("Entailment" class), contradicts h ("Contradiction" class), or neither ("Neutral" class) (Zeng et al., 2021).

We used a BART model (Lewis et al., 2020) fine-tuned on the Multi-genre Natural Language Inference dataset (Williams et al., 2018) to predict the textual entailment between each premise/conclusion input pair. We did this first with the premise as the text t and the conclusion as the hypothesis h (**TE_P2C**), and then the other way around (**TE_C2P**). In each case, the model returns the probability distribution for the three entailment classes; i.e., a vector of three real numbers adding up to 1. We chose the BART_MNLI model[3] to extract the entailment features because of its state-of-the-art performance on the RTE/NLI task (Yin et al., 2019).

3.1.2 Cosine Similarity

For each premise/conclusion input pair, we used the SBERT package (Reimers and Gurevych, 2019) to obtain $\vec{p}$ and $\vec{c}$, the vector representations of the premise and conclusion respectively. To measure the similarity between these two vectors, we calculated their cosine similarity (**CoSim**), as defined by the following equation:

$$cos(\vec{p}, \vec{c}) = \frac{\vec{p} \cdot \vec{c}}{||\vec{p}||\,||\vec{c}||} \quad (1)$$

3.1.3 BERT Predictions

We trained two separate BERT models to predict Validity and Novelty on the training set. The probabilities of validity (**BERT_pred_val**) and novelty (**BERT_pred_nov**) were used as additional neural input features.

3.2 Knowledge Graph Features

Knowledge Graphs (KGs) represent knowledge in a graph-based structure, in which nodes represent entities and edges represent relations connecting them. Within the KG formalism, the connection between two entities is denoted as the triple $\langle s, r, o \rangle$, where s, r and o represent the subject, relation and object, respectively.

KGs have many applications, including query answering (Huang et al., 2019; Yasunaga et al., 2021) and modelling 5G networks (Zhu et al., 2022; Wang et al., 2021). In this paper, we chose to work with WikiData, one of the biggest KGs in the literature (Vrandečić and Krötzsch, 2014), to extract KG features that can assist the validity/novelty classification of a conclusion c for a given premise p.

To obtain our KG features, we first extracted WikiData entities from p and c, respectively. We tested two entity extraction tools, Wikifier (Brank et al., 2017) and Falcon2.0 (Sakor et al., 2020). Both performed similarly for our task, however we

[2] https://phhei.github.io/ArgsValidNovel/

[3] https://huggingface.co/facebook/bart large mnli

		Valid?	Novel?
Premise	The notion of man's dominion over animals need not be thought of as a blank check for man to exploit animals. Indeed, it may be appropriate to connect the notion of "dominion" to stewardship" over animals. Yet, humans can be good stewards of animals while continuing to eat them. It is merely necessary that humans maintain balance, order, and sustainability in the animal kingdom. But, again, this does not require the abandonment of meat-eating.		
Conclusion	Two-party systems are more stable	no	no
	Man's "dominion" over animals does not imply abandoning meat.	yes	no
	The idea of "domiminism" is unnecessary.	no	yes
	Dominion over animals can and should be used responsibly.	yes	yes

Table 2: Example from Task A on the topic of *Vegetarianism.*

chose Wikifier for its convenient interface. Our entity extractions from p and c are written as $p \mapsto \mathbb{E}_p$ and $c \mapsto \mathbb{E}_c$, where $\mathbb{E}_p$ and $\mathbb{E}_c$ are sets of WikiData entity IDs, respectively. Having done this, we then identified the Knowledge Graph Paths connecting entities from the premise to entities from the conclusion.

Definition 3.1 (Knowledge Graph Path (KGP)) *Given a pair (e_h, e_t) in the KG, their KGP, $\mathbb{K}(e_h, e_t)$, is defined as:*

- $\emptyset$, *if e_h and e_t are disconnected;*
- $\{\langle e_h \rangle\}$, *if $e_h = e_t$;*
- $\{\langle e_h, r_1, x_1 \rangle, \langle x_1, r_2, x_2 \rangle, ..., \langle x_n, r_n, e_t \rangle\}$, *a set of n triples where the object of the former triple is the subject of the following triple, otherwise.*

Multiple KGPs can exist for a single pair of entities. Moreover, there is no guarantee for a KGP to be finite. For our task, we aimed to find the shortest KGPs with a limit. Our search of KGP over WikiData is based on SPARQL queries (Pérez et al., 2009), for which breadth-first search (BFS) was the easiest to implement. To reduce the search space of KGP, we applied an interactive depth limit to the BFS algorithm with a termination depth limit D equal to 3.[4] As a result, the search terminates with the shortest KGPs whose length is less or equal to 3, or with failure if no such path is found.

Some relations denote extremely close proximity, e.g. 'same as', while others the opposite, e.g. 'different from'. These two kinds of extreme relations are summarised $\mathbb{L}_1$ and $\mathbb{L}_2$, respectively. Both sets are given in the Appendix. Based on our test, the extreme relations in $\mathbb{L}_1$ and $\mathbb{L}_2$ make KGPs less representative in our tasks. We compute the semantic length between two entities e_1 and e_2, ($\mathcal{L}_s(e_1, e_2)$) as defined in Equation 2.

$$\mathcal{L}_s = \begin{cases} 0,\ \mathbb{K}(e_1,e_2) = \{e_1\} \bigvee \forall \langle s,r,o\rangle \in \mathbb{K}(e_1,e_2), r \in \mathbb{L}_1 \\ D+1,\ \mathbb{K}(e_1,e_2) = \emptyset \bigvee \exists \langle s,r,o\rangle \in \mathbb{K}(e_1,e_2) \wedge r \in \mathbb{L}_2 \\ |\{\langle s,r,o\rangle \mid \langle s,r,o\rangle \in \mathbb{K}(e_1,e_2) \wedge r \notin \mathbb{L}_1\}|,\ otherwise \end{cases} \quad (2)$$

Finally, we compute the final KG features, i.e. **Irrelevancy** and **Avg_Dist**, as shown below, where $p \mapsto \mathbb{E}_p$, $c \mapsto \mathbb{E}_c$, $e_p \in \mathbb{E}_p$ and $e_c \in \mathbb{E}_c$.

1. **Irrelevancy**: the number of conclusion entities e_c that are disconnected from all premise entities e_p:

$$\mathcal{I} = |\{e_c | \forall e_p,\ \mathbb{K}(e_p, e_c) = \emptyset\}| \quad (3)$$

2. **Avg_Dist**: the average minimal distance between premise entities $\mathbb{E}_p$ to conclusion entities $\mathbb{E}_c$, based on the semantic length ($\mathcal{L}_s$) of all possible pairs of entities from the premise and the conclusion.

$$\mathcal{A} = \frac{\sum_{e_p, e_c} \min |\mathcal{L}_s(e_p, e_c)|}{|\mathbb{E}_p| \times |\mathbb{E}_c|} \quad (4)$$

These two KG features were shown to be significant for our task. Other KG features that we experimented with but that were not as useful are given in the Appendix.

4 Preprocessing and Training

Once the features were computed, we applied several preprocessing steps to improve results. Given the distribution shift between the training and development data of Task A, as shown in Table 1, we used a simple upsampling strategy to ensure that all classes ($Val\&Nov$, $Val\&\neg Nov$, $\neg Val\&Nov$, $\neg Val\&\neg Nov$) were relatively balanced. To do this, we duplicated 200 $Val\&Nov$ examples and 250 $\neg Val\&\neg Nov$ examples so that we would have roughly 300 samples for each class. We also duplicated ambiguous examples, such that if a sample

[4]We choose 3 as the depth limit, because helpful KG features can be found under that limit and the program terminates within reasonable time.

Model	Precision	Recall	F1
RoBERTa	0.21	0.26	0.21
$\mathcal{KEV}i\mathcal{N}_1$	0.44	0.43	0.43
$\mathcal{KEV}i\mathcal{N}_2$	0.41	0.40	0.40

Table 3: Performance of the $\mathcal{KEV}i\mathcal{N}_1$, $\mathcal{KEV}i\mathcal{N}_2$ and a fine-tuned RoBERTa model on the test set for the combined task of validity and novelty prediction.

Model	Validity	Novelty
$\mathcal{KEV}i\mathcal{N}_1$	0.70	0.62
$\mathcal{KEV}i\mathcal{N}_2$	0.67	0.62

Table 4: F1 scores of models on task A, broken down by validity and novelty.

has ambiguous validity, it would appear once as valid and once as invalid, and likewise for novelty. Finally, MinMax scaling was applied to each feature across the training, development, and test sets to ensure that all values were between 0 and 1.

The features were then concatenated and input to a small neural network with two hidden layers of widths five and two respectively and a softmax output layer. We used the Adam optimizer (Kingma and Ba, 2014) with a constant learning rate of 0.001 with L2 regularization. To optimize the regularization term and find the best combination of features for the task we performed an exhaustive grid search using L2 parameters $\alpha \in \{0.001, 0.01, 0.1, 1.0\}$ and all possible combinations of features with a limit of five features at most.

5 Results and Analysis

Table 3 shows the performance of $\mathcal{KEV}i\mathcal{N}_1$, $\mathcal{KEV}i\mathcal{N}_2$ and a RoBERTa baseline on the test set. All models were trained on the same upsampled version of the train set. The RoBERTa baseline was fine-tuned over 3 epochs: the checkpoint that minimised loss on the dev set, obtained after the first epoch, was used for the evaluation. We see clearly that $\mathcal{KEV}i\mathcal{N}_1$ outperforms the RoBERTa baseline and the model with two independent classifiers both in precision and recall. The increase in performance mostly affects the predicition of validity as shown in Table 4.

For $\mathcal{KEV}i\mathcal{N}_1$, our validation run identified **irrelevancy**, **average KGP distance**, **TE_P2C** and **TE_C2P** as the set of features leading to the best performance. We performed an ablation study to identify the relative contribution of each feature. Table 5 shows that removing **TE_P2C** or **Irrelevancy** has the most significant impact overall. We also see that the neural features play a more important role than KG features, especially for validity classification. The results suggest that neural features are crucial to improve the model performance for the combined task of validity and novelty prediction. While KG features are also useful for detecting validity, removing them particularly harms the novelty detection. We expect this result since the existence of KGPs and their lengths reflect the semantic relatedness between the premise and the conclusion, which is relevant for novelty detection.

Removed Feature	Val	Nov	Both
TE_P2C	0.65	0.45	0.31
TE_C2P	0.67	0.61	0.39
Avg_Dist	0.59	0.59	0.40
Irrelevancy	0.67	0.57	0.35
Neural features	0.54	0.54	0.26
KG features	0.68	0.59	0.37

Table 5: Ablation study on test set showing the F1 score of $\mathcal{KEV}i\mathcal{N}_1$ when a given feature is removed. The F1 scores of $\mathcal{KEV}i\mathcal{N}_1$ for validity, novelty and the combined task are 0.70, 0.62 and 0.43, respectively. Colours represent the relative performance decrease with respect to the original $\mathcal{KEV}i\mathcal{N}_1$ model (as a percentage).

6 Related Work

This work identifies a strong similarity between argument validity and textual entailment which has been previously explored (Cabrio and Villata, 2012; Bosc et al., 2016) with mixed success for argument mining. Likewise, the introduction of external KGs into the argument mining pipeline has been studied by Fromm et al. (2019); Paul et al. (2020); Li et al. (2021). In the textual entailment literature, a substantial amount of work has shown the importance of external KGs in making accurate inferences over new domains (Wang et al., 2019, 2020).

7 Conclusion

In this paper, we have shown how features can be extracted from knowledge graphs and pre-trained neural networks that are both relevant and complementary for the task of argument novelty and validity detection. We did this by demonstrating how a small neural network trained on these features outperforms fine-tuning with large transformers.

We defined KG paths in terms of their semantic length and the corresponding KG distance features, which gave promising results and provides a basis for future work. For example, we would also like to consider semantic representations of paths, such as natural language representations, vector-based KG embedding approaches, and other KGs to improve the performance of the proposed model. In addition, it would be interesting to see if learning weights to predict the semantic length based on the relations in KG paths or if extending the graph containing the premise and conclusion concepts with semantic dependency relations would boost the performance.

Acknowledgements

This work was supported by the ELIAI (Edinburgh Laboratory for Integrated Artificial Intelligence) EPSRC (grant no EP/W002876/1); the UKRI (grant EP/S022481/1) and the University of Edinburgh; the Edinburgh-Huawei Joint Lab and Huawei's grant CIENG4721/LSC. We appreciate the time given by the shared task reviewers for their useful feedback, which contributed to improvements in our paper.

References

Tom Bosc, Elena Cabrio, and Serena Villata. 2016. Tweeties Squabbling: Positive and Negative Results in Applying Argument Mining on Social Media. *Computational Models of Argument*, pages 21–32. Publisher: IOS Press.

Janez Brank, Gregor Leban, and Marko Grobelnik. 2017. Annotating documents with relevant wikipedia concepts. *Proceedings of SiKDD*, 472.

Elena Cabrio and Serena Villata. 2012. Natural language arguments: A combined approach. In *ECAI*.

Michael Fromm, Evgeniy Faerman, and Thomas Seidl. 2019. TACAM: Topic And Context Aware Argument Mining. *IEEE/WIC/ACM International Conference on Web Intelligence*, pages 99–106. ArXiv: 1906.00923.

Xiao Huang, Jingyuan Zhang, Dingcheng Li, and Ping Li. 2019. Knowledge graph embedding based question answering. In *Proceedings of the twelfth ACM international conference on web search and data mining*, pages 105–113.

Diederik P. Kingma and Jimmy Ba. 2014. Adam: A method for stochastic optimization. Cite arxiv:1412.6980Comment: Published as a conference paper at the 3rd International Conference for Learning Representations, San Diego, 2015.

Mike Lewis, Yinhan Liu, Naman Goyal, Marjan Ghazvininejad, Abdelrahman Mohamed, Omer Levy, Veselin Stoyanov, and Luke Zettlemoyer. 2020. BART: Denoising sequence-to-sequence pre-training for natural language generation, translation, and comprehension. In *Proceedings of the 58th Annual Meeting of the Association for Computational Linguistics*, pages 7871–7880, Online. Association for Computational Linguistics.

Weichen Li, Patrick Abels, Zahra Ahmadi, Sophie Burkhardt, Benjamin Schiller, Iryna Gurevych, and Stefan Kramer. 2021. Topic-guided knowledge graph construction for argument mining. In *2021 IEEE International Conference on Big Knowledge (ICBK)*, pages 315–322.

Juri Opitz, Philipp Heinisch, Philipp Wiesenbach, Philipp Cimiano, and Anette Frank. 2021. Explainable unsupervised argument similarity rating with Abstract Meaning Representation and conclusion generation. In *Proceedings of the 8th Workshop on Argument Mining*, pages 24–35, Punta Cana, Dominican Republic. Association for Computational Linguistics.

Xiaoman Pan, Kai Sun, Dian Yu, Jianshu Chen, Heng Ji, Claire Cardie, and Dong Yu. 2019. Improving question answering with external knowledge. In *Proceedings of the 2nd Workshop on Machine Reading for Question Answering*, pages 27–37, Hong Kong, China. Association for Computational Linguistics.

Debjit Paul, Juri Opitz, Maria Becker, Jonathan Kobbe, Graeme Hirst, and Anette Frank. 2020. Argumentative Relation Classification with Background Knowledge. *Computational Models of Argument*, pages 319–330. Publisher: IOS Press.

Jorge Pérez, Marcelo Arenas, and Claudio Gutierrez. 2009. Semantics and complexity of sparql. *ACM Transactions on Database Systems (TODS)*, 34(3):1–45.

Nils Reimers and Iryna Gurevych. 2019. Sentence-bert: Sentence embeddings using siamese bert-networks. *arXiv preprint arXiv:1908.10084*.

Ahmad Sakor, Kuldeep Singh, Anery Patel, and Maria-Esther Vidal. 2020. Falcon 2.0: An entity and relation linking tool over wikidata. In *Proceedings of the 29th ACM International Conference on Information & Knowledge Management*, pages 3141–3148.

Denny Vrandečić and Markus Krötzsch. 2014. Wikidata: a free collaborative knowledgebase. *Communications of the ACM*, 57(10):78–85.

Henning Wachsmuth, Nona Naderi, Yufang Hou, Yonatan Bilu, Vinodkumar Prabhakaran, Tim Alberdingk Thijm, Graeme Hirst, and Benno Stein. 2017. Computational argumentation quality assessment in natural language. In *Proceedings of the 15th Conference of the European Chapter of the Association for Computational Linguistics: Volume 1, Long Papers*, pages 176–187, Valencia, Spain. Association for Computational Linguistics.

Fangrong Wang, Alan Bundy, Xue Li, Ruiqi Zhu, Kwabena Nuamah, Lei Xu, Stefano Mauceri, and Jeff Z Pan. 2021. Lekg: A system for constructing knowledge graphs from log extraction. In *The 10th International Joint Conference on Knowledge Graphs*, pages 181–185.

Xiaoyan Wang, Pavan Kapanipathi, Ryan Musa, Mo Yu, Kartik Talamadupula, Ibrahim Abdelaziz, Maria Chang, Achille Fokoue, Bassem Makni, Nicholas Mattei, and Michael Witbrock. 2019. Improving Natural Language Inference Using External Knowledge in the Science Questions Domain. *Proceedings of the AAAI Conference on Artificial Intelligence*, 33(01):7208–7215. Number: 01.

Zikang Wang, Linjing Li, and Daniel Zeng. 2020. Knowledge-Enhanced Natural Language Inference Based on Knowledge Graphs. In *Proceedings of the 28th International Conference on Computational Linguistics*, pages 6498–6508, Barcelona, Spain (Online). International Committee on Computational Linguistics.

Adina Williams, Nikita Nangia, and Samuel Bowman. 2018. A broad-coverage challenge corpus for sentence understanding through inference. In *Proceedings of the 2018 Conference of the North American Chapter of the Association for Computational Linguistics: Human Language Technologies, Volume 1 (Long Papers)*, pages 1112–1122. Association for Computational Linguistics.

Michihiro Yasunaga, Hongyu Ren, Antoine Bosselut, Percy Liang, and Jure Leskovec. 2021. Qagnn: Reasoning with language models and knowledge graphs for question answering. *arXiv preprint arXiv:2104.06378*.

Wenpeng Yin, Jamaal Hay, and Dan Roth. 2019. Benchmarking zero-shot text classification: Datasets, evaluation and entailment approach. In *Proceedings of the 2019 Conference on Empirical Methods in Natural Language Processing and the 9th International Joint Conference on Natural Language Processing (EMNLP-IJCNLP)*, pages 3914–3923, Hong Kong, China. Association for Computational Linguistics.

Xia Zeng, Amani S Abumansour, and Arkaitz Zubiaga. 2021. Automated fact-checking: A survey. *Language and Linguistics Compass*, 15(10):e12438.

Ricky Zhu, Xue Li, Sylvia Wang, Alan Bundy, Jeff Z Pan, Kwabena Nuamah, Stefano Mauceri, and Lei Xu. 2022. Treat: Automated construction and maintenance of probabilistic knowledge bases from logs. In *The 8th Annual Conference on Machine Learning, Optimization and Data Science*.

Appendix

The KG Features

Several KG features not described in the main body of this paper were also tested in our experiments. We provide their definition here for the record.

- **Max_Dist**: the length of the longest KGP from any e_p to any e_c.

$$\mathbb{K}_{max} = \max_{e_p,\, e_c} \mathcal{L}_s(e_p, e_c) \quad (5)$$

- **Total_Dist**: the sum of all KGPs from premise entities to conclusion entities.

$$S(t, c) = \sum_{e_p, e_c} \mathcal{L}_s(e_p, e_c) \quad (6)$$

- **Minimal KGP (MKGP):** the shortest KGPs from one entity e_c to a set of entities $\mathbb{T}$.

$$\mathbb{P}_{min}(h, \mathbb{T}) = \min_{e_t, e_c} \mathcal{L}_s(e_p, e_c) \quad (7)$$

The **Dist_max** feature was useful but was not selected as one of the optimal features during grid-search. The **Dist_max** and **MKGP** features, on the other hand, proved unhelpful for this task.

KG Relations

A set of common logical relations are summarised in Table 6, where the last two are used to invalidate a KGP. Relations not included in the list are omitted when calculating the semantic length of a KGP.

ID	Label	Type
P31	instance of	$\mathbb{L}_1$
P279	subclass of	$\mathbb{L}_1$
P527	has part(s)	$\mathbb{L}_1$
P361	part of	$\mathbb{L}_1$
P463	member of	$\mathbb{L}_1$
P1269	facet of	$\mathbb{L}_1$
P355	has subsidiary	$\mathbb{L}_1$
P460	said to be the same as	$\mathbb{L}_1$
P642	of	$\mathbb{L}_1$
P1889	different from	$\mathbb{L}_2$
P461	opposite of	$\mathbb{L}_2$

Table 6: A set of logical relations wither their WikiData IDs and type, where $\mathbb{L}_1$ represents semantic similarity and $\mathbb{L}_2$ represents semantic distance.

Task B (Comparitive Predictions)

In Task B, two conclusions are given for a single premise and the objective is to decide whether the first conclusion is more, less, or equally valid/novel as as the second. In both these tasks the model should output two labels, one for validity and one for novelty.

We approached this task by using the best model trained on Task A to predict the probability of novelty and validity of both conclusions. We then assigned the conclusion with the highest probability of validity/novelty as that which is more valid/novel. The results are given in Table 7.

	Validity			**Novelty**		
	−1	**0**	**1**	**−1**	**0**	**1**
Precision	0.39	0.00	0.38	0.26	0.00	0.32
Recall	0.67	0.00	0.66	0.64	0.00	0.57
F1	0.49	0.00	0.48	0.37	0.00	0.41
	Both (Macro)					
Precision	0.07					
Recall	0.19					
F1	0.09					

Table 7: Results of our best model on Task B.

The results show that this simple approach to Task B fails to identify cases where the two conclusions are equally valid/novel (classes 0). This can be explained by the fact that the classifier outputs continuous probabilities, which span the entire 0 to 1 range. As such, requiring both probabilities to be equal for the two conclusions to be considered equally valid/movel is an excessively stringent requirement. A better approach might require the difference between the two probabilities not to exceed a given threshold. This threshold could for instance be found using the training set provided for Task B.

Argument Novelty and Validity Assessment via Multitask and Transfer Learning

Milad Alshomary
Paderborn University
milad.alshomary@upb.de

Maja Stahl
Paderborn University
maja.stahl@upb.de

Abstract

An argument is a constellation of premises reasoning towards a certain conclusion. The automatic generation of conclusions is becoming a very prominent task, raising the need for automatic measures to assess the quality of these generated conclusions. The SharedTask at the 9th Workshop on Argument Mining proposes a new task to assess the novelty and validity of a conclusion given a set of premises. In this paper, we present a multitask learning approach that transfers the knowledge learned from the natural language inference task to the tasks at hand. Evaluation results indicate the importance of both knowledge transfer and joint learning, placing our approach in the fifth place with strong results compared to baselines.

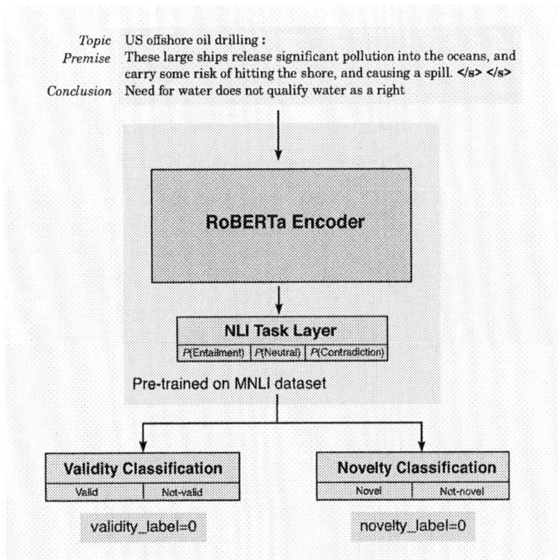

Figure 1: Our proposed model, which jointly models the validity and novelty assessment tasks, starts from a transformer-based model pre-trained on the natural language inference (NLI) task. First, we pass the input through the RoBERTa encoder. Then, the last hidden state of the encoder is projected into a probability distribution representing the NLI labels. Each classification head (novelty and validity) then learns to map this distribution into the corresponding labels.

1 Introduction

Conclusions are essential to understanding the reasoning behind their arguments. In daily life argumentation, argument conclusions are often left implicit (Alshomary et al., 2020) because they are easy to infer or for rhetorical reasons. While it is easy for humans to infer these conclusions, machines struggle with such a task. This phenomenon motivated a line of computational argumentation research to study the task of automatic generation of conclusions (Alshomary et al., 2020; Syed et al., 2021). Evaluating these approaches using traditional text generation measures like BLEU or ROUGE is not enough since multiple conclusions can be considered valid for a given argument. Additionally, one might desire specific criteria in a generated conclusion, like being informative (Syed et al., 2021).

In this regard, the SharedTask at the 9th Workshop on Argument Mining proposed two quality dimensions of argument conclusions to be assessed. The first is *validity*, defined as whether a given conclusion can be logically inferred from its premises. The second is *novelty*, assessing whether the conclusion goes beyond what is mentioned in the premises to provide novel insights. This paper describes our approach to the automatic assessment task of conclusion's validity and novelty.

We address the novelty and validity assessment tasks via a multitask learning approach, employing already acquired knowledge from the natural language inference task. In particular, the two assessed quality dimensions are orthogonal. That is, conclusions that can be easily inferred from their premises and hence valid are less likely to be novel. Similarly, the more novel a conclusion is, the harder to judge its validity. Accordingly, we believe that jointly modeling the two assessment tasks allows the model to exploit such dynamics. Moreover, the natural language inference task (NLI) is very simi-

Proceedings of the 9th Workshop on Argument Mining, co-located with the 29th International Conference on Computational Linguistics, pages 111–114
October 17, 2022.

lar and is widely studied (Wang et al., 2018). One can understand the entailment attribute between two sentences in the NLI task as a validity criterion. Hence, we start from a transformer-based model fine-tuned on the NLI task. As shown in Figure 1, this model consists of a transformer-based encoder and a classification head that predicts one of three labels, *entailment*, *contradiction*, *neutral*. We stack two classification heads on top of the model, one to predict novelty and the other for validity.

We evaluate our approach against the basic RoBERTa model trained on each task independently in our experiments. Results show the gain achieved from both the knowledge acquired from the NLI task as well as the joint learning of the two tasks. First, utilizing knowledge from the NLI task boosts the average F1-score from 0.09 to 0.15. Secondly, the joint learning of the two tasks further raises the average F1-score up to 0.42, placing our approach in the fifth place with strong competitive performance.[1]

2 Related Work

Conclusion inference is the task of generating a natural language conclusion given a set of premises. The generation of these conclusions is important for AI algorithms to understand the reasoning behind arguments. Hence, several works in computational argumentation addressed this task. Alshomary et al. (2020) reconstructed implicit conclusion targets from premises using triplet neural networks. Syed et al. (2021) studied the effectiveness of several transformer-based models on the conclusion generation across various corpora and evaluated the informativeness criteria of conclusions. Gurcke et al. (2021) automatically generated conclusions to then use them for argument quality assessment. Liu et al. (2021) worked on generating perspectives (conclusion) for news articles. (Becker et al., 2021) fine-tuned language models to generate implicit knowledge in sentences. In this work, the proposed task and approaches aim to study the quality of automatically generated conclusions along the validity and novelty dimensions.

Recent advances in natural language processing (NLP) have been driven by transfer learning, where knowledge on one task is used to learn another potentially relevant task. Indeed, it has been shown that language models trained on big corpora can excel in transferring such knowledge into downstream tasks in a zero-shot setting (Radford et al., 2019). Our proposed method uses knowledge learned the natural language inference (NLI) task (Liu et al., 2019) to solve the novelty and validity assessment tasks. Another promising learning paradigm is multitask learning (Zhang et al., 2022), in which two or more relevant tasks are learned in the same neural model, either in a soft or hard parameter sharing setting. Our approach models the validity and novelty tasks jointly in one model with hard parameter sharing.

3 Task and Data

In the SharedTask at the 9th Workshop on Argument Mining, the organizers defined the validity and novelty criteria of argument conclusions as follows:[2]

- *Validity*: The conclusion can be logically inferred from the premise.
- *Novelty*: The conclusion provides novel premise-related content and/or combines the content of the premises in a way that goes beyond what is stated in the premises.

According to these definitions, the organizers proposed two settings for this SharedTask. The first is, given a set of premises in natural language text and a corresponding conclusion, predict two scores that reflect the conclusion's novelty and validity (Subtask A). In the second Subtask, two conclusions are provided, and the task is to rank them according to their novelty and validity (Subtask B). This paper tackles Subtask A, which is the binary classification of validity and novelty dimensions.

The dataset provided by the organizers consists of premises and conclusions, which they manually annotated for validity and novelty dimensions. Additionally, the organizers include the topic of the debate and the confidence scores for the two labels. The data also contained borderline cases for both target dimensions, which are considered to be *somewhat* novel or valid. We excluded those examples from the training and validation sets, as suggested by the organizers. We ended up with 721 training and 199 development examples for validity and 718 training and 200 development examples

[1] Our model and experiments are publicly available under `https://github.com/MiladAlshomary/ArgsValidNovelTask`

[2] `https://phhei.github.io/ArgsValidNovel/`, last accessed: 2022-08-25.

Split	Novel? Yes	Novel? No	Novel? All	Valid? Yes	Valid? No	Valid? All
Train	123	595	718	401	320	721
Validation	82	118	200	125	74	199
Test	226	294	520	314	206	520

Table 1: Class distribution for both Novelty and Validity classes in each of the data split.

Model	Validity	Novelty	ValNov
RoBERTa	0.28	0.36	0.09
NLI-based RoBERTa	0.52	0.35	0.15
NLI-based Multitask	**0.71**	**0.60**	**0.42**

Table 2: Macro F1-scores for the validity and novelty tasks, as well as the combined one (ValNov) computed for our approach (NLI-based Multitask) and its baselines on the test set.

for novelty. The test set has a size of 520 instances. Table 1 shows the distribution of each label for all the data splits. We notice that the data is imbalanced in terms of novelty class. In our experiments, we report our approach's effectiveness also when trained on a training split that is balanced through oversampling.

4 Approach

As mentioned, our approach to the Subtask A is to jointly learn the two assessment tasks (*novelty* and *validity*), starting from knowledge acquired by a model trained on the NLI task (Wang et al., 2018). The motivation for our choice is two folds. On the one hand, we argue that the novelty and validity dimensions correlate such that conclusions that are easily inferred to be valid are likely not that novel. Similarly, the more novel a conclusion is, the harder to judge its validity. On the other hand, we see similarities to the natural language inference task. If an NLI model deemed the conclusion to be entailed from its premises, then the conclusion is likely valid but probably not novel.

In particular, we start from a transformer-based model fine-tuned on the NLI task. As shown in Figure 1, this model consists of a transformer-based encoder and a classification head that predicts one of three labels, *entailment, contradiction, neutral*. The input to our model is a concatenation of the topic, premise, and conclusion. We pass the input through the RoBERTa encoder to obtain the final hidden state, which is passed through the classification layer to obtain a probability distribution over the three NLI labels. We stack two classification heads on top of the model to project this distribution into the corresponding novelty and validity labels. During training, one can compute an average error with respect to the two tasks at each optimization step or consider the error subject to one task at a time. For simplicity, we chose the second option since the framework we build upon supports only this option (details in Sections 5). Although the weights are not updated according to an average loss of the two tasks, the overall training will drive the weights into an area optimal for both tasks.

5 Experiments

In our experiments, we use the RoBERTa model (Liu et al., 2019) fine-tuned on the Multi-Genre Natural Language Inference dataset (MNLI) made public by Williams et al. (2018). For each task, we train a model considering it the main task and the other as an auxiliary one with a loss discounted by a factor of α. We explored a range of α values and chose the ones that lead to the best F1-score on the validation set, that is, 0.9 and 0.7 for novelty and validity, respectively. Additionally, we explored different learning rates for each of the models independently and chose a learning rate of $2e^{-5}$ and $5e^{-6}$ for the novelty and validity models, respectively. We train both models for ten epochs with a batch size of 8. We compare our approach against the RoBERTa model without NLI fine-tuning and once with NLI fine-tuning. Both trained independently on each task. As mentioned in Section 3, the training data is imbalanced along the novelty label. To address this problem, we perform oversampling in which we randomly replicate instances of the class novel to reach a balanced situation. We then train our model and the baselines on it. Our model is built on top of the multitask learning framework made publicly available under `https://multi-task-nlp.readthedocs.io/en/latest/`.

Table 2 shows the F1-score achieved by our approach (NLI-based Multitask) and its baselines computed for the novelty and validity tasks, and the combined task on the test set [3]. We can see that using knowledge from the NLI task boosts the effectiveness of RoBERTa on the validity task

[3]Reported results were computed after the SharedTask deadline when the test set was made publicly available. Wrong prediction file was originally submitted before the deadline, however the approach and training procedure are the same.

Model	Validity	Novelty	ValNov
RoBERTa	0.28	0.52	0.13
NLI-based RoBERTa	0.52	**0.64**	**0.33**
NLI-based Multitask	**0.71**	0.46	0.32

Table 3: Macro F1-scores for the validity and novelty tasks, as well as the combined one (ValNov) computed for our approach (NLI-based Multitask) and its baselines on the test set when trained on the over sampled training split.

from 0.28 to 0.52. Moreover, modeling novelty and validity tasks jointly boost the performance to reach 0.71 and 0.60 F1-score on the validity and novelty tasks, respectively. The combined F1-score recognizes instances as correctly predicted only if validity and novelty are both correctly predicted. Among evaluated baselines in this paper, our model achieves the best combined F1-score of 0.42.

From Table 3, we can see that when training the models on the oversampled training set, we observe a boost in performance for novelty for both the normal and NLI-based RoBERTa models. On the contrary, the effectiveness of our multitask learning approach got worse when we performed the oversampling. However, the overall performance of our approach still improves over the baselines when oversampling. Overall, the best performing model in terms of the combined F1-score is achieved by our model trained on the original data.

6 Conclusion

In this paper we described our approach proposed for the SharedTask at the 9th Workshop on Argument Mining for assessing the validity and novelty of argument conclusions. Our approach jointly models the two binary tasks of novelty and validity making use of knowledge acquired from the natural language inference task. Experimental results, shows the gain achieved from both transferring knowledge from the NLI, as well as the joint modeling of the two tasks.

References

Milad Alshomary, Shahbaz Syed, Martin Potthast, and Henning Wachsmuth. 2020. Target inference in argument conclusion generation. In *Proceedings of the 58th Annual Meeting of the Association for Computational Linguistics*, pages 4334–4345, Online. Association for Computational Linguistics.

Maria Becker, Siting Liang, and Anette Frank. 2021. Reconstructing implicit knowledge with language models. In *Proceedings of Deep Learning Inside Out (DeeLIO): The 2nd Workshop on Knowledge Extraction and Integration for Deep Learning Architectures*, pages 11–24.

Timon Gurcke, Milad Alshomary, and Henning Wachsmuth. 2021. Assessing the sufficiency of arguments through conclusion generation. In *Proceedings of the 8th Workshop on Argument Mining*, pages 67–77, Punta Cana, Dominican Republic. Association for Computational Linguistics.

Siyi Liu, Sihao Chen, Xander Uyttendaele, and Dan Roth. 2021. Multioped: A corpus of multi-perspective news editorials. In *Proceedings of the 2021 Conference of the North American Chapter of the Association for Computational Linguistics: Human Language Technologies*, pages 4345–4361.

Xiaodong Liu, Pengcheng He, Weizhu Chen, and Jianfeng Gao. 2019. Multi-task deep neural networks for natural language understanding. *arXiv preprint arXiv:1901.11504*.

Alec Radford, Jeffrey Wu, Rewon Child, David Luan, Dario Amodei, Ilya Sutskever, et al. 2019. Language models are unsupervised multitask learners.

Shahbaz Syed, Khalid Al Khatib, Milad Alshomary, Henning Wachsmuth, and Martin Potthast. 2021. Generating informative conclusions for argumentative texts. In *Findings of the Association for Computational Linguistics: ACL-IJCNLP 2021*, pages 3482–3493.

Alex Wang, Amanpreet Singh, Julian Michael, Felix Hill, Omer Levy, and Samuel Bowman. 2018. Glue: A multi-task benchmark and analysis platform for natural language understanding. In *Proceedings of the 2018 EMNLP Workshop BlackboxNLP: Analyzing and Interpreting Neural Networks for NLP*, pages 353–355.

Adina Williams, Nikita Nangia, and Samuel Bowman. 2018. A broad-coverage challenge corpus for sentence understanding through inference. In *Proceedings of the 2018 Conference of the North American Chapter of the Association for Computational Linguistics: Human Language Technologies, Volume 1 (Long Papers)*, pages 1112–1122. Association for Computational Linguistics.

Zhihan Zhang, Wenhao Yu, Mengxia Yu, Zhichun Guo, and Meng Jiang. 2022. A survey of multi-task learning in natural language processing: Regarding task relatedness and training methods. *arXiv preprint arXiv:2204.03508*.

Is Your Perspective Also My Perspective? Enriching Prediction with Subjectivity

Julia Romberg
Department of Social Sciences
Heinrich Heine University Düsseldorf, Germany
julia.romberg@hhu.de

Abstract

Although argumentation can be highly subjective, the common practice with supervised machine learning is to construct and learn from an aggregated ground truth formed from individual judgments by majority voting, averaging, or adjudication. This approach leads to a neglect of individual, but potentially important perspectives and in many cases cannot do justice to the subjective character of the tasks. One solution to this shortcoming are multi-perspective approaches, which have received very little attention in the field of argument mining so far.

In this work we present *PerspectifyMe*, a method to incorporate perspectivism by enriching a task with subjectivity information from the data annotation process. We exemplify our approach with the use case of classifying argument concreteness, and provide first promising results for the recently published CIMT PartEval Argument Concreteness Corpus.

1 Introduction

The analysis of arguments and especially their properties is challenging and often subjective, which renders the creation of suitable language resources for argument mining difficult (Stab and Gurevych, 2014; Lindahl et al., 2019). Uniform annotation often requires intensive training, and this costly approach has been shown to regularly result in at most moderate agreement among annotators (Aharoni et al., 2014; Rinott et al., 2015; Habernal and Gurevych, 2017; Shnarch et al., 2018). Alternative approaches such as crowd-sourcing share this problem, especially for demanding tasks like argument quality (Toledo et al., 2019).

Although the lack of consensus might clearly indicate that the annotation task is either ambiguous (Artstein and Poesio, 2008), too complex (Aroyo and Welty, 2015), or influenced by variables such as demographics and individual bias (Sap et al., 2022; Biester et al., 2022), the established procedure is to aggregate the individual judgments into a single ground truth at the end of the annotation process (by majority vote, averaging, or adjudication).

Learning from aggregated ground truth has several drawbacks. Minority voices are ignored, however valuable they may be, and only those in line with the mainstream are heeded (Noble, 2012). This rises also a fairness concern, as certain sociodemographic groups and their perspectives may be underrepresented (Prabhakaran et al., 2021). Finally, it is questionable whether the assumption of a single truth, i.e., that there is only one correct label for an example, holds at all for subjective tasks (Ovesdotter Alm, 2011; Aroyo and Welty, 2015).

Therefore, the question of multi-perspective approaches arises (Abercrombie et al., 2022). Basile et al. (2021) introduced the paradigm of *data perspectivism* in order to "integrate the opinions and perspectives of the human subjects involved in the knowledge representation step of ML processes". One example for perspectivist data is argumentation (Hautli-Janisz et al., 2022; Romberg et al., 2022b).

However, many popular algorithms require a single ground truth to which the model can adapt. In this paper, (i) we thus introduce a method that combines collaborative and subjective viewpoints by complementing an aggregated label with a subjectivity score. More specifically, *PerspectifyMe* proposes to add the prediction of how perspectivist an input is as an additional sub-task. Providing this information can for example help a human decide when to rely on their own perspective. (ii) To exemplify our approach, we draw on a recently published perspectivist dataset for argument concreteness in public participation processes (Romberg et al., 2022b). We provide several baselines based on our proposed method for this subjective task. While these are certainly extendable, they already show promising results for automatic classification by concreteness. (iii) To the best of our knowledge, we are the first to automatically classify arguments

Proceedings of the 9th Workshop on Argument Mining, co-located with the 29th International Conference on Computational Linguistics, pages 115–125
October 17, 2022.

in an explicitely perspectivist manner.

2 Related Work

Basile et al. (2021) provide a nice summarization of the previous work towards perspectivist machine learning, dividing the field in two groups.

The first aims at building unified ground labels that involve perspectivism by either only keeping instances on which a statistically significant majority agrees (Cabitza et al., 2020), by computing a weighting according to annotator reliability (Heinecke and Reyzin, 2019; Cabitza et al., 2020; Hovy et al., 2013), by replicating or weighting instances using provided labels or disagreement measures (Plank et al., 2014; Akhtar et al., 2019), or by participatory consensus building (Chang et al., 2017; Schaekermann et al., 2018).

The second group incorporates the perspectivism into the core machine learning workflow by either training an ensemble of models that rely on different ground truths (Akhtar et al., 2020; Campagner et al., 2021), by soft loss learning (Plank et al., 2014; Uma et al., 2020; Campagner et al., 2021), or by utilizing multi-task learning (Cohn and Specia, 2013; Guan et al., 2018; Sudre et al., 2019; Fornaciari et al., 2021; Davani et al., 2022).

Our approach ties into the latter idea by transforming the original problem into multiple subtasks. However, multi-task learning approaches for multi-perspectivist tasks have primarily aimed at improving model performance. To do so, the aggregated ground truth is learned along with the distribution of individual labels. Instead, we focus on outputting an indication of how perspectivist the model predictions are (namely, by adding a subjectivity score) to help interpret the results.

The only previous studies that specifically address argument mining are, to the best of our knowledge, two recently published non-aggregated datasets: QT30nonaggr (Hautli-Janisz et al., 2022) and the CIMT PartEval Argument Concreteness Corpus (Romberg et al., 2022b).

3 Use Case: Argument Concreteness in Public Participation

Public participation is a means regularly used by democratic authorities to involve citizens in policy-making processes (Dryzek et al., 2019). The manual evaluation workflow often includes reading the contributions, detecting duplicates, identifying arguments and opinions, and thematically clustering content before drawing conclusions from the input (Romberg and Escher, 2022).

One solution to reduce the workload of human evaluators is machine learning (OECD, 2003). Although there is a general consensus that such important democratic processes cannot be fully automated, automating sub-tasks such as topic classification or argument detection and analysis can support the evaluation.

Argument Mining for public participation has received considerable attention (Kwon et al., 2007; Liebeck et al., 2016; Lawrence et al., 2017; Park and Cardie, 2018; Romberg and Conrad, 2021). While works such as Park and Cardie (2014) and Niculae et al. (2017) have already addressed the evidence and verifiability of propositions, there has been no attempt to automatically classify their concreteness. Predicting the concreteness of propositions can assist a human analyst to speed up the evaluation by ranking them, since less concrete ideas tend to be more laborious to evaluate (Romberg et al., 2022b).

The CIMT PartEval Argument Concreteness Corpus (Romberg et al., 2022a) provides argumentative text units (ATU) in German extracted from mobility-related public participation processes. Each ATU consists of one to several sentences, consecutive in the original document, and a tag that describes the argumentative function (*major positions*: proposed courses of action and policy options or *premises*: attacking/supporting reasons). In total, the dataset contains $1,127$ ATUs, 614 of which are major positions and 513 are premises.

These ATUs have been categorised into three different degrees of concreteness:

- ATUs of **high concreteness** contain comprehensive details that describe the "what", "how", and "where".
- ATUs of **intermediate concreteness** contain only partial specification of the "what", "how" and "where". There is room for interpretation in inferring specific actions (major positions) or in evaluating the actual reasons (premises).
- ATUs of **low concreteness** contain no detailed information of the "what", "how" and "where". A variety of measures could be derived and reasons remain vague.

Table 1 illustrates the three types to provide a better understanding of the dataset. Example A is a major position unit of high concreteness: it is clear what action is desired (protective cycle lanes next

Ex.	Unit text	Unit type	Concreteness
A	If the parking spaces along Friedrich-Breuer-Straße were removed, there would be enough space for protective cycle lanes next to the rails.	major position	high
B	The connection to the centre of Beuel through Obere Wilhelmsstraße is also not very pleasant to drive.	premise	intermediate
C	Rules for cycle paths	major position	low

Table 1: Examples of argumentative text units with argument types and concreteness ratings from the CIMT PartEval Argument Concreteness Corpus. To assist readers understand the content, the texts have been translated into English. (The examples presented here are cases in which the annotators were in complete agreement on the coding of concreteness.)

to the rails), where it is to be implemented (along Friedrich-Breuer-Straße) and how (free space by parking space removal). The premise unit in example B is of intermediate concreteness: it is clear, what the issue is and where (connection through Obere Wilhelmsstraße not very pleasant to drive). However, it remains unclear what makes driving through unpleasant. Example C shows a major position unit of low concreteness: the claim is very general and does not refer to specific locations, nor is it more specific about what rules are required.

The annotation of the data was performed by five coders. While finalizing the annotation guidelines, the coders annotated a selection of contributions, and inconsistencies were discussed in a group with the coders and two process supervisors. The guidelines were adjusted and the coders trained to the point where it became apparent that the divergent annotations were different perspectives rather than incorrect coding: In the discussion, the different coders were able to argue convincingly for their stance. Krippendorff's α_w (Krippendorff, 2013) of 0.46 confirms that the codings, although subjective, are not arbitrary.

4 PerspectifyMe

Previous work has incorporated perspectivism through distributions over individual labels. However, such distributions may be of limited use when provided to a human as a direct output, e.g. in human-machine interactions. In particular, providing such a diversity of perspectives that might apply (from the annotators' point of view - not necessarily from the point of view of the particular user) can be too complex and potentially confusing.

For items that trigger a subjective perception, it might make more sense (e.g., in a use case like ours) to inform the user about this and let them decide whether to make their own assessment or to go along with the collaborative opinion.

Therefore, we propose to enrich model predictions for subjective supervised machine learning tasks with the provision of a subjectivity score.

Task	Label	Support
Sub-Task $\mathcal{T}_H$: Concreteness	High	709 (62.9%)
	Intermediate	336 (29.8%)
	Low	82 (7.3%)
Sub-Task $\mathcal{T}_S$: Subjectivity	Objective	478 (42.4%)
	Rather objective	244 (21.7%)
	Rather subjective	275 (24.4%)
	Subjective	130 (11.5%)

Table 2: Overview of the label distributions for the tasks.

4.1 General Description

Given a task $\mathcal{T}$, we assume that there are both objective and subjective items in a corresponding dataset. This means that part of the dataset is annotated in a very consistent way, while the rest has elicited different views among coders. Our goal is then to predict a so-called hard label (aggregated by some method), and jointly inform on items for which there might be multiple correct outputs, depending on the perspective. We thus propose *PerspectifyMe*, a method to introduce perspectivism into the machine learning workflow by translating $\mathcal{T}$ into two sub-tasks $\mathcal{T}_\mathcal{H}$ and $\mathcal{T}_\mathcal{S}$. $\mathcal{T}_\mathcal{H}$ refers to the original prediction task using hard-labels as ground truth. $\mathcal{T}_\mathcal{S}$ refers to an artificial task of predicting the subjectivity of the input using a subjectivity score.

4.2 Application to Our Use Case

The perspectivity of judging argument concreteness is reflected in the CIMT PartEval Argument Concreteness Corpus through five single annotations. Following the previously introduced method, we conducted two transformation steps to yield the target variables for $\mathcal{T}_\mathcal{H}$ and $\mathcal{T}_\mathcal{S}$.

Concreteness Score We first built an aggregated ground truth by calculating the average concreteness per unit. For this, we mapped the categorical labels to numerical values (high: 3, intermediate: 2, low: 1) and averaged them. To retain the origi-

		Concreteness		Subjectivity (4-class)		Subjectivity (2-class)	
		Macro-F_1	Accuracy	Macro-F_1	Accuracy	Macro-F_1	Accuracy
joint	Majority Baseline	0.26	0.63	0.15	0.42	0.39	0.64
	LR (length)	0.54 ± 0.06	0.74 ± 0.03	0.30 ± 0.02	$\mathbf{0.52} \pm 0.03$	0.68 ± 0.03	0.72 ± 0.02
	LR (bow)	0.53 ± 0.04	0.75 ± 0.02	0.33 ± 0.05	0.50 ± 0.03	0.69 ± 0.03	0.71 ± 0.03
	LR (length+bow)	0.54 ± 0.04	0.74 ± 0.03	0.34 ± 0.05	0.50 ± 0.04	0.69 ± 0.03	0.72 ± 0.03
	SVM (length)	0.59 ± 0.04	0.71 ± 0.02	0.34 ± 0.03	0.48 ± 0.03	0.70 ± 0.02	0.72 ± 0.02
	SVM (bow)	0.59 ± 0.04	0.74 ± 0.03	0.37 ± 0.05	0.49 ± 0.04	0.69 ± 0.02	0.71 ± 0.03
	SVM (length+bow)	0.62 ± 0.05	0.75 ± 0.03	0.37 ± 0.03	0.50 ± 0.03	0.70 ± 0.03	0.72 ± 0.02
	BERT	$\mathbf{0.67} \pm 0.05$	$\mathbf{0.79} \pm 0.02$	$\mathbf{0.42} \pm 0.04$	$\mathbf{0.52} \pm 0.03$	$\mathbf{0.72} \pm 0.02$	$\mathbf{0.74} \pm 0.02$
major position	Majority Baseline	0.25	0.60	0.14	0.40	0.39	0.64
	LR (length)	0.49 ± 0.06	0.70 ± 0.04	0.27 ± 0.04	0.46 ± 0.04	0.59 ± 0.11	0.68 ± 0.04
	LR (bow)	0.52 ± 0.06	0.69 ± 0.03	0.28 ± 0.06	0.42 ± 0.04	0.60 ± 0.10	0.67 ± 0.04
	LR (length+bow)	0.52 ± 0.06	0.69 ± 0.04	0.31 ± 0.06	0.44 ± 0.04	0.63 ± 0.10	0.68 ± 0.05
	SVM (length)	0.56 ± 0.04	0.69 ± 0.04	0.33 ± 0.04	0.44 ± 0.04	0.64 ± 0.05	0.67 ± 0.04
	SVM (bow)	0.53 ± 0.07	0.67 ± 0.04	0.28 ± 0.08	0.42 ± 0.04	0.63 ± 0.09	0.67 ± 0.06
	SVM (length+bow)	0.55 ± 0.06	0.70 ± 0.04	0.33 ± 0.06	0.44 ± 0.04	0.64 ± 0.06	0.68 ± 0.04
	BERT	$\mathbf{0.62} \pm 0.07$	$\mathbf{0.76} \pm 0.04$	$\mathbf{0.37} \pm 0.06$	$\mathbf{0.47} \pm 0.05$	$\mathbf{0.68} \pm 0.06$	$\mathbf{0.71} \pm 0.05$
premise	Majority Baseline	0.26	0.65	0.15	0.44	0.39	0.64
	LR (length)	0.57 ± 0.07	0.80 ± 0.02	0.32 ± 0.02	$\mathbf{0.56} \pm 0.04$	$\mathbf{0.73} \pm 0.05$	0.75 ± 0.04
	LR (bow)	0.52 ± 0.06	0.69 ± 0.03	0.34 ± 0.05	0.54 ± 0.05	0.71 ± 0.03	0.74 ± 0.03
	LR (length+bow)	0.61 ± 0.08	0.80 ± 0.03	0.35 ± 0.04	0.55 ± 0.04	0.72 ± 0.04	0.74 ± 0.04
	SVM (length)	0.60 ± 0.05	0.75 ± 0.03	0.33 ± 0.04	0.48 ± 0.05	0.72 ± 0.04	0.74 ± 0.04
	SVM (bow)	0.67 ± 0.05	0.79 ± 0.03	0.36 ± 0.05	0.53 ± 0.05	0.72 ± 0.04	0.74 ± 0.04
	SVM (length+bow)	$\mathbf{0.68} \pm 0.07$	0.81 ± 0.03	0.38 ± 0.07	0.53 ± 0.07	0.71 ± 0.04	0.74 ± 0.04
	BERT	$\mathbf{0.68} \pm 0.06$	$\mathbf{0.82} \pm 0.03$	$\mathbf{0.42} \pm 0.05$	$\mathbf{0.56} \pm 0.04$	$\mathbf{0.73} \pm 0.04$	$\mathbf{0.76} \pm 0.04$

Table 3: Excerpt from the results for the classification of ATUs according to concreteness and subjectivity.

nal concreteness scale, the rounded average scores were remapped to the original categories.

Subjectivity Score For each unit, we calculated the pairwise L1 distance of the numerical labels and summed them up to calculate an overall distance. We translated the resulting distances into a four-category and a two-category scheme of subjectivity (for more details see Appendix A.1).

Table 2 provides an overview of the resulting sub-tasks. While highly concrete ATUs predominate, low concreteness is rare. Over sixty percent of the units elicited a fairly objective perception, a large proportion of which were even coded in a completely consistent manner. At the same time, there is a notable proportion of perspectivist ATUs.

5 Experiments

5.1 Classification Baselines

We evaluate several classification baselines: The traditional approaches logistic regression (LR), support vector machines (SVM), and random forests (RF) were combined with text length (in tokens) and a bag-of-words as features. The language model BERT was initialized with a case-sensitive base model for German (110M parameters) [1]. We fitted separate classifiers for the two sub-tasks.

5.2 Experimental Setup

We evaluated model performance on the dataset with and without respect to the types of arguments (major position/premise vs. joint) to see whether there are differences in predicting concreteness and subjectivity. To obtain reliable results, we used a repeated 5-fold cross-validation setup (Krstajic et al., 2014) (10 repetitions) and kept 10% for validation (i.e. splitting the dataset each time in 70/10/20 for train/val/test). The hyperparameters were tuned with a grid search in each fold (an overview of the search space is given in Appendix A.2). F_1 and accuracy are the evaluation scores.[2]

5.3 Results

Table 3 shows a selection of the results for the classification of ATUs. A complete overview, including class scores, can be found in Appendix A.3.

When predicting degrees of concreteness, BERT achieved the best results (F_1 as well as accuracy). Looking at the other models, it turned out that simple length was already a good indicator for concreteness. When analyzing correlation effects with Spearman's rank correlation coefficient this finding was supported by a strong correlation of the target variables with the text length (concreteness: $\rho = 0.657$, subjectivity: $\rho = -0.525$). Adding

[1] https://huggingface.co/bert-base-german-cased

[2] Code available at github.com/juliaromberg/ArgMining2022

		rather objective	rather subjective
Macro-F_1	LR (length)	0.50 ± 0.08	0.45 ± 0.06
	LR (bow)	0.49 ± 0.05	0.44 ± 0.05
	LR (length+bow)	0.51 ± 0.07	0.45 ± 0.05
	SVM (length)	0.64 ± 0.06	0.46 ± 0.05
	SVM (bow)	0.61 ± 0.06	0.47 ± 0.05
	SVM (length+bow)	0.64 ± 0.07	0.49 ± 0.07
	BERT	0.70 ± 0.06	0.51 ± 0.07
Accuracy	LR (length)	0.80 ± 0.03	0.62 ± 0.05
	LR (bow)	0.82 ± 0.03	0.62 ± 0.05
	LR (length+bow)	0.81 ± 0.03	0.62 ± 0.05
	SVM (length)	0.84 ± 0.04	0.49 ± 0.05
	SVM (bow)	0.83 ± 0.03	0.57 ± 0.05
	SVM (length+bow)	0.84 ± 0.03	0.57 ± 0.07
	BERT	0.88 ± 0.02	0.63 ± 0.06

Table 4: Differences in predictions (joint classification) between rather objective and rather subjective ATUs.

semantic information by bag-of-words could nevertheless mostly improve prediction, especially for SVM and with respect to premises.

We further looked at predicting the subjectivity of ATUs and considered two granularities. While in the 2-class case all classifiers scored rather similar in the joint evaluation, in the 4-class case the differences became more obvious: In terms of F_1 score, BERT can outperform the other classifiers. Overall, it appears that our baseline models can already make some meaningful predictions for the complex task of whether an ATU triggers a subjective perception regarding its concreteness.

As for the different types of arguments, it shows that predicting concreteness and subjectivity is more difficult for major positions than for premises.

To gain further insight into the relationship between the task at hand and subjectivity, we examined the differences in the models' predictions of concreteness between "rather objective" and "rather subjective" ATUs (see Table 4). We found that all models did significantly better with the objective ATUs than with the subjective ones. We therefore hypothesize that the difficulty of assigning a standardized value to subjective ATUs is also shared by machine learning models due to the perspectivist scope.

6 Discussion

The evaluation of public participation can be supported by machine learning in a human-machine interaction. Not only machine prediction, but also pointing out cases where the user might potentially disagree can help with good evaluation practice. Perspectives can differ for a variety of reasons. First, it is due to the task itself, which is subjective. In addition, personal biases of the analyst may also contribute, such as their professional background (e.g., in our application case, whether they studied urban planning or administrative sciences). Furthermore, process-related demands on the evaluation may require the analyst to adjust their view. All these factors argue for a perspectivist approach.

As exemplified, our method can be integrated into workflows by adding a model for the sub-task of predicting subjectivity. While $\mathcal{T}_H$ reflects the prevailing opinion of the crowd, $\mathcal{T}_S$ can indicate how different coders' perceptions were when rating the unit - a valuable piece of information that is lost in non-perspectivist approaches. However, a potential barrier to applying our method to further use cases is the need for a non-aggregated dataset. The publication of annotations on an individual level is not yet common (Basile et al., 2021).

We found that objective ATUs (regarding their concreteness) can already be filtered out with an F_1 score between 0.73 and 0.80, depending on the granularity level (cf. Table 7 in Appendix A.3). However, the distinction between different degrees of subjectivity yielded weak results. Further research is needed to determine whether the problem lies in the task of predicting subjectivity, insufficient classification models, the dataset itself, or the transfer of the non-aggregated annotations to the labels for $\mathcal{H}_S$.

Concerning the original task of classifying the concreteness of arguments, the degree of concreteness (hard label) could be predicted with an accuracy of 0.80 and an F_1 of 0.67, which can already be helpful for supporting the manual evaluation of public participation processes.

7 Conclusion & Future Work

We introduced PerspectifyMe, a simple method to include perspectivism in machine learning workflows. Using argument concreteness as an example, we have shown that our baseline approaches can assess the subjective perception of ATUs.

In future work, we plan to apply advanced multitask learning models as previous work has shown that they can lead to an increase in performance (Davani et al., 2022). Furthermore, we have tailored the transformation of the spectrum of annotations into a subjectivity score specific to the use case at hand. It would be of great interest to develop a more general (task-independent) algorithm.

Acknowledgements

Thanks to the anonymous reviewers for their helpful comments. This publication is based on research in the project CIMT/Partizipationsnutzen, which is funded by the Federal Ministry of Education and Research of Germany as part of its Social-Ecological Research funding priority, funding no. 01UU1904. Responsibility for the content of this publication lies with the author.

References

Gavin Abercrombie, Valerio Basile, Sara Tonelli, Verena Rieser, and Alexandra Uma, editors. 2022. *Proceedings of the 1st Workshop on Perspectivist Approaches to NLP @LREC2022*. European Language Resources Association, Marseille, France.

Ehud Aharoni, Anatoly Polnarov, Tamar Lavee, Daniel Hershcovich, Ran Levy, Ruty Rinott, Dan Gutfreund, and Noam Slonim. 2014. A benchmark dataset for automatic detection of claims and evidence in the context of controversial topics. In *Proceedings of the First Workshop on Argumentation Mining*, pages 64–68, Baltimore, Maryland. Association for Computational Linguistics.

Sohail Akhtar, Valerio Basile, and Viviana Patti. 2019. A new measure of polarization in the annotation of hate speech. In *AI*IA 2019 – Advances in Artificial Intelligence*, pages 588–603, Cham. Springer International Publishing.

Sohail Akhtar, Valerio Basile, and Viviana Patti. 2020. Modeling annotator perspective and polarized opinions to improve hate speech detection. *Proceedings of the AAAI Conference on Human Computation and Crowdsourcing*, 8(1):151–154.

Lora Aroyo and Chris Welty. 2015. Truth is a lie: Crowd truth and the seven myths of human annotation. *AI Magazine*, 36(1):15–24.

Ron Artstein and Massimo Poesio. 2008. Inter-Coder Agreement for Computational Linguistics. *Computational Linguistics*, 34(4):555–596.

Valerio Basile, Federico Cabitza, Andrea Campagner, and Michael Fell. 2021. Toward a perspectivist turn in ground truthing for predictive computing. *arXiv preprint arXiv:2109.04270*.

Laura Biester, Vanita Sharma, Ashkan Kazemi, Naihao Deng, Steven Wilson, and Rada Mihalcea. 2022. Analyzing the effects of annotator gender across nlp tasks. In *Proceedings of the 1st Workshop on Perspectivist Approaches to NLP @LREC2022*, pages 10–19, Marseille, France. European Language Resources Association.

Federico Cabitza, Andrea Campagner, and Luca Maria Sconfienza. 2020. As if sand were stone. new concepts and metrics to probe the ground on which to build trustable ai. *BMC Medical Informatics and Decision Making*, 20(1):1–21.

Andrea Campagner, Davide Ciucci, Carl-Magnus Svensson, Marc Thilo Figge, and Federico Cabitza. 2021. Ground truthing from multi-rater labeling with three-way decision and possibility theory. *Information Sciences*, 545:771–790.

Joseph Chee Chang, Saleema Amershi, and Ece Kamar. 2017. Revolt: Collaborative crowdsourcing for labeling machine learning datasets. In *Proceedings of the 2017 CHI Conference on Human Factors in Computing Systems*, CHI '17, page 2334–2346, New York, NY, USA. Association for Computing Machinery.

Trevor Cohn and Lucia Specia. 2013. Modelling annotator bias with multi-task Gaussian processes: An application to machine translation quality estimation. In *Proceedings of the 51st Annual Meeting of the Association for Computational Linguistics (Volume 1: Long Papers)*, pages 32–42, Sofia, Bulgaria. Association for Computational Linguistics.

Aida Mostafazadeh Davani, Mark Díaz, and Vinodkumar Prabhakaran. 2022. Dealing with disagreements: Looking beyond the majority vote in subjective annotations. *Transactions of the Association for Computational Linguistics*, 10:92–110.

John S. Dryzek, André Bächtiger, Simone Chambers, Joshua Cohen, James N. Druckman, Andrea Felicetti, James S. Fishkin, David M. Farrell, Archon Fung, Amy Gutmann, Hélène Landemore, Jane Mansbridge, Sofie Marien, Michael A. Neblo, Simon Niemeyer, Maija Setälä, Rune Slothuus, Jane Suiter, Dennis Thompson, and Mark E. Warren. 2019. The crisis of democracy and the science of deliberation. *Science*, 363(6432):1144–1146.

Tommaso Fornaciari, Alexandra Uma, Silviu Paun, Barbara Plank, Dirk Hovy, and Massimo Poesio. 2021. Beyond black & white: Leveraging annotator disagreement via soft-label multi-task learning. In *Proceedings of the 2021 Conference of the North American Chapter of the Association for Computational Linguistics: Human Language Technologies*, pages 2591–2597, Online. Association for Computational Linguistics.

Melody Guan, Varun Gulshan, Andrew Dai, and Geoffrey Hinton. 2018. Who said what: Modeling individual labelers improves classification. *Proceedings of the AAAI Conference on Artificial Intelligence*, 32(1).

Ivan Habernal and Iryna Gurevych. 2017. Argumentation mining in user-generated web discourse. *Computational Linguistics*, 43(1):125–179.

Annette Hautli-Janisz, Ella Schad, and Chris Reed. 2022. Disagreement space in argument analysis. In

Proceedings of the 1st Workshop on Perspectivist Approaches to NLP @LREC2022, pages 1–9, Marseille, France. European Language Resources Association.

Shelby Heinecke and Lev Reyzin. 2019. Crowdsourced pac learning under classification noise. *Proceedings of the AAAI Conference on Human Computation and Crowdsourcing*, 7(1):41–49.

Dirk Hovy, Taylor Berg-Kirkpatrick, Ashish Vaswani, and Eduard Hovy. 2013. Learning whom to trust with MACE. In *Proceedings of the 2013 Conference of the North American Chapter of the Association for Computational Linguistics: Human Language Technologies*, pages 1120–1130, Atlanta, Georgia. Association for Computational Linguistics.

Klaus Krippendorff. 2013. *Content Analysis: An Introduction to Its Methodology*. Sage publications.

Damjan Krstajic, Ljubomir J Buturovic, David E Leahy, and Simon Thomas. 2014. Cross-validation pitfalls when selecting and assessing regression and classification models. *Journal of cheminformatics*, 6(1):1–15.

Namhee Kwon, Liang Zhou, Eduard Hovy, and Stuart W. Shulman. 2007. Identifying and classifying subjective claims. In *Proceedings of the 8th Annual International Conference on Digital Government Research: Bridging Disciplines & Domains*, dg.o '07, page 76–81. Digital Government Society of North America.

John Lawrence, Joonsuk Park, Katarzyna Budzynska, Claire Cardie, Barbara Konat, and Chris Reed. 2017. Using argumentative structure to interpret debates in online deliberative democracy and erulemaking. *ACM Trans. Internet Technol.*, 17(3).

Matthias Liebeck, Katharina Esau, and Stefan Conrad. 2016. What to do with an airport? mining arguments in the German online participation project tempelhofer feld. In *Proceedings of the Third Workshop on Argument Mining (ArgMining2016)*, pages 144–153, Berlin, Germany. Association for Computational Linguistics.

Anna Lindahl, Lars Borin, and Jacobo Rouces. 2019. Towards assessing argumentation annotation - a first step. In *Proceedings of the 6th Workshop on Argument Mining*, pages 177–186, Florence, Italy. Association for Computational Linguistics.

Vlad Niculae, Joonsuk Park, and Claire Cardie. 2017. Argument mining with structured SVMs and RNNs. In *Proceedings of the 55th Annual Meeting of the Association for Computational Linguistics (Volume 1: Long Papers)*, pages 985–995, Vancouver, Canada. Association for Computational Linguistics.

Jennifer A. Noble. 2012. Minority voices of crowdsourcing: Why we should pay attention to every member of the crowd. In *Proceedings of the ACM 2012 Conference on Computer Supported Cooperative Work Companion*, CSCW '12, page 179–182, New York, NY, USA. Association for Computing Machinery.

OECD. 2003. *Promise and Problems of E-Democracy*. OECD.

Cecilia Ovesdotter Alm. 2011. Subjective natural language problems: Motivations, applications, characterizations, and implications. In *Proceedings of the 49th Annual Meeting of the Association for Computational Linguistics: Human Language Technologies*, pages 107–112, Portland, Oregon, USA. Association for Computational Linguistics.

Joonsuk Park and Claire Cardie. 2014. Identifying appropriate support for propositions in online user comments. In *Proceedings of the First Workshop on Argumentation Mining*, pages 29–38, Baltimore, Maryland. Association for Computational Linguistics.

Joonsuk Park and Claire Cardie. 2018. A corpus of eRulemaking user comments for measuring evaluability of arguments. In *Proceedings of the Eleventh International Conference on Language Resources and Evaluation (LREC 2018)*, Miyazaki, Japan. European Language Resources Association (ELRA).

Barbara Plank, Dirk Hovy, and Anders Søgaard. 2014. Learning part-of-speech taggers with inter-annotator agreement loss. In *Proceedings of the 14th Conference of the European Chapter of the Association for Computational Linguistics*, pages 742–751, Gothenburg, Sweden. Association for Computational Linguistics.

Vinodkumar Prabhakaran, Aida Mostafazadeh Davani, and Mark Diaz. 2021. On releasing annotator-level labels and information in datasets. In *Proceedings of The Joint 15th Linguistic Annotation Workshop (LAW) and 3rd Designing Meaning Representations (DMR) Workshop*, pages 133–138, Punta Cana, Dominican Republic. Association for Computational Linguistics.

Ruty Rinott, Lena Dankin, Carlos Alzate Perez, Mitesh M. Khapra, Ehud Aharoni, and Noam Slonim. 2015. Show me your evidence - an automatic method for context dependent evidence detection. In *Proceedings of the 2015 Conference on Empirical Methods in Natural Language Processing*, pages 440–450, Lisbon, Portugal. Association for Computational Linguistics.

Julia Romberg and Stefan Conrad. 2021. Citizen involvement in urban planning - how can municipalities be supported in evaluating public participation processes for mobility transitions? In *Proceedings of the 8th Workshop on Argument Mining*, pages 89–99, Punta Cana, Dominican Republic. Association for Computational Linguistics.

Julia Romberg and Tobias Escher. 2022. Automated topic categorisation of citizens' contributions: Reducing manual labelling efforts through active learning. In *Electronic Government*, pages 369–385, Cham. Springer International Publishing.

Julia Romberg, Laura Mark, and Tobias Escher. 2022a. *CIMT PartEval Corpus - Argument Concreteness (Subcorpus)*. ISLRN 776-577-161-062-9. https://github.com/juliaromberg/cimt-argument-concreteness-dataset.

Julia Romberg, Laura Mark, and Tobias Escher. 2022b. A corpus of german citizen contributions in mobility planning: Supporting evaluation through multidimensional classification. In *Proceedings of the Language Resources and Evaluation Conference*, pages 2874–2883, Marseille, France. European Language Resources Association.

Maarten Sap, Swabha Swayamdipta, Laura Vianna, Xuhui Zhou, Yejin Choi, and Noah Smith. 2022. Annotators with attitudes: How annotator beliefs and identities bias toxic language detection. In *Proceedings of the 2022 Conference of the North American Chapter of the Association for Computational Linguistics: Human Language Technologies*, pages 5884–5906, Seattle, United States. Association for Computational Linguistics.

Mike Schaekermann, Joslin Goh, Kate Larson, and Edith Law. 2018. Resolvable vs. irresolvable disagreement: A study on worker deliberation in crowd work. *Proc. ACM Hum.-Comput. Interact.*, 2(CSCW).

Eyal Shnarch, Carlos Alzate, Lena Dankin, Martin Gleize, Yufang Hou, Leshem Choshen, Ranit Aharonov, and Noam Slonim. 2018. Will it blend? blending weak and strong labeled data in a neural network for argumentation mining. In *Proceedings of the 56th Annual Meeting of the Association for Computational Linguistics (Volume 2: Short Papers)*, pages 599–605, Melbourne, Australia. Association for Computational Linguistics.

Christian Stab and Iryna Gurevych. 2014. Annotating argument components and relations in persuasive essays. In *Proceedings of COLING 2014, the 25th International Conference on Computational Linguistics: Technical Papers*, pages 1501–1510, Dublin, Ireland. Dublin City University and Association for Computational Linguistics.

Carole H. Sudre, Beatriz Gomez Anson, Silvia Ingala, Chris D. Lane, Daniel Jimenez, Lukas Haider, Thomas Varsavsky, Ryutaro Tanno, Lorna Smith, Sébastien Ourselin, Rolf H. Jäger, and M. Jorge Cardoso. 2019. Let's agree to disagree: Learning highly debatable multirater labelling. In *Medical Image Computing and Computer Assisted Intervention – MICCAI 2019*, pages 665–673, Cham. Springer International Publishing.

Assaf Toledo, Shai Gretz, Edo Cohen-Karlik, Roni Friedman, Elad Venezian, Dan Lahav, Michal Jacovi, Ranit Aharonov, and Noam Slonim. 2019. Automatic argument quality assessment - new datasets and methods. In *Proceedings of the 2019 Conference on Empirical Methods in Natural Language Processing and the 9th International Joint Conference on Natural Language Processing (EMNLP-IJCNLP)*, pages 5625–5635, Hong Kong, China. Association for Computational Linguistics.

Alexandra Uma, Tommaso Fornaciari, Dirk Hovy, Silviu Paun, Barbara Plank, and Massimo Poesio. 2020. A case for soft loss functions. *Proceedings of the AAAI Conference on Human Computation and Crowdsourcing*, 8(1):173–177.

A Appendix

A.1 Details on the Dataset Transformation

Table 5 gives further insights into the generation of the subjectivity scores for the dataset.

High	Interm.	Low	#	L1	Subjectivity 4-class	Subjectivity 2-class
5	0	0	439	0	O	RO
4	1	0	162	8	RO	RO
3	2	0	90	12	RS	RS
2	3	0	57	12	RS	RS
2	2	1	43	20	S	RS
1	3	1	38	16	RS	RS
0	3	2	38	12	RS	RS
3	1	1	37	20	S	RS
0	2	3	31	12	RS	RS
0	1	4	29	8	RO	RO
0	4	1	28	8	RO	RO
1	2	2	26	20	S	RS
1	4	0	25	8	RO	RO
0	5	0	20	0	O	RO
0	0	5	19	0	O	RO
4	0	1	18	16	RS	RS
1	1	3	11	20	S	RS
2	1	2	9	24	S	RS
1	0	4	3	16	RS	RS
2	0	3	2	24	S	RS
3	0	2	2	24	S	RS

Table 5: Overview of the different combinations of individual annotations, their occurence, the overall L1 distance and the mappings to subjectivity categories for both the 4-class and the 2-class schema. (O: Objective, RO: Rather Objective, RS: Rather Subjective, S: Subjective)

A.2 Hyperparameter-Tuning

For LR we tested the L1 and L2 norms for the penalty and set the regularization parameter C to take a value from $[0.001, 0.1, 1, 10, 100]$. Furthermore the classes were either weighted to simulate a balanced distribution or not weighted at all. We used an SVM with RBF kernel and a balanced class weighting. The regularization parameter C was set to be from $[0.001, 0.1, 1, 10, 100]$ and the kernel coefficient to be from $[1, 0.1, 0.01, 0.001]$. In RF the split quality was either measured with the Gini index or the Shannon information gain. Regarding the imbalance of the classes, we tested balancing weights and none.

For fine-tuning BERT we used the AdamW optimizer with beta coefficients of 0.9 and 0.999, and an epsilon of $1e-8$, and set the maximum sequence length to 128. We further trained for 5 epochs with a batch size from $[16, 32]$ and a learning rate from $[5e-5, 4e-5, 3e-5]$. For reproducibility of the experiments, we fixed the random seeds.

A.3 Full Overview of the Results

Table 6 and Table 7 list the full overview of results from the experiments.

		low	intermediate	high	macro-F_1	accuracy
	Baseline Majority	0.00	0.00	0.75	0.25	0.60
	RF (length)	0.19 ± 0.17	0.50 ± 0.07	0.81 ± 0.03	0.50 ± 0.07	0.69 ± 0.04
	RF (bow)	0.22 ± 0.13	0.58 ± 0.06	0.81 ± 0.03	0.54 ± 0.06	0.71 ± 0.04
	RF (length+bow)	0.17 ± 0.14	0.57 ± 0.06	0.82 ± 0.03	0.52 ± 0.06	0.71 ± 0.04
	LR (length)	0.13 ± 0.19	0.52 ± 0.08	0.81 ± 0.04	0.49 ± 0.06	0.70 ± 0.04
major position	LR (bow)	0.20 ± 0.13	0.55 ± 0.06	0.80 ± 0.03	0.52 ± 0.06	0.69 ± 0.03
	LR (length+bow)	0.22 ± 0.17	0.54 ± 0.06	0.80 ± 0.04	0.52 ± 0.06	0.69 ± 0.04
	SVM (length)	$\mathbf{0.45} \pm 0.08$	0.39 ± 0.09	0.83 ± 0.04	0.56 ± 0.04	0.69 ± 0.04
	SVM (bow)	0.28 ± 0.16	0.52 ± 0.11	0.79 ± 0.04	0.53 ± 0.07	0.67 ± 0.04
	SVM (length+bow)	0.33 ± 0.13	0.50 ± 0.09	0.82 ± 0.03	0.55 ± 0.06	0.70 ± 0.04
	BERT	0.38 ± 0.18	$\mathbf{0.63} \pm 0.07$	$\mathbf{0.86} \pm 0.02$	$\mathbf{0.62} \pm 0.07$	$\mathbf{0.76} \pm 0.04$
	Baseline Majority	0.00	0.00	0.79	0.26	0.65
	RF (length)	0.21 ± 0.18	0.63 ± 0.07	0.88 ± 0.02	0.57 ± 0.07	0.78 ± 0.03
	RF (bow)	0.32 ± 0.17	0.63 ± 0.06	0.89 ± 0.02	0.61 ± 0.06	0.79 ± 0.03
	RF (length+bow)	0.26 ± 0.17	$\mathbf{0.68} \pm 0.05$	0.90 ± 0.02	0.61 ± 0.06	0.81 ± 0.03
	LR (length)	0.16 ± 0.21	0.67 ± 0.04	0.90 ± 0.02	0.57 ± 0.07	0.80 ± 0.02
premise	LR (bow)	0.20 ± 0.13	0.55 ± 0.06	0.80 ± 0.03	0.52 ± 0.06	0.69 ± 0.03
	LR (length+bow)	0.25 ± 0.23	0.67 ± 0.05	0.90 ± 0.02	0.61 ± 0.08	0.80 ± 0.03
	SVM (length)	0.43 ± 0.09	0.47 ± 0.08	0.89 ± 0.02	0.60 ± 0.05	0.75 ± 0.03
	SVM (bow)	0.50 ± 0.12	0.63 ± 0.06	0.89 ± 0.02	0.67 ± 0.05	0.79 ± 0.03
	SVM (length+bow)	$\mathbf{0.51} \pm 0.15$	0.64 ± 0.08	0.90 ± 0.02	$\mathbf{0.68} \pm 0.07$	0.81 ± 0.03
	BERT	0.45 ± 0.16	$\mathbf{0.68} \pm 0.06$	$\mathbf{0.91} \pm 0.02$	$\mathbf{0.68} \pm 0.06$	$\mathbf{0.82} \pm 0.03$
	Baseline Majority	0.00	0.00	0.77	0.26	0.63
	RF (length)	0.15 ± 0.11	0.59 ± 0.05	0.86 ± 0.02	0.53 ± 0.04	0.75 ± 0.02
	RF (bow)	0.22 ± 0.13	0.61 ± 0.04	0.85 ± 0.02	0.56 ± 0.05	0.75 ± 0.02
	RF (length+bow)	0.28 ± 0.11	0.62 ± 0.04	0.86 ± 0.02	0.59 ± 0.05	0.76 ± 0.02
	LR (length)	0.16 ± 0.18	0.61 ± 0.04	0.84 ± 0.02	0.54 ± 0.06	0.74 ± 0.03
joint	LR (bow)	0.11 ± 0.11	0.62 ± 0.04	0.85 ± 0.02	0.53 ± 0.04	0.75 ± 0.02
	LR (length+bow)	0.16 ± 0.13	0.61 ± 0.05	0.85 ± 0.02	0.54 ± 0.04	0.74 ± 0.03
	SVM (length)	0.45 ± 0.07	0.46 ± 0.06	0.85 ± 0.02	0.59 ± 0.04	0.71 ± 0.02
	SVM (bow)	0.35 ± 0.10	0.58 ± 0.06	0.85 ± 0.02	0.59 ± 0.04	0.74 ± 0.03
	SVM (length+bow)	0.42 ± 0.11	0.58 ± 0.08	0.86 ± 0.02	0.62 ± 0.05	0.75 ± 0.03
	BERT	$\mathbf{0.47} \pm 0.12$	$\mathbf{0.66} \pm 0.04$	$\mathbf{0.88} \pm 0.02$	$\mathbf{0.67} \pm 0.05$	$\mathbf{0.79} \pm 0.02$

Table 6: Complete overview of all experiment results for sub-task $\mathcal{T}_H$: Concreteness.

		4-class					
		objective	rather objective	rather subjective	subjective	macro-F_1	accuracy
major position	Baseline Majority	0.57	0.00	0.00	0.00	0.14	0.40
	RF (length)	0.61 ± 0.04	0.21 ± 0.06	0.30 ± 0.08	0.30 ± 0.11	0.36 ± 0.05	0.42 ± 0.04
	RF (bow)	0.65 ± 0.04	0.16 ± 0.08	0.37 ± 0.08	0.18 ± 0.11	0.34 ± 0.04	0.45 ± 0.04
	RF (length+bow)	0.65 ± 0.04	0.12 ± 0.07	0.35 ± 0.08	0.20 ± 0.11	0.33 ± 0.04	0.46 ± 0.04
	LR (length)	0.65 ± 0.04	0.00 ± 0.00	$\mathbf{0.39} \pm 0.11$	0.02 ± 0.07	0.27 ± 0.04	0.46 ± 0.04
	LR (bow)	0.61 ± 0.05	0.10 ± 0.11	0.31 ± 0.13	0.11 ± 0.12	0.28 ± 0.06	0.42 ± 0.04
	LR (length+bow)	0.64 ± 0.05	0.11 ± 0.11	0.34 ± 0.10	0.15 ± 0.14	0.31 ± 0.06	0.44 ± 0.04
	SVM (length)	0.64 ± 0.05	0.09 ± 0.10	0.23 ± 0.11	$\mathbf{0.34} \pm 0.10$	0.33 ± 0.04	0.44 ± 0.04
	SVM (bow)	0.62 ± 0.05	0.10 ± 0.10	0.18 ± 0.15	0.23 ± 0.15	0.28 ± 0.08	0.42 ± 0.04
	SVM (length+bow)	0.64 ± 0.05	0.11 ± 0.09	0.26 ± 0.11	0.29 ± 0.11	0.33 ± 0.06	0.44 ± 0.04
	BERT	$\mathbf{0.69} \pm 0.05$	$\mathbf{0.24} \pm 0.10$	0.34 ± 0.08	0.22 ± 0.15	$\mathbf{0.37} \pm 0.06$	$\mathbf{0.47} \pm 0.05$
premise	Baseline Majority	0.62	0.00	0.00	0.00	0.15	0.44
	RF (length)	0.68 ± 0.05	0.19 ± 0.08	0.46 ± 0.08	0.05 ± 0.10	0.35 ± 0.04	0.49 ± 0.04
	RF (bow)	0.74 ± 0.04	0.10 ± 0.07	0.50 ± 0.06	0.19 ± 0.12	0.38 ± 0.05	0.56 ± 0.04
	RF (length+bow)	0.74 ± 0.04	0.10 ± 0.08	0.51 ± 0.06	0.18 ± 0.14	0.38 ± 0.05	$\mathbf{0.57} \pm 0.04$
	LR (length)	0.74 ± 0.04	0.01 ± 0.02	$\mathbf{0.53} \pm 0.06$	0.00 ± 0.03	0.32 ± 0.02	0.56 ± 0.04
	LR (bow)	0.72 ± 0.05	0.09 ± 0.10	0.51 ± 0.07	0.05 ± 0.08	0.34 ± 0.05	0.54 ± 0.05
	LR (length+bow)	0.73 ± 0.05	0.10 ± 0.09	0.52 ± 0.06	0.06 ± 0.09	0.35 ± 0.04	0.55 ± 0.04
	SVM (length)	0.71 ± 0.07	0.20 ± 0.10	0.19 ± 0.14	0.24 ± 0.10	0.33 ± 0.04	0.48 ± 0.05
	SVM (bow)	0.73 ± 0.05	0.11 ± 0.07	0.38 ± 0.20	0.21 ± 0.14	0.36 ± 0.05	0.53 ± 0.05
	SVM (length+bow)	0.72 ± 0.11	0.13 ± 0.10	0.40 ± 0.16	$\mathbf{0.27} \pm 0.12$	0.38 ± 0.07	0.53 ± 0.07
	BERT	$\mathbf{0.77} \pm 0.05$	$\mathbf{0.25} \pm 0.09$	0.51 ± 0.06	0.15 ± 0.13	$\mathbf{0.42} \pm 0.05$	0.56 ± 0.04
joint	Baseline Majority	0.60	0.00	0.00	0.00	0.15	0.42
	RF (length)	0.67 ± 0.03	0.15 ± 0.05	0.41 ± 0.05	0.14 ± 0.12	0.34 ± 0.04	0.47 ± 0.03
	RF (bow)	0.70 ± 0.03	0.12 ± 0.04	0.47 ± 0.06	0.18 ± 0.08	0.37 ± 0.04	0.51 ± 0.03
	RF (length+bow)	0.71 ± 0.03	0.09 ± 0.05	0.48 ± 0.06	0.18 ± 0.09	0.36 ± 0.03	$\mathbf{0.52} \pm 0.03$
	LR (length)	0.71 ± 0.03	0.00 ± 0.00	$\mathbf{0.49} \pm 0.05$	0.01 ± 0.05	0.30 ± 0.02	$\mathbf{0.52} \pm 0.03$
	LR (bow)	0.68 ± 0.04	0.09 ± 0.11	0.46 ± 0.05	0.07 ± 0.11	0.33 ± 0.05	0.50 ± 0.03
	LR (length+bow)	0.69 ± 0.04	0.11 ± 0.10	0.47 ± 0.06	0.10 ± 0.12	0.34 ± 0.05	0.50 ± 0.04
	SVM (length)	0.70 ± 0.04	0.13 ± 0.08	0.24 ± 0.09	$\mathbf{0.30} \pm 0.06$	0.34 ± 0.03	0.48 ± 0.03
	SVM (bow)	0.69 ± 0.03	0.15 ± 0.07	0.35 ± 0.14	0.27 ± 0.07	0.37 ± 0.05	0.49 ± 0.04
	SVM (length+bow)	0.70 ± 0.03	0.14 ± 0.07	0.37 ± 0.09	0.28 ± 0.08	0.37 ± 0.03	0.50 ± 0.03
	BERT	$\mathbf{0.73} \pm 0.03$	$\mathbf{0.27} \pm 0.08$	0.44 ± 0.05	0.25 ± 0.09	$\mathbf{0.42} \pm 0.04$	$\mathbf{0.52} \pm 0.03$

		2-class			
		rather objective	rather subjective	macro-F_1	accuracy
major position	Baseline Majority	0.78	0.00	0.39	0.64
	RF (length)	0.70 ± 0.05	0.49 ± 0.09	0.59 ± 0.05	0.62 ± 0.04
	RF (bow)	0.76 ± 0.03	$\mathbf{0.58} \pm 0.07$	0.67 ± 0.05	0.70 ± 0.04
	RF (length+bow)	0.77 ± 0.03	$\mathbf{0.58} \pm 0.06$	$\mathbf{0.68} \pm 0.04$	0.70 ± 0.04
	LR (length)	0.77 ± 0.04	0.42 ± 0.22	0.59 ± 0.11	0.68 ± 0.04
	LR (bow)	0.75 ± 0.04	0.45 ± 0.23	0.60 ± 0.10	0.67 ± 0.04
	LR (length+bow)	0.75 ± 0.04	0.52 ± 0.20	0.63 ± 0.10	0.68 ± 0.05
	SVM (length)	0.74 ± 0.04	0.54 ± 0.10	0.64 ± 0.05	0.67 ± 0.04
	SVM (bow)	0.73 ± 0.11	0.54 ± 0.16	0.63 ± 0.09	0.67 ± 0.06
	SVM (length+bow)	0.75 ± 0.04	0.53 ± 0.12	0.64 ± 0.06	0.68 ± 0.04
	BERT	$\mathbf{0.78} \pm 0.04$	$\mathbf{0.58} \pm 0.09$	$\mathbf{0.68} \pm 0.06$	$\mathbf{0.71} \pm 0.05$
premise	Baseline Majority	0.78	0.00	0.39	0.64
	RF (length)	0.78 ± 0.04	0.65 ± 0.04	0.71 ± 0.03	0.73 ± 0.03
	RF (bow)	0.81 ± 0.03	0.64 ± 0.06	$\mathbf{0.73} \pm 0.04$	0.75 ± 0.04
	RF (length+bow)	$\mathbf{0.82} \pm 0.03$	0.65 ± 0.06	$\mathbf{0.73} \pm 0.04$	$\mathbf{0.76} \pm 0.04$
	LR (length)	0.81 ± 0.03	0.64 ± 0.07	$\mathbf{0.73} \pm 0.05$	0.75 ± 0.04
	LR (bow)	0.79 ± 0.04	0.63 ± 0.05	0.71 ± 0.03	0.74 ± 0.03
	LR (length+bow)	0.79 ± 0.03	0.65 ± 0.05	0.72 ± 0.04	0.74 ± 0.04
	SVM (length)	0.80 ± 0.04	0.64 ± 0.05	0.72 ± 0.04	0.74 ± 0.04
	SVM (bow)	0.79 ± 0.04	0.64 ± 0.05	0.72 ± 0.04	0.74 ± 0.04
	SVM (length+bow)	0.80 ± 0.03	0.63 ± 0.06	0.71 ± 0.04	0.74 ± 0.04
	BERT	0.81 ± 0.03	$\mathbf{0.66} \pm 0.06$	$\mathbf{0.73} \pm 0.04$	$\mathbf{0.76} \pm 0.04$
joint	Baseline Majority	0.78	0.00	0.39	0.64
	RF (length)	0.76 ± 0.03	0.58 ± 0.03	0.67 ± 0.02	0.70 ± 0.02
	RF (bow)	0.79 ± 0.02	0.63 ± 0.03	0.71 ± 0.02	0.73 ± 0.02
	RF (length+bow)	$\mathbf{0.80} \pm 0.02$	0.62 ± 0.03	0.71 ± 0.02	$\mathbf{0.74} \pm 0.02$
	LR (length)	0.78 ± 0.02	0.58 ± 0.06	0.68 ± 0.03	0.72 ± 0.02
	LR (bow)	0.77 ± 0.03	0.60 ± 0.05	0.69 ± 0.03	0.71 ± 0.03
	LR (length+bow)	0.77 ± 0.03	0.61 ± 0.04	0.69 ± 0.03	0.72 ± 0.03
	SVM (length)	0.78 ± 0.02	0.63 ± 0.03	0.70 ± 0.02	0.72 ± 0.02
	SVM (bow)	0.77 ± 0.03	0.62 ± 0.04	0.69 ± 0.02	0.71 ± 0.03
	SVM (length+bow)	0.78 ± 0.02	0.61 ± 0.04	0.70 ± 0.03	0.72 ± 0.02
	BERT	$\mathbf{0.80} \pm 0.02$	$\mathbf{0.64} \pm 0.04$	$\mathbf{0.72} \pm 0.02$	$\mathbf{0.74} \pm 0.02$

Table 7: Complete overview of all experiment results for sub-task $\mathcal{T}_S$: Subjectivity.

Boundary Detection and Categorization of Argument Aspects via Supervised Learning

Mattes Ruckdeschel and **Gregor Wiedemann**
Leibniz-Institute for Media Research | Hans-Bredow-Institute, Germany
{m.ruckdeschel, g.wiedemann}@leibniz-hbi.de

Abstract

Aspect-based argument mining (ABAM) is the task of automatic *detection* and *categorization* of argument aspects, i.e. the parts of an argumentative text that contain the issue-specific key rationale for its conclusion. From empirical data, overlapping but not congruent sets of aspect categories can be derived for different topics. So far, two supervised approaches to detect aspect boundaries, and a smaller number of unsupervised clustering approaches categorizing groups of similar aspects have been proposed. In this paper, we introduce the Argument Aspect Corpus (AAC) which contains token-level annotations of aspects in 3,547 argumentative sentences from three highly debated topics. This dataset enables both the supervised learning of boundaries and the categorization of argument aspects. During the design of our annotation process, we noticed that it is not clear from the outset at which contextual unit aspects should be coded. We, thus, experiment with classification at the token, chunk, and sentence level granularity. Our finding is that the chunk level provides the most useful information for applications. At the same time, it produces the best-performing results in our tested supervised learning setups.

1 How to Code Argument Aspects?

Argument mining has become a prominent natural language processing task with several challenging sub-tasks (Lawrence and Reed, 2020). Argumentative utterances are found plentiful in online forums, newspapers, and social media debates, which offer heaps of text data for argument mining. Depending on the variety and complexity of the issues of a given topic, the number of talking points in such debates could be potentially very large. However, with the concept of theoretical or thematic 'saturation,' qualitative researchers refer to the fact that public debates typically revolve around a relatively small set of issues that can be inferred from textual data with manageable manual effort (Johnson, 2014). These issues are accompanied by a likewise limited set of prototypical arguments. To describe the width and depth of a debate on a given topic, arguments can be grouped according to their reference to the same aspects. Analog to Schiller et al. (2021), we define an aspect as a semantically distinguishable, recurring subtopic of an argument that expresses the issue-specific key rationale for its conclusion. A stance on an aspect, thus, potentially serves as a justification for the stance on the corresponding main topic that itself can but not necessarily has to be mentioned in the argument.

For example, in the argument *"Businesses are sometimes forced to [hire fewer employees] because they must pay minimum wage"* the token sequence in brackets holds the key rationale for the aspect category *(un-)employment rate*. In contrast, in a slightly modified version of this argument *"[Businesses were sometimes forced to close down] because they must pay minimum wage"* the sequence in brackets refers to the aspect category *competition/business challenges*. Both argument versions implicitly express a negative stance on statutory minimum wages as higher unemployment or increased bankruptcies of businesses are generally seen as undesired policy outcomes.

Individual arguments may refer to different aspects that perhaps even take opposing stances before giving reason for a final stance. Extracting aspects from arguments has several advantages for the analysis of debates in various disciplinary settings such as political science, social science, or economics. *First*, it adds a new semantic dimension to the established identification of structural components in argument mining. This allows for a theory-led grouping of relevant talking points that can facilitate a qualitative discourse inspection. For quantitative analysis, they allow for investigating the prevalence of aspects in specific debates and their co-occurrence with argumentative stances as well as other aspects. *Second*, aspects as semantic

Proceedings of the 9th Workshop on Argument Mining, co-located with the 29th International Conference on Computational Linguistics, pages 126–136
October 17, 2022.

categories can serve as a bridge to combining argument mining with the formal modeling of argument semantics (Baumann et al., 2020).

Often, aspects are neither explicitly stated nor consistently formulated in arguments which makes unsupervised aspect category extraction practically infeasible. Instead, we argue for the creation of well-defined and systematically controlled aspect category sets that generalize key points in similar arguments against the background of domain knowledge to serve the purpose of ABAM. This abstracts from the complexity and diversity of aspect expressions so that only a limited number of aspect categories are required to fully cover a topic. This not only enables manual coding and supervised classification, but guarantees a methodologically and theoretically sound interpretation of the classification results. It further enables comparative studies across divergent datasets that can hardly be achieved solely by relying on unsupervised methods.

To perform supervised ABAM, we created the Argument Aspect Corpus—a data set for supervised learning of aspects for three topics. In this paper, we describe the iterative process for creating aspect categories for a given topic, starting from an unsupervised clustering of arguments and refining aspect categories after coding samples from a data set in several rounds. During the design of our annotation process, we realized that it is not clear from the outset at which contextual unit aspects should be coded. We started with a multi-label sentence classification task but soon noticed that confining the label decision to a certain token sequence within a sentence not only would provide more valuable information for aspect mining, but also leads to better justified and, thus, more coherent label decisions. However, for a sequence tagging task, unlike for named entity recognition, span boundaries are much less obvious. If the annotated span is too wide it may contain unnecessary information to capture the aspect and, thus, distract a machine learning process from the actual task. If the span is too small, the annotated text may not represent the aspect properly.

In light of these considerations, we answer the research question: What is the recommended level of granularity to perform supervised ABAM? Hence, there are two main contributions of our paper:

1. We introduce the *Argument Aspect Corpus* (AAC) for supervised aspect-based argument mining. It contains 3,547 argumentative sentences from three highly debated topics: nuclear energy, minimum wages, and marijuana legalization.

2. We perform experiments to determine the optimal granularity of aspect boundaries. For this, we test token-based and chunk-based multi-class classification against multi-label sentence classification for argument aspects. We identify a sequence tagging task based on chunk-normalized tokens as the recommended approach.

In Section 2 we relate our approach to ABAM to several other approaches for the semantic grouping of arguments. We then present our data sets and explain our iterative annotation process in Section 3. Section 4, describes our experiment setup and the reasoning behind it. Section 5 describes our experiments on the automatic prediction of aspect labels with state-of-the-art transformer networks, as well as the optimal aspect granularity. We will present the main findings and conclusions of our work in section 6.

2 Related Work

During the last years, several approaches to grouping arguments into some type of semantic categories were published in the field of argument mining. To describe their task, these approaches rely on heterogeneous names, theoretical concepts, and mining strategies. A first group of approaches builds on *framing* theory that is commonly used in empirical communication and media research. In argument mining, the notion of a frame is adopted as the aspect of a discussion that is emphasized by an argument. Sets of aspects can be of varying breadth and depth. Also, approaches differ whether they assume frames to be issue-specific or should generalize across topics. Ajjour et al. (2019), for instance, define a *frame* as a set of arguments that focus on the same aspect. To identify references to the same aspects, they use an unsupervised clustering on argumentative texts. By definition then, each cluster supposedly represents one frame. However, the resulting clusters do not necessarily describe semantic frames in the sense of repeatedly occurring aspects of the corresponding discussion. The large number of optimal clusters as described in the paper also drastically reduces the usefulness for any further study. Heinisch and Cimiano (2021) define frames as the aspects a talking point discusses. They address the shortcomings of frames that are too generic and frames that are too issue-specific by clustering user-generated, specific labels into general frame categories from classic media research. Although they have shown that their approach is able to automatically identify media frames to some extent, they do not provide well-defined sets of issue-specific aspects that would allow for a deductive analysis of public debates. Daxenberger et al. (2020) describe a clustering-based grouping of arguments based on aspects for better search results. They use agglomerative hierarchical clustering of contextualized word embeddings, such as BERT-embeddings (Devlin et al., 2019), on sentence-level argument pairs. The resulting clusters based on similarity metrics also do not necessarily provide useful aspect categories, let alone semantically meaningful labels.

Bar-Haim et al. (2020) introduced *key point analysis* to generate a summary for large collections of arguments by finding *key points*. Their work also inspired the ArgMining 2021 shared task (Friedman et al., 2021) which contained one task for matching arguments to key points, and one task for the generation of key points. Hereby, key points are defined as higher-level arguments that occur frequently in debates on a given topic. Key points are formulated as full sentences and with an indication of a clear pro or contra stance on the debated issue. Besides the difference that in our definition aspects are independent of any stance, key points can play a similar role in argument classification as our proposed aspects. They also acknowledge the difficulty of the problem of argument grouping and the ineffectiveness of unsupervised methods based on contextual embeddings.

Addressing the problem of unsupervised approaches, Jurkschat et al. (2022) propose ABAM as a multi-class sentence classification task and provide a corpus containing argumentative sentences from the nuclear energy debate with manually annotated class labels. In a further development of this work, our approach to ABAM is designed as a token-level sequence tagging task that allows for multiple aspects to being mentioned in one sentence, and for the extraction of the decisive sentence parts determining these aspects.

Annotating and predicting aspects on the token level is also performed in the works of Trautmann (2020) and Schiller et al. (2021). Trautmann (2020) defines *aspects* analog to aspect-based sentiment analysis (Pontiki et al., 2016). He proposes the task of *Aspect Term Extraction (ATE)* and presents a supervised sequence tagging approach to detect the most common token n-grams that address argument aspects. However, no semantically meaningful aspect categories are created from the extracted token sequences. Similar to ATE, Schiller et al. (2021) perform aspect boundary detection as a supervised sequence tagging task trained on argumentative sentences in which token sequences were labeled with a BIO-tagging scheme to indicate the beginning (B), inside (I) and outside (O) of token aspect spans. They also address the problem of fuzzy span boundaries that motivated our research and present a crowdsourcing task based on automatic candidate ranking and manual candidate selection to create a gold standard with high inter-coder agreement. Regarding this task of aspect boundary detection, their approach to ABAM mostly resembles ours. We, however, extend the tagging and extraction of aspect terms to a classification of the predicted spans into issue-specific aspect categories.

3 The Argument Aspect Corpus

With this paper, we publish the Argument Aspect Corpus (AAC) that contains manually annotated aspect labels on token spans from argumentative sentences. The argumentative sentences were extracted from the UKP Sentential Argument Mining Corpus (UKP SAM) (Reimers et al., 2019). For the AAC, we selected only those sentences that have been annotated as either expressing a pro or a contra stance on one of the three topics: *minimum wage (MW)*, *nuclear energy (NE)*, and *marijuana legalization (MJ)*. The topics were chosen with respect to their importance within recent European political discourses.

As Bar-Haim et al. (2020) and Jurkschat et al. (2022) have already pointed out, labeling aspects in arguments is a complex task. This is mainly due to the fact that the granularity of aspects cannot be determined in a data-driven manner, but must be specified in a methodically rigorous process of developing the coding scheme. With this comes the necessity to develop definitions of aspect categories that are as precise as possible to separate the sometimes overlapping meanings of argumentative components from one another. To fulfill these requirements and, at the same time, address the heterogeneity of the empirical data, we followed a process that combined unsupervised clustering with group discussions to reach consensus definitions of our aspect categories. As a starting point, we employed unsupervised k-means clustering of sentence embeddings from S-BERT (Reimers and Gurevych, 2019). Analog to previous research on argument frames, we expect that semantic-similarity-based clusters already group aspect information to some extent. We decided on a fixed number of 15 initial clusters as a rough estimate of how many aspects per topic we expect. However, our subsequent development of aspect categories would allow for the creation of more or fewer aspect categories. With a group of three annotators, students, and researchers from the field of (computational) social science, we listed aspects that occur in these clusters as a first summary of a topic. With these initial aspects, we created a preliminary codebook and annotated a sample of 200 sentences per topic. Arguments in these samples were sorted by cosine similarity of their S-BERT representation. Annotators reported that this sorting was beneficial for speeding up the annotation and, at the same time, increasing its coherence. Annotators were encouraged to write comments about aspect categories and extend the list of aspects if necessary. Next, the inter-coder agreement (Krippendorff's alpha) for each aspect was calculated on a sentence level in order to find aspects that need clarification. In extensive discussion rounds, the category definitions were sharpened and refined. In the second and following rounds of annotating samples, we switched from the sentence level classification to an annotation of token spans to be able 1) to justify label decisions directly on text snippets, and 2) to allow for aspect term extraction in a subsequent step of machine learning. This iterative process of annotation, agreement evaluation, and discussion was repeated until a consensus for all aspect definitions was reached and the list of aspects covered the large majority of arguments for a topic. The full dataset was then annotated by all three annotators with the final codebook resulting from the aforementioned iterative process. A major challenge during annotation was determining token span boundaries since in many cases it is not possible to unambiguously decide where the mentioning of an aspect in a sentence actually starts or ends. We decided to instruct annotators to label the smallest number of tokens that provide sufficient information to label the aspect on its own. Still, this resulted in substantial disagreement about aspect boundaries in many cases while, at the same time, sentence-level agreement of labeled aspects was high. This observation led to the decision to further investigate the question of which granularity level of context units ABAM should be performed (cp. Section 5).

Final gold labels for the AAC dataset on the token level were derived in a two-step process. First, on the sentence level, we determined all labels that have been annotated by a majority of annotators as gold labels. Arguments without any majority label were reviewed once again to determine a final label. Second, for each token in a sentence, we copied the sentence gold label if at least one annotator included it in his/her annotation span. Again, rare conflicts of overlaps of sentence majority labels for individual tokens have been resolved in a final review. This strategy results in potentially more extensive gold labels on the token level compared to those of the single annotators.

Table 1 provides an overview of the dataset statistics of the AAC. Due to the challenge of achieving exact matches on span boundaries during the annotation, we opted for an inter-coder agreement measure on the sentence level. For each topic, this was calculated using Krippendorff's alpha in combination with the MASI distance (Passonneau, 2006) as a weighted agreement metric over the set of all labels that an annotator has used to label a sequence in a sentence. Thus, only if two annotators use the exact same set of labels to annotate a sentence, the resulting distance is 0. With alpha values of 0.65 and higher, we achieve acceptable agreement between coders. But the numbers also signal that argument aspect coding is a challenging task that requires a certain amount of coder training and expertise. Measures of the agreement for individual aspect categories some of which are significantly higher than the overall agreement are reported in Tables 7, 8, and 9 in the Appendix.

4 Experimenting with Aspect Boundaries

In a significant number of cases, annotators agreed upon which aspects were present in an argument but labeled slightly different token sequences as indicative of an aspect. Therefore, the strict token-level annotator agreement was relatively low compared to the agreement on the sentence level. A qualitative look into boundary disagreement for a small sample revealed that different individual an-

Topic	Aspects	N	α_K	Aspect categories
Minimum Wage (*MW*)	12	1118	0.65	motivation/chances, competition/business challenges, prices, social justice, welfare, economic impact, turnover, capital vs. labour, government intervention, un/employment rate, low-skilled and secondary wage earners
Nuclear Energy (*NE*)	12	1261	0.68	waste, accidents/security, reliability, costs, weapons, technological innovation, environmental impact, health effects, renewables, fossil fuels, energy policy, public debate
Marijuana Legalization (*MJ*)	13	1213	0.65	child and teen safety, community/societal effects, health/psychological effects, medical marijuana, drug abuse, illegal trade, personal freedom, national budget, drug policy, addiction, harm, gateway drug, legal drugs

Table 1: AAC Dataset statistics: the number of aspects, the number of arguments (N), Krippendorff's inter-coder agreement (α_K) and the aspect categories for all three topics of the current version.

notations could be considered valid regarding our guidelines. This challenge to achieve a high agreement for exact matches of token span boundaries during aspect annotation led us to the more general questions: what would be the most suitable level of granularity of context units, and what would be the best corresponding modeling approach to perform ABAM as a machine learning task?

To answer these questions, we experiment with different modifications of the AAC dataset. Since the category *Other* was used to annotate any sentence that either did not fit any aspect definition or was deemed not argumentative, we excluded the category from training. Then, we split the annotated data per topic randomly into a training (70 %), validation (10 %), and test set (20 %), Finally, we created different formats of these sets to test different ABAM task variants:

- **Sequence tagging:** Analog to named entity recognition (NER), each token is labeled either with its gold aspect category or the `O`-tag. Unlike Schiller et al. (2021), we refrained from using BIO(ES) prefixes to indicate beginning, inside, end, or single-token tags during training since our annotation guidelines do not allow adjacent sequences of distinct aspects of the same category. We further noticed during early experiments that BIO-tags significantly harmed the overall performance. With this input, we fine-tune a pre-trained transformer model with a sequence tagging head.[1]

- **Chunk normalization:** To improve the coherence of aspect boundaries within the dataset, we utilized information from a syntactic chunker.[2] We hypothesize that syntactic chunks are a more suitable level of context compared to sentences and tokens. They are more fine-grained than sentence-level annotations but more coarse-grained and, thus, coherent for machine learning and prediction than token-level annotations. Chunk normalization is performed by copying aspect labels from each annotated token to all other tokens belonging to the same chunk.

- **Multi-class chunk classification:** In this variant of the task, we do not strive for the prediction of labels of individual tokens but entire chunks. For this, we feed each target chunk and its surrounding sentence separated with a `[SEP]` token into a transformer model with a final multi-class output layer. Gold chunk labels are derived from the AAC gold labels the same way as for the chunk normalization.

- **Multi-label sentence classification:** High levels of inter-coder agreement on the sentence level might also suggest that ABAM is performed best as a sequence classification task for argumentative sentences neglecting aspect spans. In contrast to chunks, sentences can refer to multiple aspects, thus, requiring a multi-label classification. To test for this simplified version of the task analog to the

[1]All experiments are conducted with the *Flair* NLP framework (Akbik et al., 2019).

[2]We used the pre-trained English chunker model from *Flair* (Akbik et al., 2019).

Task variant	Sentence representation examples
Sequence tagging	[After] [the] [wage] [increase] [,] [that] [same] [basket]$_{\text{prices}}$ [cost]$_{\text{prices}}$ [$] [315] [.]
Chunk normalization	[After] [the] [wage] [increase] [,] [that]$_{\text{prices}}$ [same]$_{\text{prices}}$ [basket]$_{\text{prices}}$ [cost]$_{\text{prices}}$ [$] [315] [.]
Chunk classification	[that same basket [SEP] After the wage increase , that same basket cost $315.]$_{\text{prices}}$
Sentence classification	[After the wage increase , that same basket cost $315.]$_{\text{prices}}$

Table 2: Examples the four task variants tested for supervised ABAM (brackets indicate context unit boundaries, sub-scripted text indicates the aspect label).

approach by Jurkschat et al. (2022), we reformat the AAC dataset splits into full sentences with a set of gold labels from all contained tokens to fine-tune a transformer model with a multi-label classification head.

Table 2 shows the differences between the inputs for the two sequence tagging and the two sequence classification tasks. Since the token *basket* was annotated in the AAC gold labels, the entire chunk *that same basket* becomes annotated in chunk-normalization.

5 Supervised ABAM

First, we perform a step of model selection to determine the best pre-trained language model for performing ABAM. Second, we test different modeling variants of the ABAM task to learn about the most fitting context units for argument aspects.

5.1 Language model selection

We test several state-of-the-art language models on the aspect classification tasks in the variant of sequence tagging. We compare three common language models: RoBERTa-large (Liu et al., 2019), ALBERT-large (Lan et al., 2019), and ELECTRA-large (Clark et al., 2020). To ensure the stability of results, all experiments were repeated five times with different random seeds. In our first tests, XLM-RoBERTa (Conneau et al., 2020) performed significantly worse than RoBERTa and was, therefore, excluded from further testing. ALBERT-large was chosen over ALBERT-xxlarge, since the results for the xxlarge model version were not significantly better during first runs, whereas computing time increased significantly. All tests were conducted with the same set of reasonable default hyper-parameters (see Table 11 in the Appendix).

Table 3 shows the performance of the tested language models which were obtained using the *entity type* evaluation scheme of the *nervaluate*[3] python

Model	Precision	Recall	F1
	Minimum Wage		
roberta-large	**58.4±1.7**	**75.1±2.0**	**65.7±1.8**
albert-large-v2	35.8±3.8	50.1±4.9	41.7±4.3
electra-large	44.3±10.3	55.9±14.5	49.3±12.1
	Nuclear Energy		
roberta-large	**63.6±0.9**	**78.2±0.7**	**70.1±0.4**
albert-large-v2	51.8±2.9	66.9±3.8	58.3±2.2
electra-large	62.6±1.2	75.8±1.4	68.6±1.1
	Marijuana Legalization		
roberta-large	**60.5±2.4**	**76.8±1.8**	**67.4±1.9**
albert-large-v2	39.5±2.4	58.7±2.5	47.2±2.4
electra-large	42.0±20.8	52.4±23.2	46.2±22.4

Table 3: Performance of token-level aspect tagging for three different topics (metrics in %, entity-type evaluation scheme, mean and standard deviation of five repeated runs).

package.[4] Since the annotation of aspect boundaries was somewhat incoherent for individual arguments between multiple annotators, we expect coherency also to be affected across different arguments within the AAC gold annotations. For this reason, the entity type evaluation scheme appears as the right choice, because instead of exact span boundaries it considers overlapping of predicted and gold spans to be a correct prediction, as long as the annotated labels of the overlapping spans match.

With F1-scores between 65.7 % and 70.1 %, the RoBERTa model outperforms the other models on the task significantly.[5] Therefore we decided to continue granularity experiments only for

[3]`https://pypi.org/project/nervaluate/`

[4]*nervaluate* implements different evaluation schemes for sequence tagging based on Segura-Bedmar et al. (2013).

[5]The lower performance of the other models can be explained by the fact that they completely failed to predict some smaller aspect categories. We hypothesize that an extended search for more optimal hyper-parameters would lead to considerable performance increases. Since this is not the main focus of this paper, we decided to leave this for future work.

RoBERTa-large. We also observe that the recall is consistently and significantly higher than precision.

5.2 Aspect granularity evaluation

To test different variants of modeling the ABAM task, we fine-tune a RoBERTa-large model for each topic of the AAC dataset separately. To make the results of these variants comparable, we convert the predictions of all models to the coarsest granularity of sentence-level aspect labels. We compare the set of labels that were predicted for all tokens or chunks of a sentence to the set of gold standard sentence labels. Table 4 shows the micro-average performance of the various models.[6]

With F1-scores of 80.2% and higher, all models that classify aspects finer than sentence level granularity achieve not only very satisfactory results, but also significantly outperform aspect mining on the sentence level. This is a clear hint that ABAM profits from finer-grained annotation levels. The results also show that sentence-level classification achieves the best precision values, but suffers from lowered recall. This shows that labeling on the token or chunk level can provide more valuable and consistent insight into the used aspects in a sentence or argument. Sentence-level aspect classification, in contrast, often seems to overlook aspects that differ too much from the training sentences. Normalizing token-level annotations to chunk boundaries slightly improves the recall and accuracy compared to basic sequence tagging for the topics of minimum wage and nuclear energy. For the other metrics, the effect is ambiguous.[7] We conclude that chunk normalization may be useful to make annotation spans more consistent and therefore improve classification results slightly, although the effect is not large. Models trained to classify chunks along with their sentence context directly perform consistently worse compared to models trained on token-level sequence tagging.

5.3 Multi-topic aspect classification

In the last experiment, we want to find out whether combining data from several topics produces superior models for aspect classification compared to models trained on a single topic. As a basis, we use the chunk-normalized token dataset. Each argument token sequence is extended by preceding it with tokens containing their respective topic name followed by a separator token ([SEP]) (for an example, see Table 10 in the Appendix). Table 5 shows the performance of the trained multi-topic model over all three topics and the corresponding performance improvement compared to the single-topic classifiers. All topics benefit from the additional training data from other topics. The F1-scores improved significantly up to $+5.7$ %. The improvements in precision are considerably higher than for recall. The results show that more training data can improve model performance, even in a multi-topic setting. It is notable, that the improvement for the dataset about nuclear energy has the lowest improvement while being the dataset with the highest inter-coder agreement. This suggests that the multi-topic classifier was able to enhance the results of the slightly less coherently labeled datasets even further.

5.4 Error analysis

To learn about common error patterns, we take a closer, qualitative look at samples of false positives and false negatives of predicted aspect sequences, as well as wrongly classified aspect categories. Table 6 shows three example arguments from the minimum wage topic with aspect labels as predicted by our best-performing single-topic classifier.

In the first example, the model predicted additional spans for the same aspect (false positives). On closer inspection, these annotations can also be considered valid suggesting that the gold annotations are not entirely consistent. Annotating a large dataset with multiple annotators consistently is challenging. This is especially true for complex and potentially overlapping categories such as argument aspects. The example also supports the impression that for real application scenarios the precision values may indicate lower than actual model quality. The second example shows a minimal annotation span by the model that misses the wider span boundaries from the gold standard (false negatives). Here, the model was not able to see the same connectivity between *keep wages down* and *and keep unions out*, which was more apparent to a human annotator. Nonetheless, the model predicted the correct label for the correctly identified aspect token which makes the result partially useful for application scenarios. The last example

[6]Higher values of the F1-score compared to accuracy originate from the span-based evaluation with `nervaluate` compared to the token-wise evaluation for accuracy.

[7]A positive effect from chunk normalization on the results up to +3 percentage points can be observed when using the `strict` evaluation scheme of nereval that compares sequences of exact matches between predicted and gold labels.

Task variant	Precision	Recall	F1	Accuracy
Minimum Wage				
Sequence tagging	77.1±1.2	84.1±2.4	80.4±1.4	66.0±2.0
Chunk normalization	77.1±0.5	**84.7±2.1**	**80.7±1.0**	**66.0±1.0**
Chunk classification	74.9±1.4	86.2±0.9	80.2±0.7	64.3±2.5
Sentence classification	**84.3±1.4**	67.9±1.2	75.2±1.3	64.3±1.2
Nuclear Energy				
Sequence tagging	77.9±0.7	88.0±1.0	**82.6±0.6**	63.7±1.0
Chunk normalization	75.6±1.0	**88.5±2.4**	81.5±1.3	**65.7±1.9**
Chunk classification	74.4±2.3	87.8±1.3	80.5±1.1	61.9±1.9
Sentence classification	**83.8±0.9**	62.4±0.6	71.5±0.7	60.3±0.7
Marijuana Legalization				
Sequence tagging	79.4±1.3	87.1±1.8	**83.1±1.4**	**70.0±2.3**
Chunk normalization	78.0±1.6	**87.0±1.2**	82.3±1.1	68.1±1.2
Chunk classification	76.9±1.4	88.6±1.5	82.3±0.6	66.6±1.6
Sentence classification	**82.2±2.3**	68.5±1.9	73.8±2.1	68.8±1.4

Table 4: Micro-average performance (in %) of four modeling variations of aspect granularity. The test set predictions of the token and chunk-based approaches have been converted to a multi-label sentence prediction to allow for a fair comparison (mean and standard deviation of five repeated runs).

Topic	Precision	Impr.	Recall	Impr.	F1	Impr.
Minimum wage	66.2±2.6	+6.1%	76.9±1.6	+0.9%	71.1±2.1	+3.7%
Nuclear energy	64.7±1.4	+2.4%	80.2±1.5	+3.0%	71.5±1.1	+2.7%
Marijuana legalization	67.6±1.2	+8.8%	80.4±1.3	+2.1%	73.4±0.3	+5.7%

Table 5: Performance of the multi-topic sequence tagging model for argument aspects on chunk-normalized tokens (metrics in %, entity-type evaluation scheme, mean and standard deviation of five repeated runs). *Impr.* is the percentage improvement compared to single-topic models.

shows a wrongly predicted aspect category. The abstract proverb *to move up the economic ladder* was interpreted by annotators to indicate an opportunity for an employee to improve. The model, however, interpreted it as referring to low-skilled workers. This example also shows the difficulty of the task, for humans, and machines. For individual arguments, aspect categories still may have some overlap, even if they were carefully crafted to be about distinct sub-topic of the discourse. Deciding which category is the most suitable becomes even more difficult if metaphorical language is used.

6 Conclusion

In this paper, we further defined the task of supervised aspect-based argument mining based on experiments with a newly created dataset containing aspect annotations of token spans in argumentative sentences from three different topics. With our experiments,[8] we showed that ABAM performs best on a granularity level finer than multi-label sentence classification (cp. Exp. 2). We also showed that best results are achieved by fine-tuning a state-of-the-art language model such as RoBERTa on a token sequence tagging task. Despite satisfactory results up to 70 % F1-score (cp. Exp. 1), we see that especially disagreement on span boundaries for annotated aspects is a source of error. Normalizing token labels in the gold dataset to identical labels within syntactic chunks can mitigate this effect to some extent (cp. Exp. 2). Compared to sentences that can refer to multiple aspects, chunks are short enough to carry information for only one aspect. Compared to tokens, chunks contain more

[8]The AAC dataset and the experiment code for this paper is available at `https://github.com/Leibniz-HBI/argument-aspect-corpus-v1`.

Error type	Argument
False positives	Supporters of minimum wage also believe that a minimum wage stimulates consumption$_{\text{[Economic Impact]}}$ and thus puts more money$_{\text{[Economic Impact]}}$ into the economy$_{\text{[Economic Impact]}}$ by allowing low paid workers to spend more$_{\text{[Economic Impact]}}$.
False negatives	They've been using undocumented immigrants for DECADES (in violation of the law) to keep wages down , and$_{\text{[Capital vs. Labour]}}$ unions$_{\text{[Capital vs. Labour]}}$ out$_{\text{[Capital vs. Labour]}}$.
False category	Minimum wage laws can lead to labor market rigidities$_{\text{[Motivation/Chances]}}$ that make it more difficult for people to move up$_{\text{[Low-skilled]}}$ the economic ladder $_{\text{[Low-skilled]}}$.

Table 6: Examples for false predictions of the best performing aspect classification model (RoBERTa-large, chunk-normalized token sequence tagging). Text color blue indicates true positives, black true negatives. Background colour highlighting indicates errors (green: false positives, gray: false negatives; red: wrong aspect category). For the last example, the correctly identified aspect span was labelled as 'Motivation/Chances' in the gold standard.

information that can be interpreted unambiguously and have clear sequence boundaries that seem to support more consistent manual and automatic data annotations. In addition, the annotation process can be accelerated by tasking annotators with coding chunks instead of sequences or tokens.

In future work, we, therefore, concentrate on a new chunk-based annotation and classification pipeline for ABAM. The results from our third experiment on multi-topic classification will also be of additional help for ABAM research and applications. Training one model on all three topics with a merged set of aspect categories further improved the F1-score of our best model up to 5.7 %. This result is also promising for developing the approach further into a zero-shot or few-shot scenario for yet unseen topics as it was tested successfully already on the sentence level by Jurkschat et al. (2022). With this paper, we publish the Argument Aspect Corpus (AAC) in its version 1.0 containing aspect category definitions, annotation guidelines, and token-level annotated sentences for three topics. Our aim is to provide more topics in future versions, paired with the research about the efficacy of chunk-level annotation processes and few-shot classification performance.

Acknowledgements

This work was funded by the Deutsche Forschungsgemeinschaft (DFG) as part of the project "FAME: A framework for argument mining and evaluation" (project no. 406289255). The authors gratefully acknowledge the work of their coding team, Aya Alwais and Emma Neuhaus, who coded thousands of sentences and competently supported the definition of aspect categories with their social science domain expertise.

References

Yamen Ajjour, Milad Alshomary, Henning Wachsmuth, and Benno Stein. 2019. Modeling frames in argumentation. In *Proceedings of the 2019 Conference on Empirical Methods in Natural Language Processing and the 9th International Joint Conference on Natural Language Processing (EMNLP-IJCNLP)*, pages 2922–2932, Hong Kong, China. Association for Computational Linguistics.

Alan Akbik, Tanja Bergmann, Duncan Blythe, Kashif Rasul, Stefan Schweter, and Roland Vollgraf. 2019. FLAIR: An easy-to-use framework for state-of-the-art NLP. In *NAACL 2019, 2019 Annual Conference of the North American Chapter of the Association for Computational Linguistics (Demonstrations)*, pages 54–59.

Roy Bar-Haim, Lilach Eden, Roni Friedman, Yoav Kantor, Dan Lahav, and Noam Slonim. 2020. From arguments to key points: Towards automatic argument summarization. In *Proceedings of the 58th Annual Meeting of the Association for Computational Linguistics*, pages 4029–4039, Online. Association for Computational Linguistics.

Ringo Baumann, Gregor Wiedemann, Maximilian Heinrich, Ahmad Dawar Hakimi, and Gerhard Heyer.

2020. The road map to FAME: A framework for mining and formal evaluation of arguments. *Datenbank-Spektrum*, 20(2):107–113.

Kevin Clark, Minh-Thang Luong, Quoc V. Le, and Christopher D. Manning. 2020. ELECTRA: pre-training text encoders as discriminators rather than generators. In *8th International Conference on Learning Representations (ICLR)*, Addis Ababa, Ethiopia. OpenReview.net.

Alexis Conneau, Kartikay Khandelwal, Naman Goyal, Vishrav Chaudhary, Guillaume Wenzek, Francisco Guzmán, Edouard Grave, Myle Ott, Luke Zettlemoyer, and Veselin Stoyanov. 2020. Unsupervised cross-lingual representation learning at scale. In *Proceedings of the 58th Annual Meeting of the Association for Computational Linguistics*, pages 8440–8451, Online. Association for Computational Linguistics.

Johannes Daxenberger, Benjamin Schiller, Chris Stahlhut, Erik Kaiser, and Iryna Gurevych. 2020. ArgumenText: Argument classification and clustering in a generalized search scenario. *Datenbank-Spektrum*, 20(2):115–121.

Jacob Devlin, Ming-Wei Chang, Kenton Lee, and Kristina Toutanova. 2019. BERT: Pre-training of deep bidirectional transformers for language understanding. In *Proceedings of the 2019 Conference of the North American Chapter of the Association for Computational Linguistics: Human Language Technologies, Volume 1 (Long and Short Papers)*, pages 4171–4186, Minneapolis, Minnesota. Association for Computational Linguistics.

Roni Friedman, Lena Dankin, Yufang Hou, Ranit Aharonov, Yoav Katz, and Noam Slonim. 2021. Overview of the 2021 key point analysis shared task. In *Proceedings of the 8th Workshop on Argument Mining*, pages 154–164, Punta Cana, Dominican Republic. Association for Computational Linguistics.

Philipp Heinisch and Philipp Cimiano. 2021. A multi-task approach to argument frame classification at variable granularity levels. *it - Information Technology*, 63(1):59–72.

Lauren Johnson. 2014. Adapting and combining constructivist grounded theory and discourse analysis: A practical guide for research. *International Journal of Multiple Research Approaches*, 8(1):100–116.

Lena Jurkschat, Gregor Wiedemann, Maximilian Heinrich, Mattes Ruckdeschel, and Sunna Torge. 2022. Few-shot learning for argument aspects of the nuclear energy debate. In *Proceedings of the Language Resources and Evaluation Conference*, pages 663–672, Marseille, France. European Language Resources Association.

Zhenzhong Lan, Mingda Chen, Sebastian Goodman, Kevin Gimpel, Piyush Sharma, and Radu Soricut. 2019. Albert: A lite bert for self-supervised learning of language representations.

John Lawrence and Chris Reed. 2020. Argument mining: A survey. *Computational Linguistics*, 45(4):765–818.

Yinhan Liu, Myle Ott, Naman Goyal, Jingfei Du, Mandar Joshi, Danqi Chen, Omer Levy, Mike Lewis, Luke Zettlemoyer, and Veselin Stoyanov. 2019. RoBERTa: A robustly optimized BERT pretraining approach. Cite arxiv:1907.11692.

Rebecca Passonneau. 2006. Measuring agreement on set-valued items (MASI) for semantic and pragmatic annotation. In *Proceedings of the Fifth International Conference on Language Resources and Evaluation (LREC'06)*, Genoa, Italy. European Language Resources Association (ELRA).

Maria Pontiki, Dimitrios Galanis, Haris Papageorgiou, Ion Androutsopoulos, Suresh Manandhar, Mohammad Al-Smadi, Mahmoud Al-Ayyoub, Yanyan Zhao, Bing Qin, Orphée De Clercq, et al. 2016. Semeval-2016 task 5: Aspect based sentiment analysis. In *International workshop on semantic evaluation*, pages 19–30.

Nils Reimers and Iryna Gurevych. 2019. Sentence-BERT: Sentence embeddings using Siamese BERT-networks. In *Proceedings of the 2019 Conference on Empirical Methods in Natural Language Processing and the 9th International Joint Conference on Natural Language Processing (EMNLP-IJCNLP)*, pages 3982–3992, Hong Kong, China. Association for Computational Linguistics.

Nils Reimers, Benjamin Schiller, Tilman Beck, Johannes Daxenberger, Christian Stab, and Iryna Gurevych. 2019. Classification and clustering of arguments with contextualized word embeddings. In *Proceedings of the 57th Conference of the Association for Computational Linguistics, ACL 2019, Florence, Italy, July 28- August 2, 2019, Volume 1: Long Papers*, pages 567–578. Association for Computational Linguistics.

Benjamin Schiller, Johannes Daxenberger, and Iryna Gurevych. 2021. Aspect-controlled neural argument generation. In *Proceedings of the 2021 Conference of the North American Chapter of the Association for Computational Linguistics: Human Language Technologies*, pages 380–396, Online. Association for Computational Linguistics.

Isabel Segura-Bedmar, Paloma Martínez, and María Herrero-Zazo. 2013. SemEval-2013 task 9 : Extraction of drug-drug interactions from biomedical texts (DDIExtraction 2013). In *Second Joint Conference on Lexical and Computational Semantics (*SEM), Volume 2: Proceedings of the Seventh International Workshop on Semantic Evaluation (SemEval 2013)*, pages 341–350, Atlanta, Georgia, USA. Association for Computational Linguistics.

Dietrich Trautmann. 2020. Aspect-based argument mining. In *Proceedings of the 7th Workshop on Argument Mining*, pages 41–52, Online. Association for Computational Linguistics.

A Appendix

Minimum Wage Aspects	α_K
Un/employment rate	0.80
Motivation/chances	0.67
Competition/business challenges	0.58
Prices	0.88
Social justice/injustice	0.70
Welfare	0.76
Economic impact	0.80
Turnover	0.96
Capital vs labour	0.51
Government	0.65
Low-skilled	0.69
Youth and secondary wage earners	0.58
other	0.56
all topics	0.65

Table 7: Intercoder-agreement for all topics form the minimum wage dataset (Krippendorff-alpha α_K)

Nuclear Energy Aspects	α_K
Waste	0.89
Health effects	0.77
Environmental impact	0.75
Costs	0.79
Weapons	0.88
Reliability	0.59
Technological innovation	0.67
Energy policy	0.66
Renewables	0.94
Fossil fuels	0.89
Accidents/security	0.79
Public debate	0.63
Other	0.64
all topic	0.68

Table 8: Intercoder-agreement for all topics from the nuclear energy dataset (Krippendorff-alpha α_K)

Marijuana Legalization Aspects	α_K
Illegal trade	0.87
Child and teen safety	0.89
Community/Societal effects	0.54
Health/Psychological effects	0.78
Medical Marijuana	0.92
Drug abuse	0.78
Addiction	0.95
Personal freedom	0.79
National budget	0.77
Gateway drug	0.90
Legal drugs	0.91
Drug policy	0.50
Harm	0.53
Other	0.49
all topics	0.64

Table 9: Intercoder-agreement for all topics from the marijuana legalization dataset (Krippendorff-alpha α_K)

Token id	Text	Label
1	minimum	O
2	wage	O
3	[SEP]	O
4	After	O
5	the	O
6	wage	O
7	increase	O
8	,	O
9	that	PRICES
10	same	PRICES
11	basket	PRICES
12	cost	PRICES
13	$	PRICES
14	315	PRICES
15	.	O

Table 10: Example for CoNLL-formatted aspect data with preceding topic information

Parameter	Value
Learning rate	5.0e-6
Max epochs	50
Batch size	16
Scheduler	Linear with warmup
Warmup ratio	0.1
Number of repeats	5

Table 11: Hyperparameters for all experiments. The other parameters were Flairs default parameters.

Predicting the Presence of Reasoning Markers in Argumentative Text

Jonathan Clayton Rob Gaizauskas
University of Sheffield
{jaclayton2,r.gaizauskas}@sheffield.ac.uk

Abstract

This paper proposes a novel task in Argument Mining, which we will refer to as *Reasoning Marker Prediction*. We reuse the popular Persuasive Essays Corpus (Stab and Gurevych, 2014). Instead of using this corpus for Argument Structure Parsing, we use a simple heuristic method to identify text spans which we can identify as reasoning markers. We propose baseline methods for predicting the presence of these reasoning markers automatically, and make a script to generate the data for the task publicly available [1].

1 Introduction

One key task within the field of argument mining (AM) is the generation of textual summaries of arguments (Fabbri et al., 2021; Bar-Haim et al., 2020). Significant work has been done on automatic extraction of argument components from argumentative text (see Lawrence and Reed, 2020 for a survey). However, research is still needed on how to use these extracted argument components to generate a fluent and readable textual summary.

One means to improve the coherence, and hence readability, of an argument summary is for the selected components which express the content of the argument to be connected using *reasoning markers*, rather than simply placing them adjacent to each other. Reasoning Markers are words and phrases such as "because", "therefore" or "in conclusion" which can be used to structure an argumentative piece of text, acting as the "glue" to hold a text together and make it more intelligible.

Figure 1 indicates how we might envision Reasoning Marker prediction being used in an argument summarisation pipeline. Such a pipeline could consist of argumentative components being extracted from a text, followed by selecting and ordering the most relevant components to form a summary. We concentrate on the final step of a proposed system like this; deciding where to insert reasoning markers to connect the selected argumentative components and produce a fluent text.

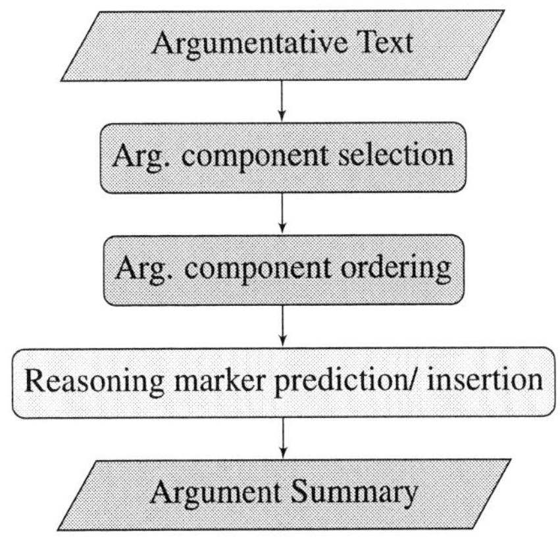

Figure 1: Our conceptualization for how Reasoning Marker Insertion could be used within an Argument Summarization pipeline.

1.1 Defining Reasoning Markers

Reasoning markers (RMs) are a proper subset of discourse markers (DMs), i.e. those words or phrases used in the organization of a spoken or written text.

Williams (2018) seems to be the first to have used the phrase "reasoning marker". However, the use of DMs in argumentative text has been noted since the notion of discourse marker was first introduced in Schiffrin (1987). The term RM excludes, for example, DMs which would typically be found in narrative text, such as "once upon a time", "eventually", or "suddenly".

RMs, specifically, are those discourse markers which are used to encode logical connections between claims and premises. The presence of RMs is argued to be positively correlated with the academic trustworthiness of a text (Williams, 2018).

We do not attempt to provide a rigorous definition of the notion of "reasoning marker" since we

[1] github.com/acidrobin/reasoning_marker_prediction

Proceedings of the 9th Workshop on Argument Mining, co-located with the 29th International Conference on Computational Linguistics, pages 137–142
October 17, 2022.

believe this is a complex linguistic problem beyond the scope of this paper. Categories of discourse marker are notoriously difficult to define, and may be best conceptualized as "family resemblance" categories rather than categories definable by a list of formal features (Bordería, 2006).

Instead we sidestep the issue by assuming that whatever linguistic material can be used to connect together argument components counts as a Reasoning Marker. For our purposes we consider this definition satisfactory, since we are not aiming at formal linguistic correctness but generating a coherent and readable text.

1.2 Related Work

RMs have been used previously in argument mining as a feature for the identification of claims and premises, and the relations between them (Stab and Gurevych, 2014; Eckle-Kohler et al., 2015; Lawrence and Reed, 2015).

Malmi et al. (2017) build a large dataset for reasoning marker prediction, which they gather from English Wikipedia. Their dataset differs from ours in that it is not specifically aimed at argumentative text, and also uses sentence pairs instead of a short-essay context as in our work. Additionally, some authors have used discourse marker prediction as an auxiliary task for generating sentence embeddings (Sileo et al., 2019).

2 Corpus Creation

We use a simple heuristic method to identify RMs in an already existing corpus, taking advantage of existing annotations.

2.1 Persuasive Essay Corpus - Existing Annotation Scheme

The corpus which we choose to use for the extraction of Reasoning Markers is the Persuasive Essay Corpus (PEC) (Stab and Gurevych, 2017). PEC is a corpus of 402 persuasive essays on a variety of controversial topics. The corpus was annotated for the task of Argumentation Structure Parsing, i.e. identifying argumentative components within these essays and the links between them.

In order to extract Reasoning Markers from PEC, we use a heuristic rule-based method. We note that PEC comes pre-segmented into Argument Components (ACs). A BIO tagging schema is used to label each token as either belonging to an AC or not; and, if a token belongs to an AC, it is labelled

> [Furthermore , RM] [investing in art could bring employment opportunities and could end in return of capital occasionally CLAIM] . [The investment could be paid back through the values of the created works of art which as a matter of fact should be considered as national possessions PREMISE] [. To sum up , RM] [not only could investing in art be considered as wasting money at any kind PREMISE] [, but also RM] [it would enriches the culture of the society PREMISE] .

Figure 2: An essay fragment from PEC with our automatically generated RM annotations applied to it. Note we show annotated spans rather than tokens for readability. Tokens in spans labelled "RM" are originally labelled "O" in PEC.

as either a Claim, a MajorClaim (the claim that is the main topic of each essay) or a Premise.

Looking at an example from PEC in Figure 2, we can observe that some ACs are separated by RMs, while others are separated only by punctuation. This suggests that it may be possible to leverage this dataset for RM prediction.

2.2 Inferring Reasoning Markers

In order to identify RMs, we use a simple two-stage pipeline: (1) carry out sentence tokenization; (2) identify those segments within a sentence containing an AC (Claim, MajorClaim or Premise) but labelled with O tags, excluding segments consisting solely of a single punctuation character.

We observe that the vast majority of these O-labelled sentence fragments can be considered as either constituting or containing an RM. This should not be surprising for two reasons: (1) as just outlined, all of these sentence fragments come attached to ACs; (2) the essays originate from `essayforum.com`, a website consisting mostly of essays composed by high-school students or learners of English as a second language – educational contexts where students are rewarded for including RMs within texts.

2.3 Corpus Contents

We find our processed version of PEC contains a total of 7426 "potential RM" datapoints, where a potential RM datapoint occurs between each pair of adjacent ACs. The data is evenly balanced between the classes RM/No RM, as can be seen in Table 1.

The corpus contains a total of 1264 reasoning marker types. While this number seems large, it is somewhat artificially inflated by a number of minor

	RM	No RM	Total
Train	2726	2550	5276
Validation	346	287	633
Test	802	715	1517
Total	3874	3552	7426

Table 1: Numbers of samples found in train, validation and test sets.

variations on what are semantically very similar RM phrases, such as "To conclude, I definitely feel that", "To conclude, I strongly believe that", "To conclude, I want to say that", and a number of similar examples. Shorter RMs are also much more common than longer RMs, as shown in Table 2 and Figure 3. 39.8% of all RMs are only a single token long. As well as concurring with Zipf's brevity law (Zipf, 1949), this reflects the length of RMs typically studied in the literature.

Reasoning Marker	Frequency in Corpus
"because"	195
"for example"	178
"therefore"	137
"however"	110
"moreover"	104

Table 2: The five most common reasoning markers appearing in PEC

The classification of some of the longer segments as RMs is somewhat dubious. For example, the following 25-token phrase would not be typically classified linguistically as a RM, but it seems to fulfil a similar function in context:

> "In conclusion, after analyzing the pros and cons of advertising, both of the views have strong support, but it is felt that... «conclusion»"

However, we refrain from filtering out discourse markers using linguistic criteria, since we treat this as an engineering task and mainly aim to add in appropriate connective material between ACs, whether or not they count as RMs in the strict sense.

2.4 The Corpus Processing Script

We release a script via our repository (`github.com/acidrobin/reasoning_marker_prediction`) which takes in the data provided in the PEC repository (`github.com/UKPLab/acl2017-neural_end2end_am`) and converts it into valid input for a language model. We describe the format of this input in Section 3.1.

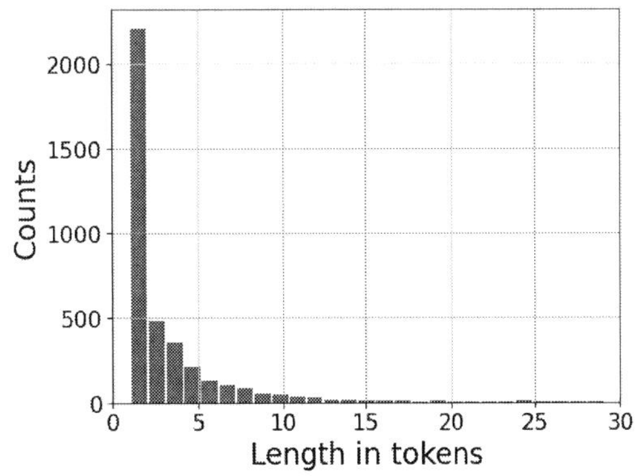

Figure 3: Counts of RM tokens in PEC by token length

3 Task and Baselines

Here we describe the task and the implementation of several pretrained language model baselines.

3.1 Reasoning Marker Prediction

In this task, we take a version of PEC with full essays represented as strings, with each essay replicated as many times as there are RMs in it. Each essay copy has a single gap where one RM may or may not appear. We then predict whether or not an RM should appear in this gap. All other RMs are included in this copy, but excluded in turn in other copies. This is a binary classification task, with two possible labels "True" (if an RM is present) and "False" (if an RM is not present).

Input: "furthermore investing in art could bring employment opportunities and could end in return of capital occasionally [RM] the investment could be paid..."
Output: "False"

Table 3: Input/output schema for RM prediction task.

We also add an additional test condition, which we denote +AC, in which we add special tokens to the input representing AC types: [claim], [majorclaim], and [premise]. For example, a paragraph containing a premise and claim would have an input similar to "[premise] *premise text* [RM] [claim] *claim text*" – so that the [premise] and [claim] special tokens indicate the beginning of these components. We reason that in at least some cases this should help provide useful information to the model; e.g. RMs such as "in conclusion" are very common in the dataset before major claims.

3.2 Implementation of Baselines

Since the ratio of RMs to no-RMs is roughly 50/50, we use a random baseline where the probability of choosing "True" is set at 0.5.

We also use two large pretrained language models, BERT (Devlin et al., 2018) and T5 (Raffel et al., 2020). The two share fundamental similarities in that they are transformer models (Vaswani et al., 2017), however they differ in the specific pretraining regime that they follow (see Raffel et al. (2020) for details).

Implementations of the two models are taken from `huggingface.com` (Wolf et al., 2019). For both models, we used lower-cased text in the input, to prevent trivial classification using the case of the word following the potential RM location.

Due to its pretraining scheme, T5 benefits from a task-specific linguistic prompt being prepended to the input. We experiment with options: no prompt, "True or False:", and "Is there a reasoning marker? True or False:". We found the prompt "True or False:" gave the best result.

For the tokenizers of both models, we add in a special [RM] token which indicates a potential reasoning marker position. For the +AC test condition, we add [claim], [majorclaim], and [premise] special tokens to the BERT tokenizer. For the T5 model, we additionally add "true" and "false" as single tokens. To use the T5 model, which can generate free text, as a classifier, we generate only a single token at inference time and ignore all logits except those corresponding to the "true" and "false" tokens.

Appendix A contains further details of our training scheme.

4 Results

We evaluate our results using precision, recall and F1-score macro-averaged between the two classes. The random baseline, as might be anticipated, achieved an F1-score of 0.50.

Model Name	Precision	Recall	F1-Score
RandomBaseline	0.50	0.50	0.50
bert-base	**0.75**	**0.70**	**0.69**
bert-base+AC	0.73	0.66	0.64
t5-small	0.63	0.60	0.59

Table 4: Performance of the baseline and three models evaluated on the test set.

As Table 4 shows us, the best-performing model was the "vanilla" bert-base-uncased. Adding in the extra tokens to indicate the beginning of argument components lowered performance. Additionally, the T5 model underperformed compared to BERT. The reasons for this are unclear – one possible explanation that could be hypothesized is that the input to this task is closest to what was seen in pretraining by the bert-base model since it was all uncased. The T5 model used was cased since an uncased variant was not available on the web. The largest source of error for both models was over-prediction of reasoning markers.

5 Conclusions and Future Work

We have presented a new task which we believe is a useful subtask for generating summaries of argumentative text: reasoning marker prediction. We have released a script that can be used to generate our derived corpus from PEC, which supports this task. Additionally, we have shown it is possible to predict the presence or absence of an RM between two argumentative components at an above-chance level. Our baseline scores show this is a challenging task, with much room for improvement.

Of course we want not only to predict *that* an RM should occur but *what* the RM should be. In the future, we aim to work on using end-to-end models to generate an appropriate RM for a given context, instead of simply predicting whether or not an RM should appear.

Another aspect of this task which we have not explored is the sub-categorization of RMs. Multiple taxonomies of DMs have been developed that could be used for this task. See Knott's (1996) taxonomy, and the development in Oates (2000).

However, it is likely that this would be a non-trivial task and require some expert labelling, due to the fact that there is not a one-to-one correspondence between DMs and their functions. A simple DM like "so" for example, has many different functions and can be used to provide justifications, for sequencing, or for expressing a purpose.

Nonetheless, since, as noted above, there are many RMs in this dataset that are more-or-less interchangeable, it may be sufficient to predict the category that a potential RM should belong to rather than attempting to generate one directly.

This work was supported by the Centre for Doctoral Training in Speech and Language Technologies (SLT) and their Applications funded by UK Research and Innovation [grant number EP/S023062/1], and by Amazon.

References

Roy Bar-Haim, Lilach Eden, Roni Friedman, Yoav Kantor, Dan Lahav, and Noam Slonim. 2020. From arguments to key points: Towards automatic argument summarization. *arXiv preprint arXiv:2005.01619*.

Salvador Pons Bordería. 2006. A functional approach to the study of discourse markers. In *Approaches to discourse particles*, pages 77–99. Brill.

Jacob Devlin, Ming-Wei Chang, Kenton Lee, and Kristina Toutanova. 2018. Bert: Pre-training of deep bidirectional transformers for language understanding. *arXiv preprint arXiv:1810.04805*.

Judith Eckle-Kohler, Roland Kluge, and Iryna Gurevych. 2015. On the role of discourse markers for discriminating claims and premises in argumentative discourse. In *Proceedings of the 2015 Conference on Empirical Methods in Natural Language Processing*, pages 2236–2242.

Alexander R Fabbri, Faiaz Rahman, Imad Rizvi, Borui Wang, Haoran Li, Yashar Mehdad, and Dragomir Radev. 2021. Convosumm: Conversation summarization benchmark and improved abstractive summarization with argument mining. *arXiv preprint arXiv:2106.00829*.

Diederik P Kingma and Jimmy Ba. 2014. Adam: A method for stochastic optimization. *arXiv preprint arXiv:1412.6980*.

Alistair Knott. 1996. A data-driven methodology for motivating a set of coherence relations.

John Lawrence and Chris Reed. 2015. Combining argument mining techniques. In *Proceedings of the 2nd Workshop on Argumentation Mining*, pages 127–136.

John Lawrence and Chris Reed. 2020. Argument mining: A survey. *Computational Linguistics*, 45(4):765–818.

Eric Malmi, Daniele Pighin, Sebastian Krause, and Mikhail Kozhevnikov. 2017. Automatic prediction of discourse connectives. *arXiv preprint arXiv:1702.00992*.

Sarah Louise Oates. 2000. Multiple discourse marker occurrence: Creating hierarchies for natural language generation. In *Proceedings of the ANLP-NAACL 2000 Student Research Workshop*.

Colin Raffel, Noam Shazeer, Adam Roberts, Katherine Lee, Sharan Narang, Michael Matena, Yanqi Zhou, Wei Li, Peter J Liu, et al. 2020. Exploring the limits of transfer learning with a unified text-to-text transformer. *J. Mach. Learn. Res.*, 21(140):1–67.

Deborah Schiffrin. 1987. *Discourse markers*. 5. Cambridge University Press.

Damien Sileo, Tim Van-De-Cruys, Camille Pradel, and Philippe Muller. 2019. Mining discourse markers for unsupervised sentence representation learning. *arXiv preprint arXiv:1903.11850*.

Christian Stab and Iryna Gurevych. 2014. Annotating argument components and relations in persuasive essays. In *Proceedings of COLING 2014, the 25th international conference on computational linguistics: Technical papers*, pages 1501–1510.

Christian Stab and Iryna Gurevych. 2017. Parsing argumentation structures in persuasive essays. *Computational Linguistics*, 43(3):619–659.

Ashish Vaswani, Noam Shazeer, Niki Parmar, Jakob Uszkoreit, Llion Jones, Aidan N Gomez, Łukasz Kaiser, and Illia Polosukhin. 2017. Attention is all you need. *Advances in neural information processing systems*, 30.

Ashley Williams. 2018. Using reasoning markers to select the more rigorous software practitioners' online content when searching for grey literature. In *Proceedings of the 22nd International Conference on Evaluation and Assessment in Software Engineering 2018*, pages 46–56.

Thomas Wolf, Lysandre Debut, Victor Sanh, Julien Chaumond, Clement Delangue, Anthony Moi, Pierric Cistac, Tim Rault, Rémi Louf, Morgan Funtowicz, et al. 2019. Huggingface's transformers: State-of-the-art natural language processing. *arXiv preprint arXiv:1910.03771*.

George Kingsley Zipf. 1949. Human behavior and the principle of least effort: an introduction to human ecology.

A Details of Training Scheme

All of our BERT and T5 models are pretrained and then fine-tuned on the task for a number of epochs chosen by early stopping, in the range of $[0 \,..\, 8]$. We used the uncased version of BERT base. We use the Adam optimizer (Kingma and Ba, 2014). The best learning rate is chosen by a grid search; for both models we explore the set $\{1e^{-4}, 5e^{-5}, 1e^{-5}, 5e^{-6}, 1e^{-6}\}$. For the BERT model, we found the optimal learning rate was $1e^{-5}$ and the best performance was achieved after 3 epochs of fine-tuning. For T5, a learning rate of $5e^{-6}$ and 5 epochs of fine-tuning were optimal.

Detecting Arguments in CJEU Decisions on Fiscal State Aid

Giulia Grundler[*1] and **Piera Santin**[*2] and **Andrea Galassi**[1 ✉] and **Federico Galli**[2]
Francesco Godano[2] and **Francesca Lagioia**[2 ✉] and **Elena Palmieri**[1]
Federico Ruggeri[1] and **Giovanni Sartor**[2] and **Paolo Torroni**[1]
[1]DISI, University of Bologna, Bologna, Italy
[2]CIRSFID-Alma AI, University of Bologna, Bologna, Italy
a.galassi@unibo.it
francesca.lagioia@unibo.it

Abstract

The successful application of argument mining in the legal domain can dramatically impact many disciplines related to law. For this purpose, we present *Demosthenes*, a novel corpus for argument mining in legal documents, composed of 40 decisions of the Court of Justice of the European Union on matters of fiscal state aid. The annotation specifies three hierarchical levels of information: the argumentative elements, their types, and their argument schemes. In our experimental evaluation, we address 4 different classification tasks, combining advanced language models and traditional classifiers.

1 Introduction

The study of argumentation in legal contexts is one of the most lively research areas at the intersection of Artificial Intelligence and Law (Bench-Capon et al., 2004, 2009). It has its roots in logic, philosophy, and linguistics, as it studies how different claims and opinions are proposed, debated, and evaluated, considering their relations and inter-dependencies. The legal domain offers a natural scenario for the application of different argument models as well as novel machine learning and natural language processing techniques in order to perform legal reasoning (Prakken and Sartor, 1996a; Atkinson and Bench-Capon, 2019, 2021), build specific ontologies (Hoekstra et al., 2009), or support the teaching of law (Ashley et al., 2002; Carr, 2003). Argumentation is relevant to legal logic (Prakken and Sartor, 1996b, 2002), case-based reasoning (Aleven, 2003; Ashley et al., 2002), the interpretation of judicial opinions and statutory laws (McCarty, 2007; Savelka and Ashley, 2016; Palau and Ieven, 2009; Mochales Palau and Moens, 2011), the summarization of judicial opinions (Hachey and Grover, 2006).

Building tools capable of automatically detecting arguments in legal texts can produce a dramatic impact on many disciplines related to law, providing valuable instruments for the retrieval of legal arguments from large corpora, for the summarization and classification of legal texts, and for the development of AI systems supporting lawyers and judges, by suggesting relevant arguments and counterarguments. A crucial obstacle to providing effective automatic support to legal argumentation pertains to the knowledge bottleneck: legal arguments are only available in natural language texts, whose content has been so far only accessible with the help of domain experts. To overcome this limitation, recourse has been made to argument mining (AM), i.e., the automated extraction of arguments from documents.

AM frameworks can be described as multi-stage pipeline systems, aimed at extracting natural language arguments and their relations from textual documents (Lippi and Torroni, 2016; Cabrio and Villata, 2018). Each stage of the pipeline addresses a sub-task of the problem. A first stage usually consists of detecting which sentences in the input document(s) are argumentative, i.e., contain an argument or part thereof. Once argumentative sentences are singled out, it is possible to detect the boundaries of the various argument components and their characteristics (Mochales Palau and Moens, 2011; Niculae et al., 2017; Bar-Haim et al., 2017). Finally, a last stage in the pipeline considers these components in order to predict the relationship between them and/or between the arguments they are part of (Lippi and Torroni, 2016; Lawrence and Reed, 2019).

In this work, we contribute to this research domain by releasing *Demosthenes*, a novel corpus of legal documents annotated for AM. Specifically, we focus on the first two stages of the pipeline in order to: (i) identify premises and conclusions; (ii) distinguish between legal and factual premises; (iii)

[*] Equal contribution

Proceedings of the 9th Workshop on Argument Mining, co-located with the 29th International Conference on Computational Linguistics, pages 143–157
October 17, 2022.

identify argumentative schemes. Additionally, we perform an experimental evaluation on all the tasks using multiple representations and classifiers.

The paper is structured as follows. In Section 2, we provide an overview of related work. Section 3 describes the corpus we have created and the annotation procedure. Section 4 concerns the experimental setting, while the results are presented in Section 5. Section 6 concludes.

2 Related work

Despite in the last decade the field of AM has become a popular research area in Natural Language Processing (NLP), there are yet limited studies focusing on legal texts and, in particular, on judicial decisions (Zhang et al., 2022b). Among them, the targets of judicial AM vary widely (Zhang et al., 2022a). Some studies aim at extracting the arguments from generic unstructured documents (Levy et al., 2014); others start from a given set of arguments and focus on aspects such as the identification of attack/support relations between them (Chesnevar et al., 2006), or the classification of argument schemes (Feng and Hirst, 2011).

One of the main obstacles in providing effective automatic support to legal argumentation pertains to the knowledge bottleneck. Like most interdisciplinary studies, creating and constructing annotated corpora is labour–intensive, as it is a complex and time-consuming task, requiring the guidance of legal experts, i.e., lawyers, being also familiar with legal arguments and the specific legal domain. Indeed, a discrepancy exists between the way NLP researchers model and annotate arguments in court decisions and the way legal experts understand and analyze legal argumentation (Habernal et al., 2022). In fact, under computational approaches, arguments are often treated as mere structures of premises and claims (Stede and Schneider, 2018). In legal research, on the contrary, it it critical to also distinguish different kinds of arguments and classify them according to the rich typology that is rooted in the theory and practice of legal argumentation (Trachtman, 2013). Finally, legal arguments may present themselves in different ways within different kinds of legal texts, depending on the on the domain of the law being addressed, and on the institutional position and legal culture of the authority that is producing such texts.

Unfortunately, there are a limited number of annotated corpora that fit the requirements just mentioned, and they include a small amount of documents, withing specific areas of the law.

Thus the research community can highly benefit from the availability of new datasets, which as is the case of Demosthenes, cover a sizable amount of examples, and include an attempt at classifying the identified arguments according to a legal typology.

Moreover, to the best of our knowledge, few works have analysed how natural-language argumentation is used in real courts (Mochales and Moens, 2011; Habernal et al., 2022). This situation leads to three urgent needs in legal AM: (1) the creation of new annotated corpora, (2) possibly addressing different domains of the law; and (3) an analysis of how and to what extent models of arguments from legal theory can be reliably operationalized in terms of discourse annotations.

The approach by Poudyal et al. (2020) represents, to date, one of the few works whose goal was to implement a full-fledged argumentation mining system, specific to a single legal domain. Mochales Palau and Moens (2011) created a corpus of 47 cases (judgments and decisions) from the open-source database of the European Court of Human Rights (ECHR), in which they applied a sentence-level annotation scheme based on Walton's model (Walton et al., 2008) where each sentence was labeled as *premise*, *conclusion* or *non-argumentative*. More recently, Poudyal et al. (2020); Mochales and Moens (2011); Teruel et al. (2018) used the same guidelines to release a similar dataset of 42 documents. Walker et al. (2011) annotated judicial decisions selected from the U.S. Court of Federal Claims also identifying sentences' inferential roles and support levels by using logical connectives to represent argumentative relations between premises and conclusions. Walker et al. (2017) published a dataset of judicial decisions from the Board of Veterans Appeals. The decisions are annotated by legal experts with semantic information about arguments, including ten sentence roles and eight propositional connectives. The corpus initially contained 20 documents but was expanded subsequently (Walker et al., 2019, 2020).

In this work, we aim to partially fill the mentioned gaps by: (1) creating a new annotated legal corpus; (2) focusing on a domain that is still unexplored in the field of legal argumentation, i.e., fiscal state aid; and (3) investigating whether argumentation schemes defined in legal theory, in particular by Walton et al. (2008, 2021) can be easily adapted to the CJEU reasoning, as made explicit in the Court discourse. In particular, we focus on the detection of argumentative elements and their classification according to a hierarchical taxonomy of three layers, as detailed in the following.

For what concerns the experimental part, previous works have addressed AM in the legal domain using Naive Bayes and Maximum Entropy (Mochales Palau and Moens, 2011), factor graphs (Niculae et al., 2017), and residual networks (Galassi et al., 2018, 2021). More recently, advanced language models based on attention such as BERT (Devlin et al., 2019) and RoBERTa (Liu et al., 2019; Poudyal et al., 2020) have been used and combined with LSTMs and CNNs (Xu et al., 2020, 2021a,b). In this work, we exploit a combination of advanced language models, namely SBERT (Reimers and Gurevych, 2019) and Legal-BERT (Chalkidis et al., 2020), and traditional classifiers. We used existing language models without fine-tuning them. This is in line with recent efforts in the NLP community toward efficient machine learning methodologies with limited computational footprint (Lai et al., 2021).

3 Corpus Creation

The source corpus consists of 40 decisions on fiscal State aids by the Court of Justice of the European Union (CJEU), written in English. The decisions range from 2000 to 2018, i.e., since the CJEU's inception as a Court of Appeal in this domain. All documents have been downloaded from the EUR-LEX database and manually labelled. We have chosen this source since: (a) CJEU decisions usually contain a rich and diverse set of legal arguments (e.g., arguments appealing to statues, principles or precedents, according to different interpretive canons); (b) they have a standard (although not fixed) structure, in which argument chains are embedded and can be easily identified; (c) the selected decisions come from the same domain–i.e., fiscal State aids–which strongly relies on judicial interpretation; and (d) our annotators have some expertise in this domain.

3.1 Annotation Procedure

CJEU decisions are structured in clearly separated sections.[1] Since our primary purpose is to capture the argumentative patterns of the CJEU reasoning process, we focused on the section *Findings of the Court*, reporting all argumentative steps leading to the final ruling. This section is characterised by a set of interacting inferences, which ultimately lead to conclusions on the parties' claims. Each inference links a set of premises to a conclusion, which may support or attack further inferences.

The annotation guidelines were written and refined through multiple stages of annotation, evaluation of the agreement, and discussion. The annotation was done at the sentence level by two experts in the legal domain, using periods, semicolons, and line breaks as delimiters. As shown in Table 1, three hierarchical levels of annotation were identified in arguments: the elements (premises and conclusions), the type of premise (legal or factual), and the scheme.

3.1.1 Argumentative Elements and Types

Sentences compose arguments, which are included in argument chains. By an argument, we mean a set of connected inferences. Each such inference consists of the link between certain premises and a conclusion. It is important to note that the conclusion of an inference can also serve as the premise for further inferences. Such intermediate conclusions/premises have been marked as premises. By an argument chain, we mean an argument supporting a final conclusion concerning a specific ground of appeal, together with all counterarguments considered by the Court (see appendix B). More than one argument chain may be provided in a single decision.

For premises and conclusions, we defined mandatory and optional attributes and their possible values, as reported in Table 1. In particular, each premise and conclusion is denoted through a unique identifier (`ID`), whose value is constructed by joining a letter (which denotes the argument chain to which the premise(s) or the conclusion belongs to, e.g. A or B), with a progressive number (which distinguishes the single premise or conclusion withing the chain, e.g., A1, A2, An; B1, B2, Bn).

We distinguished between *factual* and *legal* premises. The former describes factual situations and events (pertaining to the substance or the procedure of the case); the latter specifies the legal content (legal rules, precedents, interpretation of applicable laws and principles). Whenever a premise combines legal and factual aspects, it has been

[1] Additional details about decision's structure are indicated in Appendix A.

Argumentative elements	Tag	Mandatory attributes of the element			Optional attribute of the element		
		Name	Value	Tag	Name	Value	Tag
Premise	<prem>	Identifier	A1, A2, An B1, B2, Bn	ID="An"	/	/	/
		Type	Legal	T="L"	Argumentation scheme	Argument from Rule	S="Rule"
						Argument from Precedent	S="Prec"
						Authoritative Argument	S="Aut"
						Argument from Verbal Classification	S="Class"
						Argument from Interpretation	S="Itpr"
						Argument from Principle	S="Princ"
			Factual	T="F"	/	/	/
Conclusion	<conc>	Identifier	An, Bn, Cn	ID="An"	/	/	/

Table 1: Annotation scheme.

marked as both legal and factual. Examples of premises, their classification, and argument chains can be found in Appendix B.

3.1.2 Argumentation Schemes

In general, legal premises determine the nature of the inference in which they are used; thus we have labelled them with the corresponding type of inference, which we call argument scheme following Walton et al. (2008, 2021). As an example, consider the following legal premise marked under the Rule scheme:

> *As stated in recital 14 of the preamble to that regulation, this limitation period has been established for reasons of legal certainty.* (Case C-408/04 P, para 102)

In this work, we rely on a set of schemes inspired by the work by Walton et al. (2008, 2021), which we specifically adapted to the CJEU reasoning, as made explicit in the cases. In particular, we identified six argument schemes that are not exclusive between each other. Therefore, a single legal premise may be assigned multiple schemes.

Rule (or established rule) scheme. According to the Rule scheme, a legislative rule is applicable to the case and determines its outcome unless exceptional provisions exist whichoverride that rule. In CJEU decisions, we used this scheme to classify premises explicitly citing an EU norm as part of the relevant legislative framework. Thus, we excluded all cases where the Court refers to national laws or to norms mentioned by the Court of First Instance since such norms can not be considered a basis for the CJEU decision. As an example, consider the following premise:

> *...Article 173 of the Treaty, ...provides that any natural or legal person may on the grounds of lack of competence, infringement of an essential procedural requirement, infringement of this Treaty ...institute proceedings against a decision addressed to that person ....* (Case C-298/00 P, para 34).

Precedent scheme. According to the Precedent scheme, the *ratio decidendi* of a past case is applicable to the current case determining its outcome unless a distinction can be made (Langenbucher, 1998). Under this scheme, we marked the CJEU premises referring to its past decisions. Textual indicators signalling a precedent scheme include references to cited judgements as well as a set of expressions such as "according to settled case-law"; "as is apparent from that case-law"; "as the Court has consistently held". As an example, consider the following premise:

> *...undertakings to which aid has been granted may not, in principle, entertain a legitimate expectation that the aid is lawful unless it has been granted in compliance with the procedure laid down in that article and, second, that a diligent businessman should normally be able to determine whether that procedure has been followed (Case C-5/89 Commission v Germany [1990] ECR I-3437, paragraph 14;....*(Joined Cases C-183/02 P and C-187/02 P, para 44).

Authoritative scheme. According to the Authoritative scheme, an indication by an authority is applicable to the current case and may support its outcome, in the absence of reasons to the contrary. It is possible to distinguish three different types of authoritative inferences: (1) the *inference from administrative authority*, having a right to exercise command or influence over another party subject to that authority; (2) the *inference from expert opinion*, which is an epistemic authority having an expertise in the relevant field of knowledge; and (3) the *inference from the authority of the majority of the people or the common opinion* (Walton et al.,

2021; Walton and Koszowy, 2015). In our corpus, we marked as inferences from authority the CJEU statements reporting an opinion of the Advocate General, since such opinions can be considered as authoritative sources of knowledge on which the Court relies, even though they are not legally binding. As an example, consider the following premise:

> *It follows, as the Advocate General observed ... that recovery of such aid entails the restitution of the advantage procured by the aid for the recipient, not the restitution of any economic benefit the recipient may have enjoyed as a result of exploiting the advantage.* (Joined Cases C-164/15 P and C-165/15 P, para 92).

Classification scheme. According to the Classification scheme a concept is applicable to the current case and may support a corresponding classification unless an exception also applies. This scheme is an adaptation of the Verbal Classification scheme in (Macagno and Walton, 2015; Walton et al., 2008). The acceptability of the scheme from classification depends on the acceptability of the classification and on whether it admits possible exceptions or defaults. We marked a premise under this scheme whenever it consists of a definition of a legal concept, indicating the preconditions for a certain fact, property or entity to be qualified as falling under the concept. As an example, consider the following:

> *So, in order for there to be State aid within the meaning of that provision it is necessary, first, for there to be aid favouring certain undertakings or the production of certain goods and, second, for that advantage to come from the State or State resources.* (Case C-353/95 P, para 25)

Interpretative scheme. According to the interpretative scheme, a meaning relevant to the decision of the case is ascribed to a legal source (e.g., legislation, precedent, ...). This scheme includes different kinds of interpretative reasoning (e.g., literal, teleological, psychological, systematic interpretation, ...). Consider the following premise as an example of a psychological interpretative scheme:

> *... the intention of the EC Treaty, in providing through Article 88 EC for aid to be kept under constant review and monitored by the Commission, is that the finding that aid may be incompatible with the common market is to be arrived at, ..., by means of an appropriate procedure which it is the Commission's responsibility to set in motion.* (Case C-272/12 P, para 48)

Principle scheme. According to the Principle scheme, a general legal principle is applicable to the case and may determine its outcome.

We annotated under this scheme those premises explicitly stating that a given fact, property or entity should be qualified in a certain way for complying or not complying with a certain principle of law. As an example, consider the following premise:

> *That fact however had to be taken into consideration in relation to the obligation to recover the incompatible aid, in the light of the principles of protection of legitimate expectations and legal certainty, ...* (Case C-272/12 P, para 53).

Whenever a premise is relevant under more than one scheme, such premise has been marked accordingly (see Appendix B for examples).

3.2 Inter-Annotator Agreement

To measure the inter-annotator agreement regarding the classification of sentences as premises and conclusions, 14 documents were tagged by the two annotators, reaching a Cohen's kappa (Cohen, 1960) of 0.95, which indicates an almost perfect agreement. We have also measured the agreement considering only the argumentative sentences, obtaining a kappa of 0.86, which indicates strong agreement.

In order to calculate the agreement for the type attribute (legal/factual), we considered only the sentences that both annotators had labelled as premises, to avoid the propagation of error from one annotation layer to the other. We compute the Cohen's kappa on each value separately, treating it as a binary classification problem and obtained a strong agreement for both the classes: 0.87 for *factual* and 0.82 for *legal*.

To avoid error propagation, the agreement for the scheme attribute was measured on 10 documents on which the annotators had already solved previous conflicts, to consider only sentences that are legal premises according to both annotators. We computed the Cohen's kappa, as done for the type attribute, obtaining the results reported in Table 2. The agreement for the *class* (classification) scheme was none and the one for the *princ* (principle) scheme was weak. This evaluation is highly

	Aut	Class	Itpr	Prec	Princ	Rule
Only Ann. 1	2	0	14	3	2	2
Only Ann. 2	0	2	29	7	3	3
Both Ann.	4	0	80	82	2	76
κ	0.79	0.00	0.46	0.88	0.43	0.93

Table 2: Number of sentences labelled for each scheme by each annotator and agreement between them.

Element	#
documents	40
sentences	9320
prem	2375
conc	160
factual	1575
legal	906

Element	#
aut	53
class	56
itpr	296
prec	503
princ	15
rule	322

Table 3: Composition of the dataset.

influenced by the fact that these schemes were represented only in very few sentences. Another class for which the agreement was weak is *itpr* (interpretative), probably motivated by the fact that this is a mixed category, that groups together different kinds of interpretative schemes. Despite having only a few samples, there was moderate agreement on the *aut* (autoritative) scheme, while the agreement was strong for *prec* (precedent) and *rule*.

Most disagreements were due to: (i) the ambiguity of some argumentative sentences, often embedding multiple schemes; (ii) the fuzzy and overlapping boundaries between different schemes; (iii) the lack of clear language qualifiers and rhetorical clues characterizing some schemes; (iv) the different subject matters potentially falling under the same scheme. This is particularly true with regard to the interpretative scheme, which includes, as noted above, the application of different argumentative canons, each referring to different substantive grounds. Finally, while argument schemes are separately characterised and clearly analysed in theoretical studies, often in the judicial discourse complex argument patterns are present, where multiple inferences are merged and premises are left implicit.

3.3 Demosthenes Corpus

The conflicts between annotators have been solved by a third legal expert, who considered the source of the divergence and discussed with the two annotators the possible solutions. The final corpus is publicly available[2] and its composition can be found in Table 3.

The annotation regarding argumentative elements and their type can be considered reliable due to the strong agreement between annotators. Conversely, the annotation of the schemes can be considered reliable only for some of them, namely *Aut*, *Prec*, and *Rule*, while the other schemes must be considered potentially noisy.

4 Experimental Setting

In this study, we addressed four tasks. Two are general argument mining tasks, namely argument detection and argument classification. The other two are rather domain specific and are type classification and scheme classification. They are defined as follows:

- **Argument Detection (AD)**: given a sentence, classify it as *premise*, *conclusion*, or *neither*;
- **Argument Classification (AC)**: given a sentence that is known to be argumentative, classify it as *premise* or *conclusion*;
- **Type Classification (TC)**: a multi-label classification problem where a sentence that is known to be a premise is classified as *legal* (L) and/or *factual* (F);
- **Scheme Classification (SC)**: a multi-label classification task where a sentence, known to be a legal premise, is classified according to its scheme; due to the low number of samples in the dataset, the *Princ* scheme has not been considered.

We structured TC and SC as multi-label classification tasks since in both cases a single input sentence can have multiple labels. However, it is important to highlight that each sentence considered in these tasks has at least one label: there are no premises without a type, nor legal premises without a scheme. We did not enforce this constraint in our experiments and leave it for future work.

For AD, as a first step, we pre-processed the documents removing periods from some common abbreviations (e.g., 'p.' for 'paragraph' and 'n.' for 'number'). The sentence segmentation was then performed based on periods, semicolons, and newlines. For all the tasks, we pre-processed the

[2] `https://github.com/adele-project/demosthenes`.

sentences by removing stop-words and punctuation symbols.

Experiments were conducted using 5-fold cross-validation with folds determined at the document level, so that sentences of the same document belong to the same fold. The folds were created manually to balance their composition and guarantee that all scheme classes were represented in each fold.

For all tasks we adopted three different representations of the input text:

- **TF-IDF**: vectorization based on the term frequency-inverse document frequency statistic;
- **Sentence-BERT (SBERT)** (Reimers and Gurevych, 2019): a modification of the BERT model that produces semantically meaningful sentences embeddings, mapping sentences with similar semantic content into vectors close to each other;[3]
- **Legal-BERT** (Chalkidis et al., 2020): a family of BERT models adapted to the legal domain.[4]

As classifiers, we have chosen a set of traditional machine learning techniques that have low computational requirements. We focused on these efficient techniques to assess if they are effective enough or if there is the need to adopt more advanced methods such as fine-tuned language models. Specifically, we experimented with the following models: linear svc, svc, random forest, Gaussian naive Bayes and k-neighbours.[5]

5 Results and Discussion

For each task, we report the results obtained by each combination of embeddings and classifiers. We also report the performance of two simple baselines: a classifier that outputs a random value and one that always predicts the majority class. We measure the F1 score obtained for each class and their macro-average.

AD. As can be seen in Table 4, most models perform well in the majority class (*neither*), including the majority baseline. They have more difficulties

Embedding	Classifier	Avg	prem	conc	neither
-	Random	0.26	0.28	0.03	0.47
-	Majority	0.28	0.00	0.00	0.84
TF-IDF	Linear SVC	**0.70**	**0.58**	0.65	**0.88**
TF-IDF	Random Forest	0.65	0.48	0.60	**0.88**
TF-IDF	Gaussian NB	0.40	0.40	0.23	0.55
TF-IDF	K Neighbors	0.62	0.42	0.59	0.85
TF-IDF	SVC	0.53	0.14	0.59	0.86
SBERT	Linear SVC	0.69	0.55	**0.67**	0.85
SBERT	Random Forest	0.60	0.35	0.59	0.86
SBERT	Gaussian NB	0.52	0.54	0.34	0.69
SBERT	K Neighbors	0.65	0.50	0.64	0.82
SBERT	SVC	0.67	0.51	0.64	0.86
Legal-BERT	Linear SVC	0.69	**0.58**	0.62	0.87
Legal-BERT	Random Forest	0.59	0.44	0.46	0.87
Legal-BERT	Gaussian NB	0.59	0.54	0.55	0.67
Legal-BERT	K Neighbors	0.68	0.56	0.66	0.82
Legal-BERT	SVC	0.69	0.56	0.64	0.87

Table 4: Detailed results of the AD task.

in recognizing argumentative sentences. The task can be considered not trivial since both baselines obtain an average score lower than 0.30. It is interesting to notice that the *conclusion* class obtains a higher score than *premise* despite the lower number of samples. Random Forests and Gaussian Naive Bayes perform poorly with all the embeddings. All the other models obtain good results when using Legal-BERT representation, which can be considered the best representation for this task. Nonetheless, the best result is obtained by the combination of Linear SVC and TF-IDF representation.

AC. Table 5 shows the results of this classification task. The results are satisfactory, with all the models obtaining an average score above 0.80. They also obtain a score close to 1.00 for the premise class, but this also holds for the majority baseline. From our observation, random forests seem to be the best classifiers independently from the embedding used, obtaining the best score with TF-IDF representation and a similar result with the other ones.

TC. All the models perform better on the majority class (*factual*) obtaining a score between 0.75 and 0.89, as shown in Table 6. This is not surprising considering that the majority baseline reaches a score of 0.80. The best result on the *legal* label reaches a score of 0.80, for a macro average of 0.85, which can be considered a good result against the 0.60 score obtained by the best baseline. The SBERT representation is entirely dominated by the Legal-BERT one, while TF-IDF changes a lot depending on the classifier. The SVC per-

[3]We used the `bert-base-nli-mean-tokens` model.

[4]We used the `legal-bert-small` model.

[5]We used the default hyper-parameters offered by the `sci-kit learn` library.

Embedding	Classifier	Avg	prem	conc
-	Random	0.37	0.63	0.10
-	Majority	0.48	0.97	0.00
TF-IDF	Linear SVC	0.87	0.98	0.75
TF-IDF	Random Forest	**0.88**	**0.99**	**0.77**
TF-IDF	Gaussian NB	0.84	0.98	0.69
TF-IDF	K Neighbors	0.81	0.97	0.65
TF-IDF	SVC	0.82	0.98	0.66
SBERT	Linear SVC	0.85	0.98	0.71
SBERT	Random Forest	0.86	0.98	0.73
SBERT	Gaussian NB	0.81	0.97	0.66
SBERT	K Neighbors	0.84	0.98	0.71
SBERT	SVC	0.87	0.98	0.75
Legal-BERT	Linear SVC	0.80	0.98	0.63
Legal-BERT	Random Forest	0.86	0.98	0.73
Legal-BERT	Gaussian NB	0.86	0.98	0.74
Legal-BERT	K Neighbors	**0.88**	0.98	**0.77**
Legal-BERT	SVC	0.85	0.98	0.72

Table 5: Results of the AC task.

Embedding	Classifier	Avg	L	F
-	Random	0.60	0.50	0.69
-	Majority	0.40	0.00	0.80
TF-IDF	Linear SVC	0.83	0.77	0.88
TF-IDF	Random Forest	0.82	0.75	**0.89**
TF-IDF	Gaussian NB	0.68	0.61	0.75
TF-IDF	K Neighbors	0.76	0.70	0.82
TF-IDF	SVC	0.61	0.38	0.83
SBERT	Linear SVC	0.77	0.70	0.84
SBERT	Random Forest	0.74	0.64	0.85
SBERT	Gaussian NB	0.72	0.66	0.78
SBERT	K Neighbors	0.72	0.64	0.80
SBERT	SVC	0.80	0.73	0.87
Legal-BERT	Linear SVC	0.81	0.75	0.87
Legal-BERT	Random Forest	0.77	0.67	0.87
Legal-BERT	Gaussian NB	0.73	0.66	0.79
Legal-BERT	K Neighbors	0.78	0.72	0.85
Legal-BERT	SVC	**0.85**	**0.80**	**0.89**

Table 6: Results of the TC task.

form very well with Legal-BERT and with SBERT, outperforming the other classifiers, but when combined with TF-IDF leads to the worst performance instead.

SC. As shown in Table 7, the only class for which the baselines reach a good score is the *Prec* scheme; therefore we can consider the scheme classification problem to be not trivial. The results for the *Aut* scheme vary widely: the worst result is 0.00, while the best is 0.94. We hypothesize that this may be due to the limited amount of samples present in the dataset. The best result is obtained with Random Forest and TF-IDF, while Linear SVC classifiers perform well (above 0.60) with all the embeddings. Linear SVC obtains good results also for the *Class* scheme, outperforming all the other classifiers. SBERT and Legal-BERT representation perform similarly and they are outperformed by TF-IDF in most cases. The *Itpr* scheme seems to be the most challenging to predict, with the best value of 0.63 and no visible pattern in the performance of the models, probably due to the noisiness of the label. For the *Prec* scheme, all models outperform the baselines; Legal-BERT embeddings lead to good results (between 0.80 and 0.90), but the best result is obtained with Random Forest and TF-IDF. The classification as *Rule*, presents a lot of variance, with linear SVCs outperforming the other classifiers. The best results in terms of macro average are obtained with TF-IDF representation and Linear SVC (0.75), TF-IDF and Random Forest (0.73), and Legal-BERT and Linear SVC (0.74). Since *Itpr* and *Class* labels are potentially noisy, we also computed the macro average score excluding them. The best models are the same even according to this alternative metric, with TF-IDF and Random Forest outperforming the others.

Feature analysis Since the LinearSVC classifier trained on the TF-IDF representation performs well in all the proposed tasks, we analyzed which features are assigned more weight to understand which words can be considered good indicators for the prediction. For each task, in Table 8 we report the 10 most relevant words associated with each class. We can see that the words "must", "follows", "light", "well", "consequently", and "rejected" are associated with *conc* both in AD and AC. Conversely, the only word associated with *prem* both in AD and AC is the word "directed". This result suggests a more robust characterization of the *conc* class with respect of *prem*, and partially motivates the better result obtained in AD for *conc*. We can also see that some indicators of the *prem* class are also used to determine premises' types or schemes. For example, the word "see" (which is often used to direct the reader to other judicial precedents) is associated with *prem* in AD and *legal* in TC, while the words "argument", "claims", and "general" are associated with *prem* in AC and the scheme *prec* in SC. The same consideration holds between *legal* premises and schemes: the words "article" and "ecr" are associated with *legal* in TC, while in SC

Embedding	Classifier	Avg	Aut	Class	Itpr	Prec	Rule	$Avg_{reliable}$
-	Random	0.33	0.10	0.12	0.42	0.55	0.44	0.36
-	Majority	0.14	0.00	0.00	0.00	0.71	0.00	0.24
TF-IDF	Linear SVC	**0.75**	0.85	**0.72**	0.48	0.88	0.83	0.85
TF-IDF	Random Forest	0.73	**0.94**	0.57	0.30	**0.91**	**0.91**	**0.92**
TF-IDF	Gaussian NB	0.44	0.00	0.62	0.34	0.74	0.51	0.42
TF-IDF	K Neighbors	0.60	0.72	0.57	0.28	0.75	0.68	0.72
TF-IDF	SVC	0.31	0.00	0.50	0.07	0.72	0.24	0.32
SBERT	Linear SVC	0.66	0.62	0.67	0.49	0.83	0.71	0.72
SBERT	Random Forest	0.46	0.07	0.48	0.49	0.81	0.46	0.45
SBERT	Gaussian NB	0.54	0.33	0.40	0.59	0.80	0.59	0.57
SBERT	K Neighbors	0.47	0.00	0.58	0.43	0.79	0.56	0.45
SBERT	SVC	0.51	0.11	0.48	0.47	0.83	0.65	0.53
Legal-BERT	Linear SVC	0.74	0.85	0.66	0.53	0.85	0.79	0.83
Legal-BERT	Random Forest	0.51	0.04	0.52	0.52	0.87	0.60	0.50
Legal-BERT	Gaussian NB	0.64	0.58	0.39	**0.63**	0.85	0.73	0.72
Legal-BERT	K Neighbors	0.53	0.29	0.58	0.32	0.80	0.67	0.59
Legal-BERT	SVC	0.64	0.49	0.48	0.58	0.90	0.77	0.72

Table 7: Results of the SC task. The last column reports the macro-average computed excluding the *Itpr* and *Class* scheme.

AD		AC		TC		$SC_{reliable}$		
conc	**prem**	**conc**	**prem**	**factual**	**legal**	**aut**	**prec**	**rule**
must	paragraph	must	argument	contested	see	advocate	paragraph	article
follows	noted	aside	complaint	present	ecr	opinion	caselaw	tfeu
admissible	recalled	dismissed	event	general	may	point	see	treaty
light	err	well	directed	appeal	member	observed	settled	ec
consequently	see	rejected	claims	issue	must	general	commission	regulation
accordingly	apparent	consequently	also	claims	jurisdiction	points	judgment	871
well	directed	entirety	declared	appellants	irrespective	essence	ecr	meaning
circumstances	paragraphs	follows	ndsht	assessment	article	noted	effect	1071
ground	vitiated	light	general	argument	party	orange	held	within
rejected	settled	qualifying	wam	notice	effect	goodwill	others	659199

Table 8: Most relevant features for each task and class, obtained from the LinearSVC classifier trained on the TF-IDF representation.

are indicators for *rule* and *prec* in SC respectively.

6 Conclusion

We presented *Demosthenes*, a new corpus for legal AM in the fiscal state aid domain. The corpus consists in 40 decisions by the CJEU, which have been annotated on three hierarchical levels, identifying argumentative elements, their type, and argumentative scheme.

We have defined 4 AM tasks: AD, AC, TC, SC. Our results highlight that Legal-BERT consistently obtains good scores in most settings and tasks. Surprisingly, the TF-IDF embeddings were often successful, suggesting that the lexical information may be informative enough to solve such tasks. For what concerns the classifiers, Linear SVC performed well in most of the settings. Our results suggest that traditional classifiers are effective in many of the proposed tasks. We believe that these models can be considered strong baselines for further experiments involving state-of-the-art classifiers such as fine-tuned language models.

In future work, we want to improve the scheme labelling by splitting the *Itpr* class into multiple ones, and annotate the relationships between sentences. Experimentally, we aim to implement oversampling and data augmentation techniques to overcome the strong unbalance of classes in each task. We also want to study the impact of pre-processing and the use of alternative classifiers such as logistic regression. Finally, we want to improve the robustness of our experimental findings. For example, by considering multiple seed runs or applying the method proposed by Lai et al. (2021).

Acknowledgements

This work has been partially funded by the European Union's Horizon 2020 Research and Innovation Programme under grant agreement 101017142 (StairwAI), by the European Union's Justice programme under grant agreement 101007420 (ADELE), by the European Horizon 2020 ERC project CompuLaw (Computable Law) under grant agreement 833647, and by the Italian Ministry of Education and Research's PRIN programme under grant agreement 2017NCPZ22 (LAILA).

References

Vincent Aleven. 2003. Using background knowledge in case-based legal reasoning: A computational model and an intelligent learning environment. *Artif. Intell.*, 150(1-2):183–237.

Kevin D. Ashley, Ravi Desai, and John M. Levine. 2002. Teaching case-based argumentation concepts using dialectic arguments vs. didactic explanations. In *Intelligent Tutoring Systems*, volume 2363 of *Lecture Notes in Computer Science*, pages 585–595. Springer.

Katie Atkinson and Trevor J. M. Bench-Capon. 2019. Reasoning with legal cases: Analogy or rule application? In *ICAIL*, pages 12–21. ACM.

Katie Atkinson and Trevor J. M. Bench-Capon. 2021. Argumentation schemes in AI and law. *Argument Comput.*, 12(3):417–434.

Roy Bar-Haim, Indrajit Bhattacharya, Francesco Dinuzzo, Amrita Saha, and Noam Slonim. 2017. Stance classification of context-dependent claims. In *EACL (1)*, pages 251–261. Association for Computational Linguistics.

Trevor J. M. Bench-Capon, James B. Freeman, Hanns Hohmann, and Henry Prakken. 2004. Computational models, argumentation theories and legal practice. In *Argumentation Machines*, volume 9 of *Argumentation Library*, pages 85–120. Springer.

Trevor J. M. Bench-Capon, Henry Prakken, and Giovanni Sartor. 2009. Argumentation in legal reasoning. In *Argumentation in Artificial Intelligence*, pages 363–382. Springer.

Elena Cabrio and Serena Villata. 2018. Five years of argument mining: a data-driven analysis. In *IJCAI*, pages 5427–5433. ijcai.org.

Chad S. Carr. 2003. Using computer supported argument visualization to teach legal argumentation. In *Visualizing Argumentation*, Computer Supported Cooperative Work, pages 75–96. Springer.

Ilias Chalkidis, Manos Fergadiotis, Prodromos Malakasiotis, Nikolaos Aletras, and Ion Androutsopoulos. 2020. LEGAL-BERT: The muppets straight out of law school. In *Findings of EMNLP 2020*, pages 2898–2904, Online. Association for Computational Linguistics.

Carlos Chesnevar, Sanjay Modgil, Iyad Rahwan, Chris Reed, Guillermo Simari, Matthew South, Gerard Vreeswijk, Steven Willmott, et al. 2006. Towards an argument interchange format. *The knowledge engineering review*, 21(4):293–316.

Jacob Cohen. 1960. A coefficient of agreement for nominal scales. *Educational and Psychological Measurement*, 20:37 – 46.

Jacob Devlin, Ming-Wei Chang, Kenton Lee, and Kristina Toutanova. 2019. BERT: pre-training of deep bidirectional transformers for language understanding. In *NAACL-HLT (1)*, pages 4171–4186. Association for Computational Linguistics.

Vanessa Wei Feng and Graeme Hirst. 2011. Classifying arguments by scheme. In *ACL*, pages 987–996. The Association for Computer Linguistics.

Andrea Galassi, Marco Lippi, and Paolo Torroni. 2018. Argumentative link prediction using residual networks and multi-objective learning. In *Proceedings of the 5th Workshop on Argument Mining, ArgMining@EMNLP 2018, Brussels, Belgium, November 1, 2018*, pages 1–10. Association for Computational Linguistics.

Andrea Galassi, Marco Lippi, and Paolo Torroni. 2021. Multi-task attentive residual networks for argument mining. *CoRR*, abs/2102.12227.

Ivan Habernal, Daniel Faber, Nicola Recchia, Sebastian Bretthauer, Iryna Gurevych, Christoph Burchard, et al. 2022. Mining legal arguments in court decisions. *arXiv preprint arXiv:2208.06178*.

Ben Hachey and Claire Grover. 2006. Extractive summarisation of legal texts. *Artificial Intelligence and Law*, 14(4):305–345.

Rinke Hoekstra, Joost Breuker, Marcello Di Bello, and Alexander Boer. 2009. LKIF core: Principled ontology development for the legal domain. In *Law, Ontologies and the Semantic Web*, volume 188 of *Frontiers in Artificial Intelligence and Applications*, pages 21–52. IOS Press.

Tuan Lai, Heng Ji, and ChengXiang Zhai. 2021. BERT might be overkill: A tiny but effective biomedical entity linker based on residual convolutional neural networks. In *Findings of the Association for Computational Linguistics: EMNLP 2021*, pages 1631–1639, Punta Cana, Dominican Republic. Association for Computational Linguistics.

Katja Langenbucher. 1998. Argument by analogy in european law. *The Cambridge Law Journal*, 57(3):481–521.

John Lawrence and Chris Reed. 2019. Argument mining: A survey. *Comput. Linguistics*, 45(4):765–818.

Ran Levy, Yonatan Bilu, Daniel Hershcovich, Ehud Aharoni, and Noam Slonim. 2014. Context dependent claim detection. In *COLING*, pages 1489–1500. ACL.

Marco Lippi and Paolo Torroni. 2016. Argumentation mining: State of the art and emerging trends. *ACM Trans. Internet Techn.*, 16(2):10:1–10:25.

Yinhan Liu, Myle Ott, Naman Goyal, Jingfei Du, Mandar Joshi, Danqi Chen, Omer Levy, Mike Lewis, Luke Zettlemoyer, and Veselin Stoyanov. 2019. Roberta: A robustly optimized BERT pretraining approach. *CoRR*, abs/1907.11692.

Fabrizio Macagno and Douglas Walton. 2015. Classifying the patterns of natural arguments. *Philosophy & Rhetoric*, 48(1):26–53.

L. Thorne McCarty. 2007. Deep semantic interpretations of legal texts. In *ICAIL*, pages 217–224. ACM.

Raquel Mochales and Marie-Francine Moens. 2011. Argumentation mining. *Artificial Intelligence and Law*, 19(1):1–22.

Raquel Mochales Palau and Marie-Francine Moens. 2011. Argumentation mining. *Artificial Intelligence and Law*, 19(1):1–22.

Vlad Niculae, Joonsuk Park, and Claire Cardie. 2017. Argument mining with structured svms and rnns. In *ACL (1)*, pages 985–995. Association for Computational Linguistics.

Raquel Mochales Palau and Aagje Ieven. 2009. Creating an argumentation corpus: do theories apply to real arguments?: a case study on the legal argumentation of the ECHR. In *ICAIL*, pages 21–30. ACM.

Prakash Poudyal, Jaromir Savelka, Aagje Ieven, Marie Francine Moens, Teresa Goncalves, and Paulo Quaresma. 2020. ECHR: Legal corpus for argument mining. In *ArgMining@COLING*, pages 67–75, Online. Association for Computational Linguistics.

Henry Prakken and Giovanni Sartor. 1996a. A dialectical model of assessing conflicting arguments in legal reasoning. *Artif. Intell. Law*, 4(3-4):331–368.

Henry Prakken and Giovanni Sartor. 1996b. A dialectical model of assessing conflicting arguments in legal reasoning. *Artif. Intell. Law*, 4(3-4):331–368.

Henry Prakken and Giovanni Sartor. 2002. The role of logic in computational models of legal argument: A critical survey. In *Computational Logic: Logic Programming and Beyond*, volume 2408 of *Lecture Notes in Computer Science*, pages 342–381. Springer.

Nils Reimers and Iryna Gurevych. 2019. Sentence-bert: Sentence embeddings using siamese bert-networks. In *EMNLP/IJCNLP (1)*, pages 3980–3990. Association for Computational Linguistics.

Jaromír Savelka and Kevin D. Ashley. 2016. Extracting case law sentences for argumentation about the meaning of statutory terms. In *ArgMining@ACL*. The Association for Computer Linguistics.

Manfred Stede and Jodi Schneider. 2018. Argumentation mining. *Synthesis Lectures on Human Language Technologies*, 11(2):1–191.

Milagro Teruel, Cristian Cardellino, Fernando Cardellino, Laura Alonso Alemany, and Serena Villata. 2018. Legal text processing within the mirel project. In *1st Workshop on Language Resources and Technologies for the Legal Knowledge Graph*, page 42.

Joel P Trachtman. 2013. The tools of argument: How the best lawyers think, argue, and win. *Argue, and Win (July 29, 2013)*.

Vern R. Walker, Nathaniel Carie, Courtney C. DeWitt, and Eric Lesh. 2011. A framework for the extraction and modeling of fact-finding reasoning from legal decisions: lessons from the vaccine/injury project corpus. *Artif. Intell. Law*, 19(4):291–331.

Vern R. Walker, Ji Hae Han, Xiang Ni, and Kaneyasu Yoseda. 2017. Semantic types for computational legal reasoning: propositional connectives and sentence roles in the veterans' claims dataset. In *ICAIL*, pages 217–226. ACM.

Vern R. Walker, Krishnan Pillaipakkamnatt, Alexandra M. Davidson, Marysa Linares, and Domenick J. Pesce. 2019. Automatic classification of rhetorical roles for sentences: Comparing rule-based scripts with machine learning. In *ASAIL@ICAIL*, volume 2385 of *CEUR Workshop Proceedings*. CEUR-WS.org.

Vern R. Walker, Stephen R. Strong, and Vern E. Walker. 2020. Automating the classification of finding sentences for linguistic polarity. In *ASAIL@JURIX*, volume 2764 of *CEUR Workshop Proceedings*. CEUR-WS.org.

Douglas Walton and Marcin Koszowy. 2015. Two kinds of arguments from authority in the ad verecundiam fallacy. In *Proceedings of the 8th Conference of the International Society for the Study of Argumentation*, pages 1483—-1492.

Douglas Walton, Fabrizio Macagno, and Giovanni Sartor. 2021. *Statutory interpretation: Pragmatics and argumentation*. Cambridge University Press.

Douglas Walton, Chris Reed, and Fabrizio Macagno. 2008. *Argumentation Schemes*. Cambridge University Press.

Huihui Xu, Jaromír Savelka, and Kevin D. Ashley. 2020. Using argument mining for legal text summarization. In *JURIX*, volume 334 of *Frontiers in Artificial Intelligence and Applications*, pages 184–193. IOS Press.

Huihui Xu, Jaromír Savelka, and Kevin D. Ashley. 2021a. Accounting for sentence position and legal domain sentence embedding in learning to classify case sentences. In *JURIX*, volume 346 of *Frontiers in Artificial Intelligence and Applications*, pages 33–42. IOS Press.

Huihui Xu, Jaromír Savelka, and Kevin D. Ashley. 2021b. Toward summarizing case decisions via extracting argument issues, reasons, and conclusions. In *ICAIL*, pages 250–254. ACM.

Gechuan Zhang, Paul Nulty, and David Lillis. 2022a. A decade of legal argumentation mining: Datasets and approaches. In *NLDB*, volume 13286 of *Lecture Notes in Computer Science*, pages 240–252. Springer.

Gechuan Zhang, Paul Nulty, and David Lillis. 2022b. Enhancing legal argument mining with domain pre-training and neural networks. *CoRR*, abs/2202.13457.

Appendix

A Source Documents' Structure

CJEU decisions are structured as follows:

- *The Preamble*, containing information on the parties, i.e., on the one hand, the Commission, and on the other hand a member State and/or a private competitor, the appealed judgement of the Court of First Instance, and the composition of the Court;
- *Case background*, including facts and the procedural case history before the General Court;
- *The judgement under appeal*, reporting the assessment of the General Court in the first instance decision;
- *The Appeal*, reporting *The Grounds of Appeal*, i.e., the error of law or facts alleged by an Appellant as the defect in the Judgment appealed against upon which reliance has been placed to set it aside. Thus, grounds of appeal concern the reason(s) why the decision is considered wrong by the aggrieved party. For each ground of appeal, two subsections can be identified: (i) the *Arguments of the Parties*, supporting or attacking each ground of appeal; and (ii) the *Findings of the Court*, i.e., the Court reasoning process, characterised by a set of argument chains, which lead to conclusions with regard to parties' claims, as described in the grounds of appeal;
- *Costs*, i.e., the attribution of costs;
- The *Ruling*, i.e., the final decision and orders to the parties.

In analysing the CJEU decisions, we did not consider sections related to *the preamble*, *the case background*, and *the judgment under appeal*, where no arguments are put forward. The same is true with regard to the *costs* and the *final ruling* sections, the latter usually repeating the conclusion of each argument chain and reporting orders to the parties. Since our primary purpose is to capture the argumentative patterns of the CJEU reasoning process, we also excluded the section related to the *arguments of the parties*. Thus, the most relevant part is the *Findings of the Court*, reporting all argumentative steps leading to the final ruling.

B Detailed Examples

B.1 Type of Premise

The following statements respectively consist in factual and legal premises:

> *In the present case the main appeal, taken as a whole, specifically seeks to challenge the position adopted by the Court of First Instance on various points of law raised before it at first instance. It indicates clearly the aspects of the judgment under appeal which are criticised and the pleas in law and arguments on which it is based.* (Case C–321/99 P, para 50).

> *Where an appellant alleges distortion of the evidence by the General Court, he must, under Article 256 TFEU, the first paragraph of Article 58 of the Statute of the Court of Justice of the European Union and Article 168(1)(d) of the Rules of Procedure of the Court, indicate precisely the evidence alleged to have been distorted by the General Court and show the errors of appraisal which, in his view, led to such distortion.* (Case C-431/14 P, para 32).

Example of a premise that combines legal and factual arguments:

> *It is apparent from the judgment under appeal and the documents included in the file that the appellants submitted before the General Court that, contrary to what the Commission stated in point 97 of the grounds of the contested decision, the normal tax rules for company profits could not be used as a valid basis for comparison and thus as a reference framework for the assessment of the selectivity of the tax scheme at issue.* (Case C—452/10 P, para 57).

B.2 Types of Schemes

In the following, we provide examples of legal premises marked according to the schemes presented in section 3.1.2.
Examples of legal premises marked under the **Rule scheme**.

> *It must be recalled that Article 173 of the Treaty, by virtue of which the Court of Justice is to review the legality of Community acts, provides that any natural or legal person may on grounds of lack of competence, infringement of an essential procedural requirement, infringement of this Treaty or of any rule of law relating to its application, or misuse of powers institute proceedings against a decision addressed to that person or against a decision which, although in the form of a regulation or a decision addressed to another person, is of direct and individual concern to the former.* (Case C-298/00 P, para 34).

> *Consequently, given that Article 1 of the Third Steel Aid Code prohibited both aid that was and aid that was not specific to the steel sector, the Commission could not implicitly withdraw the 1971 Decision.* (Case C-408/04 P, para 89)

Examples of legal premises marked under the **Precedent scheme**.

> *It should be borne in mind, first, that in view of the mandatory nature of the review of State aid by the Commission under Article 93 of the Treaty, undertakings to which aid has been granted may not, in principle, entertain a legitimate expectation that the aid is lawful unless it has been granted in compliance with the procedure laid down in that article and, second, that a diligent businessman should normally be able to determine whether that procedure has been followed (Case C-5/89 Commission v Germany [1990] ECR I-3437, paragraph 14; Case C-169/95 Spain v Commission [1997] ECR I-135, paragraph 51; and Case C-24/95 Alcan Deutschland [1997] ECR I-1591, paragraph 25).*(Joined Cases C-183/02 P and C-187/02 P, para 44).

> *Also, it is clear from consistent case-law that Articles 4 CS and 67 CS concern two distinct areas, the first abolishing and prohibiting certain actions by Member States in the field which the ECSC Treaty places under Community jurisdiction, the second intended to prevent the distortion of competition which exercise of the residual powers of the Member States inevitably entails.* (Case C-408/04 P, para 32).

Examples of legal premises marked under the **Authoritative scheme**.

> *It follows, as the Advocate General observed, in essence, in point 62 of his Opinion, that recovery of such aid entails the restitution of the advantage procured by the aid for the recipient, not the restitution of any economic benefit the recipient may have enjoyed as a result of exploiting the advantage.* (Joined Cases C-164/15 P and C-165/15 P, para 92).

Accordingly, as the Advocate General noted in points 72 and 76 of his Opinion, nothing prevents the recipient of the aid from invoking the applicability of that test and, if the recipient does invoke that test, it falls to the Commission to assess whether the test needs to be applied and, if so, to assess its application. (Case C-300/16 P, para 26)

Examples of legal premises marked under the **Classification scheme**.

So, in order for there to be State aid within the meaning of that provision it is necessary, first, for there to be aid favouring certain undertakings or the production of certain goods and, second, for that advantage to come from the State or State resources. (Case C-353/95 P, para 25)

Any activity consisting in offering services on a given market, that is, services normally provided for remuneration, is an economic activity. (Joined Cases C-622/16 P to C-624/16 P, para 104)

Examples of legal premises marked under the **Interpretative scheme**. The first premise below constitutes an example of a teleological interpretation, while the second one constitutes an example of a psychological interpretation.

The effectiveness of Article 107 TFEU would be substantially diminished if the Commission were required, before classifying a measure as State aid within the meaning of that provision, to wait for the decision of the courts with jurisdiction regarding any reimbursement of excess tax or tax paid by certain taxpayers. (Joined Cases C-164/15 P and C-165/15 P, para 78)

As the Court held in paragraphs 29 to 31 of Case C-110/02 Commission v Council [2004] ECR I-6333, the intention of the EC Treaty, in providing through Article 88 EC for aid to be kept under constant review and monitored by the Commission, is that the finding that aid may be incompatible with the common market is to be arrived at, subject to review by the General Court and the Court of Justice, by means of an appropriate procedure which it is the Commission's responsibility to set in motion. (Case C-272/12 P, para 48)

Examples of legal premises marked under the **Principle scheme**

That fact however had to be taken into consideration in relation to the obligation to recover the incompatible aid, in the light of the principles of protection of legitimate expectations and legal certainty, as was done by the Commission in the contested decision when it declined to order the recovery of aid granted before the date of publication in the Official Journal of the European Communities of the decisions to initiate the procedure laid down in Article 88(2) EC (Case C-272/12 P, para 53).

Those arguments cannot, however, be upheld, since, as is apparent from the case-law, the question whether a selective advantage complies with the principle of proportionality arises at the third stage of the examination of selectivity, which examines whether that advantage can be justified by the nature or general scheme of the tax system of the Member State concerned. (Joined Cases C-51/19 P and C-64/19 P, para 140)

Examples of legal premises marked under more than one scheme.
The following is an example of a premise marked under both the **Precedent scheme** and the **Principle scheme**.

The principle of legal certainty – which is one of the general principles of European Union law – requires that rules of law be clear and precise and predictable in their effect, so that interested parties can ascertain their position in situations and legal relationships governed by European Union law (see, to that effect, Case C-63/93 Duff and Others [1996] ECR I-569, paragraph 20; Case C-76/06 P Britannia Alloys; Chemicals v Commission [2007] ECR I-4405, paragraph 79; and Case C-158/07 Förster [2008] ECR I-8507, paragraph 67). (Case C-81/10 P, para 100).

The following is an example of a premise marked under both the **Rule scheme** and the **Precedent scheme**.

In that regard, it must be observed that it follows from Article 58 of the Statute of the Court of Justice, in conjunction with Article 113(2) of the Rules of Procedure of the Court of Justice, that, on appeal, an appellant may put forward any relevant argument, provided only that the subject-matter of the proceedings before the General Court is not changed in the appeal (Case

C-229/05 P PKK and KNK v Council [2007] ECR I-439, paragraph 66, and Case C-8/06 P Herrero Romeu v Commission [2007] ECR I-10333, paragraph 32) (Case C-322/09 P, para 41).

B.3 Argument Chain

The following is an example of sentences that constitute an argument chain.

<prem ID="C1" T="L" S="Prec"> *According to the case-law of the Court of Justice, for infringement of the principle of the protection of legitimate expectations to be established, it is necessary for an EU institution, by giving a citizen precise assurances, to have led that person to entertain justified expectations.* </prem> <prem ID="C2" T="L" S="Prec|Class"> *Information which is precise, unconditional and consistent, in whatever form it is given, constitutes such assurances (judgment of 12 October 2016, Land Hessen v Pollmeier Massivholz, C-242/15 P, not published, EU:C:2016:765, paragraph 63).* </prem>

<prem ID="C3" T="F"> *In that regard, in its 2004 letter, the Commission merely expressed a preliminary opinion on a draft of the promotion scheme which was adopted only the following year, the precise conditions of which were not then fully known.*</prem> <prem ID="C4" T="F"> *Consequently, that letter did not give precise assurances that the initial scheme was not in the nature of State aid.* </prem> <prem ID="C5" T="F"> *Therefore, the General Court did not err in its legal characterisation by holding in paragraph 70 of the judgment under appeal that that letter could not give rise to any legitimate expectation.* </prem>

<prem ID="C6" T="F"> *Nor can the General Court be criticised for not taking the view that such an expectation could result from the alleged '2006 decision'.*</prem> <prem ID="C7" T="F"> *As the General Court pointed out in paragraph 60 of the judgment under appeal, that decision had not been placed on the file, nor even specifically identified by the appellants.*</prem>

<prem ID="C8" T="F"> *Nor do the appellants demonstrate that the General Court incorrectly characterised the Commission's conduct between 2004 and the adoption of the decision at issue in finding, in paragraph 78 of the judgment under appeal, that that conduct could not be regarded as having provided precise, unconditional and consistent assurances that there was no State aid.*</prem>

<prem ID="C9" T="L|F"> *Moreover, the appellants may criticise the General Court for failing to take into account certain other factors, which they claim to have submitted to it, only if that evidence proves that they could rely on a legitimate expectation that the initial scheme for the promotion of electricity production from RES would be maintained.*</prem> <prem ID="C10" T="F"> *The appellants have not shown that that evidence was sufficient to justify the legitimate expectation alleged.*</prem>

<prem ID="C11" T="L|F" S="Prec"> *In particular, the appellants do not effectively challenge the finding, in paragraph 79 of the judgment under appeal, that exceptional circumstances should not be taken into account in the present case, in so far as that consideration was envisaged, in the judgment of 11 July 1996, SFEI and Others (C-39/94, EU:C:1996:285), only in order to establish that, in certain cases, the repayment of State aid sought before a national court is inappropriate.*</prem>

<conc ID="C12"> *It follows from the foregoing that the third ground of appeal must be rejected.*</conc>

(Case C-850/19 P, para 34–40).

Multimodal Argument Mining: A Case Study in Political Debates

Eleonora Mancini and **Federico Ruggeri**[✉] and **Andrea Galassi** and **Paolo Torroni**
DISI, University of Bologna, Bologna, Italy
federico.ruggeri6@unibo.it

Abstract

We propose a study on multimodal argument mining in the domain of political debates. We collate and extend existing corpora and provide an initial empirical study on multimodal architectures, with a special emphasis on input encoding methods. Our results provide interesting indications about future directions in this important domain.

1 Introduction

Argument mining (AM) aims to extract arguments and their relations from natural language sources (Lippi and Torroni, 2016b). Performing AM usually entails tackling one or more tasks like argumentative component detection and classification, link prediction, relation classification, or stance classification (Lawrence and Reed, 2020) in a particular domain of interest. Among the many areas and genres where AM was investigated, the political domain allows for intuitive applications with the final aim of detecting fallacies, persuasiveness degree (Cano-Basave and He, 2016), truthfulness (Nakov et al., 2018; Kopev et al., 2019) and coherence in the candidate's argumentation (Cabrio and Villata, 2018; Lippi and Torroni, 2016a), or summarizing the candidate's positions (Vilares and He, 2017). So far, most of AM research has focused on textual inputs. Political debates and speeches have been no exception. However, differently from other domains, this particular one is especially rich in audio input sources. This could be important, since the audio input, in addition to text, may leverage the exploitation of para-linguistic cues related to the argumentation process, improving the performance of argumentative component detection and other AM tasks (Lippi and Torroni, 2016a; Villata et al., 2017; Polo et al., 2016). To date, partly owing to the scarcity of non-textual corpora for AM (Haddadan et al., 2019), only a couple of attempts have been made in this direction. Conversely, outside of AM, in the broader area of Natural Language Processing (NLP), Multimodal Deep Learning (MMDL) is attracting growing interest, also owing to remarkable progress made in the field. Current research in MMDL focuses on advanced input representations and fusion solutions. These include end-to-end architectures fully based on transfer learning for input representation (Toto et al., 2021) and attention-based architectures for efficient input management (Lian et al., 2019; Tsai et al., 2019; Gu et al., 2018). These noteworthy developments suggest that time is ripe to rethink multimodal AM in light of the latest findings in multimodal NLP research.

In spite of a wide availability of raw audio sources, processing and annotating good quality data can be very costly. To the best of our knowledge, the only two multimodal AM corpora on political speeches are UKDebates (Lippi and Torroni, 2016a), which addresses the task of claim detection, and M-Arg (Mestre et al., 2021), which focuses on argumentative relations between sentences. These are small-sized corpora where a handful of speakers debate in one or a few occasions over a year's time span. On the other hand, USElecDeb60To16 is a corpus curated by Haddadan et al. (2019), where a significant number of US presidential candidates debate over a time span of several decades. However, it only contains annotated transcripts, with no link to the audio source.

In an effort to push the envelope in multimodal AM, with this work we release MM-USElecDeb60To16, an extended version of the USElecDeb60To16 corpus, where the text input is complemented by and aligned to the audio input. At the time of writing, this is the largest multi-modal resource for AM in the domain of political debates, as well as the one with the largest number of speakers, and longest time span covered. These features make MM-USElecDeb60To16 a particularly challenging

Proceedings of the 9th Workshop on Argument Mining, co-located with the 29th International Conference on Computational Linguistics, pages 158–170
October 17, 2022.

corpus, since para-linguistic cues are very much speaker-dependent (Lippi and Torroni, 2016a) and political communication, argumentation, and language have greatly evolved in such a long time span (Haddadan et al., 2019).

Alongside this new resource, we offer a preliminary but rigorous and reproducible experimental study of multimodal AM in political debates. Our benchmarks are all the relevant corpora available: UKDebates, M-Arg, and MM-USElecDeb60To16. We build and compare architectures inspired to proposals from literature, in order to study the effect of changing the encoding of the audio input. In particular, we compare the more traditional feature-based audio encoding, with a more advanced input encoding technique that builds on recent findings in MMDL for NLP. Our results indicate that the encoding of the audio input has a noticeable effect on performance, but they also suggest that a better fusion of textual and audio input encodings and more advanced architectural solutions might be needed in order to make progress in the more challenging tasks and corpora.

The paper is structured as follows. In Section 2 we overview related work in multimodal AM and multimodal deep learning (MMDL), with a focus on architectures for text and audio processing. In Section 3 we discuss corpora and in Section 4 we define the AM tasks addressed. Section 5 presents the experimental setup and describes models, input encodings and training. Section 6 discusses the results of our experimental study. Section 7 concludes. In appendix we report all the information needed for reproducibility. The corpus and the code are publicly released.[1]

2 Related Work

There exists a strong connection between the argumentation process and the emotions felt by people involved in such a process (Benlamine et al., 2015). This observation motivated the hypothesis that para-linguistic elements encoded in the audio data are significant indicators that might aid identify arguments made in a debate. Recent studies confirmed this hypothesis. In particular, in the domain of political debates, Lippi and Torroni (2016a) presented a case study in AM from speech using a televised debate from the 2015 UK political elections. They built a first-of-a-kind political debate corpus by annotating arguments uttered by three prime ministerial candidates, and showed that audio features helped claim detection when used as input to a Support Vector Machine (SVM) classifier together with their textual transcript. More recently, Mestre et al. (2021) built the M-Arg corpus, which consists in 4,104 labelled pairs of sentences selected from debates of the 2020 US political elections. They experimented on this new corpus using a different multimodal input model. Outside of political speeches, a corpus that couples transcript and audio of several debates was developed by Mirkin et al. (2018a,b). However, differently from the previous corpora, here non-political debates are carried out by paid actors on a set of controversial topics taken from the iDebate web site.

To the best of our knowledge, at least in political debates, multimodal AM has not been further explored. Reasons for that lie partly in the difficulty and heterogeneity of AM tasks, partly in the scarcity of multimodal data for AM, partly in the inherent challenges of multimodal deep learning (MMDL). One such challenge is in endowing models with the ability to digest and actually benefit from different, complementary modalities. In this respect, the works by Lippi and Torroni (2016a), Villata et al. (2017) and Mestre et al. (2021) could be viewed as proofs-of-concept of the potential of multimodality in AM. They used mostly traditional methods for categorising data and encoding audio, such as SVM classifiers and MFCCs. Like most other studies in AM, they were carried out on a single corpus and a specific task.

Recent MMDL solutions suggest a number of promising directions for improvement. These include full transfer learning-based frameworks to alleviate the problem of multimodal data shortage (Zhang et al., 2022; Naderi et al., 2019; Harati et al., 2018) and attention mechanisms to handle interactions among and between different modalities (Lian et al., 2019; Tsai et al., 2019; Gu et al., 2018). For example, AudiBERT (Toto et al., 2021), a recent MMDL architecture, integrates pre-trained text and audio models via a dual self-attention mechanism. In our work, we examine the architectural designs presented in earlier studies (Lippi and Torroni, 2016a; Mestre et al., 2021) and also suggest a multimodal architecture comparable to AudiBERT, based on text and audio embedding taken from pre-trained models like GloVe (Pennington et al., 2014), BERT (Devlin et al., 2019)

[1]https://github.com/federicoruggeri/multimodal-am/

and Wav2Vec (Schneider et al., 2019).

3 Data

We experiment on three different debate corpora, designed to address four separate but strictly correlated argument mining tasks. Table 1 summarizes the corpora's key figures.

3.1 UKDebates Corpus

UKDebates, by Lippi and Torroni (2016a), was the first corpus released for multimodal argument mining. Its context is the UK Prime Ministerial elections of 2015. It is based on the two-hour debate aired by Sky News on April 2, 2015 and it comprises the audio sequences of 3 candidates: David Cameron, Nick Clegg, and Ed Miliband. UKDebates contains 386 audio samples (122 for David Cameron, 104 for Nick Clegg, 160 for Ed Miliband) of varying length, accompanied by a human-built transcript. Two domain experts annotated the collected transcripts for the task of claim detection, by labeling each sentence as containing or not containing a claim. Regarding Inter-Annotator Agreement (IAA), the authors report $\kappa = 0.53$, "fair to good" agreement. Because audio features are markedly speaker-dependent, Lippi and Torroni (2016a) addresses the claim detection (CD) task for each individual politician candidate in turn. The authors report a F1-score in the range of $\sim$59-62%.

3.2 M-Arg Corpus

M-Arg, by Mestre et al. (2021), is built around the 2020 US Presidential debates. The debates involve 5 different speakers (4 candidates and a moderator) and are related to 18 topics. A carefully designed crowd-sourcing exercise resulted in 4,104 labelled sentence pairs for the task of argumentative relation detection. In particular, each sentence pair was labeled as *support*, *attack*, or *neither*. To account for crowd-workers' annotation quality, each label is enriched with an *annotator agreement confidence* γ. A smaller but higher-quality subset of M-Arg is thus obtained by only selecting the links with confidence $\gamma \geq 0.85$. The price of this reduction in the annotations' noise is a reduced size of the dataset, which results in harder training and an IAA of $\alpha = 0.43$. Mestre et al. (2021) report a macro F1-score of 22.5% and 11.0% for the argumentative relation classification (ARC) task regarding the full corpus and the ($\gamma \geq 0.85$) subset, respectively. The macro F1-score regards the *support* and *attack* labels only.

3.3 MM-USElecDeb60to16 Corpus

USElecDeb60To16, by Haddadan et al. (2019), is the largest collection of annotated textual documents for argument mining in the political debates domain. It contains presidential candidates' debate transcripts aired from 1960 to 2016. Annotations are at the sentence level. Each sentence is labeled as a claim, a premise, or neither of them. The authors used this corpus to address the argumentative sentence detection (ASD) and argumentative component classification (ACC) tasks. Regarding IAA, they report a $\kappa = 0.57$ (moderate agreement) for ASD and of $\kappa = 0.40$ (fair agreement) for ACC. As for classification performance, Haddadan et al. report a macro F1-score of 73.0% and 76.95% for the ASD and ACC, respectively.

We build MM-USElecDeb60To16 by augmenting USElecDeb60To16 with the audio modality. We remark that we do not add any additional label, nor we modify existing ones. We obtained the debates audio files from the PBS NewsHour YouTube channel.[2] Before aligning transcripts with corresponding audio files, we carried out a preliminary pre-processing phase. First, we manually trimmed audio files to remove content that is not included in the paired transcripts, such as some of the opening and closing remark of the moderators. In some cases, audio files can contain cuts spanning from a few seconds to several minutes. We removed the transcripts' sentences that were matched to these cuts. Second, we removed transcripts that did not match their paired audio files or incomplete ones. Third, we removed metadata like the speaker's information from each transcript to avoid spurious alignments. Fourth, we tokenized transcripts; thus, the resulting transcripts contain one sentence per line. See Appendix A for additional details.

After pre-processing, we split each audio file into 20-minute chunks to improve the alignment quality. We manually extract the transcripts' text corresponding to the created audio files. We used Aeneas[3] to automatically retrieve the start and end timestamps of each utterance. Lastly, we post-processed our corpus by removing (i) sentences misaligned with their audio sample (ii) sentences not matching any of the aligned utterances

[2] https://www.youtube.com/channel/UC6ZFN9Tx6xh-skXCuRHCDpQ

[3] https://github.com/readbeyond/aeneas/

Corpus	Sentences	Debates	Speakers	Years	Class Distribution	Task(s)
UKDebate (Lippi and Torroni, 2016a)	386	1	3	2015	152 claim, 234 not-claim	CD
M-Arg (Mestre et al., 2021)	4,104 pairs	5	4	2020	120 attack, 384 support, 3600 neither	ARC
M-Arg ($\gamma \geq 0.85$) (Mestre et al., 2021)	2,443 pairs	5	4	2020	29 attack, 132 support, 2282 neither	ARC
MM-USElecDeb60to16 (Ours)	26,781	39	26	1960-2016	10,882 claim, 9,683 premise, 6,226 not-arg	ASD, ACC

Table 1: Corpora for multimodal argument mining. For M-Arg, we also consider the corpus version where samples have high annotation confidence γ. The acronyms used in column Task are spelled out in Section 4.

(e.g., transcription tags like "applause") (iii) non-argumentative duplicated sentences, such as *Thank You* or *Ok*. Finally, we verified the quality of the alignments by spot checks. In particular, we checked several different parts of each debate, and no major misalignments were found.

As a result of the mentioned pre- and post-processing phases, we removed about 2,000 samples from the original USElecDeb60to16 corpus. The resulting MM-USElecDeb60to16 corpus contains 26,791 annotated textual sentences and their corresponding audio samples.

Our corpus differs from previous multimodal AM corpora in terms of size, variety and annotation quality. First off, it is the largest multimodal AM corpus to date, by a significant margin. Second, it offers a wider range of speakers over a much longer time span (1976-2016), possibly paving the way to new research perspectives, such as the analysis of the evolution of political communication, argumentation and language over time. The greater number of different speakers could also facilitate the creation of more robust classification models. Finally, the corpus includes expert annotations, as opposed to crowd-sourced ones.

4 Methodology

We consider four distinct classification tasks:

- **Argumentative Sentence Detection (ASD)**: an input sentence x is classified as containing an argument (*arg*), or not containing an argument (*not-arg*);
- **Argumentative Component Classification (ACC)**: an argumentative sentence x is classified as containing a *claim* or a *premise*;
- **Claim Detection (CD)**: a sentence x is classified as containing a *claim* or not containing a claim (*not-claim*);
- **Argumentative Relation Classification (ARC)**: a pair of sentences x_i and x_j is classified as yielding an argumentative relation $x_i \rightarrow x_j$ of *support*, *attack*, or *neither* (if no argumentative relation exists).

Each input is characterized by two modalities: the textual input x_t and the audio input x_a. To assess the impact of each modality, we consider three distinct input configurations: *text-only* (TO), *audio-only* (AO), and *text-audio* (TA), where both modalities are given as input.

5 Experimental Setup

We define a reproducible and robust experimental setup to evaluate the contribution of each modality to AM tasks, and to assess the impact of different input representations and classifiers. The limited amount of data, especially in UKDebates and M-Arg, caused our setup to differ in several ways from previous studies. Hence our results are not directly comparable with those published in the relevant literature. Nonetheless, our setting includes all the classifiers used in such studies, in addition to more recent representation techniques.

Regarding UKDebates, Lippi and Torroni (2016a) address the CD task by experimenting on each politician individually. In particular, the authors evaluate a multimodal SVM classifier via a

10-fold cross-validation routine. In contrast, we evaluate our models on all speaker sentences via a repeated 5-fold cross-validation routine. Such a design choice was made to curb the high variance usually observed in a model's performance when neural models are trained with little data (Bengio, 2012). We set the number of repetitions to 3.

For the same reason, we evaluate our models on M-Arg via a repeated 5-fold cross-validation routine. We set the number of repetitions to 3. Our approach differs from the one proposed by Mestre et al. (2021), where the corpus is divided into train and validation splits.

For MM-USElecDeb60to16 we follow the same experimental setup as in (Haddadan et al., 2019). Despite the different number of samples, we keep the same train, validation, and test splits proposed for the original corpus. We define a repeated training and evaluation routine for model benchmark, setting the number of repetitions to 3. See Appendix B for additional details on our experimental setting, number of samples and data splitting.

5.1 Models

We defined three models, according to the high-level schema illustrated in Figure 1. In all our models, each modality is processed separately by either a *text module* or an *audio module*. Each module is part of a classification model defined for a particular input modality. Different input configurations use different modules. The TO and AO input configurations only consider the text module or the audio module, respectively. In the TA multimodal setting, instead, the outputs of the two modules are concatenated and passed through a final *classification module*. The classification module receives the encoded representation of one or multiple modalities according to the considered input configuration and produces a classification label.

For each model we experiment with two different audio signal encoding methods: a set of widely-adopted spectral features (Rejaibi et al., 2022) and the Wav2vec embeddings (Schneider et al., 2019). Such encoding methods represent a preliminary pre-processing step of the audio signal, which is then passed in input to the audio module.

The models are defined as follows.

- **SVM** follows Lippi and Torroni (2016a). The text module encodes input textual sentences as TF-IDF vectors. The audio module is an identity function, that is, the encoded audio signal remains unaltered. The classification module is an SVM classifier.

- **M-ArgNet** reflects the neural architecture presented in Mestre et al. (2021). The text module is defined by a pre-trained BERT (Devlin et al., 2019) model. The audio module is a stack of CNN layers with a BiLSTM layer on top. The classification module is a MLP.

- **BiLSTM** is a third architecture where the text module comprises a pre-trained GloVe (Pennington et al., 2014) embedding layer to encode input textual sentences and a stack of BiLSTM layers. The audio module is defined by another stack of BiLSTM layers. The classification module is a MLP.

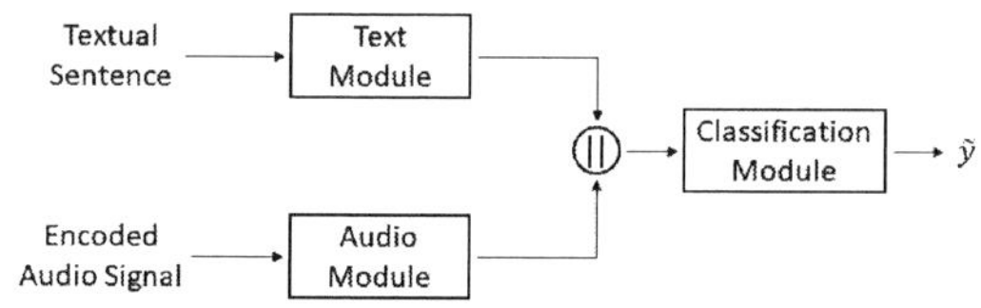

Figure 1: The proposed schema for multimodal argument mining.

M-ArgNet and BiLSTM, when used with Wav2vec embeddings, resemble AudiBERT (Toto et al., 2021) since they are all based on text and audio embedding taken from pre-trained models.

In addition to the above models, we also consider a weighted random baseline classifier, i.e. **Random**, which acts as a lower bound for each task of interest.

5.2 Audio Representation

In this section, we provide additional details regarding the described audio signal encoding methods. The first method, denoted as *feature-based* encoding, is a set of widely-adopted spectral features (Rejaibi et al., 2022), such as the Mel-frequency cepstral coefficients (MFCCs), spectral centroids, spectral bandwidth, spectral roll-off, spectral contrast and a 12-bit chroma vector. The result of this extraction process is a two-dimensional feature matrix of shape (no. frame, no. features). Following Mestre et al. (2021), we consider 25 MFCCs and 20 other spectral features, for a total of 45 features.[4] Regarding the number of frames, their amount is proportional to the duration of the audio

[4]We used the `librosa` library with default parameters.

signal. In our experimental setup it is in the order of hundreds. To reduce the number of frames we adopt average pooling. This applies a moving average with a parametric window size on the frame dimension. We experiment with different window sizes to reduce the computational demand and the number of parameters of our models, without degrading the informative content of the audio signal.

The second method, denoted as *embedding-based* encoding, uses the end-to-end audio encoding neural architecture Wav2vec (Schneider et al., 2019).[5] In particular, we directly extract the pooled embedding vector given by the model. We denote this setting as *embedding-based* encoding. The final size of the representation is a 768-dimensional embedding vector according to the chosen Wav2vec model.

5.3 Optimization

We train our neural models using cross-entropy as the optimization objective and Adam (Kingma and Ba, 2015) as an optimizer. Additionally, we regularize neural models by applying early stopping on the validation loss with patience set to 10 epochs and using dropout (Srivastava et al., 2014).

All models undergo a preliminary hyper-parameters calibration phase. In particular, for each input configuration (i.e., TO, AO, and TA) we calibrate the models to assess the contribution of individual modalities. Additional details about model calibration are reported in Appendix C.

6 Results

We report the classification results on each dataset. Additionally, we perform an ablation study regarding the models trained in the TA configuration to evaluate the contribution of each input modality.

UKDebates Table 2 reports classification results for the CD task on the UKDebates corpus. In particular, we compute the average binary F1-score on the test set for each input configuration and audio encoding method. We provide the F1-score as a customary performance indicator in unbalanced classification situations. We observe that the best-performing input configuration for each model is the TA with embedding-based audio encoding. However, the gap with respect to the TO input configuration is marginal, suggesting that the audio modality is not efficiently handled by the

		Feature-based		*Embedding-based*	
Model	**TO**	**AO**	**TA**	**AO**	**TA**
SVM	<u>66.24</u>	48.62	49.13	46.20	**66.71**
M-ArgNet	<u>67.20</u>	47.20	65.94	50.12	**68.68**
BiLSTM	<u>66.81</u>	45.40	65.29	50.20	**66.84**
Random			40.90		

Table 2: Average binary F1-score regarding the *claim* class on the test set of UKDebates. For each row, we report the best results in bold, second best results are underlined instead.

		Feature-based		*Embedding-based*	
Model	**TO**	**AO**	**TA**	**AO**	**TA**
SVM	<u>14.70</u>	11.96	12.33	14.09	**16.73**
M-ArgNet	16.24	<u>18.45</u>	18.27	8.88	**19.02**
BiLSTM	<u>16.78</u>	9.18	15.89	9.84	**20.21**
Random			2.79		

Table 3: Average macro F1-score concerning the *attack* and *support* classes on the test set of M-Arg ($\gamma \geq 0.85$). For each row, we report the best results in bold, second best results are underlined instead.

employed models or is not sufficiently informative. Regarding audio encoding, we observe that the embedding-based method leads to better performance than the feature-based approach. This is evident for the SVM classifier, where the TA setting with embedding-based audio encoding leads to an improvement of more than 17 F1-score percentage points compared to its feature-based counterpart.

M-Arg Table 3 reports the average macro F1-score regarding the *attack* and *support* classes on the test of the M-Arg corpus for the ARC task. We focus on the M-Arg corpus version with annotation confidence $\gamma \geq 0.85$ to consider high-quality examples only. We observe that the TA input configuration with the embedding-based audio representation is the best performing one for all the considered classifiers. In particular, such a configuration outperforms the TO input configuration by 2.03, 2.78 and 3.43 F1-score percentage points for SVM, M-ArgNet, and BiLSTM classifiers, respectively. In contrast, the TA input configuration with feature-based audio representation yields mixed results. More precisely, only the M-ArgNet model outperforms its TO counterpart. This is in agreement with the results obtained in CD on UKDebates. The feature-based AO input configuration is remarkably on par with its TA counterpart.

[5] We use the *facebook/wav2vec2-base-960h* model version.

MM-USElecDeb60to16 Table 4 reports classification performance concerning the ASD and ACC tasks evaluated on the test set of the MM-USElecDeb60to16 corpus. In general, the embedding-based audio encoding appears to perform better than the feature-based one. This agrees with the behaviour observed in the previous experiments. However, we observe that the TA configuration does not always perform better than TO. We hypothesize that the characteristics of this corpus, with multiple speakers spanning several decades, bring in additional challenges that these architectures are not addressing effectively. Concerning ASD, we observe that the TA input configuration is the best performing one for the BiLSTM and the M-ArgNet models. In contrast, the TO input configuration leads to superior performance for the SVM model. Overall, there is no significant performance gap between the TA and TO input configurations. However, the AO input configurations with both audio signal representations are not far behind their TO and TA counterparts. All this suggests that the encoded audio signal is informative to address the task, but the fusion of both modalities is non-trivial depending on the given audio representation. We observe similar behaviours concerning the ACC task. In particular, the TA input configurations do not lead to consistent performance benefits for the employed models. Nonetheless, the AO input configuration with embedding-based audio representation significantly outperforms its feature-based counterpart. These observations confirm a known fact, that merging multiple input modalities is still a major challenge in current multimodal models.

		Feature-based		*Embedding-based*	
Model	**TO**	**AO**	**TA**	**AO**	**TA**
ASD					
SVM	**67.18**	49.37	49.02	61.20	<u>65.38</u>
M-ArgNet	<u>65.64</u>	52.71	60.89	61.04	**68.38**
BiLSTM	67.19	58.89	**68.57**	60.40	<u>68.23</u>
Random			50.54		
ACC					
SVM	**65.85**	50.19	51.66	58.44	<u>64.75</u>
M-ArgNet	**67.40**	50.05	60.09	65.33	<u>67.38</u>
BiLSTM	<u>65.99</u>	49.58	**66.25**	58.86	65.80
Random			50.51		

Table 4: Average macro F1-score on the test set of MM-USElecDeb60to16. For each row, we report the best results in bold, second best results are underlined.

Discussion The results presented so far warrant the following considerations:

1. Embedding-based audio encoding generally yields better results than feature-based encoding. This is consistent with recent findings in MMDL (Schneider et al., 2019) and confirms that investigating the ramifications of those findings for multimodal AM is a worthwhile endeavour, which should be pursued.

2. The TA input configuration is superior to its TO counterpart, or at least on part with it, in all described corpora. This reinforces our belief that audio can benefit AM tasks. This is also supported by the observed performance of models trained in the AO input configuration. For instance, the performance gap between TO and TA configurations is only ~2-8 F1-score points for the ASD and ACC tasks in the MM-USElecDeb60to16 corpus.

3. The definition of effective methods for input encoding and fusion represent major challenges of multimodal AM, as observed in our extended case study.

6.1 Ablation Study

To assess the contribution of each individual input modality, we carried out an ablation study on models trained with the TA input configuration, by alternatively masking either input modalities. To this end, we zeroed out the output embedding vector of the input module corresponding to the modality to be masked.

Table 5 reports the results of the ablation study regarding the UKDebates corpus. We observe that the BiLSTM model with feature-based audio representation reaches the same performance in both the TA and TO (i.e., w/o Audio) configurations. This result suggests that the audio modality does not provide informative content in addition to text for the task. From a reversed perspective, the SVM classifier with feature-based audio representation focuses solely on the audio modality. We interpret this as an effect of the difficulty of combining text and audio modalities for the SVM classifier. We observe similar behaviours when considering the embedding-based audio representation as well. In contrast, the M-ArgNet model behaves in line with our initial expectations regarding the ablation study. In particular, the model achieves superior performance compared to the random baseline when one

Input	BiLSTM	SVM	M-ArgNet
Feature-based			
TA	65.29	49.13	65.94
w/o Text	21.00	49.13	46.04
w/o Audio	65.29	0.00	57.02
Embedding-based			
TA	66.84	66.71	68.68
w/o Text	3.81	16.40	11.27
w/o Audio	66.78	0.00	68.48

Table 5: Ablation test regarding TA model configuration on the UKDebates test set.

Input	BiLSTM	SVM	M-ArgNet
Feature-based			
TA	15.89	12.33	18.27
w/o Text	0.0	12.33	9.21
w/o Audio	10.00	0.00	3.78
Embedding-based			
TA	20.21	16.73	19.02
w/o Text	0.0	9.30	1.16
w/o Audio	12.80	0.00	18.24

Table 6: Ablation test regarding TA model configuration on the M-ARG ($\gamma \geq 0.85$) test set.

of the input modalities is removed, while being inferior to the default TA case. The only exception concerns the embedding-based audio representation setting. In this setting, the text modality significantly contributes to the task compared to the audio modality.

Likewise, with the M-Arg corpus (see Table 6), we observe odd results similar to those observed with UKDebates. In particular, the BiLSTM and SVM models show symmetrical effects concerning performance metrics when one of the input modalities is removed. Independently of the audio representation method, the BiLSTM model heavily relies on text information to perform the task. In contrast, the SVM model fails to address the task when audio is removed. This evidence suggest that the way input is encoded also plays an important role in a multimodal model concerning the impact of each modality.

Furthermore, we observe similar issues in the MM-USElecDeb60to16 corpus when addressing the ASD and ACC tasks. Table 7 reports the results of the ablation study concerning the ASD task. Again, we observe that the BiLSTM and SVM models have symmetric behaviours. Additionally, the BiLSTM reaches superior classification performance when removing the audio modality in both audio representation settings. Despite a small improvement, this surprising result suggests that the audio modality might be noisy and, thus, detrimental to the task. This observation is further supported by the low performance achieved when removing the text modality. We observe this phenomenon also in the ACC task as reported in Table 8. In particular, the M-ArgNet with embedding-based audio representation has superior performance when removing the audio modality compared to the default TA input configuration.

Input	BiLSTM	SVM	M-ArgNet
Feature-based			
TA	68.57	49.02	60.89
w/o Text	17.26	49.02	23.11
w/o Audio	69.40	17.26	48.04
Embedding-based			
TA	68.23	65.38	68.38
w/o Text	17.26	61.11	44.35
w/o Audio	68.44	17.26	33.95

Table 7: Ablation test regarding TA model configuration on the MM-USElecDeb60to16 test set for the ASD task.

Input	BiLSTM	SVM	M-ArgNet
Feature-based			
TA	66.25	51.66	60.09
w/o Text	32.71	51.66	44.25
w/o Audio	66.24	32.71	55.25
Embedding-based			
TA	65.80	64.75	67.38
w/o Text	32.71	48.86	33.95
w/o Audio	65.80	33.57	67.57

Table 8: Ablation test regarding TA model configuration on the MM-USElecDeb60to16 test set for the ACC task.

7 Conclusion

Political debates and speeches are an important domain where audio data is abundant. The automated argumentative analysis of such data could leverage a variety of innovative applications and open promising research avenues. Yet, AM research so far has mostly focused on textual transcripts. Motivated by recent advances in MMDL and in an effort to push the envelope in multimodal AM research, we release the largest-to-date multimodal AM dataset. We thus run an empirical study on three multimodal AM datasets differing from one another in many respects like size, topics, annotations, and speaker variety. To this end, we defined three architectures, inspired from literature baselines. Our results indicate that embedding-based audio encodings have an edge over feature-based encodings. They also suggest that there is a significant margin for improvement, hence the need for different architectures to enable a tighter mutual interaction between input modalities. We speculate that current trends in MMDL, in particular attention-based methods for multimodal input fusion, should be investigated in this domain. We hope that our dataset will facilitate such endeavor. A remarkable result is the performance of the AO configuration, which in some cases is observed to be competitive with TA. This could indicate that, independently of automated speech recognition and transcription systems that may or may not be available for different languages, useful AM systems could be devised to work only based on the audio signal. Possible applications include systems to support debate summarization and news reporting. Future research directions include a more extensive exploration of the possible architectural configurations and embedding methods, and the introduction of attention-based architectural innovations.

Acknowledgements

This work has been partially funded by the European Union's Horizon 2020 Research and Innovation programme under grant agreement 101017142 (StairwAI: Stairway to AI).

References

Yoshua Bengio. 2012. Practical recommendations for gradient-based training of deep architectures. In *Neural networks: Tricks of the trade*, pages 437–478. Springer.

M. Sahbi Benlamine, Maher Chaouachi, Serena Villata, Elena Cabrio, Claude Frasson, and Fabien Gandon. 2015. Emotions in argumentation: an empirical evaluation. In *IJCAI*, pages 156–163. AAAI Press.

Elena Cabrio and Serena Villata. 2018. Five years of argument mining: a data-driven analysis. In *Proceedings of the Twenty-Seventh International Joint Conference on Artificial Intelligence, IJCAI 2018, July 13-19, 2018, Stockholm, Sweden.*, pages 5427–5433.

Amparo Elizabeth Cano-Basave and Yulan He. 2016. A study of the impact of persuasive argumentation in political debates. In *Proceedings of the 2016 Conference of the North American Chapter of the Association for Computational Linguistics: Human Language Technologies*, pages 1405–1413, San Diego, California. Association for Computational Linguistics.

Jacob Devlin, Ming-Wei Chang, Kenton Lee, and Kristina Toutanova. 2019. BERT: pre-training of deep bidirectional transformers for language understanding. In *NAACL-HLT (1)*, pages 4171–4186. Association for Computational Linguistics.

Yue Gu, Kangning Yang, Shiyu Fu, Shuhong Chen, Xinyu Li, and Ivan Marsic. 2018. Multimodal affective analysis using hierarchical attention strategy with word-level alignment. In *ACL (1)*, pages 2225–2235. Association for Computational Linguistics.

Shohreh Haddadan, Elena Cabrio, and Serena Villata. 2019. Yes, we can! mining arguments in 50 years of US presidential campaign debates. In *Proceedings of the 57th Annual Meeting of the Association for Computational Linguistics*, pages 4684–4690, Florence, Italy. Association for Computational Linguistics.

Sahar Harati, Andrea Crowell, Helen S. Mayberg, and Shamim Nemati. 2018. Depression severity classification from speech emotion. In *EMBC*, pages 5763–5766. IEEE.

Diederik P. Kingma and Jimmy Ba. 2015. Adam: A method for stochastic optimization. In *ICLR*.

Daniel Kopev, Ahmed Ali, Ivan Koychev, and Preslav Nakov. 2019. Detecting deception in political debates using acoustic and textual features. In *2019 IEEE Automatic Speech Recognition and Understanding Workshop (ASRU)*, pages 652–659.

John Lawrence and Chris Reed. 2020. Argument mining: A survey. *Computational Linguistics*, 45(4):765–818.

Zheng Lian, Jianhua Tao, Bin Liu, and Jian Huang. 2019. Conversational emotion analysis via attention mechanisms. In *INTERSPEECH*, pages 1936–1940. ISCA.

Marco Lippi and Paolo Torroni. 2016a. Argument mining from speech: Detecting claims in political debates. In *Proceedings of the Thirtieth AAAI*

Conference on Artificial Intelligence, AAAI'16, pages 2979–2985. AAAI Press.

Marco Lippi and Paolo Torroni. 2016b. Argumentation mining: State of the art and emerging trends. *ACM Trans. Internet Technol.*, 16(2):10:1–10:25.

Rafael Mestre, Razvan Milicin, Stuart Middleton, Matt Ryan, Jiatong Zhu, and Timothy J. Norman. 2021. M-arg: Multimodal argument mining dataset for political debates with audio and transcripts. In *ArgMining@EMNLP*, pages 78–88. Association for Computational Linguistics.

Shachar Mirkin, Michal Jacovi, Tamar Lavee, Hong-Kwang Kuo, Samuel Thomas, Leslie Sager, Lili Kotlerman, Elad Venezian, and Noam Slonim. 2018a. A recorded debating dataset. In *LREC*. European Language Resources Association (ELRA).

Shachar Mirkin, Guy Moshkowich, Matan Orbach, Lili Kotlerman, Yoav Kantor, Tamar Lavee, Michal Jacovi, Yonatan Bilu, Ranit Aharonov, and Noam Slonim. 2018b. Listening comprehension over argumentative content. In *Proceedings of the 2018 Conference on Empirical Methods in Natural Language Processing*, pages 719–724, Brussels, Belgium. Association for Computational Linguistics.

Habibeh Naderi, Behrouz Haji Soleimani, Sheri Rempel, Stan Matwin, and Rudolf Uher. 2019. Multimodal deep learning for mental disorders prediction from audio speech samples. *CoRR*, abs/1909.01067.

Preslav Nakov, Alberto Barrón-Cedeño, Tamer Elsayed, Reem Suwaileh, Lluís Màrquez, Wajdi Zaghouani, Pepa Atanasova, Spas Kyuchukov, and Giovanni Da San Martino. 2018. Overview of the clef-2018 checkthat! lab on automatic identification and verification of political claims. In *Experimental IR Meets Multilinguality, Multimodality, and Interaction*, pages 372–387, Cham. Springer International Publishing.

Jeffrey Pennington, Richard Socher, and Christopher D. Manning. 2014. Glove: Global vectors for word representation. In *EMNLP*, pages 1532–1543.

Claire Polo, Kristine Lund, Christian Plantin, and Gerald P. Niccolai. 2016. Group emotions: the social and cognitive functions of emotions in argumentation. *Int. J. Comput. Support. Collab. Learn.*, 11(2):123–156.

Emna Rejaibi, Ali Komaty, Fabrice Meriaudeau, Said Agrebi, and Alice Othmani. 2022. Mfcc-based recurrent neural network for automatic clinical depression recognition and assessment from speech. *Biomedical Signal Processing and Control*, 71:103107.

Steffen Schneider, Alexei Baevski, Ronan Collobert, and Michael Auli. 2019. wav2vec: Unsupervised pre-training for speech recognition. In *INTERSPEECH*, pages 3465–3469. ISCA.

Nitish Srivastava, Geoffrey Hinton, Alex Krizhevsky, Ilya Sutskever, and Ruslan Salakhutdinov. 2014. Dropout: a simple way to prevent neural networks from overfitting. *The Journal of Machine Learning Research*, 15(1):1929–1958.

Ermal Toto, M. L. Tlachac, and Elke A. Rundensteiner. 2021. Audibert: A deep transfer learning multimodal classification framework for depression screening. In *CIKM*, pages 4145–4154. ACM.

Yao-Hung Hubert Tsai, Shaojie Bai, Paul Pu Liang, J. Zico Kolter, Louis-Philippe Morency, and Ruslan Salakhutdinov. 2019. Multimodal transformer for unaligned multimodal language sequences. In *ACL (1)*, pages 6558–6569. Association for Computational Linguistics.

David Vilares and Yulan He. 2017. Detecting perspectives in political debates. In *Proceedings of the 2017 Conference on Empirical Methods in Natural Language Processing*, pages 1573–1582, Copenhagen, Denmark. Association for Computational Linguistics.

Serena Villata, Elena Cabrio, Imène Jraidi, M. Sahbi Benlamine, Maher Chaouachi, Claude Frasson, and Fabien Gandon. 2017. Emotions and personality traits in argumentation: An empirical evaluation. *Argument Comput.*, 8(1):61–87.

Yiming Zhang, Ying Weng, and Jonathan Lund. 2022. Applications of explainable artificial intelligence in diagnosis and surgery. *Diagnostics*, 12(2).

A Dataset Pre-Processing Details

In this section, we provide information on the debates that were removed owing to issues with the audio file's quality or discrepancy between the audio content and the corresponding transcript. We removed the samples corresponding to the first parliamentary debate in 1988 (Bush vs Dukakis) since the transcript is incomplete and this would have caused alignment mismatches. Regarding the two presidential debates of 2016 (Clinton vs Trump), there was no correspondence between the audio content and corresponding transcripts. Thus, we removed these debates from the original dataset.

The transcript of the first Clinton-Bush-Perot debate of 1992 has been divided into two sections by the Commission. However, the second section did not match the audio file and, thus, we removed the samples corresponding to the second section from the dataset. In the first Carter-Ford debate in 1976, the audio contains a cut of about 30 minutes. Thus, we trimmed the audio file and kept only the audio content before the cut.

B Experimental Setup Details

Table 9 reports the number of samples for each cross-validation fold splits regarding the UKDebates corpus. Likewise, Table 10 provides training statistics for the M-Arg corpus. Table 11 reports the number of samples for the training, validation and test splits of MM-USElecDeb60To16. We used the following seeds for the repeated cross-validation routine: 15371, 15372, 15373. Lastly, Table 12, Table 13 and Table 14 report the class distribution for each train, validation and test split for the UKDebates, M-Arg and MM-USElecDeb60to16 corpora, respectively.

	Fold 1	**Fold 2**	**Fold 3**	**Fold 4**	**Fold 5**
Train	246	247	247	247	247
Validation	62	62	62	62	62
Test	78	77	77	77	77

Table 9: The number of samples for each train, validation and test fold split regarding the UKDebates corpus.

C Model Calibration

In this section, we report the hyper-parameters set used to calibrate each described classification model. We distinguish between input configurations TA, TO, and AO. In particular, the calibration space for input configuration TA is the combination of those regarding input configurations TO and AO. Table 15 reports the hyper-parameter set used to calibrate the BERT model. Similarly, Table 17 and 16 describe the calibration space of the SVM and Bi-LSTM baselines, respectively.

	Fold 1	**Fold 2**	**Fold 3**	**Fold 4**	**Fold 5**
Train	1563	1563	1563	1564	1564
Validation	391	391	391	391	391
Test	489	489	489	488	488

Table 10: The number of samples for each train, validation and test fold split regarding the M-Arg ($\gamma \geq 0.85$) corpus.

	No. Sentences
Train	12423
Validation	6894
Test	7464

Table 11: The number of samples for each train, validation and test split regarding the MM-USElecDeb60to16 corpus.

D Performance on Validation Splits

Table 18 reports classification performance on the validation set of the UKDebates corpus. Likewise, Table 19 and 20 report classification metrics for M-Arg and MM-USElecDeb60to16 corpora, respectively.

	Fold 1		Fold 2		Fold 3		Fold 4		Fold 5	
	claim	not-claim	claim	not-claim	claim	not-claim	claim	not-claim	claim	not-claim
Train	96	150	98	149	98	149	98	149	97	150
Validation	25	37	24	38	24	38	24	38	24	38
Test	31	47	30	47	30	47	30	47	31	46

Table 12: Class distribution for each train, validation and test split regarding the UKDebates corpus.

	Fold 1			Fold 2			Fold 3			Fold 4			Fold 5		
	neither	attack	support	neither	attack	support	neither	attack	support	neither	attack	support	neither	attack	support
Train	1460	19	84	1460	19	84	1460	19	84	1460	20	84	1460	19	85
Validation	365	4	22	365	4	22	366	4	21	366	4	21	366	4	21
Test	457	6	26	457	6	26	456	5	27	456	5	27	456	6	26

Table 13: Class distribution for each train, validation and test split regarding the M-Arg corpus.

	ASD		ACC	
	arg	not-arg	claim	premise
Train	9456	2967	5029	4427
Validation	5199	1695	2814	2385
Test	5907	1557	3036	2871

Table 14: Class distribution for each train, validation and test split regarding the MM-USElecDeb60to16 corpus.

Hyper-parameter	Search Space
Input Configuration TO	
Input dropout	$[0., 0.1, 0.2, 0.3, 0.4, 0.5]$
Classification units	$[64, 100, 128, 256, 512]$
Pre-classification dropout	$[0., 0.1, 0.2, 0.3, 0.4, 0.5]$
Input Configuration AO	
Input dropout	$[0., 0.1, 0.2, 0.3, 0.4, 0.5]$
Classification units	$[64, 100, 128, 256, 512]$
Pre-classification dropout	$[0., 0.1, 0.2, 0.3, 0.4, 0.5]$
L2 regularization	$[1e^{-2}, 1e^{-3}, 5e^{-3}, 1e^{-04}, 5e^{-04}]$
Bi-LSTM units	$[64, 100, 128, 256, 512]$
Audio pooling	$[None, [10, 2], [5, 5], [5, 5, 5], [5], [10, 10]$
CNN filters	$[8, 64]$
CNN kernel size	$[3, 7]$

Table 15: The hyper-parameters search space of the BERT model.

Hyper-parameter	Search Space
Input Configuration TO	
Input dropout	$[0., 0.1, 0.2, 0.3, 0.4, 0.5]$
Classification units	$[64, 100, 128, 256, 512]$
Pre-classification dropout	$[0., 0.1, 0.2, 0.3, 0.4, 0.5]$
L2 regularization	$[1e^{-2}, 1e^{-3}, 5e^{-3}, 1e^{-04}, 5e^{-04}]$
Bi-LSTM units	$[32, 64, 128]$
Bi-LSTM layers	$[1, 2]$
GloVe embedding	$[50, 100, 200, 300]$
Learning rate	$[1e^{-3}, 1e^{-4}, 2e^{-4}]$
Input Configuration AO	
Input dropout	$[0., 0.1, 0.2, 0.3, 0.4, 0.5]$
Classification units	$[64, 100, 128, 256, 512]$
Pre-classification dropout	$[0., 0.1, 0.2, 0.3, 0.4, 0.5]$
L2 regularization	$[1e^{-2}, 1e^{-3}, 5e^{-3}, 1e^{-04}, 5e^{-04}]$
Bi-LSTM units	$[64, 100, 128, 256, 512]$
Bi-LSTM layers	$[1, 2]$
Audio pooling	$[None, [10, 2], [5, 5], [5], [5, 5, 5], [10, 10]]$

Table 16: The hyper-parameters search space of the Bi-LSTM model.

Hyper-parameter	Search Space
Kernel	$[rbf, linear]$
γ	$[5e^{-2}, 1e^{-2}, 1e^{-1}, 5e^{-1}, 1.]$
C	$[0.01, 0.1, 1., 10, 100]$

Table 17: The hyper-parameters search space of the SVM model.

		Feature-based		*Embedding-based*	
Model	**TO**	**AO**	**TA**	**AO**	**TA**
SVM	**66.18**	49.86	48.00	51.58	64.45
M-ArgNet	**71.64**	53.07	63.25	55.02	70.52
BiLSTM	**68.80**	52.90	67.88	49.86	68.06
Random			37.78		

Table 18: Average binary F1-score on the validation set of UKDebates. For each row, we report the best results in bold, second best results are underlined instead.

		Feature-based		*Embedding-based*	
Model	**TO**	**AO**	**TA**	**AO**	**TA**
SVM	13.26	11.54	12.75	13.50	**24.09**
M-ArgNet	23.69	20.35	23.66	13.04	**26.56**
BiLSTM	21.83	11.98	20.34	11.43	**24.62**
Random			2.62		

Table 19: Average macro F1-score on the validation set of M-Arg ($\gamma \geq 0.85$). For each row, we report the best results in bold, second best results are underlined instead.

		Feature-based		*Embedding-based*	
Model	**TO**	**AO**	**TA**	**AO**	**TA**
ASD					
SVM	**68.01**	56.34	56.76	64.40	67.24
M-ArgNet	66.71	56.14	62.30	63.59	**68.53**
BiLSTM	68.71	58.86	69.35	63.01	**69.39**
Random			50.26		
ACC					
SVM	**66.17**	49.28	49.23	57.72	64.34
M-ArgNet	**68.48**	50.43	67.28	58.36	68.01
BiLSTM	67.78	48.27	68.38	58.30	**68.49**
Random			49.43		

Table 20: Average macro F1-score on the validation set of MM-USElecDeb60to16. For each row, we report the best results in bold, second best results are underlined instead.

A Robustness Evaluation Framework for Argument Mining

Mehmet Sofi[*], **Matteo Fortier**[*], and **Oana Cocarascu**[†]
Department of Informatics, King's College London
{mehmet.sofi, matteo.fortier, oana.cocarascu}@kcl.ac.uk

Abstract

Standard practice for evaluating the performance of machine learning models for argument mining is to report different metrics such as accuracy or F_1. However, little is usually known about the model's stability and consistency when deployed in real-world settings. In this paper, we propose a robustness evaluation framework to guide the design of rigorous argument mining models. As part of the framework, we introduce several novel robustness tests tailored specifically to argument mining tasks. Additionally, we integrate existing robustness tests designed for other natural language processing tasks and re-purpose them for argument mining. Finally, we illustrate the utility of our framework on two widely used argument mining corpora, UKP topic-sentences and IBM Debater Evidence Sentence. We argue that our framework should be used in conjunction with standard performance evaluation techniques as a measure of model stability.

1 Introduction

Deep learning models have obtained state-of-the-art results on a wide range of Natural Language Processing (NLP) tasks and have even achieved superhuman performance on benchmark tasks (Wang et al., 2019). The standard approach for evaluating machine learning models is to use held-out data and report various performance metrics such as accuracy and F_1.

However, reporting an aggregate statistic on benchmarks does not reflect the model's performance and robustness when applied to real-world texts. Indeed, recent works have shown that NLP models are not robust to perturbations. For instance, natural language inference (NLI) models classify a permuted example where word positions are randomly changed, as they would classify the original input (Sinha et al., 2021), and sentiment analysis models give a lower sentiment score when a positive phrase is added to the original example (Ribeiro et al., 2020). Koch et al. (2021) argue for rigorous evaluation to avoid poor generalisability, whereas Raji et al. (2021) propose systematic development of test suites. Several frameworks have been developed for evaluating the robustness of NLP models, for example CheckList (Ribeiro et al., 2020), TextAttack (Morris et al., 2020), Robustness Gym (Goel et al., 2021), and TextFlint (Wang et al., 2021). There is limited work on evaluating the robustness of argument mining models (Mayer et al., 2020; Schiller et al., 2021), and the linguistic and logical reasoning required in argument mining tasks have so far been ignored.

In this paper we propose a robustness evaluation framework for machine learning-based argument mining models. In particular, we propose a variety of *simulation functions* that, given a *seed dataset*, automatically create *simulated datasets*. The simulated datasets are designed to mimic realistic settings which can be used to test the model's robustness.

Our framework is model-agnostic and only requires access to the data. We propose several novel robustness tests tailored to the argument mining task (e.g. argument removal, motion syntax inversion, motion negation, motion synonym/antonym verb replacement, etc.) as well as re-purpose robustness tests previously applied to other NLP tasks (e.g. contract/expand contraction, verb tense change, back-translation, etc.). We focus on two major corpora available for argument mining: the UKP topic-based sentential argument mining corpus (Stab et al., 2018) where the task is to determine whether a sentence is an argument for a topic and whether it supports or opposes the topic, and the IBM Debater Evidence Sentences corpus (Ein-Dor et al., 2020) where the task is to determine whether a sentence includes evidence for a given

[*] Equal contribution.
[†] Corresponding author.

Proceedings of the 9th Workshop on Argument Mining, co-located with the 29th International Conference on Computational Linguistics, pages 171–180
October 17, 2022.

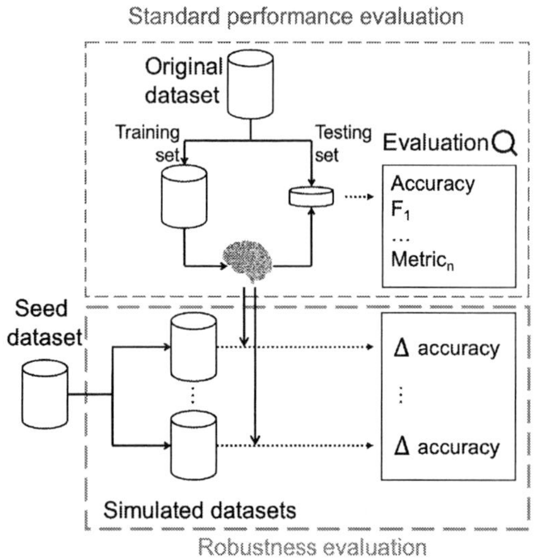

Figure 1: An overview of our proposed robustness evaluation framework for argument mining and how it complements standard performance evaluation.

motion. While other works on robustness focus on adversarial training (e.g. Morris et al. (2020)), our contributions are a range of *functions* that generate *simulated datasets* that reflect real-world examples. We believe our robustness evaluation framework can be used to enhance the standard performance evaluation in order to create better models for argument mining. Figure 1 gives an overview of our proposed robustness evaluation framework.

2 Related Work

There is a plethora of work in evaluating the robustness of NLP models that cover a variety of tasks: sentiment analysis (Ribeiro et al., 2020; Goel et al., 2021; Kiela et al., 2021; Moradi and Samwald, 2021; Wu et al., 2021; Jin et al., 2020; Wang et al., 2021; Li et al., 2020), machine translation (Sai et al., 2021; Morris et al., 2020; Wang et al., 2021), natural language inference (Tarunesh et al., 2021; Goel et al., 2021; Kiela et al., 2021; Morris et al., 2020; Wu et al., 2021; Jin et al., 2020; Wang et al., 2021; Li et al., 2020), question answering (Goel et al., 2021; Moradi and Samwald, 2021; Kiela et al., 2021), duplicate question detection (Ribeiro et al., 2020; Wu et al., 2021), and fake news classification (Jin et al., 2020; Li et al., 2020).

Robustness is evaluated by perturbing data and checking whether the model responds correctly to these changes. Amongst the most commonly used transformations (note that we use "perturbation" and "transformation" interchangeably in this paper) we find: punctuation errors (Sai et al., 2021), typos (Ribeiro et al., 2020; Sai et al., 2021; Wang et al., 2021), synonym replacement (Ribeiro et al., 2020; Moradi and Samwald, 2021; Sai et al., 2021; Morris et al., 2020; Jin et al., 2020; Wang et al., 2021), contractions (Sai et al., 2021; Wang et al., 2021), verb tense change (Wang et al., 2021; Moradi and Samwald, 2021), entity replacement (Ribeiro et al., 2020), back-translation (Goel et al., 2021; Wang et al., 2021), negation (Ribeiro et al., 2020; Moradi and Samwald, 2021; Wu et al., 2021), and using BERT (Devlin et al., 2019) for word replacement (Li et al., 2020). In this paper, we draw from previous works and apply commonly used data transformations in NLP tasks to argument mining.

Regarding task-specific perturbations, TextFlint includes perturbations for NLI, machine translation, and sentiment analysis amongst others, while Tarunesh et al. (2021) extend CheckList with templates tailored for the NLI task to cover more linguistic and logical reasoning such as causal, spatial, and pragmatic.

To the best of our knowledge, only two works have considered the robustness of argument mining models, for topic-dependent argument classification models (Mayer et al., 2020) and stance detection (Schiller et al., 2021). Schiller et al. (2021) used simple linguistic transformations such as two typos and negation by adding the tautology "and false is not true" after each sentence. Mayer et al. (2020) proposed more transformations such as punctuation errors, entity replacement, replacing a noun with its hyponym, using topic alternatives (e.g. *death penalty* → *capital punishment*), and adding speculative adverbs in the evidence text (e.g. *cannabis leads to other drugs* → *cannabis indeed leads to other drugs*), and used these transformations in adversarial training. In both works, the sentence-level topic information within an argument or motion, which we believe to be a key aspect in argument mining, is ignored. In this paper, we propose a robustness evaluation framework and introduce a variety of novel transformations tailored for the argument mining task as well as use existing transformations for NLP tasks and apply them to argument mining.

3 Robustness Tests for Argument Mining

We first introduce the terminology used in this paper. Given an original dataset with N instances

Topic	Sentence	Label
nuclear energy	It has been determined that the amount of greenhouse gases have decreased by almost half because of the prevalence in the utilization of nuclear power.	supporting arg
minimum wage	A 2014 study [...] found that minimum wage workers are more likely to report poor health, suffer from chronic diseases, and be unable to afford balanced meals.	opposing arg
minimum wage	We should abolish all Federal wage standards and allow states and localities to set their own minimums.	non-arg

Table 1: Examples from the UKP dataset.

Motion	Sentence	Label
We should legalize doping in sport	Although the number of cases is low, the Basque regional governments started introducing anti-doping measures in 1997 and created the office of Official Veterinarian in 2005 to help ensure good practice.	arg
We should legalize doping in sport	Contador signed a commitment in which he stated: "I am not involved in the Puerto affair nor in any other doping case".	non-arg
We should lower the drinking age	Alcohol and minors: initiatives seek to discourage underage drinking by providing tools and supporting parents and teachers to engage with minors.	arg
We should lower the drinking age	Some bottles now carry a warning stating that they are not for consumption by people under the legal drinking age (under 18 in the UK and 21 in the United States).	non-arg

Table 2: Examples from the IBM dataset.

$\mathcal{X} = \{X_1, X_2, ..., X_N\}$, where X_i is a pair of texts, and a corresponding set of N labels $\mathcal{Y} = \{Y_1, Y_2, ..., Y_N\}$, we train a model $F : \mathcal{X} \rightarrow \mathcal{Y}$ that maps the inputs $\mathcal{X}$ to the label space $\mathcal{Y}$.

We define a *simulation function* sim to be a function that takes a labelled dataset, called *seed dataset*, and creates a new, labelled *simulated dataset* $\mathcal{S}$ with the corresponding set of labels $\mathcal{Y}'$. For example, we may have $(\mathcal{S}, \mathcal{Y}') = sim(\mathcal{X}, \mathcal{Y})$, but other sub-sets of $\mathcal{X}$ could be used, such as the training set or the validation set.

A *robustness test* consists of applying a *simulation function* to obtain a *simulated dataset* and then evaluating a model's robustness on the *simulated dataset* (see Figure 1 for an overview). The model robustness is recorded as the difference between the model's performance on the original dataset and the model's performance on the simulated dataset.

Next, we describe the two argument mining datasets we use as *seed datasets* and the *simulation functions* we propose for obtaining *simulation datasets* that can be used to test the robustness of argument mining models.

3.1 Seed Datasets

There are two major corpora available for argument mining: UKP topic-based sentential argument mining corpus (Stab et al., 2018) and IBM Debater Evidence Sentences corpus (Ein-Dor et al., 2020).

The UKP dataset consists of 25,492 sentences for 8 topics (abortion, cloning, death penalty, gun control, marijuana legalization, minimum wage, nuclear energy, school uniforms), labelled as *supporting*, *opposing*, or *non-argument*. A text is deemed to be an argument if it provides evidence or reasoning that can be used to support or oppose a given topic. Table 1 shows examples from UKP.

The IBM dataset consists of 29,429 sentences for 221 motions that have a "dominant concept" (e.g. higher education, distance education, athletic scholarship, olympic games, alcoholic drink, hydroelectricity). Each sentence in a motion-sentence pair has an acceptance rate between 0 and 1 reflecting whether the sentence can be considered as evidence supporting or opposing the motion. Here, we consider sentences with an acceptance rate above 0.5 as *arguments*, and sentences with an acceptance rate below 0.5 as *non-arguments*. Table 2 shows examples from the IBM dataset.

3.2 Simulation Functions for Robustness Tests

We propose 15 simulation functions for testing the robustness of argument mining models. We define novel robustness tests tailored for the argument classification task which exploit the sentence-level topic information within an argument or motion: topic change, argument removal, motion syntax inversion, motion negation, motion verb replacement, and motion replacement. In addition, we integrate existing robustness tests and apply them to argument mining: motion topic synonym, motion adverbial modifier, punctuation error, typo, contract/expand contraction, synonym replacement, verb tense change, entity replacement, back-translation. Some simulation functions result in a change in the label (i.e. topic change, argument removal, motion replacement), while the rest of the simulation functions keep the label unchanged.

In the following, we describe our simulation functions, and indicate in brackets if a function can be applied to only one of the datasets.

Topic change (UKP): In this simulation function, we randomly change the topic of the argument to one of the other topics in the dataset. As an argument for a topic (e.g. "abortion") cannot be an argument for another topic (e.g. "minimum wage"),[1] the model should classify the new text as *non-argument*. This test is also applied to instances labelled *non-argument* to check whether the model can consistently classify texts that are unrelated or provide no evidence for the topic as *non-argument*.

Argument removal (UKP): An argument expresses evidence for/against a topic, thus a sentence that expresses an opinion for/against a topic but does not provide evidence would be classified as *non-argument*. In this test, we remove the evidence from an argument and expect the model to classify the new text as *non-argument*. We use premise and conclusion indicators to implement this test. In particular, premise indicators can be found before the evidence, thus removing the text after the indicators would remove the evidence; similarly, conclusion indicators can be found after the evidence and removing the text before the indicators would remove the evidence. We remove the evidence based on the occurrence of certain keywords used in discourse that indicate the presence of a premise or conclusion. We use the following *conclusion indicators*: {"therefore", "thus", "hence", "consequently", "ergo", "it proves that", "in conclusion", "suggests that", "so", "it follows that", "implies that", "we can infer that", "we can conclude that"}, and the following *premise indicators*: {"because", "since", "supposing that", "assuming that", "given that", "as indicated by", "the fact that", "it follows from", "for", "as", "follows from", "as shown by", "the reason is that"}. We implement two variations of this test on the instances labelled as *supporting/opposing argument*: *i)* testing whether removing the evidence using indicators will result in the model classifying the text as *non-argument*, and *ii)* confidence testing which uses the model's output for each label and evaluates whether the text with the argument removed has a higher confidence in the *non-argument* label when compared with the text where the evidence is preserved.

Motion topic synonym (IBM): In this simulation function, we replace the topic of a motion with a synonymous topic. The topic can be the passive nominal subject or direct object of the motion sentence. We use spaCy[2] to identify the motion topic and sense2vec (Trask et al., 2015) to obtain topic alternatives and their similarity scores, and select the top-scoring alternative topic with similarity score above 80%.

Motion syntax inversion (IBM): This simulation function recognises and reconstructs motion sentences using a different syntax. We identify four types of motion syntax, defined by the dependency of the topic within the motion: passive nominal subject topic, nominal subject topic, direct object topic, and object of preposition topic. We use spaCy, in particular dependency tags and part-of-speech tags to recognise the motion syntax, and then invert it.

Motion negation (IBM): We negate a motion by adding the word *not*. We expect the model to predict the label of the instance in the seed dataset as negation does not affect whether a sentence is or is not an argument for the motion, distinguishing the argument classification task from a supporting/opposing relation prediction task.

Motion adverbial modifier (IBM): In this simulation function, we add adverbial modifiers (i.e. *absolutely*, *indeed*, *certainly*, and *definitely*) or use them to replace existing adverbial modifiers. We use dependency tags and part-of-speech tags to ensure the adverbial modifier is added in the correct location in the sentence.

Motion verb replacement (IBM): We replace the root verb in a motion with a synonymous or antonymous verb. Similarly to motion negation, using an antonym of the root verb does not affect whether a sentence is or is not an argument for the motion. We use SupWSD (Papandrea et al., 2017), a supervised Word Sense Disambiguation (WSD) model, to obtain the WordNet (Fellbaum, 1998) senses of words in a sentence from which we determine the synonyms and antonyms that we use to replace the root verbs. We also ensure that all verbs replaced are conjugated as in the original sentence.

Motion replacement (IBM): In this test, we replace the motion text of a motion-sentence pair with another motion text from the dataset, and ex-

[1] Note that this is possible due to the non-overlapping topics in the UKP dataset.

[2] `https://spacy.io/`

pect the model to predict *non-argument*. We implement two variations of this test: *i)* replacing the motion with the most similar motion in the dataset given the motion topic and *ii)* replacing the motion with the most different motion in the dataset given the motion topic. We use sense2vec on the "dominant concept" in the IBM dataset to sort motions based on their similarity score to a given motion. If the concept cannot be found in the sense2vec model, we use spaCy's similarity score computed using the average vector of word embeddings.

The remaining simulation functions are applied to the sentences in the topic/motion sentence pairs.

Punctuation error: Punctuation errors arise from the misuse or absence of punctuation marks. In this simulation function, we use CheckList that adds/removes a single punctuation mark. Given that texts found in online sources often omit several or all punctuation marks, to test the model's robustness we also implement a simulation function where all punctuation marks are removed.

Typo: Typos represent mistakes made when typing. As the datasets were collected from online sources where typos are common, it is important to test the model's robustness against these errors. We use CheckList to implement this simulation function as CheckList has support for adding typos. We introduce different number of typos: 1, 2, and 3 typos, respectively.

Contract/Expand contraction: Contractions represent shortened versions of words. In this simulation function, we expand contractions (e.g. *aren't* $\rightarrow$ *are not*) or contract the expanded contractions (e.g. *are not* $\rightarrow$ *aren't*), depending on the form used in the sentence. We use Checklist to contract and to expand contractions in texts.

Synonym replacement: Synonyms are words that are similar or have a related meaning and we use them to increase the language variety. In this simulation function, we replace each word in the text with a context appropriate synonym using CheckList's inbuilt synonym replacement feature.

Verb tense change: Grammar errors occur frequently in online sources. We introduce grammar errors by changing the verb tense. We use spaCy and LemmInflect[3] to identify the verbs in text and to change their tense. We create a new text for each verb inflection; if an argument contains several verbs, we create a new text for each verb.

Entity replacement: We identify entities (e.g. date, event, location, etc.) using spaCy and replace them with 10 words/phrases chosen randomly from their respective categories. We limit the number of replacements to 10 due to the high number of entities in each category.[4]

Back-translation: Back-translation is the process by which a text is translated from one language L_1 to another language L_2 and then back to L_1, resulting in a text with similar meaning, but different structure. We experiment with 3 configurations to capture the linguistic variance between the original sentence and its back-translated counterpart: English $\rightarrow$ French $\rightarrow$ English, English $\rightarrow$ Russian $\rightarrow$ English, and English $\rightarrow$ Arabic $\rightarrow$ English. We use the OPUS-MT (Tiedemann and Thottingal, 2020) model from EasyNMT[5] to translate texts from English to the target languages and back.

Table 3 shows examples from the simulated datasets obtained from UKP and IBM.

4 Experiments

In this section, we apply our proposed *simulation functions* and evaluate the robustness of argument mining models. We use UKP and IBM, respectively, as seed datasets. We adopt the methodology in Wang et al. (2021) and apply each simulation function on the original dataset to generate the corresponding simulated dataset. Depending on the simulation function used, the simulated dataset may be of different size compared to the seed dataset. For example, some functions are not applicable to all instances in the seed dataset (e.g. contraction), while other functions may result in creating one example (e.g. punctuation error) or several examples for each instance in the dataset (e.g. synonym replacement, entity replacement).

We experiment with BERT (Devlin et al., 2019), a pre-trained transformer network (Vaswani et al., 2017) which set state-of-the-art performance on various sentence classification and sentence-pair classification tasks. We use bert-base-cased and fine-tune on each dataset. For UKP, we train using the proposed train-test-validation sets and we obtain 71.7% accuracy and 67.4% macro F_1, using e-3 as learning rate and training for 21 epochs. For IBM, we split the dataset into 70% for training, 15% for testing and 15% for validation, and obtain 83.4% accuracy and 71% F_1, using 2e-5 as

[3]http://github.com/bjascob/LemmInflect

[4]We experimented with higher values, but the results were similar and hence decided not to include them.

[5]https://github.com/UKPLab/EasyNMT

Simulation function	Original text in seed dataset	New text in simulated dataset
Topic change	(Abortion, Abortion is wrong because it is taking a human life.)	(Minimum Wage, Abortion is wrong because it is taking a human life.)
Argument removal	Abortion is wrong because it is taking a human life.	Abortion is wrong.
Motion topic synonym	We should ban alternative medicine	We should ban naturopathy
Motion syntax inversion	Private universities should be banned	We should ban private universities
Motion negation	We should subsidize cultivation of tobacco	We should not subsidize cultivation of tobacco
Motion adverbial modifier	We should ban lotteries	We should absolutely ban lotteries
Motion adverbial modifier	We should further exploit wind turbines	We should indeed exploit wind turbines
Motion syn verb replacement	We should abolish the monarchy	We should get rid of the monarchy
Motion ant verb replacement	We should prohibit flag burning	We should permit flag burning
Motion similar replacement	We should fight global warming	Tattoos should be banned
Motion different replacement	We should fight global warming	We should subsidize renewable energy
Punctuation (single)	The war on poverty has not had any effect in the 40 + years that it has been going on.	The war on poverty has not had any effect in the 40 + years that it has been going on
Punctuation (all)	It is true, as conservative commentators often point out, that some minimum-wage workers are middle-class teenagers or secondary earners in fairly well-off households.	It is true as conservative commentators often point out that some minimumwage workers are middleclass teenagers or secondary earners in fairly welloff households
Typo	Milton Friedman called them a form of discrimination against low-skilled workers.	Milton Friedman calledt hem a form of discriminatio nagainst lwo-skilled workers.
Contraction	Not true: The typical minimum wage worker is not a high school student earning weekend pocket money.	Not true: The typical minimum wage worker isn't a high school student earning weekend pocket money.
Synonym replacement	And those employers, in turn, would be unable to hire as many people – an undesirable result when unemployment continues to hover at about 8 percent.	And those employers, in turn, would be unable to hire as many people – an undesirable outcome when unemployment continues to hover at {around/nearly} 8 percent.
Verb tense change	You really want your kids on that?	You really wanting your kids on that?
Entity replacement	In 2012 the richest 1% of the US population earned 22.83% of the nation 's total pre-tax income resulting in the widest gap between the rich and the poor since the 1920s.	In 1934 the richest 1% of the US population earned 22.83% of the nation's total pre-tax income resulting in the widest gap between the rich and the poor since the 1920s.
Back-translation	A woman can not sincerely be considered to have equal standing in society if she does not at least have the choice to remove the challenges that will come with a pregnancy.	A woman cannot sincerely be considered equal in society if she does not at least have the option to overcome the difficulties of pregnancy.

Table 3: Examples from the simulated datasets. The orange highlights indicate the portions of the original text in the seed dataset on which the function is applied and the green highlights indicate the changes in the new text.

learning rate and training for 3 epochs. Our results are higher than those previously reported on UKP (63.25% macro F_1) and on a smaller, but similar IBM dataset (81.37% accuracy) (Reimers et al., 2019).

Robustness has been evaluated in different ways: Ribeiro et al. (2020) check that the model's output is invariant when certain transformations are applied to the input, while others calculate the accuracy on the transformed set (Wang et al., 2021; Morris et al., 2020). We experiment with both methods and discuss model robustness and model consistency.

4.1 Model Robustness

We evaluate the robustness of the model in predicting the labels $\mathcal{Y}'$ of each simulated dataset $\mathcal{S}$. We report the percentage point change between the accuracy on the seed dataset and the accuracy on the simulated dataset in Table 4. In this paper, we used a single metric per transformation function, however additional metrics can be used. Overall, the results show that the BERT model trained on the UKP dataset is more robust than the model trained on the IBM dataset.

The tests topic change and argument removal are only applicable to UKP as the dataset contains topics rather than motions and three labels, *non-argument*, *supporting* and *opposing* argument, in contrast to the IBM dataset that has motions and two labels only, *argument* and *non-argument*. The results for the topic change test show that the model struggles to draw a distinction between an argument and its relation to the topic input. For example, the model classified the argument "But those predisposed to defending the interests of cor-

Simulation function	Simulated UKP datasets (3 classes) Data size	Δ	Simulated IBM datasets (2 classes) Data size (# motions)	Δ
Topic change	25,492	-8.99	n/a	n/a
Argument removal	5,963	-45.77	n/a	n/a
Argument removal (confidence)	5,963	-11.83	n/a	n/a
Motion topic synonym	n/a	n/a	10,455 (63)	-5.39
Motion syntax inversion	n/a	n/a	29,429 (221)	-5.65
Motion negation	n/a	n/a	29,429 (221)	-4.2
Motion adverbial modifier	n/a	n/a	29,429 (221)	-4.34
Motion synonym verb replacement	n/a	n/a	11,834 (205)	-2.64
Motion antonym verb replacement	n/a	n/a	6,781 (86)	-4.46
Motion similar replacement	n/a	n/a	29,429 (221)	-16.91
Motion different replacement	n/a	n/a	29,429 (221)	-0.82
Punctuation (single)	25,492	-0.18	29,429	-8.56
Punctuation (all)	25,492	-0.47	29,429	-8.31
One Typo	25,492	-1.26	29,429	-2.08
Two Typos	25,492	-3.52	29,429	-4.16
Three Typos	25,492	-5.69	29,429	-5.72
(Expand) Contraction	5,226	-1.67	4,182	-2.35
Synonym replacement	53,867	-0.97	53,867	+0.62
Verb tense change	201,786	-0.94	313,121	-2.06
Entity replacement	267,916	-0.44	772,870	+0.24
Back-Translation (French)	25,492	-2.56	29,42	+3.17
Back-Translation (Russian)	25,492	-5.88	29,42	-4.23
Back-Translation (Arabic)	25,492	-11.25	29,42	-3.75

Table 4: The percentage point change between the model's accuracy on the seed dataset and the accuracy on the simulated dataset for each simulation function.

porate America - including retailers and fast-food restaurants - oppose any increase" as an *opposing argument* for topic "school uniforms", when this is in fact an argument against the topic "minimum wage". We run two types of tests when removing the argument, the first in which we expect the model to predict *non-argument* and the second in which we expect an increase in the model's confidence for the class *non-argument*. The results of the confidence test show that the model is not robust, however the absence of premise and conclusion indicators increases the model's confidence that the argument has no reasoning or evidence.

For the IBM tests where we modified the motion, we sample ten instances from the simulated datasets and check their correctness. The results for motion topic synonym show that the model struggles with topics that it has not seen during training. The model failed when the following topic synonyms were used: "alternative medicine" → "naturopathy", "assisted suicide" → "euthanasia". Whilst we generate tests at large and thus improve over existing manual methods for generating similar tests (Mayer et al., 2020), we acknowledge that the automatic generation of synonyms is not a perfect task. For example, we noticed that the topic "fraternities" was replaced with "sororities" and topic "abortions" with "legal abortions"; assuming the concepts overlap sufficiently, the evidence sentences should still be arguments. In addition, we also observed incorrect topic synonyms such "wealth distribution" → "progressive taxation".

Regarding the other simulation functions that modify the motion, we evaluate the generated texts in the simulated datasets and find that they match their intended design. The motion syntax inversion test evaluates the models' ability for predicting motion-evidence relations by identifying the subject or topic in texts with different syntax. The motion negation test checks whether the model is able to identify motion-evidence relation even in the presence of the word *not* in the motion, while the motion adverbial modifier evaluates the model's robustness to adding or replacing adverbs. The motion synonym/antonym verb replacement tests are useful in determining the model's robustness towards the role of the root verb in predicting the motion-evidence relation. Similarly to previous cases when synonyms were used, we noticed one replacement to be incorrect: "We should ban fast food" → "We should censor fast food", otherwise, the simulated dataset matches the intended designs. For motion different replacement, all generated examples appear to be correct and the model classifies the motion-evidence as *non-argument*. However, for motion similar replacement, the motion concepts may overlap significantly, and thus the expected label should not change to *non-argument*. For example, “We should protect endangered species" and “We should increase eco-tourism" may share several arguments, as well as “We should ban lotteries" and “Casinos should be banned". Thus, further work is required to assess the suitability of the *motion similar replacement* test.

Regarding simulation functions applied to the sentences in the topic/motion sentence pairs, while the UKP model's accuracy is relatively unaffected by the absence or addition of punctuation marks, the IBM model is sensitive to these types of changes. As the number of typos in a single argument increases, the model's performance in identifying the correct label for the argument decreases. Upon inspection, we noticed that shorter arguments from UKP that were correctly classified under the one typo setup were misclassified under the two typo setup. Regarding the contraction test, the model struggled with the less common contractions such as “that would" $\rightarrow$ “that'd". The performance for this test was lower than expected; we believe that a BERT model with a large training set should be robust to contractions as they do not change the meaning of the sentence. The verb tense change result shows that the UKP model is able to identify the relation between sentences and the topic regardless of a verb's tense, highlighting the fact that it can correctly classify the stance of an argument even in the presence of grammar errors. With respect to synonym replacement and entity replacement, the models for both datasets appear to be robust, with the UKP model yielding a small decrease in robustness while the IBM model yielded a small increase. We experimented with three languages for the back-translation tests: French, Russian and Arabic. As expected, French back-translation performed the best as English shares more similarities with French than with the other languages. We observed that the model failed on all three languages in cases where the translation model added noise and resulted in the argument losing its meaning.

4.2 Model Consistency

Beyond model robustness measured as the difference in accuracy between the seed dataset and the simulated dataset, we also evaluate whether the model is consistent in making predictions, i.e. we compare whether the model predicts the same label for an instance in the seed dataset and for its corresponding instance in the simulated dataset.

Simulation function	UKP (%)	IBM (%)
Punctuation (single)	99.08	95.19
Punctuation (all)	97.76	94.99
One Typo	93.24	95.01
Two Typos	86.73	90.32
Three Typos	81.91	86.71
(Expand) Contraction	97.95	99.47

Table 5: Model consistency results.

Thus, we evaluate model consistency using the simulation functions that introduce minimal changes to the syntax (i.e. punctuation errors, typos, and contraction/expand contraction).

Table 5 shows the model consistency results. On the UKP dataset, the model's prediction for adding/removing a single punctuation mark is consistent, while we see a decrease in consistency when removing all the punctuation marks. In contrast, the model's prediction on the IBM dataset is less consistent. The consistency of both models' predictions decreased as the number of typos increased, highlighting that the models are sensitive to small changes in the argument. The model consistency is higher on the IBM dataset than on the UKP dataset for typos and contractions.

5 Conclusion

We proposed a robustness evaluation framework for machine learning-based argument mining models. Our framework is model-agnostic and only requires access to the data. We presented 15 simulation functions, amongst which 6 are novel and tailored for the argument classification task by exploiting sentence-level topic information within an argument or motion, with the rest of the functions re-purposed for argument mining tasks. These can be used to automatically create simulated datasets, designed to mimic realistic settings which can be used to test the model's robustness. We illustrated the utility of our framework on two widely used argument mining corpora, UKP topic-sentences and IBM Debater Evidence Sentence and showed that, while robust, BERT models can still be vulnerable to new inputs.

Our robustness evaluation framework can be used to enhance the standard performance evaluation in order to create better models for argument mining by measuring model stability. We experimented with the major corpora available for argument mining, however our framework can be applied to datasets for relation prediction in argument mining (Cocarascu et al., 2020).

There are several avenues for future work. First, we plan to apply our framework to other datasets and models used in argument mining. We also plan to use the simulated datasets in adversarial training to evaluate whether model robustness can be improved. Further, it would be useful to explore combining several simulation functions to create simulated datasets. Finally, one interesting line of research is to provide explanations and/or summaries of failures on the simulated datasets that can be used to understand why a model fails and thus work on improving it.

References

Oana Cocarascu, Elena Cabrio, Serena Villata, and Francesca Toni. 2020. Dataset independent baselines for relation prediction in argument mining. In *Computational Models of Argument - Proceedings of COMMA*, volume 326 of *Frontiers in Artificial Intelligence and Applications*, pages 45–52. IOS Press.

Jacob Devlin, Ming-Wei Chang, Kenton Lee, and Kristina Toutanova. 2019. BERT: pre-training of deep bidirectional transformers for language understanding. In *Proceedings of the 2019 Conference of the North American Chapter of the Association for Computational Linguistics: Human Language Technologies, NAACL-HLT*, pages 4171–4186. Association for Computational Linguistics.

Liat Ein-Dor, Eyal Shnarch, Lena Dankin, Alon Halfon, Benjamin Sznajder, Ariel Gera, Carlos Alzate, Martin Gleize, Leshem Choshen, Yufang Hou, Yonatan Bilu, Ranit Aharonov, and Noam Slonim. 2020. Corpus wide argument mining - A working solution. In *The Thirty-Fourth AAAI Conference on Artificial Intelligence, AAAI*, pages 7683–7691. AAAI Press.

Christiane Fellbaum. 1998. *WordNet: An Electronic Lexical Database*. Bradford Books.

Karan Goel, Nazneen Fatema Rajani, Jesse Vig, Zachary Taschdjian, Mohit Bansal, and Christopher Ré. 2021. Robustness gym: Unifying the NLP evaluation landscape. In *Proceedings of the 2021 Conference of the North American Chapter of the Association for Computational Linguistics: Human Language Technologies: Demonstrations, NAACL-HLT*, pages 42–55. Association for Computational Linguistics.

Di Jin, Zhijing Jin, Joey Tianyi Zhou, and Peter Szolovits. 2020. Is BERT really robust? A strong baseline for natural language attack on text classification and entailment. In *The Thirty-Fourth AAAI Conference on Artificial Intelligence, AAAI*, pages 8018–8025. AAAI Press.

Douwe Kiela, Max Bartolo, Yixin Nie, Divyansh Kaushik, Atticus Geiger, Zhengxuan Wu, Bertie Vidgen, Grusha Prasad, Amanpreet Singh, Pratik Ringshia, Zhiyi Ma, Tristan Thrush, Sebastian Riedel, Zeerak Waseem, Pontus Stenetorp, Robin Jia, Mohit Bansal, Christopher Potts, and Adina Williams. 2021. Dynabench: Rethinking benchmarking in NLP. In *Proceedings of the 2021 Conference of the North American Chapter of the Association for Computational Linguistics: Human Language Technologies, NAACL-HLT*, pages 4110–4124. Association for Computational Linguistics.

Bernard Koch, Emily Denton, Alex Hanna, and Jacob G. Foster. 2021. Reduced, reused and recycled: The life of a dataset in machine learning research. In *Proceedings of the Neural Information Processing Systems (NeurIPS) Track on Datasets and Benchmarks 1*.

Linyang Li, Ruotian Ma, Qipeng Guo, Xiangyang Xue, and Xipeng Qiu. 2020. BERT-ATTACK: adversarial attack against BERT using BERT. In *Proceedings of the 2020 Conference on Empirical Methods in Natural Language Processing, EMNLP*, pages 6193–6202. Association for Computational Linguistics.

Tobias Mayer, Santiago Marro, Elena Cabrio, and Serena Villata. 2020. Generating adversarial examples for topic-dependent argument classification. In *Computational Models of Argument - Proceedings of COMMA*, volume 326 of *Frontiers in Artificial Intelligence and Applications*, pages 33–44. IOS Press.

Milad Moradi and Matthias Samwald. 2021. Evaluating the robustness of neural language models to input perturbations. In *Proceedings of the 2021 Conference on Empirical Methods in Natural Language Processing, EMNLP*, pages 1558–1570. Association for Computational Linguistics.

John X. Morris, Eli Lifland, Jin Yong Yoo, Jake Grigsby, Di Jin, and Yanjun Qi. 2020. Textattack: A framework for adversarial attacks, data augmentation, and adversarial training in NLP. In *Proceedings of the 2020 Conference on Empirical Methods in Natural Language Processing: System Demonstrations, EMNLP*, pages 119–126. Association for Computational Linguistics.

Simone Papandrea, Alessandro Raganato, and Claudio Delli Bovi. 2017. SupWSD: A flexible toolkit for supervised word sense disambiguation. In *Proceedings of the 2017 Conference on Empirical Methods in Natural Language Processing, EMNLP*, pages 103–108. Association for Computational Linguistics.

Inioluwa Deborah Raji, Emily Denton, Emily M. Bender, Alex Hanna, and Amandalynne Paullada. 2021. AI and the everything in the whole wide world benchmark. In *Proceedings of the Neural Information Processing Systems (NeurIPS) Track on Datasets and Benchmarks 1*.

Nils Reimers, Benjamin Schiller, Tilman Beck, Johannes Daxenberger, Christian Stab, and Iryna Gurevych. 2019. Classification and clustering of arguments with contextualized word embeddings. In *Proceedings of the 57th Conference of the Association for Computational Linguistics, ACL*, pages 567–578. Association for Computational Linguistics.

Marco Túlio Ribeiro, Tongshuang Wu, Carlos Guestrin, and Sameer Singh. 2020. Beyond accuracy: Behavioral testing of NLP models with checklist. In *Proceedings of the 58th Annual Meeting of the Association for Computational Linguistics, ACL*, pages 4902–4912. Association for Computational Linguistics.

Ananya B. Sai, Tanay Dixit, Dev Yashpal Sheth, Sreyas Mohan, and Mitesh M. Khapra. 2021. Perturbation checklists for evaluating NLG evaluation metrics. In *Proceedings of the 2021 Conference on Empirical Methods in Natural Language Processing, EMNLP*, pages 7219–7234. Association for Computational Linguistics.

Benjamin Schiller, Johannes Daxenberger, and Iryna Gurevych. 2021. Stance detection benchmark: How robust is your stance detection? *Künstliche Intell.*, 35(3):329–341.

Koustuv Sinha, Prasanna Parthasarathi, Joelle Pineau, and Adina Williams. 2021. Unnatural language inference. In *Proceedings of the 59th Annual Meeting of the Association for Computational Linguistics and the 11th International Joint Conference on Natural Language Processing, ACL/IJCNLP*, pages 7329–7346. Association for Computational Linguistics.

Christian Stab, Tristan Miller, Benjamin Schiller, Pranav Rai, and Iryna Gurevych. 2018. Cross-topic argument mining from heterogeneous sources. In *Proceedings of the 2018 Conference on Empirical Methods in Natural Language Processing EMNLP*, pages 3664–3674. Association for Computational Linguistics.

Ishan Tarunesh, Somak Aditya, and Monojit Choudhury. 2021. Trusting RoBERTa over BERT: insights from checklisting the natural language inference task. *CoRR*, abs/2107.07229.

Jörg Tiedemann and Santhosh Thottingal. 2020. OPUS-MT - building open translation services for the world. In *Proceedings of the 22nd Annual Conference of the European Association for Machine Translation, EAMT*, pages 479–480. European Association for Machine Translation.

Andrew Trask, Phil Michalak, and John Liu. 2015. sense2vec - A fast and accurate method for word sense disambiguation in neural word embeddings. *CoRR*, abs/1511.06388.

Ashish Vaswani, Noam Shazeer, Niki Parmar, Jakob Uszkoreit, Llion Jones, Aidan N. Gomez, Lukasz Kaiser, and Illia Polosukhin. 2017. Attention is all you need. In *Advances in Neural Information Processing Systems 30: Annual Conference on Neural Information Processing Systems*, pages 5998–6008.

Alex Wang, Yada Pruksachatkun, Nikita Nangia, Amanpreet Singh, Julian Michael, Felix Hill, Omer Levy, and Samuel R. Bowman. 2019. SuperGLUE: A stickier benchmark for general-purpose language understanding systems. In *Advances in Neural Information Processing Systems 32: Annual Conference on Neural Information Processing Systems, NeurIPS*, pages 3261–3275.

Xiao Wang, Qin Liu, Tao Gui, Qi Zhang, Yicheng Zou, Xin Zhou, Jiacheng Ye, Yongxin Zhang, Rui Zheng, Zexiong Pang, Qinzhuo Wu, Zhengyan Li, Chong Zhang, Ruotian Ma, Zichu Fei, Ruijian Cai, Jun Zhao, Xingwu Hu, Zhiheng Yan, Yiding Tan, Yuan Hu, Qiyuan Bian, Zhihua Liu, Shan Qin, Bolin Zhu, Xiaoyu Xing, Jinlan Fu, Yue Zhang, Minlong Peng, Xiaoqing Zheng, Yaqian Zhou, Zhongyu Wei, Xipeng Qiu, and Xuanjing Huang. 2021. TextFlint: Unified multilingual robustness evaluation toolkit for natural language processing. In *Proceedings of the Joint Conference of the 59th Annual Meeting of the Association for Computational Linguistics and the 11th International Joint Conference on Natural Language Processing, ACL*, pages 347–355. Association for Computational Linguistics.

Tongshuang Wu, Marco Túlio Ribeiro, Jeffrey Heer, and Daniel S. Weld. 2021. Polyjuice: Generating counterfactuals for explaining, evaluating, and improving models. In *Proceedings of the 59th Annual Meeting of the Association for Computational Linguistics and the 11th International Joint Conference on Natural Language Processing, ACL/IJCNLP*, pages 6707–6723. Association for Computational Linguistics.

On Selecting Training Corpora for Cross-Domain Claim Detection

Robin Schaefer and **René Knaebel** and **Manfred Stede**
Applied Computational Linguistics
University of Potsdam
14476 Potsdam, Germany
{robin.schaefer|rene.knaebel|stede}@uni-potsdam.de

Abstract

Identifying claims in text is a crucial first step in argument mining. In this paper, we investigate factors for the composition of training corpora to improve cross-domain claim detection. To this end, we use four recent argumentation corpora annotated with claims and submit them to several experimental scenarios. Our results indicate that the "ideal" composition of training corpora is characterized by a large corpus size, homogeneous claim proportions, and less formal text domains.

1 Introduction

In the last decade, argument mining (AM) has grown into a fruitful area of research (Stede and Schneider, 2018; Lawrence and Reed, 2020). While early studies tended to focus on the annotation and detection of argument components in edited text domains (Levy et al., 2014), more recently the field progressed in different new directions. This includes intensified work on social media texts such as Twitter, e.g. by Schaefer and Stede (2022), argument quality assessment (Wachsmuth et al., 2017) and the identification of argumentation strategies (Al-Khatib et al., 2017).

Arguments consist of several components, and their identification is traditionally split into several subtasks, such as detecting argumentative text segments, specifying their function, and finding the relations among them. Given that a claim is the central component of an argument, claim detection often constitutes a crucial part of an AM pipeline.

In this paper, we combine work in claim detection with recent advances in learning contextualized word representations in order to study cross-domain claim detection on the following set of recent English argumentation corpora: Change My View (CMV) posts (Hidey et al., 2017), persuasive essays (Stab and Gurevych, 2017), micro texts (Peldszus and Stede, 2015) and political US debates (Haddadan et al., 2019). We selected them for achieving variation in genre or register, formality level, and topic. In principle, these dimensions should be distinguished, but for present purposes we do not study them separately, and thus we follow the common practice to use "domain" as an unspecific cover term. Ultimately, we are interested in investigating the "ideal" composition of a training corpus for detecing claims in new domains or corpora.

The paper is structured as follows. In Section 2, we present relevant related work. In Section 3, we describe the used corpora, and we outline our methods in Section 4. We present our results in Section 5 and provide a discussion in Section 6.

2 Related Work

Early work on claim detection was presented by Levy et al. (2014), who introduced the concept of context-dependent claims for finding claims that are relevant for a particular predetermined topic and context. Based on this idea, Lippi and Torroni (2015) proposed an approach to more general topic-independent claim detection, where the context of the argumentation was not given to the detection model as input.

Haddadan et al. (2019) focus on political debates and approach argument detection with the two subtasks of identifying argumentative sentences and subsequent classification of claims and premises. They report 0.84 F1 and 0.67 F1 scores for both tasks, respectively. Our work differs from their study by only focusing on claims and classifying them directly, i.e., against "all other" material.

Stab and Gurevych (2017) propose models for argument role classification with mostly handcrafted features. Later, in their work on a large heterogeneous corpus of argumentive sentences, Stab et al. (2018) develop an LSTM cell that incorporates topic information in the process of sentence-level claim detection. They demonstrate the beneficial effect of this additional information of about 0.05

Proceedings of the 9th Workshop on Argument Mining, co-located with the 29th International Conference on Computational Linguistics, pages 181–186
October 17, 2022.

Corpus	Domain	Type	#Docs	#Sentences	#Claims
CMV	web	monologue	107	3966	1356 (34%)
Essay	student essays	monologue	402	6743	2108 (31%)
Micro	various	monologue	112	451	112 (25%)
USDEB	politics	dialogue (spoken)	42	38309	14418 (38%)

Table 1: Overview of studied corpora.

F1 score compared to LSTM cells without topic information. Reimers et al. (2019) build on top of previously proposed recurrent architectures and successfully examine the positive influence of different contextualized word embeddings on the task of classifying argument components.

Daxenberger et al. (2017) investigate cross-domain claim identification in order to shed light on differences and similarities in claim conceptualizations across domains. They utilize linguistic feature-based and neural approaches (with and without pre-trained word embeddings). Their study is a direct precursor of our work—we use some more recent data, and in addition, incorporate recent contextualized word embeddings that serve as input for our recurrent neural network classifier. For claim detection, their best feature-free models report 0.62 F1 and 0.67 F1 for persuasive essays and micro texts, respectively.

3 Data

For determining factors influencing claim detection, we chose four English argumentation corpora of varying register (monologue and dialogue), formality level (written text and transcribed speeches), and topics. See Table 1 for statistics.

To facilitate the task, we also ensured that our corpora have less variety in claim proportions than those used by Daxenberger et al. (2017). All our corpora contain further annotations, e.g., premises, but we only use claim annotations in this study.

CMV. Hidey et al. (2017) annotate claims, premises and semantic types of argument components on the Change My View corpus from Tan et al. (2016), reporting an IAA of 0.63 for claims. We segment this user-generated data into 3966 sentences. 34% sentences contain a claim.

Essay. The corpus of argumentative essays (Stab and Gurevych, 2017) consists of 402 persuasive essays annotated for three argument components (major claim, claim, and premise) and their relations (support and attack). Annotators achieved IAA scores of 0.88 and 0.64 for major claims and claims, respectively. All argument components are annotated on clause level. We combine *major claim* and *claim* into one single claim class. After sentence splitting, we obtain 6743 units, 31% of which contain a claim.

Micro. The argumentative microtext corpus (Peldszus and Stede, 2015) was developed in a controlled setting where participants created short texts containing a single argument. Annotators then built a complete argumentation graph per text, the agreement was 0.83. Texts were originally written in German and then professionally translated to English. We work on this version; it consists of 451 sentences, 25% of which contain a claim.

USDEB. The USElecDeb60To16 corpus of Haddadan et al. (2019) is a collection of transcripts of political TV debates between 1960 and 2016. Annotators labeled argumentativeness of sentences and sentences containing argument components, i.e., claim and premise. They achieved an IAA for component annotation of 0.40, which indicates the challenge for analyzing spoken language of this kind. This is the only corpus in our set where the number of claims exceeds those of premises. After sentence splitting, we obtain 38309 sentences. 38% contain a claim.

To account for potential positional effects, we calculated percentages of claim positions by dividing a sentence into three equal parts on a token basis: beginning, middle and ending. A claim could potentially occur in individual parts or the combination of beginning and middle, middle and ending or all three parts. The percentages show that for the vast majority of sentences containing a claim, the claim occurs in all three parts. Only in 1%-4% of sentences do the claims occur in two parts. See Table 2 for details.

4 Method

For preprocessing, we perform tokenization and sentence segmentation with the Trankit toolkit (Nguyen et al., 2021). Following Daxenberger et al. (2017), we label a sentence as a claim if any token

Corpus	B & M	M & E	B & M & E
CMV	3%	2%	26%
Essay	2%	4%	25%
Micro	2%	1%	20%
USDEB	3%	3%	30%

Table 2: Claim position percentages of combined sentence parts (B=Beginning; M=Middle, E=Ending). The percentages refer to full corpus size.

within the sentence is part of a claim. However, note that this may lead to some imprecision in classification, as sentences with a claim may contain additional premises or non-argumentative parts. To study this potential issue we additionally experimented with *elementary discourse units* (EDU) (Mann and Thompson, 1988) replacing sentences as the unit of classification. For EDU identification, we use an end-to-end neural segmentation approach proposed by Wang et al. (2018) that works on already-split sentences. We adopt the previously described mapping for sentences and label individual EDUs containing at least one token referring to a claim as positive training instances. In this step, a single claim might be split into two separate discourse units, which increases the number of training instances. In general, classifying EDUs instead of full sentences is more precise, since the proportion of positive labels within a positively labeled instance is higher than on the sentence level.

We conduct one in-domain and four cross-domain experiments in order to identify promising scenarios for claim detection:

1. Train and test models on single corpora (in-domain; S1).
2. Train and test models on the union of all four corpora (S2).
3. Utilize the same test sets as in S2 but train only on three corpora, which allows us to identify the effects of removing individual corpora (S3).
4. Adopt a leave-one-out approach by training across three corpora and testing on the remaining one (S4).
5. Allow for pair comparisons by training on individual corpora and testing on a different one (S5).

We apply 10-fold cross-validation and compute the average model performance in all experiments.

		Claim Class			Macro
		F1	P	R	F1
S1)	CMV	0.72	0.74	0.69	0.79
	Essay	0.67	0.70	0.64	0.76
	Micro	0.73	0.82	0.69	0.82
	USDEB	0.73	0.75	0.71	0.78
S2)	All Corpora	0.72	0.72	0.72	0.78
S3)	No CMV	0.71	0.71	0.71	0.77
	No Essay	0.71	0.70	0.71	0.77
	No Micro	0.72	0.71	0.73	0.78
	No USDEB	0.49	0.72	0.37	0.65
S4)	CMV	0.46	0.56	0.39	0.62
	Essay	0.55	0.56	0.55	0.67
	Micro	0.59	0.52	0.68	0.71
	USDEB	0.37	0.75	0.25	0.58

Table 3: Results for experiments (except S5). *In-Domain* (S1): Training, validating and testing within a single domain. *Cross-Domain*: S2) Training/validating and testing on union of all corpora; S3) Training/validating with all except the mentioned corpus and testing with the same 4-corpora sets as in S2; S4) Training/validating with three corpora and testing with the mentioned corpus (leave-one-out).

For S1 (in-domain) and S2, we reserve 10% of the data for validation and testing, respectively. In S3, however, the validation set is <10% while the test set is larger given that we use the same test sets for S3 as for S2 while removing individual corpora from the training and validation sets. In S4 (leave-one-out) and S5 (pair comparison), 20% of the training corpora are used for validation while the whole respective testing corpus is used for testing.

Our classification pipeline was implemented using the FLAIR framework (Akbik et al., 2019), which offers a simple interface for training BERT-related models (Devlin et al., 2019), among others. We use a simple recurrent neural network on top of context-sensitive embeddings extracted using RoBERTa (Liu et al., 2019). In particular, we make use of *roberta-argument* (Stab et al., 2018), which was pre-trained on roughly 25,000 sentences annotated for +/- argumentative. The last hidden state is finally processed by a linear layer with softmax activation. The full neural network, including the pre-trained RoBERTa embeddings, is updated during training. In addition, we trained models using the classic *base-cased* BERT model (Devlin et al., 2019) for comparison.

Pair (Train - Test)	Claim Class F1	P	R	Macro F1	Pair (Train - Test)	Claim Class F1	P	R	Macro F1
CMV - Essay	0.55	0.49	0.63	0.65	Micro - CMV	0.13	0.24	0.09	0.43
CMV - Micro	0.45	0.38	0.57	0.60	Micro - Essay	0.11	0.50	0.06	0.46
CMV - USDEB	0.47	0.66	0.37	0.62	Micro - USDEB	0.30	0.36	0.28	0.46
Essay - CMV	0.21	0.66	0.13	0.51	USDEB - CMV	0.54	0.53	0.55	0.64
Essay - Micro	0.33	0.61	0.24	0.60	USDEB - Essay	0.57	0.52	0.65	0.67
Essay - USDEB	0.22	0.86	0.13	0.50	USDEB - Micro	0.57	0.44	0.82	0.67

Table 4: Results for corpus pair experiments (S5). Models were trained and validated on the first corpus and tested on the second corpus.

5 Results

All results presented in this section are produced with the RoBERTa architecture trained on sentence units. We conducted additional experiments with BERT models and with EDUs, which on the whole lead to worse results. For EDUs, this is especially the case for the claim class, which we are particularly interested in. We will discuss this briefly in Section 6. In the following, we report macro F1 scores and F1, precision, and recall for the claim class. See Table 3 for result of S1-S4 and Table 4 for results of S5.

5.1 In-Domain

S1 shows good results for all corpora. The best macro F1 score was achieved for the Micro corpus (0.82). However, the less formal CMV and USDEB still come relatively close. F1 scores for the claim class are considerably lower, which is to be expected, as it is the smaller class for all corpora.

5.2 Cross-Domain

Models trained and tested across all four corpora (S2) yield results comparable to S1. Removing the CMV, Essay, or Micro corpus from the training set while still testing on all corpora (S3) does not influence results. However, removing the USDEB corpus reduces the recall of the claim class, which leads to a drop in F1.

Leave-one-out experiments (S4) show mixed results. Best results were achieved when the Micro corpus was not part of the training set (macro F1: 0.71; claim F1: 0.59). Testing on the Essay corpus also works comparatively well. Results obtained from removing the USDEB corpus from the training set, however, are low (macro F1: 0.58; class F1: 0.37).

S5 (pair comparison; Table 4) shows substantial variance, especially with respect to the claim class results. Models trained on USDEB yield the most robust results with comparatively little variance in F1 scores. Models trained on CMV show the best results when tested with the Essay corpus. In comparison, Essay and Micro perform worse as training corpora. While models trained on the Essay corpus yield the best results when tested with the Micro corpus, all pairs show low results for the claim class (F1: 0.21-0.33). The lowest results occur for the Micro corpus with F1 scores of 0.11-0.30 for the claim class.

6 Discussion & Conclusion

As noted above, our BERT and EDU results cannot compete with the sentence-level RoBERTa results. We surmise that RoBERTa may have outperformed BERT as it was pre-trained on an argument detection task; likewise, since it was trained on sentences, EDU performance may be lower.

While being a potentially interesting factor, we argue that the claim position in a sentence does not substantially affect our results. Statistics on claim position show that claims in the vast majority of claim sentences occur in the beginning, middle, and ending, i.e. they cover more than 66% of tokens in a sentence. Only in 1%-4% of sentences of a given corpus, claims merely occur in the beginning and middle or middle and ending, i.e. they cover a span of 34%-66% tokens in a given sentence. Of course, this does not mean that position cannot have an effect in general, and justifies more research in the future.

In contrast, our results suggest that different factors influence the choice of a suitable corpus for training claim detection models. First, corpus size seems to play a crucial role. This is especially the case when several corpora are combined for training. Removing individual corpora from the training set while testing on all corpora (S3) shows that only the removal of the largest corpus (USDEB) has a profound effect on the results. Our leave-one-out experiments (S4) confirm this finding, as models trained on all corpora except USDEB obtain worse results than models trained in other leave-one-out scenarios. Also, training on USDEB in a corpus pair scenario (S5) consistently yields good results, indicating that a large training size has a beneficial effect, while training on the small Micro corpus yields the worst results.

Second, although claim proportions vary less in our corpora than in those used by Daxenberger et al. (2017), differences in claim proportions may still have an effect. For instance, while USDEB is the largest corpus in our set, it also contains the highest proportion of claims, which may render it difficult for models trained on corpora with lower claim proportions to sufficiently capture the class distribution in USDEB. Still, it appears that size effects outweigh claim proportion effects given that claim detection results improve when the Micro corpus is left out for training, which is the corpus that is both the smallest and the one with the lowest claim proportion.

Third, our results suggest that domain plays a role. Recall that the Essay and Micro corpora represent relatively "edited" text types, while CMV and USDEB contain web data and oral debates, which can be described as less formal. This may affect the way argumentation takes place. Our corpus pair experiments show that models trained on the less formal CMV and USDEB yield better results than models trained on Essay and Micro. Note that corpus size does not explain this pattern given that the CMV corpus is smaller than the Essay corpus.

Conclusion. In this paper we present several experiments to investigate cross-domain claim detection. Our results indicate that corpus size, differences in claim proportions, and content domain influence the composition of an effective training corpus. We argue that a large training set size, homogeneous claim proportions, and less formal language improve the results, and we plan to investigate this in further experiments that examine the broad notion of "domain" more closely and consider factors like monologue/dialogue or formality level as separate dimensions. Also, we plan to extend the work to premise detection and thus move closer to "full" arguments. Finally, we are interested in investigating the effect of claim position in units larger than sentences, for instance by using sequence labeling techniques.

Acknowledgements

This research has been supported by the German Research Foundation (DFG) with grant number 455911521, project "LARGA" in SPP "RATIO". We would like to thank the anonymous reviewers for their valuable feedback.

References

Alan Akbik, Tanja Bergmann, Duncan Blythe, Kashif Rasul, Stefan Schweter, and Roland Vollgraf. 2019. FLAIR: An easy-to-use framework for state-of-the-art NLP. In *Proceedings of the 2019 Conference of the North American Chapter of the Association for Computational Linguistics (Demonstrations)*, pages 54–59, Minneapolis, Minnesota. Association for Computational Linguistics.

Khalid Al-Khatib, Henning Wachsmuth, Matthias Hagen, and Benno Stein. 2017. Patterns of argumentation strategies across topics. In *Proceedings of the 2017 Conference on Empirical Methods in Natural Language Processing*, pages 1351–1357, Copenhagen, Denmark. Association for Computational Linguistics.

Johannes Daxenberger, Steffen Eger, Ivan Habernal, Christian Stab, and Iryna Gurevych. 2017. What is the essence of a claim? cross-domain claim identification. In *Proceedings of the 2017 Conference on Empirical Methods in Natural Language Processing*, pages 2055–2066, Copenhagen, Denmark. Association for Computational Linguistics.

Jacob Devlin, Ming-Wei Chang, Kenton Lee, and Kristina Toutanova. 2019. BERT: Pre-training of deep bidirectional transformers for language understanding. In *Proceedings of the 2019 Conference of the North American Chapter of the Association for Computational Linguistics: Human Language Technologies, Volume 1 (Long and Short Papers)*, pages 4171–4186, Minneapolis, Minnesota. Association for Computational Linguistics.

Shohreh Haddadan, Elena Cabrio, and Serena Villata. 2019. Yes, we can! mining arguments in 50 years of US presidential campaign debates. In *Proceedings of the 57th Annual Meeting of the Association for Computational Linguistics*, pages 4684–4690, Florence, Italy. Association for Computational Linguistics.

Christopher Hidey, Elena Musi, Alyssa Hwang, Smaranda Muresan, and Kathy McKeown. 2017. Analyzing the semantic types of claims and premises in an online persuasive forum. In *Proceedings of the 4th Workshop on Argument Mining*, pages 11–21,

Copenhagen, Denmark. Association for Computational Linguistics.

John Lawrence and Chris Reed. 2020. Argument Mining: A Survey. *Computational Linguistics*, 45(4):765–818.

Ran Levy, Yonatan Bilu, Daniel Hershcovich, Ehud Aharoni, and Noam Slonim. 2014. Context dependent claim detection. In *Proceedings of COLING 2014, the 25th International Conference on Computational Linguistics: Technical Papers*, pages 1489–1500, Dublin, Ireland. Dublin City University and Association for Computational Linguistics.

Marco Lippi and Paolo Torroni. 2015. Context-independent claim detection for argument mining. In *Proceedings of the 24th International Conference on Artificial Intelligence*, IJCAI'15, page 185–191. AAAI Press.

Yinhan Liu, Myle Ott, Naman Goyal, Jingfei Du, Mandar Joshi, Danqi Chen, Omer Levy, Mike Lewis, Luke Zettlemoyer, and Veselin Stoyanov. 2019. Roberta: A robustly optimized bert pretraining approach. *ArXiv*, abs/1907.11692.

William C. Mann and Sandra A. Thompson. 1988. Rhetorical structure theory: Toward a functional theory of text organization. *Text & Talk*, 8:243 – 281.

Minh Van Nguyen, Viet Dac Lai, Amir Pouran Ben Veyseh, and Thien Huu Nguyen. 2021. Trankit: A lightweight transformer-based toolkit for multilingual natural language processing. In *Proceedings of the 16th Conference of the European Chapter of the Association for Computational Linguistics: System Demonstrations*, pages 80–90, Online. Association for Computational Linguistics.

Andreas Peldszus and Manfred Stede. 2015. An annotated corpus of argumentative microtexts. In *Argumentation and Reasoned Action: Proceedings of the 1st European Conference on Argumentation*, volume 2, pages 801—-816, Lisbon. College Publications, London.

Nils Reimers, Benjamin Schiller, Tilman Beck, Johannes Daxenberger, Christian Stab, and Iryna Gurevych. 2019. Classification and clustering of arguments with contextualized word embeddings. In *Proceedings of the 57th Annual Meeting of the Association for Computational Linguistics*, pages 567–578, Florence, Italy. Association for Computational Linguistics.

Robin Schaefer and Manfred Stede. 2022. GerCCT: An annotated corpus for mining arguments in german tweets on climate change. In *Proceedings of the Language Resources and Evaluation Conference*, pages 6121–6130, Marseille, France. European Language Resources Association.

Christian Stab and Iryna Gurevych. 2017. Parsing argumentation structures in persuasive essays. *Computational Linguistics*, 43(3):619–659.

Christian Stab, Tristan Miller, Benjamin Schiller, Pranav Rai, and Iryna Gurevych. 2018. Cross-topic argument mining from heterogeneous sources. In *Proceedings of the 2018 Conference on Empirical Methods in Natural Language Processing*, pages 3664–3674, Brussels, Belgium. Association for Computational Linguistics.

Manfred Stede and Jodi Schneider. 2018. *Argumentation Mining*, volume 40 of *Synthesis Lectures in Human Language Technology*. Morgan & Claypool.

Chenhao Tan, Vlad Niculae, Cristian Danescu-Niculescu-Mizil, and Lillian Lee. 2016. Winning arguments: Interaction dynamics and persuasion strategies in good-faith online discussions. In *Proceedings of the 25th International Conference on World Wide Web, WWW 2016, Montreal, Canada, April 11 - 15, 2016*, pages 613–624. ACM.

Henning Wachsmuth, Nona Naderi, Yufang Hou, Yonatan Bilu, Vinodkumar Prabhakaran, Tim Alberdingk Thijm, Graeme Hirst, and Benno Stein. 2017. Computational argumentation quality assessment in natural language. In *Proceedings of the 15th Conference of the European Chapter of the Association for Computational Linguistics: Volume 1, Long Papers*, pages 176–187, Valencia, Spain. Association for Computational Linguistics.

Yizhong Wang, Sujian Li, and Jingfeng Yang. 2018. Toward fast and accurate neural discourse segmentation. In *Proceedings of the 2018 Conference on Empirical Methods in Natural Language Processing*, pages 962–967, Brussels, Belgium. Association for Computational Linguistics.

Entity-based Claim Representation Improves Fact-Checking of Medical Content in Tweets

Amelie Wührl and **Roman Klinger**
Institut für Maschinelle Sprachverarbeitung, University of Stuttgart, Germany
{amelie.wuehrl,roman.klinger}@ims.uni-stuttgart.de

Abstract

False medical information on social media poses harm to people's health. While the need for biomedical fact-checking has been recognized in recent years, user-generated medical content has received comparably little attention. At the same time, models for other text genres might not be reusable, because the claims they have been trained with are substantially different. For instance, claims in the SCIFACT dataset are short and focused: "*Side effects associated with antidepressants increases risk of stroke*". In contrast, social media holds naturally-occurring claims, often embedded in additional context: "*'If you take antidepressants like SSRIs, you could be at risk of a condition called serotonin syndrome' Serotonin syndrome nearly killed me in 2010. Had symptoms of stroke and seizure.*" This showcases the mismatch between real-world medical claims and the input that existing fact-checking systems expect. To make user-generated content checkable by existing models, we propose to reformulate the social-media input in such a way that the resulting claim mimics the claim characteristics in established datasets. To accomplish this, our method condenses the claim with the help of relational entity information and either compiles the claim out of an entity-relation-entity triple or extracts the shortest phrase that contains these elements. We show that the reformulated input improves the performance of various fact-checking models as opposed to checking the tweet text in its entirety.

1 Introduction

People use social media platforms like Twitter to discuss medical issues. This can expose them to false health-related information and poses immediate harm to people's well-being (Suarez-Lledo and Alvarez-Galvez, 2021). While the necessity for fact-checking biomedical or scientific information has been recognized and addressed in recent years, naturally occurring arguments and claims as they are shared by social media users have received less attention.

Id	Source	Claim
1	SCIFACT	A mutation in HNF4A leads to an increased risk of diabetes by the age of 14 years.
2	PubHealth	Scientists find clues to why binge-drinking causes binge-eating.
3	Zuo et al. (2020)	Scientists discover gene mutation involved in paraplegia and epilepsy
4	COVID-Fact	Baricitinib restrains the immune dysregulation in covid-19 patients
5	HealthVer	Frequent touching of contaminated surfaces in public areas is therefore a potential route of SARS-CoV-2 transmission.
6	CoVERT	So, they die from lung failure caused by extreme pneumonia or heart failure from sludgy blood but the root cause is #COVID19 (which can be confirmed post-mortem) so the death is counted as due to the #coronavirus & NOT due to natural causes of pneumonia or heart attack

Table 1: Claims from different fact-checking datasets.

Unfortunately, systems trained on datasets from other domains might not be reusable: The datasets that underly existing pretrained models work with atomic, edited or summarized claims (e.g., from datasets like SCIFACT, Wadden et al., 2020), cover claims that have been selected to be well-formed (COVID-Fact, Saakyan et al., 2021), or contain editorial content such as news headlines (Zuo et al., 2020). Examples 1–5 in Table 1 convey complex biomedical processes, they are relatively short and coherently worded. In addition, they make statements covering only one claim or fact. On the other hand, medical statements as they organically occur for example on Twitter are complex, wordy, imprecise and often ambiguous (Example 6). This makes them substantially different to the claims in established fact-checking datasets for the medical domain. To address the limitations of using only

Proceedings of the 9th Workshop on Argument Mining, co-located with the 29th International Conference on Computational Linguistics, pages 187–198
October 17, 2022.

well-formed claims, Sarrouti et al. (2021) propose a custom dataset and fact-checking model. Their analysis indicates that naturally occurring claims contain multiple, inter-related facts compared to claims in other fact-verification datasets. Along with Zuo et al. (2022), they show that real-world medical claims in user-generated and news content are more complex and longer. In addition, Kim et al. (2021) show that fact-checking systems do not transfer robustly to colloquial claims.

This mismatch motivates extracting a check-worthy main claim from user-generated content before continuing with fact-checking. This claim detection task, which is also a central task in argument mining, can be addressed as a sequence labeling problem (Zuo et al., 2022, i.a.). While this approach requires dedicated annotated data, we propose an alternative that requires an entity annotation and relation detection system – something that has been developed for various purposes across domains (Yepes and MacKinlay, 2016; Giorgi and Bader, 2018; Scepanovic et al., 2020; Lamurias et al., 2019; Doan et al., 2019; Akkasi and Moens, 2021, i.a.). We hypothesize that the main information relevant to a claim is encoded in entities and their relations, because they convey the key semantic information within a statement and describe how they interact with each other. For our approach we propose to use that information to either find the claim token sequence or to generate a sentence representation based on entity and relation classes. Our results show that entity-based claim extraction supports fact-checking for user-generated content, effectively making it more accessible to MultiVerS (Wadden et al., 2022), an architecture recently suggested for scientific claim verification.

2 Related Work

2.1 Biomedical & Scientific Fact-Checking

The task of fact-checking is to determine the truthfulness of a claim (Thorne and Vlachos, 2018). This has been addressed for various domains (Guo et al. (2022) provide a comprehensive review). For the general domain, some work has explored judging the truthfulness of claims based on its linguistic features (Rashkin et al., 2017) or using the knowledge stored in language models as evidence (Lee et al., 2020). Fact-checking for biomedical and scientific content typically leverages external evidence sources. In biomedicine this is vital as novel research that might change or overturn an existing view on a medical claim can only be taken into account if we tap into up to date, external evidence. In other fact-checking contexts (e.g., in a political context), this requirement is not as strong since the veracity of a statement made at a particular point in time is relatively stable. In the biomedical context, given a claim, fact-checking is typically modeled as a two-step process: evidence retrieval (on document and/or sentence-level) and predicting a verdict. This verdict either determines the veracity of the claim or indicates if the evidence supports or refutes the claim. We can group existing approaches by the genre of text from which claims and evidence stem. Wadden and Lo (2021) formalize scientific claim verification in the SCIVER shared task, in which evidence and claims both originate from expert-written text. Pradeep et al. (2021) approach this task with a pipeline model, while Li et al. (2021a); Zhang et al. (2021) propose modeling one or multiple subtasks in a multi-task learning setup. Recently, Wadden et al. (2022) showed that providing more context, i.e., by representing the claim, full evidence abstract and title in a single encoding, is beneficial for inferring a final verdict.

Moving away from expert-written text, Kotonya and Toni (2020) explore verdict prediction for public health claims and use fact-checking and news articles as evidence. Hossain et al. (2020) classify a tweet into predefined categories of known misconceptions about COVID-19. Mohr et al. (2022) automatically verify tweets with COVID-19-related claims with the help of excerpts from online sources. Finally, some studies explore settings in which the claim and evidence texts originate from different genres. Zuo et al. (2020) investigate retrieving scientific evidence for biomedical claims in news texts. Sarrouti et al. (2021) check user-generated, online claims against scientific articles and Saakyan et al. (2021) explore this task for COVID-19-related claims from Reddit.

2.2 Datasets & Their Claim Characteristics

Various datasets have been proposed to facilitate scientific and medical fact-checking. One common characteristic lies in the claims contained in these datasets: they are typically well-formed and sometimes synthetic. This attribute presents a misalignment with the type of data as it occurs on social media.

In SCIFACT (Wadden et al., 2020) claims are synthetic. They are atomic summaries of claims within scientific articles. As evidence, the dataset provides abstracts from scientific literature as well as sentence-level rationales for the claims within those abstracts. PubHealth (Kotonya and Toni, 2020) and the dataset released by Zuo et al. (2020) include claims from editorial content. Kotonya and Toni (2020) provide claims and evidence texts from health-related news and fact-checking articles while Zuo et al. (2020) identify the headlines of health news articles as claims and provide the scientific papers referenced in the news article as evidence. While this genre of claims and content is targeted towards non-experts, it undergoes journalistic editing and can therefore not be characterized as occurring naturally.

We are aware of three datasets that cover user-generated claims, all with a focus on COVID-19. *COVID-Fact* (Saakyan et al., 2021) contains medical claims shared on a COVID-19-specific Sub-Reddit. They use the scientific articles that the users reference as evidence documents. The claims have been filtered to retain only well-formed statements. Sarrouti et al. (2021) contribute the *HealthVer* corpus of real-world statements from online users. To find relevant claims, they query a search engine with COVID-19 questions and use the resulting texts as claims. The provided evidence consists of abstracts from scientific articles. Similar, but exclusively focused on COVID-19 information on Twitter, *Co*VERT (Mohr et al., 2022) provides fact-checked tweets along with evidence texts from online resources. To the best of our knowledge, only *HealthVer* and *Co*VERT cover naturally occurring medical claims from a broad audience.

2.3 Detecting, Extracting & Generating Claims

The task of claim detection is relevant to the field of fact-checking as well as the area of argument mining. From an argument mining perspective, claim detection requires identifying the claim as the core component within the argument structure (Daxenberger et al., 2017). While mainly rooted in the political domain and social sciences (Lawrence and Reed, 2019; Vecchi et al., 2021, i.a.), some work has explored claim detection in scientific text. Achakulvisut et al. (2019); Mayer et al. (2020); Li et al. (2021b, i.a.) extract claims from clinical and biomedical articles, Wührl and Klinger (2021) classify tweets that contain medical claims.

At the same time, detecting a checkable and check-worthy claim is considered the first task within a fact-checking pipeline (Guo et al., 2022). The task of claim-check-worthiness detection is to determine if a given claim should be fact-checked. Typically this is framed as a document, sentence or claim-level classification or ranking task: Gencheva et al. (2017); Jaradat et al. (2018); Wright and Augenstein (2020, i.a.) study this task for general domain claims, in the *CLEF-CheckThat!* shared task (Nakov et al., 2022) participants are tasked to identify tweets that contain check-worthy claims about COVID-19. To the best of our knowledge, Zuo et al. (2022) are the first to explore this on the token level by extracting check-worthy claim sequences from health-related news texts. This shows that identifying biomedical claim sequences in longer documents for the purpose of fact-checking is understudied. The focus in fact-checking datasets and shared tasks (e.g., FEVER (Thorne et al., 2018) or SCIVER (Wadden and Lo, 2021)) is typically to infer the relationship between a claim-evidence pair or on retrieving evidence for a given claim.

While in the studies described above the original phrasing of a document or claim is kept intact, some work has proposed extracting relevant semantic information to reconstruct the content that is being conveyed. Recently, Magnusson and Friedman (2021) show that fine-grained biomedical information within scientific text can be extracted into a knowledge graph to model claims. Related to our work is Yuan and Yu (2019) who extract triplets from health-related news headlines to capture medical claims. Their focus is on classifying the triples as claim or non-claim which leaves fact-checking for future work. Our objective is to extract a concise claim representation and to explore its impact on fact-checking.

Moving even further away from the original text, Wright et al. (2022) suggest generating claims from scientific text to address the data bottleneck for the downstream fact-checking task. They report comparable performances for models trained on automatically generated claims compared to a model trained on the manually labeled SCIFACT claims. Their work is related to Pan et al. (2021) who generate claims to facilitate zero-shot fact

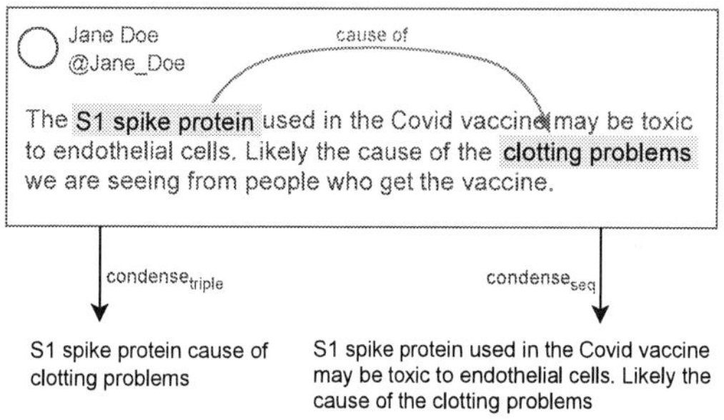

Figure 1: Presented with an input document that has entity and relation labels, $\text{condense}_{\text{triple}}$ and $\text{condense}_{\text{seq}}$ extract two concise claims.

verification for the general domain.

3 Methods

With this work we investigate if knowledge about biomedical entities allows us to extract a concise claim representation from user-generated text that enables fact-checking systems to predict a verdict. To explore this, we suggest two methods to extract and construct entity-based, claim-like statements. We assume we have a sequence of tokens $\mathbf{t} = (t_1, \ldots, t_n)$. In addition, we have a set of m annotations

$$A = \{(e^{\mathbf{a}_1}_{\text{subj}}, r^{\mathbf{a}_1}, e^{\mathbf{a}_1}_{\text{obj}}), \ldots, (e^{\mathbf{a}_m}_{\text{subj}}, r^{\mathbf{a}_m}, e^{\mathbf{a}_m}_{\text{obj}})\},$$

which encode entity and relation information, respectively e and r. The entities are located within the token sequence $\mathbf{t}$ and identified by their character-level onset k and offset ℓ such that $e = (k, \ell)$, with $1 \leq k, \ell \leq n$. The relation r is a string representing the relation type (e.g., "cause of").

Building on data of this type, we suggest two claim condensation methods of the form

$$\text{condense}(\mathbf{t}, \mathbf{a}) \rightarrow c$$

that transform the sequence $\mathbf{t}$ along with its annotation a into a claim-like token sequence c. We propose two variants:

Representing Claims as Triples. We reduce the claim to what we hypothesize to be its core components: two medical entities and the relation between them. We hypothesize that the entities express the most relevant information with regard to the claim.

In this representation the claim is a concatenation $\circ$ of the subject entity tokens, the name of the relation r and the object entity tokens:

$$\text{condense}_{\text{triple}}(\mathbf{t}, \mathbf{a}) = \mathbf{t}_{e^{\mathbf{a}}_{\text{subj}_k}:e^{\mathbf{a}}_{\text{subj}_\ell}} \circ r^{\mathbf{a}} \circ \mathbf{t}_{e^{\mathbf{a}}_{\text{obj}_k}:e^{\mathbf{a}}_{\text{obj}_\ell}}$$

This approach ignores tokens that are not part of the relation or entity annotation.

Extracting Claim Sequences. Alternatively, we extract a subsequence from the original text. For each annotation $\mathbf{a}$ in $\mathbf{t}$, we apply

$$\text{condense}_{\text{seq}}(\mathbf{t}, \mathbf{a}) = \mathbf{t}_{e^{\mathbf{a}}_{\text{subj}_k}} \cdots \circ \cdots \mathbf{t}_{e^{\mathbf{a}}_{\text{obj}_\ell}}.$$

This retains the way the author of the original text chose to express the relation, including all tokens that are mentioned between the entities. Commonly, this also involves words that indicate the relation class, but we do not ensure that. Figure 1 shows examples of both condensation methods. The example is taken from Mohr et al. (2022).

4 Experiments

We investigate whether we can reduce the complexity of user-generated claims in order to make the information that they convey accessible to pretrained "off-the-shelf" fact-checking models and circumvent the necessity of custom training data and specialized models. We specifically explore the use of entity information to formulate a condensed version of a claim (see Section 3). More concretely, we compare how the claim representation impacts the performance of a fact-checking model.

4.1 Experimental Setting

4.1.1 Data

To test our claim condensation methods as outlined in Section 3, we assume the availability of entity and relation information. This is not an unrealistic assumption: Entity and relation extraction systems exist (Yepes and MacKinlay, 2016; Giorgi and Bader, 2018; Scepanovic et al., 2020; Lamurias et al., 2019; Doan et al., 2019; Akkasi and Moens, 2021, i.a.). For our experiments, we build on top of data that has such annotations to focus the evaluation on the extraction method instead of evaluating the quality of a NER/RE system. To the best of our knowledge, the only dataset that provides both fact checking as well as entity and relation information is the CoVERT corpus (Mohr et al., 2022). The dataset consists of fact-checked medical claims in tweets about COVID-19 and includes evidence texts that the annotators provided to substantiate their verdicts (SUPPORT, REFUTE, NOT ENOUGH INFORMATION). Importantly, the dataset also contains the span and type of medical entities and type of relations for each Twitter post. The entity classes cover *Medical Condition*, *Treatment*, *Symptom/Side-effect* and *Other*. Each tweet is also labeled with causative relations *(not_)cause_of* and *causative_agent_of* between a subject and an object entity. We use these annotations to formulate the condensed claims.

CoVERT includes 300 tweets with a total of 722 entities and 300 relations. In instances where multiple objects have been annotated for an entity, we choose the triple which appears first in the document under the assumption that the first claim is the main claim of the statement. For short texts, such as tweets, we hypothesize that people will mention their central, main claim at the beginning of their statement. Additionally, this emulates the atomic nature of claims in SCIFACT. CoVERT is crowd-annotated and provides three evidence texts per claim. From those, we choose the first snippet that is in line with the majority fact-checking verdict as the gold evidence. While SCIFACT assigns the NOT ENOUGH INFO (NEI) label if a given abstract does not provide enough information to come to a verdict, in CoVERT a tweet is labeled as NEI if annotators were not able to find any evidence or if there was no majority w.r.t. the verdict. We therefore drop the 36 tweets labeled NEI for our experiments, as there is no agreement w.r.t. the verdict class or no available evidence. This leaves us with 264 extracted claims (198 SUPPORT, 66 REFUTES).

4.1.2 Fact-checking Models

We use the MultiVerS architecture which has recently been suggested for evidence-based scientific fact verification (Wadden et al., 2022). At the time of writing, this approach ranks first for the shared task SCIVER.[1] It takes as input a claim-evidence pair and represents both in a single encoding to predict a fact-checking label and identify rationales with the evidence. Claim, title and evidence abstract sentences are concatenated using separator tokens and assigned global attention during training. The model subsequently uses a classifier over the separator token that identifies the claim to predict the fact-checking verdict and an additional classification head over the separator tokens between the evidence sentences.

Based on this architecture, Wadden et al. (2022) provide various models.[2] *fever* is trained on the FEVER dataset for general domain fact-checking. *fever_sci* is trained on a combination of FEVER data and weakly-labeled biomedical fact-checking data. The other models build on top of *fever_sci* and are subsequently fine-tuned on gold-labeled, in-domain data for verdict prediction and rationale selection using *scifact*, *covidfact* and *healthver*.

In order to test the impact of the claim representations, we do not adapt the fact-checking model, but alter the input claims.

4.1.3 Baseline: Predicting Claim Sequences

To provide a baseline and gauge the impact of entity-based claim representation as opposed to predicting a claim sequence without relying on entities, we compare to the model by Zuo et al. (2022). They train a Bi-LSTM-CRF sequence labeling model to detect check-worthy claims in medical news articles. Such articles are similar to tweets in that they are also non-expert-written text conveying medical information. Using their code base and provided training data[3], we recreate their best performing model which encodes the input with a combination of BioBERT and FLAIR embeddings.[4] We use the resulting model to predict claim sequences in the CoVERT tweets[5]. For tweets where the model predicted more than one claim sequence in a tweet we use the prediction with the highest confidence score. Note that for 6 tweets the model does not predict any claim. This leaves us with 258 claims.

4.1.4 Evaluation

We evaluate the claim condensation techniques on the downstream task of predicting a fact-checking

[1] https://leaderboard.allenai.org/scifact/submissions/public

[2] We use their code base https://github.com/dwadden/multivers and the provided model checkpoints from there.

[3] https://github.com/chzuo/jdsa_cross_genre_validation

[4] Zuo et al. (2022) use the position of hyperlinks to a source publication within the news articles as additional input to their model. However, they report that the performance gains using this information is not statistically significant. As the CoVERT data does not contain this type of information, we do not include it when recreating their model.

[5] We make predictions for 264 CoVERT tweets not labeled as NEI (see Sec. 4.1.1).

verdict for a claim-evidence pair. Following Wadden et al. (2022) we report the *Label-Only* F_1 on abstract level from the SCIFACT task[6]. It measures the F_1-score of the model for predicting the correct fact-checking verdict given a claim and evidence candidate. A true positive is therefore a claim-evidence pair with a correctly predicted verdict.

4.2 Results

We report results for four approaches to represent the claim. Our baselines are:

full Full text of the tweet which contains a claim.

Zuo et al. (2022) A sequence predicted by a claim detection model, not informed by entity or relation knowledge.

The methods that we propose are:

condense$_{\text{triple}}$ Claim represented by an entity–relation triple.

condense$_{\text{seq}}$ Shortest token sequence which contains all entities.

Table 2 reports the results. The columns indicate which type of claim the models receive as input. For each claim type and model we report precision, recall and F_1 as well as the difference Δ in F_1 to the prediction performance for the **full** tweet. The table rows denote which model is used for prediction. The models (*fever, fever_sci, scifact, covidfact, healthver*) are based on the MultiVerS architecture and vary w.r.t. the type of data they were trained on.

Overall, we observe three major patterns from the results: (1) All models show limited performance when presented with the full tweet. (2) Delimiting the claim sequence always improves verdict prediction. (3) Representing the claim based on the entities and relations is highly beneficial and leads to the most successful predictions. In the following, we discuss the results in more detail.

Fact-checking models struggle to predict verdicts for full tweets. In the first block of Table 2, we see that the performance is generally low (avg. F_1 =12.4) when the models are tasked to check the full tweet. The *fever* model fails to predict fact-checking verdicts for this type of input. The *healthver* model is the most successful (F_1 =45.2), presumably because its training data fits the CoVERT data best.

[6]We use their evaluation script: `https://github.com/allenai/scifact-evaluator`

Delimiting the claim sequence is beneficial. Using the claim sequence prediction obtained with the Zuo et al. (2022) model as claim input shows an improved performance across all models (increases between 2.3 and 13.8pp in F_1 compared to predictions for the full tweet). *healthver* remains the most successful model (48.2 F_1). Notably, the *covidfact* model benefits most from the adapted input (Δ 13.8pp in F_1).

Entity-based claim condensation improves verdict prediction. Across all models, one of the entity and relation-based claim representations achieves the best results. For three out of five models, condense$_{\text{triple}}$ claims facilitate the best prediction compared to other input types. *fever, fever_sci* and *covidfact* achieve F_1-scores of 6.5, 32.8 and 41.3, respectively. For the *scifact* and *healthver* model, using the condense$_{\text{seq}}$ extracted claims leads to the most reliable predictions: we observe 14.0 F_1 for *scifact* and 62.0 F_1 for *healthver*. *healthver*'s prediction for the condense$_{\text{seq}}$ claims is the most successful across all models and settings.

Across the board, the *covidfact* model benefits the most from delimiting the claim sequence. Here, we observe increases in F_1 of 13.8, 33.4 and 29.7pp when comparing the performance on the full tweet with that for a Zuo et al. (2022) claim, condense$_{\text{triple}}$ and condense$_{\text{seq}}$ claim, respectively.

The results show that both condense methods improve the performance of the fact-checking models. While the F_1-scores and the improvements (Δ values) vary across models, we observe the same pattern across our experiments: providing a concise claim as input leads to a more reliable verdict prediction. We also see that claims from both condense methods are more successfully checked than the predicted claim sequence identified by the Zuo et al. (2022) model. This shows that entities and relations do capture the core information of a claim relatively well. It is important to note that the condense claims are constructed using gold annotated entities and relations from CoVERT, while the predicted sequence is not. This needs to be taken into account when comparing the results for those claim representations.

5 Analysis and Discussion

We aim to understand in which cases condensing the claim is helpful and when it harms the

	Claim Representation														
	full tweets			Zuo et al. (2022)				$\text{condense}_{\text{triple}}$				$\text{condense}_{\text{seq}}$			
model	P	R	F_1	P	R	F_1	Δ	P	R	F_1	Δ	P	R	F_1	Δ
fever	0.0	0.0	0.0	75.0	1.2	2.3	+2.3	81.8	3.4	**6.5**	+6.5	83.3	1.9	3.7	+3.7
fever_sci	91.7	4.2	8.0	100	10.1	18.3	+10.3	89.8	20.1	**32.8**	+24.8	87.2	15.5	26.4	+18.4
scifact	100	0.4	0.8	100	2.7	5.3	+4.5	86.4	7.2	13.3	+12.5	90.9	7.6	**14.0**	+13.2
covidfact	30.8	4.5	7.9	48.6	14.0	21.7	+13.8	65.0	30.3	**41.3**	+33.4	55.6	28.4	37.6	+29.7
healthver	82.8	31.1	45.2	86.9	33.3	48.2	+3.0	79.7	41.7	54.7	+9.5	85.9	48.5	**62.0**	+16.8
average	61.1	8.0	12.4	82.1	12.3	19.2	+6.8	80.5	20.5	**29.7**	+17.3	80.6	20.4	28.7	+16.3

Table 2: Fact-checking performance of MultiVerS-based models (*fever, fever_sci, scifact, covidfact, healthver*) on CoVERT data. As the claim input, we present the model with the full tweets, a sequence predicted to contain the claim (Zuo et al., 2022), and the claims that we obtain from our entity and relation-based extraction methods $\text{condense}_{\text{triple}}$ and $\text{condense}_{\text{seq}}$. We report precision, recall and F_1. For each model, Δ captures the difference in F_1 between the full tweet as input and the claims obtained from the respective claim detection or extraction methods. The last row denotes the average across all models. The best performance for each model is printed in bold face.

performance. We therefore conduct an error analysis where we compare the predictions of the best model (*healthver*) with the full tweet as input with predictions of that model using the claims from the most successful condensation method $\text{condense}_{\text{seq}}$. The examples mentioned in the following section are displayed in Table 3. For the sake of brevity, we provide the relevant evidence documents in the Appendix, Table 4.

In total, there are 54 instances in which both claim inputs lead to a correct label. In those instances, the tweet itself tends to be fairly short (see Ex. 1a) or relatively well-formed (see Ex. 1b).

There are 74 instances in which the condensed claim sequence produces a correctly predicted label while the check based on the full tweet input does not lead to a correct result. For 66 out of 74, we observe that the label flips from NEI to the correct label (see Ex. 2a). This shows that the condensation can make the evidence more accessible to the fact-checker. In addition, Ex. 2b shows how a condensed claim is assigned a correct label, while the full tweet is not. This might be the case because the claim is presented as a question in the tweet.

In 28 cases condensing the claim leads to an incorrect prediction while checking the full tweet leads to a correct output. In 20 cases, condensing the claim changes the predicted label from the gold verdict to NEI (see Ex. 3a). This indicates that condensation can render evidence unusable. In Example 3b the condensation actually misrepresents the statement because it cuts of the phrase 'no evidence' before the claim. We recognize that this is a potential pitfall of the claim extraction methods.

There are 108 instances where both claim types lead to incorrectly predicted labels. In 90 out of 108 cases, both are labeled with NEI. The evidence did not provide sufficient information to check the claim. Example 4a exemplifies that, to a certain degree, the NEI label makes sense. The evidence (see Table 4) does not specifically mention long-term consequences of mRNA (vaccines). To conclude that the claim is supported by the evidence, we need to infer that long-term effects are improbable, because the mRNA does not stay in the body or affect the DNA. Similarly, in 4b, the evidence (see Table 4) requires reasoning, because 'pneunomia' and 'flu-like symptoms' which the tweet claims are primary causes of death in COVID-19 patients are not mentioned directly in the evidence. In addition, the comparative statement in the evidence of septic shock and multi-organ failure being the more prevalent causes of death as opposed to respiratory failure might pose difficulties for the model.

6 Conclusion and Future Work

Based on the substantial mismatch between the biomedical claims as they are most typically expected by existing fact-checking models and the nature of real-world, user-generated medical statements made on Twitter, we propose to extract entity-based claim representations. We use the entities as the core information relevant to the claim, and extract condensed claims from tweets. When presented with the adapted claim input, the fact-checking models we experiment with are able to verify the claims more reliably as opposed to when they are tasked to infer a verdict for a full

id	claim input: full tweet	claim input: $cond_{seq}$	Pred. F	Pred. C	Pred. G
1a	Actually wearing masks causes bacterial pneumonia which people can die from NOT covid19. Most people do not know how to don/doff PPE properly. Follow the science Big Guy!	masks causes bacterial pneumonia	R	R	R
1b	Up to half of hospitalized COVID patients have elevated levels of antiphospholipid antibodies, or antibodies that cause blood clots to form. Patients with these antibodies are much more likely to have severe respiratory disease and kidney injury. #COVID19	elevated levels of antiphospholipid antibodies, or antibodies that cause blood clots to form	S	S	S
2a	"It's unclear if his death was related to the virus." This is why we perform autopsies. There is a significant likelihood that #COVID19 played a role in that it is known to affect endothelial cells & has been shown to cause neurological symptoms including stroke.	COVID19 played a role in that it is known to affect endothelial cells & has been shown to cause neurological symptoms	N	S	S
2b	Are you aware that the vaccines could cause miscarriage? The real data regarding covid is that there are tiny numbers, percentage wise, of generally healthy people under the age of 60 that die from COVID or that get admitted into ICU. Are you worried about cancer too?	vaccines could cause miscarriage	S	R	R
3a	The predominant symptoms of 'long COVID' are psychological in nature, with anxiety and depression being most common. But those of course are also exactly the conditions which have been caused in, literally, millions of people, especially young people, by the lockdowns.	long COVID' are psychological in nature, with anxiety	S	N	S
3b	Know the facts! There is no evidence that #COVID19 #vaccines cause #infertility, says @username @username & @username #NIAW2021 #InfertilityAwareness	COVID19 #vaccines cause #infertility	S	R	S
4a	Covid is no joke, this is why we need the vaccine. We know that mRNA doesn't cause long term effects since it decomposes in your body within 1-2 hours. Please everyone, get vaccinated as soon as you can!	mRNA doesn't cause long term effects	N	N	S
4b	I never said Covid-19 wasn't a real coronavirus. And deaths linked to Covid-19 are primarily caused directly from pneumonia, or flu-like symptoms. The classifications for influenza and pneumonia reporting changed when Covid-19 appeared. Facts.	deaths linked to Covid-19 are primarily caused directly from pneumonia	S	S	R

Table 3: Example predictions for full tweets vs. $condense_{seq}$ claims. For each error category, we provide two examples (a and b). The predictions are made by the *healthver* model. F: full tweet as input, C: condensed with method $condense_{seq}$, G: gold annotation. S: Supports, R: Refutes, N: Not enough information.

tweet.

In this study, we focused the analysis on an existing dataset with a comparably narrow focus. While we intuitively believe that the findings also hold for other domains, this remains to be proven. Therefore we propose that future work explores entity- and relation-based claim extraction for other types of medical relations. CoVERT focuses on causative claims which are by design of the dataset explicitly mentioned in the tweet. Exploring if claims about other types of relations can be extracted in a similar manner is up to future research. Similarly, it is important to explore how this method translates to statements with more than one entity-relation-entity triple.

Another limitation of our analysis is its focus on one fact-checking architecture. It is important to evaluate if the impact of claim condensation carries over to other claim checking methods. A possible alternative to our approach (change the claim at test time) could also be to adapt the system (adapt the claims at training time). The degree of which the difference in genre and structure of the evidence document might impact the models' performances is another important perspective for future research.

Finally, we performed studies based on correct annotations of entities. While this is a reasonable approach in a research environment, it is important to explore the impact of error propagation from a named entity recognizer to claim condensation.

Apart from verdict prediction, entity-based claim representation could also facilitate discovering suitable evidence for user-generated medical content as entity knowledge has been shown to benefit evidence retrieval as well (Hanselowski et al., 2018).

7 Ethical Considerations

Unreliable fact-checking evidence and verdicts potentially exacerbate the spread of misinformation because they lend false credibility to harmful health-related information. Therefore, it is greatly important to carefully evaluate and analyze automatic fact-checking systems before their predictions can be used reliably.

It is important to acknowledge that by extracting a claim sequence from a broader statement, we might omit essential context. This could impact the statement's meaning, its intended gravity or generally misrepresent the claim that the author originally meant to convey. To alleviate this and contextualize an automatically generated verdict, it is important to design applications which are transparent with respect to the input claims and prediction process.

Acknowledgements

This research has been conducted as part of the FIBISS project which is funded by the German Research Council (DFG, project number: KL 2869/5-1). We thank the anonymous reviewers for their valuable feedback.

References

Titipat Achakulvisut, Chandra Bhagavatula, Daniel E. Acuna, and Konrad P. Körding. 2019. Claim extraction in biomedical publications using deep discourse model and transfer learning. *CoRR*, abs/1907.00962.

Abbas Akkasi and Mari-Francine Moens. 2021. Causal relationship extraction from biomedical text using deep neural models: A comprehensive survey. *Journal of Biomedical Informatics*, 119:103820.

Johannes Daxenberger, Steffen Eger, Ivan Habernal, Christian Stab, and Iryna Gurevych. 2017. What is the essence of a claim? cross-domain claim identification. In *Proceedings of the 2017 Conference on Empirical Methods in Natural Language Processing*, pages 2055–2066, Copenhagen, Denmark. Association for Computational Linguistics.

Son Doan, Elly W. Yang, Sameer S. Tilak, Peter W. Li, Daniel S. Zisook, and Manabu Torii. 2019. Extracting health-related causality from twitter messages using natural language processing. *BMC Medical Informatics and Decision Making*, 19(3):79.

Pepa Gencheva, Preslav Nakov, Lluís Màrquez, Alberto Barrón-Cedeño, and Ivan Koychev. 2017. A context-aware approach for detecting worth-checking claims in political debates. In *Proceedings of the International Conference Recent Advances in Natural Language Processing, RANLP 2017*, pages 267–276, Varna, Bulgaria. INCOMA Ltd.

John M Giorgi and Gary D Bader. 2018. Transfer learning for biomedical named entity recognition with neural networks. *Bioinformatics*, 34(23):4087–4094.

Zhijiang Guo, Michael Schlichtkrull, and Andreas Vlachos. 2022. A survey on automated fact-checking. *Transactions of the Association for Computational Linguistics*, 10:178–206.

Andreas Hanselowski, Hao Zhang, Zile Li, Daniil Sorokin, Benjamin Schiller, Claudia Schulz, and Iryna Gurevych. 2018. UKP-athene: Multi-sentence textual entailment for claim verification. In *Proceedings of the First Workshop on Fact Extraction and VERification (FEVER)*, pages 103–108, Brussels, Belgium. Association for Computational Linguistics.

Tamanna Hossain, Robert L. Logan IV, Arjuna Ugarte, Yoshitomo Matsubara, Sean Young, and Sameer Singh. 2020. COVIDLies: Detecting COVID-19 misinformation on social media. In *Proceedings of the 1st Workshop on NLP for COVID-19 (Part 2) at EMNLP 2020*, Online. Association for Computational Linguistics.

Israa Jaradat, Pepa Gencheva, Alberto Barrón-Cedeño, Lluís Màrquez, and Preslav Nakov. 2018. ClaimRank: Detecting check-worthy claims in Arabic and English. In *Proceedings of the 2018 Conference of the North American Chapter of the Association for Computational Linguistics: Demonstrations*, pages 26–30, New Orleans, Louisiana. Association for Computational Linguistics.

Byeongchang Kim, Hyunwoo Kim, Seokhee Hong, and Gunhee Kim. 2021. How robust are fact checking systems on colloquial claims? In *Proceedings of the 2021 Conference of the North American Chapter of the Association for Computational Linguistics: Human Language Technologies*, pages 1535–1548, Online. Association for Computational Linguistics.

Neema Kotonya and Francesca Toni. 2020. Explainable automated fact-checking for public health claims. In *Proceedings of the 2020 Conference on Empirical Methods in Natural Language Processing (EMNLP)*, pages 7740–7754, Online. Association for Computational Linguistics.

Andre Lamurias, Diana Sousa, Luka A. Clarke, and Francisco M. Couto. 2019. BO-LSTM: classifying relations via long short-term memory networks along biomedical ontologies. *BMC Bioinformatics*, 20(1):10.

John Lawrence and Chris Reed. 2019. Argument mining: A survey. *Computational Linguistics*, 45(4):765–818.

Nayeon Lee, Belinda Z. Li, Sinong Wang, Wen-tau Yih, Hao Ma, and Madian Khabsa. 2020. Language models as fact checkers? In *Proceedings of the Third Workshop on Fact Extraction and VERification (FEVER)*, pages 36–41, Online. Association for Computational Linguistics.

Xiangci Li, Gully Burns, and Nanyun Peng. 2021a. A paragraph-level multi-task learning model for scientific fact-verification. In *Proceedings of the Workshop on Scientific Document Understanding co-located with 35th AAAI Conference on Artificial Inteligence (AAAI 2021)*, Online.

Xiangci Li, Gully Burns, and Nanyun Peng. 2021b. Scientific discourse tagging for evidence extraction. In *Proceedings of the 16th Conference of the European Chapter of the Association for Computational Linguistics: Main Volume*, pages 2550–2562, Online. Association for Computational Linguistics.

Ian Magnusson and Scott Friedman. 2021. Extracting fine-grained knowledge graphs of scientific claims: Dataset and transformer-based results. In *Proceedings of the 2021 Conference on Empirical Methods in Natural Language Processing*, pages 4651–4658, Online and Punta Cana, Dominican Republic. Association for Computational Linguistics.

Tobias Mayer, Elena Cabrio, and Serena Villata. 2020. Transformer-based Argument Mining for Healthcare Applications. In *ECAI 2020 - 24th European Conference on Artificial Intelligence*, Santiago de Compostela / Online, Spain.

Isabelle Mohr, Amelie Wührl, and Roman Klinger. 2022. Covert: A corpus of fact-checked biomedical covid-19 tweets. In *Proceedings of the Language Resources and Evaluation Conference*, pages 244–257, Marseille, France. European Language Resources Association.

Preslav Nakov, Alberto Barrón-Cedeño, Giovanni Da San Martino, Firoj Alam, Rubén Míguez, Tommaso Caselli, Mucahid Kutlu, Wajdi Zaghouani, Chengkai Li, Shaden Shaar, Hamdy Mubarak, Alex Nikolov, Yavuz Selim Kartal, and Javier Beltrán. 2022. Overview of the CLEF-2022 CheckThat! lab task 1 on identifying relevant claims in tweets. In *Working Notes of CLEF 2022—Conference and Labs of the Evaluation Forum*, CLEF '2022, Bologna, Italy.

Liangming Pan, Wenhu Chen, Wenhan Xiong, Min-Yen Kan, and William Yang Wang. 2021. Zero-shot fact verification by claim generation. In *Proceedings of the 59th Annual Meeting of the Association for Computational Linguistics and the 11th International Joint Conference on Natural Language Processing (Volume 2: Short Papers)*, pages 476–483, Online. Association for Computational Linguistics.

Ronak Pradeep, Xueguang Ma, Rodrigo Nogueira, and Jimmy Lin. 2021. Scientific claim verification with VerT5erini. In *Proceedings of the 12th International Workshop on Health Text Mining and Information Analysis*, pages 94–103, online. Association for Computational Linguistics.

Hannah Rashkin, Eunsol Choi, Jin Yea Jang, Svitlana Volkova, and Yejin Choi. 2017. Truth of varying shades: Analyzing language in fake news and political fact-checking. In *Proceedings of the 2017 Conference on Empirical Methods in Natural Language Processing*, pages 2931–2937, Copenhagen, Denmark. Association for Computational Linguistics.

Arkadiy Saakyan, Tuhin Chakrabarty, and Smaranda Muresan. 2021. COVID-fact: Fact extraction and verification of real-world claims on COVID-19 pandemic. In *Proceedings of the 59th Annual Meeting of the Association for Computational Linguistics and the 11th International Joint Conference on Natural Language Processing (Volume 1: Long Papers)*, pages 2116–2129, Online. Association for Computational Linguistics.

Mourad Sarrouti, Asma Ben Abacha, Yassine Mrabet, and Dina Demner-Fushman. 2021. Evidence-based fact-checking of health-related claims. In *Findings of the Association for Computational Linguistics: EMNLP 2021*, pages 3499–3512, Punta Cana, Dominican Republic. Association for Computational Linguistics.

Sanja Scepanovic, Enrique Martin-Lopez, Daniele Quercia, and Khan Baykaner. 2020. Extracting medical entities from social media. In *Proceedings of the ACM Conference on Health, Inference, and Learning*, CHIL '20, pages 170–181. Association for Computing Machinery. Event-place: Toronto, Ontario, Canada.

Victor Suarez-Lledo and Javier Alvarez-Galvez. 2021. Prevalence of health misinformation on social media: Systematic review. *Journal of medical Internet research*, 23(1):e17187.

James Thorne and Andreas Vlachos. 2018. Automated fact checking: Task formulations, methods and future directions. In *Proceedings of the 27th International Conference on Computational Linguistics*, pages 3346–3359, Santa Fe, New Mexico, USA. Association for Computational Linguistics.

James Thorne, Andreas Vlachos, Oana Cocarascu, Christos Christodoulopoulos, and Arpit Mittal. 2018. The fact extraction and VERification (FEVER) shared task. In *Proceedings of the First Workshop on Fact Extraction and VERification (FEVER)*, pages 1–9, Brussels, Belgium. Association for Computational Linguistics.

Eva Maria Vecchi, Neele Falk, Iman Jundi, and Gabriella Lapesa. 2021. Towards argument mining for social good: A survey. In *Proceedings of the 59th Annual Meeting of the Association for Computational Linguistics and the 11th International Joint Conference on Natural Language Processing (Volume 1: Long Papers)*, pages 1338–1352, Online. Association for Computational Linguistics.

David Wadden, Shanchuan Lin, Kyle Lo, Lucy Lu Wang, Madeleine van Zuylen, Arman Cohan, and Hannaneh Hajishirzi. 2020. Fact or fiction: Verifying scientific claims. In *Proceedings of the 2020 Conference on Empirical Methods in Natural Language Processing (EMNLP)*, pages 7534–7550, Online. Association for Computational Linguistics.

David Wadden and Kyle Lo. 2021. Overview and insights from the SCIVER shared task on scientific claim verification. In *Proceedings of the Second Workshop on Scholarly Document Processing*, pages 124–129, Online. Association for Computational Linguistics.

David Wadden, Kyle Lo, Lucy Wang, Arman Cohan, Iz Beltagy, and Hannaneh Hajishirzi. 2022. MultiVerS: Improving scientific claim verification with weak supervision and full-document context. In *Findings of the Association for Computational Linguistics: NAACL 2022*, pages 61–76, Seattle, United States. Association for Computational Linguistics.

Dustin Wright and Isabelle Augenstein. 2020. Claim check-worthiness detection as positive unlabelled learning. In *Findings of the Association for Computational Linguistics: EMNLP 2020*, pages 476–488, Online. Association for Computational Linguistics.

Dustin Wright, David Wadden, Kyle Lo, Bailey Kuehl, Arman Cohan, Isabelle Augenstein, and Lucy Wang. 2022. Generating scientific claims for zero-shot scientific fact checking. In *Proceedings of the 60th Annual Meeting of the Association for Computational Linguistics (Volume 1: Long Papers)*, pages 2448–2460, Dublin, Ireland. Association for Computational Linguistics.

Amelie Wührl and Roman Klinger. 2021. Claim detection in biomedical Twitter posts. In *Proceedings of the 20th Workshop on Biomedical Language Processing*, pages 131–142, Online. Association for Computational Linguistics.

Antonio Jimeno Yepes and Andrew MacKinlay. 2016. NER for medical entities in twitter using sequence to sequence neural networks. In *Proceedings of the Australasian Language Technology Association Workshop 2016*, pages 138–142.

Shi Yuan and Bei Yu. 2019. HClaimE: A tool for identifying health claims in health news headlines. *Information Processing & Management*, 56(4):1220–1233.

Zhiwei Zhang, Jiyi Li, Fumiyo Fukumoto, and Yanming Ye. 2021. Abstract, rationale, stance: A joint model for scientific claim verification. In *Proceedings of the 2021 Conference on Empirical Methods in Natural Language Processing*, pages 3580–3586, Online and Punta Cana, Dominican Republic. Association for Computational Linguistics.

Chaoyuan Zuo, Narayan Acharya, and Ritwik Banerjee. 2020. Querying across genres for medical claims in news. In *Proceedings of the 2020 Conference on Empirical Methods in Natural Language Processing (EMNLP)*, pages 1783–1789, Online. Association for Computational Linguistics.

Chaoyuan Zuo, Kritik Mathur, Dhruv Kela, Noushin Salek Faramarzi, and Ritwik Banerjee. 2022. Beyond belief: a cross-genre study on perception and validation of health information online. *International Journal of Data Science and Analytics*, pages 1–16.

A Appendix

Table 4 shows examples from the CoVERT dataset along with gold evidence documents and fact-checking verdicts.

id	full tweet	evidence	Gold
1a	Actually wearing masks causes bacterial pneumonia which people can die from NOT covid19. Most people do not know how to don/doff PPE properly. Follow the science Big Guy!	There's no evidence that mask-wearing causes bacterial pneumonia.	R
1b	Up to half of hospitalized COVID patients have elevated levels of antiphospholipid antibodies, or antibodies that cause blood clots to form. Patients with these antibodies are much more likely to have severe respiratory disease and kidney injury. #COVID19	The NIH-supported study, published in Science Translational Medicine, uncovered at least one of these autoimmune antiphospholipid (aPL) antibodies in about half of blood samples taken from 172 patients hospitalized with COVID-19. Those with higher levels of the destructive autoantibodies also had other signs of trouble. They included greater numbers of sticky, clot-promoting platelets and NETs, webs of DNA and protein that immune cells called neutrophils spew to ensnare viruses during uncontrolled infections, but which can lead to inflammation and clotting. These observations, coupled with the results of lab and mouse studies, suggest that treatments to control those autoantibodies may hold promise for preventing the cascade of events that produce clots in people with COVID-19.	S
2a	"It's unclear if his death was related to the virus." This is why we perform autopsies. There is a significant likelihood that #COVID19 played a role in that it is known to affect endothelial cells & has been shown to cause neurological symptoms including stroke.	Some people with COVID-19 either initially have, or develop in the hospital, a dramatic state of confusion called delirium. Although rare, COVID-19 can cause seizures or major strokes. Muscular weakness, nerve injury, and pain syndromes are common in people who require intensive care during infections.	S
2b	Are you aware that the vaccines could cause miscarriage? The real data regarding covid is that there are tiny numbers, percentage wise, of generally healthy people under the age of 60 that die from COVID or that get admitted into ICU. Are you worried about cancer too?	Miscarriages have been reported following vaccination, but there's no evidence to show vaccines were the cause. The number of miscarriages reported after vaccination does not appear to exceed the number you would ordinarily expect.	R
3a	The predominant symptoms of 'long COVID' are psychological in nature, with anxiety and depression being most common. But those of course are also exactly the conditions which have been caused in, literally, millions of people, especially young people, by the lockdowns.	This phenomenon has led to short term as well as long term psychosocial and mental health implications for children and adolescents. The quality and magnitude of impact on minors is determined by many vulnerability factors like developmental age, educational status, pre-existing mental health condition, being economically underprivileged or being quarantined due to infection or fear of infection.	S
3b	Know the facts! There is no evidence that #COVID19 #vaccines cause #infertility, says @username @username & @username #NIAW2021 #InfertilityAwareness	There's no evidence that approved vaccines cause fertility loss. Although clinical trials did not study the issue, loss of fertility has not been reported among thousands of trial participants nor confirmed as an adverse event among millions who have been vaccinated.	S
4a	Covid is no joke, this is why we need the vaccine. We know that mRNA doesn't cause long term effects since it decomposes in your body within 1-2 hours. Please everyone, get vaccinated as soon as you can!	It's important to know that mRNA doesn't affect your genes in any way because it never enters the nucleus of cells, where your DNA is kept. After the mRNA does its job, it breaks down and is flushed out of your system within hours.	S
4b	I never said Covid-19 wasn't a real coronavirus. And deaths linked to Covid-19 are primarily caused directly from pneumonia, or flu-like symptoms. The classifications for influenza and pneumonia reporting changed when Covid-19 appeared. Facts.	We found that septic shock and multi organ failure was the most common immediate cause of death, often due to suppurative pulmonary infection. Respiratory failure due to diffuse alveolar damage presented as immediate cause of death in fewer cases.	R

Table 4: Examples from CoVERT with gold evidence and fact-checking verdicts.

QUALIASSISTANT: Extracting Qualia Structures from Texts

Manuel Biertz
Trier University
biertz@uni-trier.de

Lorik Dumani
Trier University
dumani@uni-trier.de

Markus Nilles
Trier University
nillesm@uni-trier.de

Björn Metzler
Trier University
s4bjmetz@uni-trier.de

Ralf Schenkel
Trier University
schenkel@uni-trier.de

Abstract

In this paper, we present QUALIASSISTANT, a free and open-source system written in Java for identification and extraction of Qualia structures from any natural language texts having many application scenarios such as argument mining or creating dictionaries. It answers the call for a Qualia bootstrapping tool with a ready-to-use system that can be gradually filled by the community with patterns in multiple languages. Qualia structures express the meaning of lexical items. They describe, e.g., of what kind the item is (formal role), what it includes (constitutive role), how it is brought about (agentive role), and what it is used for (telic role). They are also valuable for various Information Retrieval and NLP tasks. Our application requires search patterns for Qualia structures consisting of POS tag sequences as well as the dataset the user wants to search for Qualias. Samples for both are provided alongside this paper. While samples are in German, QUALIASSISTANT can process all languages for which constituency trees can be generated and patterns are available. Our provided patterns follow a high-precision low-recall design aiming to generate automatic annotations for text mining but can be exchanged easily for other purposes. Our evaluation shows that QUALIASSISTANT is a valuable and reliable tool for finding Qualia structures in unstructured texts.

1 Introduction

In the field of Natural Language Processing, knowledge bases and thesauri are often used to improve methods such as information extraction (Stevenson and Greenwood, 2006), question answering (Choi et al., 2003), the validation of statements (Hassan et al., 2017) or the generation of arguments (Alshomary and Wachsmuth, 2021; Schiller et al., 2021). In the domain of argument retrieval, for example, there is usually a set of arguments pre-stored in an argument base to improve performance. Given a query entered by a user, these arguments are returned in a ranking (Stab et al., 2018; Wachsmuth et al., 2017). When there are arguments suitable for the query, this ranking works well up to now (Stab et al., 2018). As the arguments are pre-stored in the bases, they are consequently finite and cannot be used for arbitrary queries. With the help of thesauri such as WORDNET, it is possible to modify existing arguments in the base to fit the query.[1] For instance, if the user enters the query *Does every worker get a pension?*, and the most appropriate argument in the base is *Each employee is eligible for pension*, a system applying a thesaurus should be able to recognize, for example, that the category of employees is wider and includes workers. Hence, given the appropriate context, the argument could be evolved to *Each worker is eligible for a pension*. However, thesauri and knowledge bases are also limited because they also have only a finite number of entries, although there could be many more arguments. While they only contain given truths such as that a worker can be seen as employee, this approach could not straightforwardly determine more nuanced facts, like they occur in topics that are discussed in parliaments. For instance, given a query *Should I rely on state pension?*, one result could be that *Pensions are no insurance sum that is simply paid out once*[2], containing valuable though very nuanced knowledge dealing with common misconceptions.

In this paper we present a free and open-source tool called QUALIASSISTANT which is written in Java and helps to create dictionaries, e.g., to mitigate the aforementioned problem of thesauri and knowledge bases.[3] It is based on the work of

[1] https://wordnet.princeton.edu/

[2] This is an actual example from our corpus translated from German.

[3] The datasets as well as a ready to use JAR file are available at https://doi.org/10.5281/zenodo.6805590. The full source code is available at https://github.com/recap-utr/qualiAssistant.

Proceedings of the 9th Workshop on Argument Mining, co-located with the 29th International Conference on Computational Linguistics, pages 199–208
October 17, 2022.

Saint-Dizier (2017), who uses Qualia roles – multi-dimensional aspects of meaning – for automatized argument mining (more on Qualia roles in Section 2) and it answers his call for a "bootstrapping method". One issue with his approach is that it takes a lot of time to acquire a high-quality corpus of such roles (his estimate: several months). While this manual approach facilitates quality control, it is also laborious and should be supported with automatized methods where possible. One such method has been introduced by Cimiano and Wenderoth (2007) in their paper on automatized creation of Qualia roles, using a set of clues, corresponding syntactic patterns (see Section 3), and a large corpus of Web documents in English language. In this paper, we not only enhance their approach so that it becomes applicable to other languages than English (German for instance), we also provide a more extensive list consisting of 142 patterns, and a tool that allows to query arbitrary words such as *pension* in user provided texts in order to extract and return their Qualia roles.[4]

The contributions of this paper are the following:

(1) We introduce the Java application QUALIASSISTANT, which (i) can pre-process texts so that Qualia roles can be found in them and (ii) can also search for Qualia roles in these pre-processed texts.[5] Further, we also explain the abstract concept and the straightforward handling of the application.

(2) We provide a set of 142 patterns to find the four roles as well as two pre-processed datasets in German language which only need queries to be searched in them. Note that QUALIASSISTANT can be easily extended to other languages. Backing up this assertion, we adapted Cimiano and Wenderoth's (Cimiano and Wenderoth, 2007) English patterns and used them to extract Qualia structures in election programs from 2000 to 2020 from seven English-speaking countries.

2 Foundations and Related Work

In this section, we start by defining Qualia structures and discuss related work and how it differs from our work.

Qualia structures were first introduced by Pustejovsky (Pustejovsky, 1991; Pustejovsky and Jezek, 2015) in 1991 as part of his 'Generative Lexicon' (GL) which "emerged from Aristotle's notion of modes of explanation" and structures "lexical semantics knowledge in conjunction with domain knowledge" (Saint-Dizier, 2016). Qualia roles structure multiple layers of meaning around an entity and form a knowledge repository which can be put to good use in many relevant areas in information retrieval (Cimiano and Wenderoth, 2007), including for reference resolution (Bos et al., 1995) and query expansions (Voorhees, 1994). They are also used in areas of natural language processing like argument mining, most prominently by Saint-Dizier (2017).

Pustejovsky's work is based on Moravcsiks's re-interpretation of Aristotle's "doctrine of four causes" as four viewpoints for understanding the meaning of lexical items (*aitia*) (Cimiano and Wenderoth, 2007; Pustejovsky and Jezek, 2015). In Qualia structures, the meaning of a lexical item is thus divided into four roles: *formal*, *constitutive*, *agentive*, and *telic* as shown and described in more detail in Table 1. In our work, the lexical item will be referred to as the *query* (usually a noun) for which we want to find the corresponding *Qualia roles*. For example, given the query *pension*: A formal role would be *income* (what is it?), a constitutive role would be *monthly payments to the retiree* (what does it include?), an agentive role would be *previously regularly paid contributions by the retiree* (what does it need), and a telic role would be *retirement security* (what is it used for?). For the proposed, condensed notation of a Qualia structure see Figure 1. This is an example for a complete Qualia structure with all four roles; but note that not all Qualia structures need all the roles.

$$\text{Pension:}\quad \begin{bmatrix} \text{FORMAL} : [\text{INCOME}], \\ \text{CONSTITUTIVE} : [\text{MONTHLY PAYMENTS}], \\ \text{AGENTIVE} : [\text{REGULAR CONTRIBUTIONS}], \\ \text{TELIC} : [\text{RETIREMENT SECURITY}] \end{bmatrix}$$

Figure 1: An exemplary Qualia structure for *pension*. Notation as proposed by Saint-Dizier (2016).

[4]In their paper, they work with 27 patterns, 13 of which are plural derivatives of other patterns.

[5]Note that the division into (i) and (ii) is made here solely for performance reasons. Reason being is that (i) is computationally intensive, but only needs to be done once beforehand. In contrast, (ii) depends on the query.

[6]Saint-Dizier uses a broader definition stating that all distinguishing features are part of the formal role, though his examples show only categories (Saint-Dizier, 2016).

Table 1: The four Qualia roles of a lexical item describing its semantic meaning.

Qualia role	description
formal	The categories of an entity (Pustejovsky and Jezek, 2015) or its superclass (Yamada et al., 2007) and how it can be distinguished in a larger domain (Cimiano and Wenderoth, 2007) such as orientation, dimensionality, magnitude, shape, or position. For example, a formal role of "dog" would be "animal".[6]
constitutive	Presents the (physical) properties of an object, such as material, weight, components, etc. (Cimiano and Wenderoth, 2007).
agentive	Explains how an entity is brought about, e.g. how it is produced or what its causal chain looks like (Yamada et al., 2007; Cimiano and Wenderoth, 2007).
telic	Expresses the function or purpose of an entity (Saint-Dizier, 2016), e.g. law is used to govern.

According to Saint-Dizier (2016), a general challenge with Qualia structures is that they must be manually retrieved. Saint-Dizier estimates that one would need about 50 Qualia structures to completely represent a knowledge domain (Saint-Dizier, 2016). Acquiring them by hand would be a tedious and laborious task, so he calls for "a bootstrapping method" (Saint-Dizier, 2017). One of the most promising approaches is presented by Cimiano and Wenderoth (2007). They create clues (i.e. general ideas about how terms or combinations of terms indicate a certain role), and patterns for those clues. They then apply those to a large, scraped Web corpus and find Qualia roles for given entities, i.e. nouns, in English. For their gold standard, they rely on 30 words based on the dataset of Yamada and Baldwin (2004), who developed a supervised Machine Learning technique for automatic acquisition of telic and agentive roles. In their approach, they use template-based contextual features extracted from nouns and provide a ranked list of verbs per noun.[7] In contrast to Yamada and Baldwin, the approach of Cimiano and Wenderoth (2007) is more oriented towards high precision results, which is a goal that we share. However, as Machine Learning methods are sensitive to training data, they can only benefit from our approach in the future since they can use the pattern and the automated annotations.

[7] Yamada and Baldwin continued their research in Yamada et al. (2007).

The aforementioned promising approach of Cimiano and Wenderoth (2007) has two main shortcomings which we aim to overcome with this paper: First, there is no ready-made tool available to apply their concept, find additional patterns, and execute the whole pipeline. This greatly hinders its application. Second and related, they provide only English clues and patterns. In this paper, we build upon Cimiano and Wenderoth's approach to answer the call of Saint-Dizier (2017) for a Qualia bootstrapping tool with a ready-to-use system that can be gradually filled by the community with patterns in multiple languages. Since the code is also open-source, it is easy to modify if required.

3 Extracting Qualia Roles

3.1 Concept

In this section, we limit ourselves to explaining the concept behind our Qualia structure extraction pipeline (as illustrated in Figure 2), but make the technical details available on the Web page.[8] Our system is based on the approach of Cimiano and Wenderoth (2007) as it uses *Part-of-Speech* (POS) to identify Qualia structures. Given a CSV file, QUALIASSISTANT derives a *constituency tree* that represents the syntactic structure of each sentence from a column specified by the user. We use constituency trees because they contain more detailed information w.r.t. phrases and their hierarchy than 'flat' POS tagging. For instance, some linguistic units in Figure 3 are encircled by a noun phrase (`NP`) tag.[9] These additional POS tags are crucial for a better division in sub clauses, which we rely on when identifying Qualia roles.

The user is expected to provide some specifications in a JSON file from which the application then extracts important information for further processing. These specifications contain information such as the language which is among others nec-

[8] `https://github.com/recap-utr/qualiAssistant`.

[9] The POS tags in the figure are the ones CoreNLP uses for the German language and can be viewed here: `https://www.coli.uni-saarland.de/projects/sfb378/negra-corpus/negra-corpus.html`

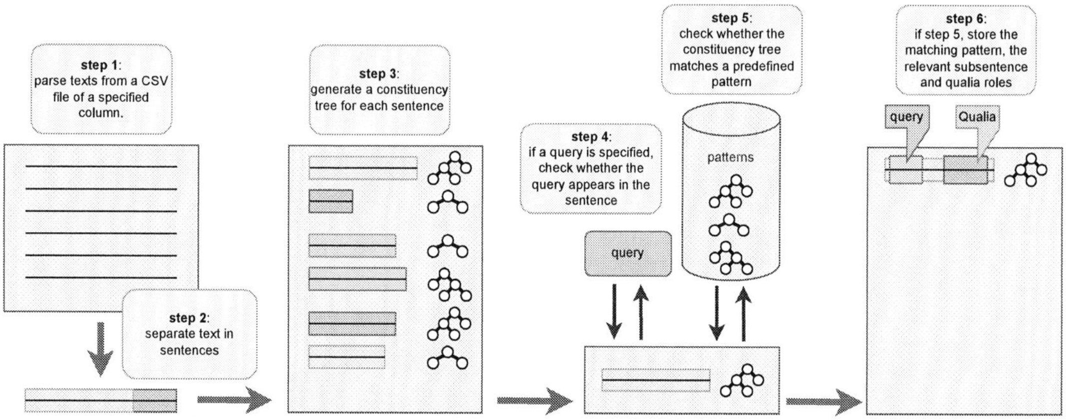

Figure 2: The whole process of QUALIASSISTANT consisting of the dataset pre-processing and the extraction of Qualia roles.

essary to generate the correct constituency trees, paths to input and output CSV files, the name of the column to which the texts should be pre-processed, whether the search for Qualia roles should be limited to a set of queries or be conducted independent from the query, or whether to use stemming (i.e. the heuristic reduction of a word to a common base term) or not to influence precision and recall. A positive example of a match between a pattern and a part of a text can be seen in Figure 3. Then, these entries with matches taken together with the found patterns, the relevant sub-sentences and the identified Qualia roles will be output.

3.2 Rules for Finding POS Tag Sequences

In order to find Qualia roles, we developed a simple convention to search for POS sequences in constituency trees, namely:

1. A *sequence of POS tags* is defined by using **white spaces** between them, e.g.

   ```
   NOUN AUX NP.
   ```

2. In order to allow *multiple selection of POS tags* where exactly one has to be chosen, we use **square brackets**, e.g.

   ```
   NOUN AUX [CNP,NP,NOUN].
   ```

3. For *optional POS tags*, we use **round brackets**, e.g.

   ```
   (DET) NOUN AUX (DET)
   [CNP,NP,NOUN].
   ```

4. To allow only *specific texts for POS tags*, ideally derived from pre-conceptualized clues, we use **slashes** after the POS tags and write the desired text, e.g.

   ```
   (DET) NOUN AUX/ist (DET)
   [CNP,NP,NOUN].
   ```
   [10]

5. The specification of the *Qualia role* and the *query* in a pattern can be done by the use of the XML tags **<qualia>** and **<query>**, respectively, e.g.

   ```
   (DET) <query>NOUN</query>
   AUX/ist (DET) <qualia>
   [CNP,NP,NOUN]</qualia>.
   ```

3.3 Finding Qualia Roles

If multiple selection of POS tags is used, the system internally works with derivative patterns. Given the aforementioned pattern (used to find *formal* roles)

```
(DET) <query>NOUN</query>
AUX/ist (DET) <qualia>
[CNP,NP,NOUN]</qualia>
```

QUALIASSISTANT derives 12 ($= 2 \cdot 2 \cdot 3$) different search patterns from this input, i.e., by including or excluding the optional POS tags and picking one

[10]The German word *ist* can be translated to the English word *is*.
Note that specifying the POS tag is essential because a specification could be represented by multiple POS tags and thus semantics could be lost. For example, the term *ist* ('is') could also be a specification for the POS tag VERB.

of the options in the multiple selection.[11] One of these derivatives is

```
<query>NOUN</query>
AUX/ist
<qualia>NP</qualia>.
```

where the two optional POS tags (DET) are not included and NP is chosen to be the searched Qualia role from the multiple selection. With regard to the initial phrase

> *Die Sicherheit ist die Grundlage für Freiheit und Wohlstand.*"
> ('Security is the basis for freedom and prosperity.')

the Stanford CoreNLP library provides the (pretty printed) constituency tree shown in Figure 3. Together with the above-mentioned derivation

```
(ROOT
  (NUR
    (S
      (NP (DET Die) (NOUN Sicherheit))
      (AUX ist)
      (NP (DET die) (NOUN Grundlage)
        (PP (ADP für)
          (CNP (NOUN Freiheit)
            (CCONJ und)
            (NOUN Wohlstand)))) )
    (PUNCT .)))
```

Figure 3: Constituency tree of the sentence *Die Sicherheit ist die Grundlage für Freiheit und Wohlstand.* ('Security is the basis for freedom and prosperity.).'

```
<query>NOUN</query>
AUX/ist
<qualia>NP</qualia>
```

of the pattern (the pattern's components are highlighted with double underlining), as well as the query *Sicherheit* (highlighted with wavy underlining; 'security') we get a match with the subsentence

> *die Grundlage für Freiheit und Wohlstand*
> ('the basis for freedom and prosperity')

In the constituency tree, the Qualia role consisting of the content inside the NP tag is highlighted with a yellow background and can be extracted for further usage such as creating and updating knowledge bases or argument mining. QUALIASSISTANT finds matching sequences and, if the query matches, it outputs the Qualia role in form of its leaves by traversing the tree. We thus derive that the term *Sicherheit* ('*security*') contains the formal role *die Grundlage für Freiheit und Wohlstand* ('the basis for freedom and prosperity').

4 Evaluation

In this section, we outline our evaluation, where we measured the performance of QUALIASSISTANT in comparison to a baseline on two datasets quantitatively and qualitatively. To this end, we involved a human annotator.

4.1 Dataset

As already remarked in Section 1, we tested QUALIASSISTANT on two German datasets and one English dataset. One of the German datasets consists of parliamentary speeches from the German Bundestag with 1,367,655 sentences (henceforth: OFFENESPARLAMENT).[12] The other represents written language and consists of user-generated arguments occurring in a forum of German petitions with 124,034 sentences (henceforth: OPENPETITION).[13] These datasets differ fundamentally in language style but they both belong to the domain of politics so they are generally comparable. The difference in language style allows for more meaningful conclusions in the evaluation. While the former dataset is available in JSON format, we scraped the debates of the latter source and converted both into CSVs so that the desired texts could be easily identified and processed based on the corresponding specified column label. The English dataset consists of 179,398 sentences which originate from election programs from 2000 to 2020 from seven English-speaking countries. In addition, we developed a file consisting of 142 search patterns for the German language. For English, we adapted the search patterns from Cimiano and Wenderoth (2007), to show that our application can be used for languages other than German. We intend for these files to be extended and adapted in future work.

[11] Line breaks are added only for improved readability.

[12] https://offenesparlament.de/

[13] https://www.openpetition.de/

4.2 Setup

Since QUALIASSISTANT is able to find Qualia structures for queries as well as independent from queries, we conducted our evaluation for both. W.r.t. the query dependent approach, we selected 52 German query terms with high political relevance in Germany such as *Rente* ('pension'), *Sicherheit* ('security'), or *Bildung* ('education') and obtained 869 Qualia structures for the dataset OFFENESPARLAMENT and 207 Qualia structures for OPENPETITION. W.r.t. the query independent approach, we let the system search for queries and Qualia roles and obtained 16,090 Qualia roles for 5,210 different identified queries for OFFENESPARLAMENT as well as and 2,811 Qualia roles for 1,833 different queries for OPENPETITION.

Since our preliminary experiments showed that single terms are not always useful as queries, e.g. because they only make sense in context (as with genitive constructions), we expanded the queries by traversing the constituency tree if they are surrounded by a certain tag - for the German patterns we took NP. In this way, for the example in Figure 3, we only get the extension *Die Sicherheit* ('The security') because there are no other NP tags placed higher. However, assuming the query was *Grundlage* ('basis') in the same example, then the extended query *Die Grundlage für Freiheit und Wohlstand* ('the basis for freedom and prosperity') would be derived. Thus, we obtained triples of the form (query, expanded query, Qualia role), where "expanded query" is the top level of extensions for a given tag. Since some queries did not include an expanded query, we ignored them for the evaluation of the four datasets. Further, we did not include more than 10 triples for each query for each the two query dependent datasets for the evaluation. Thus, w.r.t. the query dependent approach, we obtained 231 Qualia structures for the dataset OFFENESPARLAMENT and 89 Qualia structures for OPENPETITION. From each of the two sets following the query independent approach, we drew a random sample of 50 Qualia structures that also include expanded queries. Thus, our final evaluation set consists of 420 (=231+89+50+50) (query, expanded query, Qualia role) triples. Figure 4 visualizes the setup to obtain the evaluation set. Among these, 414 hold the role "formal", 4 hold the role "constitutive" and 2 hold the role "agentive". Obviously, formal roles appear most often. On the one hand, this is due to the fact that we were able to find more patterns for these roles because these are easier to determine. On the other hand, this is a result of the texts in which formal roles are more likely to be found. However, we do not see this as a disadvantage since we are currently only using small datasets as a proof of concept. In the future, we plan to use huge datasets like Wikipedia and datasets of different domains, where we can find the other roles as well.

4.3 Baseline

Since we are not aware of any existing system for finding Qualia structures, we developed an intuitive baseline. For a given query, this baseline first searches for all subtrees of the constituency tree that branch off NP tags and then randomly picks one in which the query does not occur. If no query is given, a random noun is chosen from the original input sentence and used as the query for the process described above. The intuition behind this is the following:

(1) Queries are mostly nouns. Thus, it makes sense to randomly select a noun as a query if none is supplied by the user. Apart from that, the number of nouns in a sentence is moderate.

(2) Qualia roles to queries are mostly noun phrases. Hence, it makes sense to select such as Qualia roles. Particularly in this case, the number of noun phrases in a sentence is small as there cannot be that many noun phrases of this kind, since we are only considering constituency trees of sentences here.

We ran this baseline system for all of the four datasets. W.r.t. the two query independent datasets, similar to our proposed system, we drew a random sample of 50 triples for each. W.r.t. the two query dependent datasets, we obtained 142 triples for OFFENESPARLAMENT and 70 for OPENPETITION. Overall, this resulted in 312 (=50+50+142+70) triples delivered by the baseline system. Assuming that this process provided reasonable Qualia structures, the approach still fails in assigning the roles agentive, constitutive, formal, and telic. Since our approach mostly retrieved formal roles, we assigned the role formal for the baseline to each found Qualia structure so that the annotator should not be able to recognize from the assigned role which system returned it.

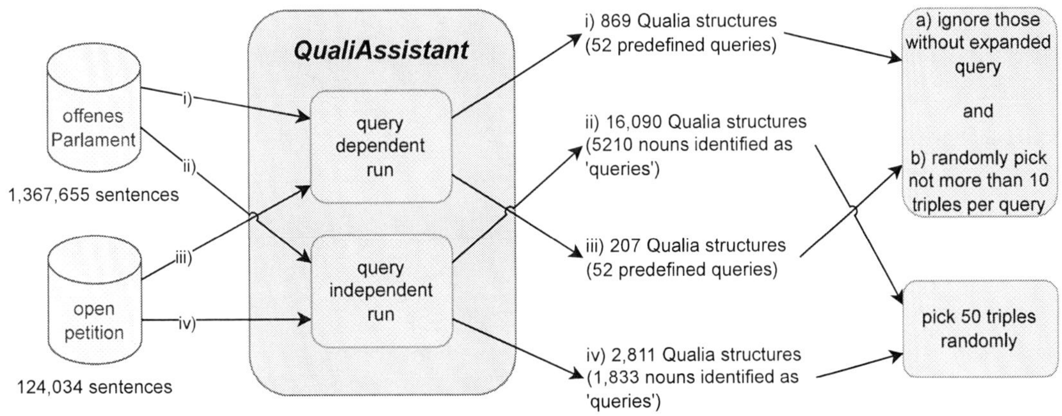

Figure 4: Setup to obtain the final evaluation set.

4.4 Annotation

Then, we aggregated the 732 (=420+312) triples in a single file and asked a human annotator to assess these triples with respect to their meaningfulness on a three fold scale. The annotator is a doctoral student in computer science working on computational argumentation for more than four years. Note that we veiled the triples' origins to the annotator and shuffled the order. For both query and expanded query, the annotator assigned the value `0` with respect to the Qualia role if the role does not make any sense to be included in a text mining process. For example, if the query was *poverty* and the Qualia role was *work*. If the Qualia role was a perfect fit without compromises and could be seen as a gold standard in further systems, the annotator assigned the value `2`. For example, if the query was *employment* and the (constitutive) Qualia role was *work*. If the Qualia structure could be seen as tenable (even with only little drawbacks) the annotator assessed it with the value `1`. This could be, e.g., when the Qualia role to the query was in the genitive form.

4.5 Results of the Quantitative Evaluation

We measured the annotations with micro average precision. Table 2 shows these results for standard as well as expanded queries for the two datasets OFFENESPARLAMENT and OPENPETITION. There, we not only distinguish between query dependent and query independent searches but also compare perfect pairs (label = `2`) to pairs that need to be processed (label = `1` and label = `2`) to be included in a database.

We can observe from the table that our method performs significantly better than the baseline for both datasets and for both query dependent and query independent searches. We can also notice that for each method and dataset, the results improve by expanding the queries with their context. The query dependent search seems to perform better on the dataset OFFENESPARLAMENT, which consists of sophisticated texts, while the query independent search performs better on the dataset OPENPETITION which consists of user-generated content. Nevertheless, these results should be treated with some caution, since only one annotator carried out the assessments. It is therefore more important to pay attention to the tendency, which clearly shows the value of QUALIASSISTANT, and less to the absolute numbers.

4.6 Results of the Qualitative Evaluation

Some observations of the annotations were that queries without context rarely make sense, and thus it is good to provide additional contexts. For example, for the query *Armut* ('poverty') we get the wrong Qualia role *Arbeit* ('work'). Adding the extension of the query, we obtain the expanded and reasonable query *Das beste Mittel gegen Armut* ('the best remedy for poverty'). Sometimes queries without context also made sense, but then there is the risk of losing the semantics of the text. For example, for the query *Gesundheit* ('health') we get the Qualia role *keine Nebensächlichkeit* ('no minor matter'), which is completely reasonable. However, expanding the query automatically to include context provides the expanded query *Schutz der Gesundheit* ('protection of health'), which provides a more accurate description of the text. Therefore, we recommend including the expanded query when intending to reflect the text for future tasks.

Table 2: Precision values for standard as well as expanded queries for the datasets OFFENESPARLAMENT and OPENPETITION when only **perfect** matching pairs (label = 2) are considered to be true positives (left side) as well as when also **tenable** matching pairs (label = 1 and label = 2) are considered to be matching pairs (right side). The upper part shows the results for the **query dependent** search. The lower part shows the results for the **query independent** search.

query dependent search	**method**	**consider only perfect pairs** OFFENESPARLAMENT	OPENPETITION	**consider also tenable pairs** OFFENESPARLAMENT	OPENPETITION
✓	QUALIASSISTANT$_{expanded}$	**0.714**	**0.551**	**0.887**	**0.73**
✓	QUALIASSISTANT$_{standard}$	0.377	0.36	0.736	0.64
✓	BASELINE$_{expanded}$	0.218	0.186	0.415	0.414
✓	BASELINE$_{standard}$	0.134	0.057	0.415	0.357
✗	QUALIASSISTANT$_{expanded}$	**0.46**	**0.64**	**0.8**	**0.8**
✗	QUALIASSISTANT$_{standard}$	0.22	0.34	0.5	0.6
✗	BASELINE$_{expanded}$	0.02	0.06	0.04	0.16
✗	BASELINE$_{standard}$	0.0	0.0	0.04	0.14

In order to shed more light on the numbers of Table 2, we randomly picked a sample of the four datasets to qualitatively inspect the results and will now discuss these impressions.

In general, we can state that formal roles can be found very well in German texts. Agentive and constitutive roles also provide quite good but few results. We also found Qualia structures which could be declared as telic, but they were classified as formal. Nevertheless, in the found cases the results are also valid as formal roles, underscoring the general ambiguity of language(s). For example, the query *Arbeit* ('work') provided the formal Qualia role *ein wichtiger Hebel für Integration* ('an important lever for integration') as it also matched such a pattern. However, this role could also be considered telic, since the role not only shows what it is (formal), but also what it is needed for (telic). At least in German, there is a need for much more specific telic patterns catching different grammar, such as active and passive. The current telic patterns could not throw any results, underscoring that development of good patterns remains a continuous task and challenge.

Since the dataset OPENPETITION, contrary to the dataset OFFENESPARLAMENT, is user-generated, there were occasionally grammatical errors made by users, thus leading to minimally incorrect constituency trees. Still, the extracted Qualia roles were semantically meaningful, although they could include syntactical errors. For example, the query *Abtreibung* ('abortion') yielded the Qualia role *Mord an einem Menschen das* ('Murder of a human being the') since there was no punctuation mark between two sentences in the corresponding text and the second sentence started with *das* ('the'), so only this article was appended to the end of a Qualia role.[14]

Apart from that, we noticed that good queries can produce properly good results, some of which we will briefly mention below. For example, for the query *Rente* ('pension') we get the Qualia role *keine Versicherungssumme , die einfach nur einmal ausbezahlt wird* ('no insurance sum that is simply paid out once') and for the query *Subsidiarität* ('subsidiarity') we get the role *der Violinschlüssel dafür, dass dieser Ausgleich in angemessener Form gelingen kann* ('the treble clef for this compensation to succeed in an appropriate form'). These cases show that QUALIASSISTANT is able to grasp a complex political issue. We noticed that in particular those roles that contain a negation seem to contain strong political demarcations. The query *Bildung* ('education'), for example, returns the Qualia role *Schlüssel zu einem erfolgreichen Berufsleben* ('key to a successful professional life'), which could as well have been passable as telic. The query *Staatsverschuldung* ('national debt') yields, among other things, the Qualia role *die Basis für eine weiter schlechte wirtschaftliche Entwickung* ('basis for still deteriorating economic development'), which can also be seen as an argument, e.g., when asking an argument search engine for reasons against increasing national debts. Note that argument search engines work in such a way that they take queries such as "*should national debts be taken care of?*" as input and output a list of ranked arguments either supporting or attacking the query's topic. In this case *basis for still deteriorating economic development* would be an attacking argument. That means that QUALIASSISTANT

[14]This issue disappeared after updating CoreNLP to version 4.4.0, i.e., CoreNLP correctly recognized the superfluous term *the* and does not include it in that sentence anymore.

might also help in argument mining tasks (see Section 1).

For the query *Parlament* ('parliament') we got the Qualia role *keine Versammlung von Helden und Heiligen* ('not a gathering of heroes and saints'), which on the one hand shows that the application is able to reflect the point of view of the texts. On the other hand, it shows that it is a find that would most likely not be found in such a way in a knowledge base or thesaurus.

If the query was not carefully designed (or automatically assigned if the user does not provide any), the results could become more noisy. For example, for the query *Redner* ('speaker') we get Qualia roles such as *the colleague x* (where x is a name of a politician), which offers no genuine added value. Especially with references we noticed problems in the German language at an early stage. For example, for the query *Krankheit* ('illness') the role *ein Grundbedürfnis* ('a basic need') was assigned, which is nonsense. In fact, the original sentence is *Die Versorgung bei Krankheit ist ein Grundbedürfniss* ('the care in case of illness is a basic need'). This kind of false results can be easily removed by taking only sentences that start with the desired pattern. However, in the future we want to enable researchers to explore other possibilities, namely how the results change when the context of a query is automatically included. Thus, we added an additional column in the output that contains expanded queries. As the manual investigations in the last section showed this query expansion immensely helps to understand the relationships between query and Qualia role.

5 Conclusion and Future Work

In this paper, we presented QUALIASSISTANT for finding Qualia structures in texts. In our evaluation utilizing two different datasets in German and one in English, we showed that our approach works reasonably well. However, in this research, the most challenging part remains the gathering of patterns in the form of POS sequences for texts. This is an ongoing process that can take years of development to become sophisticated. We hope for the community to assist in this process by contributing to updating the patterns in our repository since Qualia structures are important for many NLP tasks such as argument mining which is a growing area of research.

In the future, we aim to identify Qualia structures on larger datasets such as Wikipedia using our application, e.g., to set up knowledge bases with them, or for mining arguments. Furthermore, we will investigate the development of further patterns in multiple languages as we believe that many fields of research benefit from having Qualia structures with high-precision, e.g., the validation of statements. Moreover, we want to develop Machine Learning methods that are able to find new Qualia Roles by making use of the automated annotations. We will also improve usability, for example by returning complete Qualia objects as query response.

Acknowledgements

The authors sincerely thank both anonymous reviewers 2 and 3 for their invaluable feedback.

This work has been funded by the Deutsche Forschungsgemeinschaft (DFG) within the projects ReCAP and ReCAP-II, Grant Number 375342983 - 2018-2024, as part of the Priority Program "Robust Argumentation Machines (RATIO)" (SPP-1999).

References

Milad Alshomary and Henning Wachsmuth. 2021. Toward audience-aware argument generation. Patterns, 2(6):100253.

Johan Bos, Paul Buitelaar, and Anne-Marie Mineur. 1995. Bridging as coercive accommodation. arXiv preprint cmp-lg/9508001.

Key-Sun Choi, Jae-Ho Kim, Masaru Miyazaki, Jun Goto, and Yeun-Bae Kim. 2003. Question-answering based on virtually integrated lexical knowledge base. In Proceedings of the Sixth International Workshop on Information Retrieval with Asian Languages, 2003, Sappro, Japan, July 7, 2003, pages 168–175. ACL.

Philipp Cimiano and Johanna Wenderoth. 2007. Automatic acquisition of ranked qualia structures from the web. In ACL 2007, Proceedings of the 45th Annual Meeting of the Association for Computational Linguistics, June 23-30, 2007, Prague, Czech Republic. The Association for Computational Linguistics.

Naeemul Hassan, Gensheng Zhang, Fatma Arslan, Josue Caraballo, Damian Jimenez, Siddhant Gawsane, Shohedul Hasan, Minumol Joseph, Aaditya Kulkarni, Anil Kumar Nayak, Vikas Sable, Chengkai Li, and Mark Tremayne. 2017. Claimbuster: The first-ever end-to-end fact-checking system. Proc. VLDB Endow., 10(12):1945–1948.

James Pustejovsky. 1991. The generative lexicon. Comput. Linguistics, 17(4):409–441.

James Pustejovsky and Elisabetta Jezek. 2015. A Guide to Generative Lexicon Theory.

Patrick Saint-Dizier. 2016. Argument mining: the bottleneck of knowledge and language resources. In Proceedings of the Tenth International Conference on Language Resources and Evaluation LREC 2016, Portorož, Slovenia, May 23-28, 2016. European Language Resources Association (ELRA).

Patrick Saint-Dizier. 2017. Knowledge-driven argument mining based on the qualia structure. Argument Comput., 8(2):193–210.

Benjamin Schiller, Johannes Daxenberger, and Iryna Gurevych. 2021. Aspect-controlled neural argument generation. In Proceedings of the 2021 Conference of the North American Chapter of the Association for Computational Linguistics: Human Language Technologies, NAACL-HLT 2021, Online, June 6-11, 2021, pages 380–396. Association for Computational Linguistics.

Christian Stab, Johannes Daxenberger, Chris Stahlhut, Tristan Miller, Benjamin Schiller, Christopher Tauchmann, Steffen Eger, and Iryna Gurevych. 2018. Argumentext: Searching for arguments in heterogeneous sources. In Proceedings of the 2018 Conference of the North American Chapter of the Association for Computational Linguistics, NAACL-HLT 2018, New Orleans, Louisiana, USA, June 2-4, 2018, Demonstrations, pages 21–25. Association for Computational Linguistics.

Mark Stevenson and Mark A Greenwood. 2006. Learning information extraction patterns using wordnet. In Proceedings of the 5th Intl. Conf. on Language Resources and Evaluations (LREC), pages 95–102.

Ellen M. Voorhees. 1994. Query expansion using lexical-semantic relations. In Proceedings of the 17th Annual International ACM-SIGIR Conference on Research and Development in Information Retrieval. Dublin, Ireland, 3-6 July 1994 (Special Issue of the SIGIR Forum), pages 61–69. ACM/Springer.

Henning Wachsmuth, Martin Potthast, Khalid Al Khatib, Yamen Ajjour, Jana Puschmann, Jiani Qu, Jonas Dorsch, Viorel Morari, Janek Bevendorff, and Benno Stein. 2017. Building an argument search engine for the web. In Proceedings of the 4th Workshop on Argument Mining, ArgMining@EMNLP 2017, Copenhagen, Denmark, September 8, 2017, pages 49–59. Association for Computational Linguistics.

Ichiro Yamada and Timothy Baldwin. 2004. Automatic discovery of telic and agentive roles from corpus data. In Proceedings of the 18th Pacific Asia Conference on Language, Information and Computation, PACLIC 18, Waseda University, Tokyo, Japan, December 8-10, 2004. ACL.

Ichiro Yamada, Timothy Baldwin, Hideki Sumiyoshi, Masahiro Shibata, and Nobuyuki Yagi. 2007. Automatic acquisition of qualia structure from corpus data. IEICE transactions on information and systems, 90(10):1534–1541.

Author Index

Association for Computational Linguistics
209 N. Eighth Street
Stroudsburg, Pennsylvania 18360

ISBN 978-1-7138-9103-1

CURRAN ASSOCIATES INC.
proceedings.com